Fighting Poverty

FIGHTING POVERTY
What Works and What Doesn't

Edited by
Sheldon H. Danziger
and Daniel H. Weinberg

Harvard University Press
Cambridge, Massachusetts, and London, England

Library of Congress Cataloging-in-Publication Data
Main entry under title:

Fighting poverty.

   Revised versions of papers presented at a conference held in Williamsburg, Va., in Dec. 1984, sponsored by the University of Wisconsin—Madison's Institute for Research on Poverty and the U.S. Dept. of Health and Human Services.
   Bibliography: p.
   Includes index.
   1. Economic assistance, Domestic—United States—Congresses.   2. Poor—United States—Congresses.   3. Public welfare—United States—Congresses.   I. Danziger, Sheldon.   II. Weinberg, Daniel H.   III. University of Wisconsin—Madison. Institute for Research on Poverty.   IV. United States. Dept. of Health and Human Services.
HC110.P63F54   1986   362.5′8′0973   85-24848
ISBN 0-674-30085-8 (cloth)
ISBN 0-674-30086-6 (paper)

Preface

The December 1984 conference at which the chapters in this volume were originally presented was sponsored by the Institute for Research on Poverty and the U.S. Department of Health and Human Services. A number of people helped to make the conference a success. Anthony Pellechio suggested the format, Joyce Collins handled many of the arrangements, Christine Ross compiled background material for participants, Nancy Rortvedt provided clerical assistance, and Elizabeth Evanson assisted both in organizing the conference and in preparing this volume.

We are grateful to the contributors for their prompt responses to the editors' requests for revisions and to Peter Gottschalk, Robert Helms, Robert Lampman, Eugene Smolensky, and the members of the Institute's National Advisory Committee for their aid, from the conference planning period through the review of the chapters.

Any views expressed in this book are those of the authors and should not be construed as representing the official position or policy of the University of Wisconsin, the Institute for Research on Poverty, the Department of Health and Human Services, or the institutions with which individual authors are affiliated.

S.H.D.
D.H.W.

Contents

Fighting Poverty

1   Introduction

Sheldon H. Danziger
Daniel H. Weinberg

POVERTY WAS AT THE TOP of the nation's agenda when the War on Poverty was declared twenty years ago. Now it is only one of several concerns. The chapters in this volume, whose goal is to refocus attention on the continuing problems of the poor, take stock of which antipoverty policies have worked and which have not.

In 1964 no official estimates of the nature or extent of poverty in the United States existed, nor was poverty a focus of government studies or programs. In the aftermath of the Great Depression of the 1930s, poverty commanded little academic attention and few legislative initiatives explicitly designed to aid the poor were proposed. The situation changed dramatically in the 1960s. John Kennedy, influenced by the poverty he observed while campaigning in West Virginia and by contemporary accounts of the plight of the poor (Harrington, 1962), directed his Council of Economic Advisers to study the problem. After Kennedy's assassination, Lyndon Johnson accelerated the work of the Council and, in his first State of the Union speech in January 1964, declared war on poverty. Shortly thereafter he announced a set of companion programs designed to enhance the general welfare and create the Great Society.

In the next decade, as a result of these initiatives, new programs were introduced and old programs were expanded; the emphasis of the federal budget shifted from military spending toward social welfare spending. The prevailing view during that period was optimistic. If stable growth could be maintained, government actions could solve the poverty problem if only sufficient resources were devoted to the task. However, economic growth would not serve as the sole antipoverty policy: "We cannot and need not wait for the gradual growth of the economy to lift this forgotten fifth of our Nation above the poverty line . . . We know what must be done, and this Nation of abundance can surely afford to do it" (Johnson, 1964, p. 15).

That optimism soured as the war in Vietnam replaced the War on Poverty in the headlines and helped destroy faith in the government's ability to solve any problem (Aaron, 1978). Arguments that social problems could not be solved by "throwing money" at them and that the antipoverty attempts had failed were increasingly popular.

By the late 1970s two revisionist views were heard. One suggested that even though the earlier efforts had reduced measured poverty, they had not provided sufficient opportunities for the able-bodied poor to earn their way out of poverty. We had nevertheless learned enough from this experience to reorient antipoverty policy (Danziger, Haveman, and Plotnick, 1980). A second view argued that social spending had grown too large and had become a drag on economic growth. Income poverty had been "virtually eliminated" (Anderson, 1978), but work incentives had been eroded for both the poor and the rich, and the incentive to save had been weakened. As a result, these programs should be scaled back or eliminated (Murray, 1984). By 1982 the latter view had become official policy: "With the coming of the Great Society, government began eating away at the underpinnings of the private enterprise system. The big taxers and big spenders in the Congress had started a binge that would slowly change the nature of our society and, even worse, it threatened the character of our people . . . By the time the full weight of Great Society programs was felt, economic progress for America's poor had come to a tragic halt" (Reagan, 1982, p. 1154). Rather than ask what government could do for the poor, official policy now emphasized what it could not accomplish and how it could be counterproductive.

In 1984, twenty years after the declaration of War on Poverty, the facts were clear—social spending had increased rapidly in real terms and as a percentage of the Gross National Product (GNP), yet poverty as officially measured had declined little. But these facts do not speak for themselves. Simple comparisons of spending trends and poverty trends obscure the diversity of the poverty population and the complexity of evaluating government policies.

In order to explain these facts and trends, the authors of the chapters in this volume were commissioned by the Institute for Research on Poverty at the University of Wisconsin-Madison and the Office of the Assistant Secretary for Planning and Evaluation at the U.S. Department of Health and Human Services to review the research of the past two decades and discuss the appropriate roles for antipoverty policy. The papers were presented in December 1984 at a conference in Williamsburg, Virginia, before a group of analysts from the academic community and government agencies. The participants spent three days assessing and debating the achievements, failures, and diverse lessons of government efforts over the past twenty years to reduce poverty in America.

The papers, revised after the conference, form the contents of this volume. They address the following questions:

> What is the nature of antipoverty programs and what are their effects?
>
> How do economic growth and the business cycle affect the poor?
>
> What are the causes of family structure changes and their consequences for poverty?
>
> How have social movements and changes in welfare institutions affected the poor?
>
> What are the economic and political constraints to antipoverty initiatives?

Even though poverty had not been eliminated by 1984, as some War on Poverty and Great Society planners had envisioned, the papers suggest that we have learned a great deal about which programs have worked and which have not. As a result, some provide recommendations for future antipoverty strategies.

The Nature and Effects of Antipoverty Programs

A broad range of government programs and policies directly or indirectly aid the poor. However, because the official definition of poverty is based solely on cash income available during a calendar year, the antipoverty effects of direct cash payments—income transfers—have received the most attention. Yet employment and training, education, health care, food and nutrition, and housing programs are all designed to reduce the short-term and long-term impacts of poverty. Even though the official measure is based on money income, poverty is a broader concept; it involves at its source the inability to achieve participation in societal institutions, an adequate diet, shelter from the elements (housing and clothes), health care, and other necessities.

The first three chapters in the volume trace the course of public anti-poverty spending over the past two decades and examine its effects on poverty. Gary Burtless categorizes government antipoverty programs into three types—means-tested income transfers, social insurance transfers, and education, training, and employment (human capital) programs.

Social insurance transfers (primarily Social Security retirement, survivors, and disability payments, Medicare, and unemployment insurance) account for both the majority of spending in any year and for much of the spending growth: they rose from 3.3 percent of GNP in 1966 to 7.1 percent in 1984. None of these programs was specifically designed to reduce poverty. Their stated goals are to protect workers and their dependents against loss of earnings owing to retirement or to unexpected events such as unemployment, disability, death, and extraordinary health care costs. Nevertheless, their benefits remove more persons from poverty than do means-tested transfers, which have the explicit intent of aiding those with low incomes.

Means-tested income transfers rose from 2.3 to 3.9 percent of GNP between 1965 and 1984. Noncash transfers (mainly Medicaid, food stamps and other nutrition assistance, and housing) rose steadily during that period, while cash assistance, mainly Aid to Families with Dependent Children (AFDC) and Supplemental Security Income (SSI), fell slightly. Burtless speculates that the emphasis on noncash assistance reflects the public's unwillingness to let specific needs (for food, health care, or shelter) go unmet. These benefits did reach those in need, but their magnitude was too limited to remove many from poverty. It is those who receive both social insurance and means-tested transfers that are most likely to escape poverty.

Education and training programs, intended to raise the skills and abilities necessary for the poor to succeed in the marketplace, were a cornerstone of the War on Poverty. However, federal spending on them has never been large relative to that on transfers, rising from almost nothing to 0.85 percent of GNP in 1978, but accounting for less than 0.45 percent of GNP in 1984. Burtless emphasizes that these programs, which seek to raise future earnings, cannot substitute for cash assistance, which raises present well-being, and vice versa.

Sheldon Danziger, Robert Haveman, and Robert Plotnick present trends in poverty as measured in different ways. They show that although poverty, both as officially measured and as measured after accounting for in-kind transfers, has declined since the beginning of the War on Poverty, pre-transfer poverty (measured before any government transfers are included) has not. For example, the poverty rate declined from 17.3 percent in 1965 to 15.2 percent in 1983 (to about 13.0 percent in 1983 if noncash transfers are counted as income), while the pretransfer rates rose over these years from 21.3 to 24.2 percent. The authors interpret these divergent trends as showing that income transfers became increasingly effective in reducing poverty. Danziger, Haveman, and Plotnick also note the wide variations in poverty trends for different demographic groups: poverty declined much more for the elderly than for the nonelderly, and more for blacks than for whites. The poverty declines of the elderly result from increased transfers—mainly expansion and indexation for inflation of Social Security payments and the introduction of Medicare and SSI.

Danziger, Haveman, and Plotnick conclude that the lack of progress in reducing pretransfer poverty for the able-bodied and their increased reliance on income transfers are serious problems on their own account. However, they are especially troublesome because the War on Poverty sought to cure what were then regarded as the fundamental causes of poverty: a stagnant economy, deficiencies in the job skills and qualifications of the poor, and discrimination by those who controlled access to employment or goods or services. As a result, the authors emphasize the continuing need for policies to raise the earnings of the able-bodied poor.

They also provide a rough estimate of the gains and losses from antipoverty policies for those not poor—those who paid for most of the increased public spending. However, many of the gains they identify are nonquantifiable (for example, satisfaction from lower poverty and reduced economic insecurity in the society at large). They estimate that the quantifiable elements produce a net loss to the nonpoor of 2 to 3 percent of personal income, an amount more than offset, in their opinion, by the nonquantifiable benefits to both the poor and the nonpoor.

David Ellwood and Lawrence Summers examine the antipoverty effectiveness and disincentive effects of income transfers for three demographic groups—the disabled, single women with children, and unemployed black youth. They conclude that while government is frequently indicted for discouraging work, disrupting families, and reducing labor force participation, the actual damage attributable to government programs is quite small.

In the case of the disabled, Ellwood and Summers find little support for the claim that the Social Security disability program has distorted the earnings patterns of older men. As evidence, they note that most unsuccessful applicants for benefits did not return to employment. They conclude that "disability insurance appears to be an example of a carefully targeted program that can provide generous benefits without generating large adverse incentive effects.''

Welfare payments, particularly AFDC, have been charged with encouraging illegitimacy and marital dissolution and fostering economic dependency. Using a variety of tests, Ellwood and Summers conclude that these adverse effects are at worst modest. They highlight in particular two issues that contradict the popular belief that AFDC is largely responsible for changes in family structure: the real value of welfare payments has declined since the early 1970s while family dissolution continued to rise, and variations in benefit levels across states do not lead to corresponding variations in divorce rates, illegitimacy rates, or percentages of children in single-parent families. On the other hand, there is some evidence that welfare may promote long-term dependency for a small portion of the caseload.

The problem of black youth unemployment is particularly acute (see also the discussion of family structure effects, below). While the gap between black and white youth unemployment rates has widened, Ellwood and Summers conclude that current policy can have little if any effect on this trend, since young single men are eligible for little in the way of welfare benefits (generally only food stamps), and these benefits have not increased. They also question whether the receipt of welfare has created a culture of nonwork and dependence, since black youth employment rates differ little by family type (two-parent versus single-parent) or by geographic region, although welfare benefits vary greatly across these categories. Ellwood and Summers suggest that something more fundamental than the growth of welfare programs is to blame for the rise in black youth unemployment but can find in the literature no consensus for a cause.

The effects of programs that seek to raise the health, educational level, and job skills of the poor are examined by Paul Starr, Laurie Bassi, Orley Ashenfelter, Nathan Glazer, and Christopher Jencks.

Starr highlights a major success of the War on Poverty: Medicare, Medicaid, and other programs have expanded access to medical care for the poor and have probably improved their health status. These gains have come at substantial budgetary cost, however, and a large and growing portion of the poor still have either no health insurance or inadequate coverage.

Starr emphasizes that a number of "historical encumbrances" burden the provision of health care to the poor: (1) the channeling of health care services to the poor through public assistance via Medicaid, rather than through social insurance, the course chosen in other countries, has prevented universal access; (2) political accommodations made with doctors and hospitals when Medicare and Medicaid were first established have allowed spending to grow without adequate controls; (3) the subsidization of employer-provided medical care through the tax system has encouraged continued spending for the nonpoor, while direct expenditures on the poor have been reduced; and (4) the public has misperceived medical spending as benefiting mainly a "welfare class," whereas two-thirds of these expenditures go to the aged and the disabled.

Nevertheless, in contrast with studies from the 1970s, Starr concludes that increased government intervention in health care financing is correlated with improvements in several indicators of health status. Overall life expectancy at birth, after remaining almost unchanged in the decade preceding the War on Poverty, began to increase in 1968 and by 1980 had lengthened by four years. Mortality rates fell 20 percent over that period and infant mortality rates were cut in half, with declines for blacks even greater.

Bassi and Ashenfelter review studies that evaluate the effect of employment and training programs on the subsequent employment and earnings levels of participants. The evaluations generally find that earnings gains are larger for women than for men. Employment and training programs have increased earnings for women chiefly by raising their hours of work rather than their hourly wage. Since women generally worked fewer hours prior to the program than did men, it is easier for them to improve their earnings. Individuals who benefited most from programs under the Comprehensive Employment and Training Act often were those with the least prior work experience, a result confirmed by recent analyses of the San Diego Workfare Demonstration (Manpower Demonstration Research Corporation, 1984). Thus, greater benefits are likely if training slots are targeted on poor youth and women rather than prime-age men.

There have been a handful of success stories. The Supported Work Demonstration, the Job Corps, and the Youth Incentive Entitlement Pilot Projects all appear to have resulted in social benefits exceeding program costs. Social benefits are measured in terms of goods and services produced by participants, increased tax payments on postprogram income, reduced transfer payments, reduced criminal activity, and a decline in other federally provided services.

Bassi and Ashenfelter conclude that "employment and training programs have been neither an overwhelming success nor a complete failure in terms of their ability to increase the long-term employment and earnings of disadvantaged workers." Employment and training programs never covered a very large proportion of the target group, but even if they had, there is little evidence to suggest they could have significantly reduced pretransfer poverty.

Nathan Glazer, reviewing the literature on the effects of education programs, challenges the view that "nothing works"—the view that despite expensive and intensive efforts to provide compensatory education to disadvantaged students, to give children from poor families a head start in the classroom, and to offer job training to high school dropouts and delinquents, cognitive skills were little improved and the later earnings of program participants were not increased. The current perspective is different, Glazer asserts, in part because recent studies have found long-term (albeit modest) educational effects from preschool interventions such as Head Start and from compensatory services at the elementary level. Glazer suggests that increased spending in the elementary schools will have a higher payoff than spending on work-training programs for dropouts, since only a few dropouts "manage to get much from these programs."

Christopher Jencks takes issue with some of Glazer's optimistic conclusions. He points out that most gains in elementary education disappear by the time students are in secondary school. Positive evaluations, he asserts, are due to a "revolution of declining expectations" that focuses on improvements in deportment and in dropout rates and not on the failure to close the gap in achievement between rich and poor children. Jencks argues that the availability of resources in secondary schools is of prime importance because students there, unlike those in elementary schools, will not have another chance to improve their skills.

In sum, even though income transfers were not a major component of the early War on Poverty and Great Society initiatives, their growth has accounted for the greatest portion of the rise in social spending and is responsible for much of the observed decline in poverty. While this has meant great success for the elderly, transfers have not promoted self-sufficiency among the able-bodied poor, an important goal of the poor and taxpayers alike.

Success is also reflected in greater access to medical care and improved health of the poor, another area in which spending growth was rapid and expenditures massive. However, gains from education and employment and training programs have been rather limited. This is troublesome, since improving the skills and capabilities of the poor, particularly the young, was a key goal of the War on Poverty. Part of the problem was that these programs never received the funds that planners intended. However, even if these funds had been available, we did not learn and still do not know enough about how to improve the education and employment prospects of the poor to achieve that goal.

Effects of Economic Growth and the Business Cycle

While it is a truism that there are fewer poor in good times than in bad, it is quite difficult to sort out the effects of macroeconomic activity on the poor. Secular economic growth, reflected in higher productivity per hour at work, leads both to increased earnings, which can directly reduce poverty, and to increased tax revenues, which can be used to increase antipoverty spending. But if the rewards of economic growth are not shared, poverty may not decline. Cyclical changes in economic activity, reflected in changes in employment and inflation rates, also can affect the poor directly or indirectly. Three chapters in this volume address these effects.

Danziger, Haveman, and Plotnick discuss three factors that affect the trend in poverty over time: economic performance, government transfers, and demographic change. They divide the years 1965–1983 into four periods. In the first, from 1965 to 1969, the strong economy reduced pretransfer poverty and the antipoverty effect of transfers increased as spending on them grew. With both forces working together, poverty fell rapidly. From 1969 to 1975 poverty remained more or less steady as the poverty-increasing impacts of economic stagnation and rising unemployment were offset by growing transfers. The postrecession years of 1975 to 1978 were characterized by a small decline in poverty as the economy improved somewhat and transfers remained mostly unchanged. After 1978 decline in the real value of transfers and severe recession both contributed to substantial increases in the poverty rate. Furthermore, for the past two decades increases in the size of demographic groups with above-average poverty rates (in particular, female-headed families and individuals living alone) tended to increase the aggregate poverty rate.

Ellwood and Summers also discuss the importance of macroeconomic influences on poverty. They focus on the close connection between median family income and the poverty rate of the nonelderly, suggesting that poverty did not decline in the 1970s because real median family income did not rise. Among the reasons offered by Ellwood and Summers for this lack of growth are demographic shifts and the productivity slowdown; the growth of welfare programs, they contend, is not responsible. The authors conclude that "a restoration of the rapid productivity growth enjoyed by the American economy . . . would do more to alleviate poverty than any plausible policy initiative . . . The problem is that we do not really know how to restore rapid growth."

Rebecca Blank and Alan Blinder investigate the effects of the business cycle and the structure of taxation on the poor. The authors focus on cyclical changes rather than economic growth, because "while a permanent increase in the growth rate of per capita income would . . . probably do wonderful things for the poor, no one has any idea how to achieve it." The authors find that unemployment, not inflation, is the larger contributor to poverty: a one percentage point increase in unemployment has seven times the effect of a one percentage point decrease in inflation. Also, the effects of unemployment vary by group: nonwhite and young workers are the most adversely affected by increased unemployment; female and older workers, the least affected.

Had unemployment and inflation not increased over the 1973–1983 decade, Blank and Blinder estimate that the official poverty rate among persons would have fallen from 11.1 to 10.7 percent instead of rising to 15.2 percent. Most of that increased poverty was due to increased unemployment. The authors find no evidence that inflation has seriously lowered the relative income levels of the poor; some transfer benefits have lost real value (particularly AFDC), but most transfers have been adequately indexed to account for inflation.

Changes in the structure of taxation, mainly the rapid and continuing growth of the payroll tax, have made federal, state, and local taxation much more regressive. By 1983 a family of four at the poverty line was paying more than 16 percent of its income in direct taxes, almost double the percentage paid in 1965. These changes result from tax policy, not fluctuations in economic activity.

Blank and Blinder forecast that by 1989 poverty for all persons will have fallen from the 1983 peak of 15.2 back to the 1973 level of 11.1 percent, if the economy does not experience a recession or a resurgence of inflation. Thus, poverty, as officially measured, will remain a problem, particularly for minorities and female-headed households.

In sum, these three papers conclude that economic growth is necessary but not sufficient to reduce poverty. Because it is very difficult to raise the secular economic growth rate, the most feasible way to reduce poverty is to achieve high employment rates. This would have a large impact for the able-bodied poor of working age, particularly minorities.

Changes in Family Structure and Their Consequences for Poverty

The "feminization" of poverty, the fact that women living alone or with their children are disproportionately represented among the poor, signals one of the major changes in the poverty population since the War on Poverty was declared (another is the rapid decline in poverty among the aged). Mary Jo Bane points out that the proportion of the poor who are members of female-headed and single-person households rose between 1959 and 1979 from 30 to 60 percent. This increase resulted from the combined effects of changes in the family composition of the population as a whole and changes in the relative poverty rates of various household groups. Bane estimates that 42 percent of the increased feminization of poverty over this twenty-year period was due to differential changes in poverty rates—that is, even though the rate declined for female-headed households, it declined less for them than for other groups. The remainder, 58 percent, was due to changes in the household composition of the population. Bane shows that changes in household composition caused poverty in 1979 to be two percentage points higher than if household composition had remained as it was in 1959 (it would have been 9.7 percent instead of 11.6 percent).

Nonetheless, Bane argues that changes in family structure have less causal influence on poverty than is commonly thought. She suggests that much poverty, especially among blacks, is the result of "reshuffling"—that is, already poor two-parent households break up, producing poor female-headed households. The longitudinal data she analyzes suggest that only about one-fifth to one-quarter of the poor fell into poverty at the time their family structure changed. Most poverty, even among female-headed families, comes about because of income or job changes.

William Julius Wilson and Kathryn Neckerman examine changes in fertility, out-of-wedlock births, and the age structure of the population to see whether the changes in the composition of the poverty population are caused by or are independent of the structure of antipoverty programs. The chapter reviews the substantial changes in family structure that have occurred since 1940. The proportion of illegitimate births to blacks has risen dramatically, not because of a rising rate of out-of-wedlock births, but in large part because the rate of marital fertility and the percentage of women married and living with their husbands both declined significantly. The sharp reduction of the latter is due to the rise in black divorce and separation, blacks' lower rates of remarriage, and an increase in the proportion of never-married women. Linked with these trends is change in the age structure, resulting in increases in the fraction of births occurring to young women. The net result is a 41-percent increase in the number of black children growing up in fatherless families during the decade of the 1970s (in most of these families the mother was never married). These trends are especially disturbing because female-headed families are far more likely than married-couple families to be not only poor but poor for long periods.

Changing cultural and social trends—for example, attitudes and expectations concerning marriage and parenthood, the availability of birth control, the rise of feminism—appear to have more relevance for explaining changes in white family structure than in explaining changes in black family structure. And contrary to popular opinion, but in accord with Ellwood and Summers, Wilson and Neckerman argue that welfare is not a primary cause of family break-ups, female-headed households, or out-of-wedlock births. If welfare does have an influence, it is on the living arrangements of single mothers, encouraging or permitting more of them to live independently.

Wilson and Neckerman point to male joblessness as the major determinant of changes in the structure of black families. Because of the poor labor market prospects of black men, black women are more likely to delay marriage and are less likely to remarry. The authors construct a "male marriageable pool index"—the ratio of employed civilian men to women of the same race and age group—and find that black women, especially young black women, face a shrinking pool of marriageable black men. The pool has not shrunk for white women; rather, the increase in white separation and divorce is due chiefly to the increased economic independence of white women rather than the absence of marriageable men.

Thus, the chapters described in this and the previous section address the issue of whether the growth of social spending since the mid-1960s—especially welfare—increased poverty or disrupted families. Each rejects the view that spending growth was a major cause of recent adverse trends in poverty or family structure. They instead single out economic stagnation, particularly high unemployment, as the main determinant of both trends.

Social Movements and Changes in Welfare Institutions

Michael Sosin analyzes changes in AFDC regulations, its appeals procedures, and other administrative practices brought about in part by the legal rights movement. Mobilized by the civil rights movement and related events in the 1960s, legal rights advocates contended that discretionary administrative practices denied welfare benefits to many who were eligible; they sought to change the perception of welfare from a discretionary award to a right under law. Sosin argues that the movement was successful in reducing discretion and increasing the welfare rolls, but that the bureaucratic reaction to it has reduced the sensitivity of the welfare system to the diversity of needs among clients.

Lawrence Mead favors a more political and less bureaucratic explanation for the welfare reforms of the late 1960s and early 1970s. He argues that welfare rolls expanded not primarily because of the legal rights movement but because of liberal changes in all social policies. He considers the current bureaucratic emphasis on rules and procedures as necessary to enforce the social obligations of work and child support that had previously been enforced through discretion. Mead concludes that welfare cannot become a right until obligations are conceded—benefit receipt must be reciprocated by a contribution, such as work.

Charles Hamilton and Dona Hamilton discuss the issues that have formed the agenda of civil rights organizations since the New Deal of the 1930s. They note that these organizations have favored government intervention on behalf of the poor, have preferred national action over that of state and local governments, and have generally advocated jobs over welfare. In the late 1960s and early 1970s, however, these organizations paid scant attention to direct job creation measures. In the Hamiltons' view, the acceptance by civil rights activists of a service-oriented welfare strategy during this period and their failure to support Richard Nixon's Family Assistance Plan were detrimental to the long-run economic well-being of blacks. Despite the advances of the past two decades, the Hamiltons conclude that civil rights organizations must continue to emphasize the elimination of job discrimination and reemphasize the need for increased employment opportunities.

The message of both Sosin and the Hamiltons is that the poor achieved lasting gains from the welfare rights and civil rights movements of the late 1960s and early 1970s, even though much of the momentum of those movements has been lost. What remains is the need to focus attention both on the way the welfare system treats recipients and the way minorities are treated in society in general and the labor market in particular.

Economic and Political Constraints on Antipoverty Initiatives

Hugh Heclo reminds us that antipoverty policy is dependent on favorable public opinion, but that support for such policy is difficult to sustain. Reflecting on both the New Deal and the Great Society, he finds that the War on Poverty initiatives suffered from four political weaknesses. First, the policy community lacked strong links to the politicians whose support was necessary for enactment of programs in forms that made implementation feasible. Second, major policy initiatives require strong presidential leadership, but the War on Poverty suffered when public support for President Johnson wavered. Third, association of the War on Poverty with the activism of a black-dominated coalition provoked a backlash. Finally, the political compromises required to obtain the necessary support undermined the operational feasibility of the programs.

Heclo then turns to analyses of public preferences. He argues that the public regards as suspect any grand ideological justifications for social action. Consequently, "Americans favor government action to help the poor, but they generally dislike the subset of government programs that are intended to be targeted on the poor." Thus, "the main political problem with antipoverty policy is that it is antipoverty policy." Only when antipoverty programs are disguised within "the protective coloration" of a larger social agenda can the programs obtain the political support necessary for passage in any effective form. The best example of successful use of that strategy is the Social Security system and its effectiveness in reducing poverty among the aged.

Burtless discusses the economic limits to social spending. Even though one additional dollar going to the poor rather than to defense does not necessarily affect national output (absent incentive effects of the expenditure), the current size of the federal deficit places an enormous obstacle in the way of increased antipoverty spending. To put the U.S. experience in perspective, Burtless compares social expenditures and economic growth in six major industrial nations. He rejects the notion of a trade-off between growth and redistribution, since countries with higher spending on social programs do not necessarily have lower growth rates. He therefore concludes that the limits to antipoverty spending are political, not economic.

Given the current economic and political climate, neither Heclo nor Burtless is optimistic about the near-term prospects for a renewed antipoverty effort.

Research Summary and Agenda

The final two chapters in this volume summarize what we have learned from the research of the past two decades and offer suggestions for future research.

Edward Gramlich focuses on three issues—the ways in which family structure relates to poverty; the problem of joblessness, particularly as it affects black men; and the preference for a categorical strategy to deliver benefits to the needy. His discussion of the family structure problem emphasizes several questions that remain unanswered: How does family splitting affect individual welfare? How do splits affect long-run economic mobility and poverty? His discussion of the employment problem stresses that we already have much evidence on the effects of work and training programs, but the results suggest that we do not know enough to increase significantly employment opportunities for the disadvantaged. In contrast to his pessimism about creating jobs, Gramlich concludes that categorization of support for specific groups among the poor and by means of specific goods and services is both economically and politically efficient.

Drawing on each of the chapters in the volume, Daniel Weinberg offers a poverty research agenda for the next decade. He suggests seven categories in which research is needed, each including both broad areas and narrow lines of research: family and household structure, work and welfare, in-kind transfer programs, labor market studies, the relationship of poverty to the broader society, intergovernmental relations, and methodological issues.

A Synthesis of Policy Themes and Prescriptions

Given the varying disciplinary backgrounds of the authors and their diverse views as to the appropriate role for antipoverty policy, it should not be surprising that no formal policy agenda emerged from the conference. But a number of common themes and policy prescriptions are apparent.

First, the authors reject the view that government programs do not work. Rather, as suggested by Burtless, a more appropriate conclusion is that, except for the substantial reduction in poverty among the aged, nothing works miracles. On the positive side, Starr documents gains in access to medical care and improvements in health; Bassi and Ashenfelter find modest returns from some employment and training programs; Glazer, modest successes in some education programs. Although it is clear in each of these areas that significant problems remain, neither these authors nor those of the other chapters advocate abandonment of public efforts to reduce poverty. Rather, they conclude that new policies must build on what we have learned does work and abandon what does not.

What Glazer suggests in his discussion of education is relevant to most areas of antipoverty policy—that we can accomplish more, particularly if we lower our expectations and establish realistic policy goals. The realization that we cannot work miracles leads to a second policy recommendation, explicitly defended by Ellwood and Summers but consistent with most other papers: because there is no single program or policy that can eliminate poverty, categorization by target groups as well as program area is important. The chapters contain no call for a national health insurance program or a guaranteed annual income or any such comprehensive reform. In fact, several advocate pursuing only some types of programs and targeting them on certain groups among the poor. For example, policies that are most appropriate for the elderly and other groups not expected to work are less appropriate or even not desirable for those able to work; some programs will work for women and not for men; the causes of black poverty differ from those of white poverty.

The third theme relates to the tension between income transfer and employment strategies. The planners of the War on Poverty and the American public in general have always preferred a "hand up" to a "handout." Yet most of the increased public spending since 1965 is accounted for by cash and in-kind income transfers. Transfers have been far more successful in reducing poverty than have education or employment and training programs. To quote Aaron Wildavsky (1977), we are "doing better, but feeling worse." We are doing better because the income transfer strategy has worked to alleviate poverty, but we are feeling worse because large numbers remain dependent on transfers. Mead's emphasis on reciprocity characterizes transfers for the able-bodied not as a right but as a return for work. This issue was the subject of much discussion which highlighted two obstacles to implementation: lack of jobs for low-skilled workers and mixed societal feelings about expecting single mothers with young children to work.

Finally, there is consensus that antipoverty policies cannot begin to be effective if unemployment rates remain high and if the economy fails to grow. Declines in poverty were rapid during the late 1960s when the economy was expanding and unemployment was low, but in the past fifteen years we have been unable to achieve such favorable macroeconomic conditions. Since 1983 the economy has grown, but unemployment remains high; when unemployment rates were lower, during the 1970s, growth was also lower. And Blank and Blinder conclude that even if we avoid recession and inflation over the 1983–1989 period, the poverty rate in 1989 will not fall below the rate of the early 1970s.

Although no general agreement was reached, specific recommendations for antipoverty policy proposed by the authors include the following:

Achievement of high employment rates (Danziger-Haveman-Plotnick, Ellwood-Summers, Blank-Blinder, Wilson-Neckerman, Hamilton-Hamilton)

Continued experimentation with education, employment, and training programs, especially those that emphasize the integration of welfare and work (Bassi-Ashenfelter, Glazer, Jencks, Mead)

Maintenance of transfers for those not expected to work (a "safety net") (Burtless, Danziger-Haveman-Plotnick, Ellwood-Summers)

A national minimum AFDC benefit (Danziger-Haveman-Plotnick, Bane)

Expansion and extension of the Earned Income Tax Credit and other tax changes to reduce the burden of taxation on the working poor (Danziger-Haveman-Plotnick, Blank-Blinder)

Expanded access to health insurance for those who lack coverage, along with better treatment of the poor who are covered (Starr)

These then are the findings, themes, and policy recommendations derived from an extensive review of the experience of the past twenty years. While no reader is likely to agree with them all, we hope that they serve to stimulate both poverty research and antipoverty policy formation.

2   Public Spending for the Poor: Trends, Prospects, and Economic Limits

Gary Burtless

THE PAST FIVE YEARS have seen a major break in the trend toward more generous support of transfer and training programs for the American poor. During the two decades after 1960 the federal government mounted or expanded a variety of expensive programs to assist the poor and near-poor: Medicaid, food stamps, subsidized housing, Supplemental Security Income, targeted student loans, low-income scholarships, comprehensive employment training, an earned income tax credit, and work incentives for able-bodied recipients of welfare. Many of these programs have been trimmed or even eliminated since 1979.[1] Although total outlays for the poor have continued to mount, all of the recent rise is attributable to inflation and rising poverty, with much of the latter caused by the impact of severe economic contraction. None of the rise has been due to more generous government provision for the low-income population.

The political reaction against poverty programs has occurred at least partly in response to adverse economic trends. Many voters, politicians, and economists believe that programs for the poor must be curtailed in an era when the real incomes of working taxpayers have failed to rise. Some would go further and argue that real income growth has stagnated precisely because poverty programs have been so generous; in their view these programs are not only redistributing the economic pie but also limiting its size.

Here I review the goals, design, and recent budget histories of the main forms of government aid to the poor, with specific consideration of the role of means-tested income transfers, social insurance, and federal programs to educate and train low-income workers. I discuss the trends and prospects of spending in each area and summarize the evidence regarding the effectiveness of each form of aid in reducing poverty. The chapter also includes·an examination of the adverse impacts of poverty spending on efficiency and economic growth. The economic limits to poverty spending can be viewed in two ways. There may be a natural limit on spending imposed by macroeconomic considerations—the current budget situation or the share of national income that can be devoted to government spending. Alternatively, the poverty programs themselves may have undesirable microeconomic effects on beneficiaries. If these effects are sufficiently harmful, the programs may actually increase the incidence of poverty rather than reduce it. Both of these economic limits are considered. The chapter concludes with a brief examination of prospects for future progress against poverty.

The Trend in Poverty Spending

The United States has established three kinds of programs to help equalize incomes and reduce poverty: means-tested income transfers, social insurance, and targeted education and training programs. Means-tested programs distribute money and other resources directly to poor or near-poor families. Participation in such programs is limited; the affluent need not apply. In certain cases benefits are restricted even more narrowly to particular classes of the poor—the aged, the disabled, single parents and their children. Judged according to traditional measures of antipoverty effectiveness, means-tested programs are highly efficient. A high proportion of benefits reaches families that would otherwise be poor or near-poor, and almost no benefits are received by families significantly above the poverty line.

A second type of redistribution takes place in the nation's far more popular social insurance programs—Social Security, Medicare, and unemployment insurance. These programs are largely financed by payroll taxes paid by the currently employed and their employers. Benefits are paid to groups that have low current earnings—the retired, the disabled, dependents of deceased workers, and the insured unemployed. As a whole, these recipient groups are less affluent than wage earners, at least as measured by current money income. With a one-year accounting period, social insurance programs undeniably redistribute income from the better off to the less well off.

This charitable view of the redistributive impact of social insurance must, however, be modified if we take a longer term perspective. Viewed over an individual's lifetime, social insurance redistributes income from periods of gainful employment when an individual has high income to periods of unemployment, disability, or retirement when wage income is low. Benefits received in adversity are assumed to be a rightful repayment of taxes paid during flush times. This lifetime redistribution takes place for insured workers whether they are poor, middle-class, or wealthy.

The last form of redistribution aims at equalizing incomes in the future rather than in the present. Instead of redistributing current incomes, human capital enhancement programs provide special education, training, and employment help that is directed toward raising the future earnings of disadvantaged children and adults. Head Start, targeted aid to elementary schools, basic educational opportunity grants, the Job Corps, and the Job Training Partnership Act are among the better-known human capital enhancement programs. One would expect that these programs would enjoy greater popularity than means-tested income transfers since their goal is to reduce poverty and public dependency. But education and training programs have been cut much more severely than means-tested transfers in the past few years.

Social scientists, and economists in particular, have usually shown greater enthusiasm for targeted human capital programs than for income transfers. In part this preference arises from a theoretical bias. The case for pure income redistribution has left many economists uneasy. Taking a dollar from rich Mr. Smith to give to poor Mr. Jones lowers the welfare of the first and raises that of the second but has an unknown effect on the combined utility of the two, even if the total amount of income to be divided between Mr. Smith and Mr. Jones remains unchanged. But there are good economic reasons to believe that income will not remain unchanged; it may fall, possibly *lowering* the combined utility of the two men.

The case for targeted human capital investment appears stronger. Rich Mr. Smith is required to contribute one dollar to training or educating poor Mr. Jones, and in consequence the latter is transformed into a better earner. Since the combined income of Messrs. Smith and Jones may thereby be raised, economists have found it easier to persuade themselves that the combined utility of the two men has been enhanced. But combined after-tax income can only be raised if poor Mr. Jones's earnings are ultimately raised by more than one dollar. If they are raised by less than that amount, Mr. Smith has paid more for Mr. Jones's training than that training has been worth to Mr. Jones. Mr. Smith could have raised the poorer man's income more cheaply simply by transferring money to him directly. In practice, one cannot be sure of the return on investing in human capital programs. This element of uncertainty may explain why the nation invests so little in such progams, although lip service is paid to the idea that these programs are preferable to the dole. Both the poor and the nonpoor may prefer that society help impoverished breadwinners earn their way out of poverty, but there is no guarantee that education and training programs can achieve that goal, in either the short or the long run.

MEANS-TESTED TRANSFERS

Means-tested transfers are paid out by programs specifically aimed at raising money incomes or consumption levels of poor families and individuals. State, local, and federal government agencies distribute means-tested transfers in two forms, as cash grants and as earmarked or in-kind transfers. The programs popularly referred to as "welfare" distribute cash payments. The main cash programs include AFDC, general assistance, and categorical aid programs for the blind, disabled, and destitute elderly. These last programs were combined in the federally administered Supplemental Security Income in 1974. The federal government also offers means-tested cash aid to impoverished veterans and their families. All of the cash assistance programs except general assistance and means-tested veterans' benefits trace their origins to the Social Security Act of 1935. Until the mid-1960s cash transfers accounted for an overwhelming fraction of all means-tested transfers distributed to the poor. In 1966, for example, 88 percent of means-tested transfers were distributed in the form of cash aid.

Over the past quarter-century, spending on cash assistance programs has gone through several distinct phases, as may be seen in Figure 2.1. From 1960 to 1973 there was a quintupling of federal, state, and local spending on AFDC, as average benefit levels rose and participation in the program mounted.[2] Real spending on AFDC rose again in 1975 and 1976 in response to the severe 1974–75 recession. But since 1976 AFDC outlays have fallen substantially. In the eight years after 1976 real outlays declined by 20 percent, as nominal benefit levels failed to keep pace with the rate of inflation and, more recently, as eligibility limits were tightened.

Spending on the other cash assistance programs grew much more slowly after 1960. Means-tested veterans' payments actually declined in real terms. Real outlays for other public assistance also remained relatively flat, except in the two years after 1973, when the federal government assumed responsibility for aid to the blind, disabled, and elderly. Between 1973 and 1975 real outlays for aid to those groups rose 36 percent, but since that

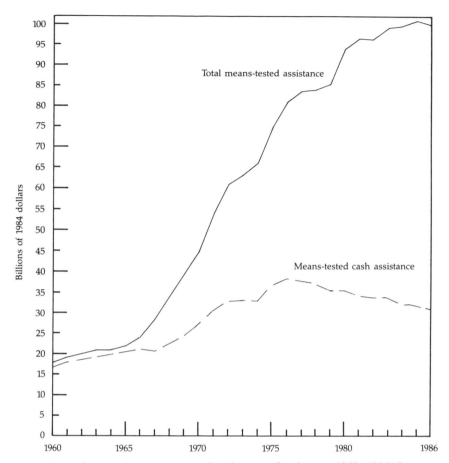

Figure 2.1.   Outlays for means-tested assistance, fiscal years 1960–1986. Sources: U.S. Department of Health, Education, and Welfare (1971); U.S. House of Representatives (1984); U.S. Department of Health and Human Services, Social Security Administration (1984); U.S. Office of Management and Budget, *Budget of the U.S. Government,* various years.

time outlays have remained relatively unchanged. Total real spending on cash assistance rose to a peak in 1976 and has fallen about 15 percent since that year. Thus, contrary to a popular perception that welfare spending was soaring at the time President Reagan took office, real cash assistance outlays rose only 16 percent in the decade from 1971 to 1980 and actually fell 7 percent in the four years before 1981.

The recent history of in-kind assistance programs is markedly different from that of the cash programs: Real spending on means-tested in-kind programs has risen strongly and without interruption since the mid-1960s, although the rate of increase fell after 1981 (see Figure 2.1). In-kind assistance is provided in three main forms: as food (through food commodity distribution, subsidized school meals, and food stamps); as housing (through public housing projects and other housing subsidy programs); and as medical care (primarily through the federal-state Medicaid program). Government spending on each of these forms of assistance has soared since 1965, although the growth in Medicaid has far outpaced that in either food or housing aid. The period of fastest growth of food assistance programs was 1969 through 1981, when federal spending on means-tested food and nutrition aid rose from less than $1.5 billon to $18 billion. Real spending on these programs has declined since 1981 and is expected to remain flat in the future. Housing and energy aid grew somewhat more slowly than food assistance and has also leveled off.

The most striking expansion of means-tested assistance has occurred in the Medicaid program. Begun in 1965, the program accounted for less than 5 percent of means-tested program outlays in 1966; this figure rose to 30 percent in 1972 and is expected to be 40 percent in fiscal year 1985. Part of the rapid growth of Medicaid in the late 1960s and early 1970s consisted of the predictable expansion associated with any new transfer program: the number of beneficiaries grew quickly as states initiated or extended their means-tested medical assistance programs. Since the mid-1970s, however, the number of Medicaid recipients has stabilized at about 22 million (Russell, 1983). Nonetheless, inflation-adjusted outlays for Medicaid have risen by two-thirds since 1975. This increase has occurred both because medical inflation has been far higher than general inflation and because more resources have been devoted to providing medical care to each patient.

To be sure, measurable health gains have resulted from this higher level of expenditure (see Chapter 5). But it is doubtful that needy families would have spent as much to achieve those gains as the gains have cost taxpayers. If they had been given $40 billon in cash rather than $40 billion worth of direct medical assistance, recipients of Medicaid would almost certainly have spent far less than the full amount on medical care. The same may be true for government assistance provided in the form of free or low-cost food, housing, and energy. The value of the assistance to poor recipients is lower than the cost of providing it. Yet three dollars out of every ten that is transferred through means-tested programs is provided in the form of subsidized food, housing, and energy, and four dollars is transferred as free medical care. Only three out of the ten dollars is transferred as cash.

By contrast, in the early 1960s about *nine* dollars out of ten was transferred as cash.

Whatever the preferences of assistance recipients, taxpayers and voters have demonstrated a growing preference for transferring earmarked aid rather than cash to the needy. As the total amount of means-tested assistance has risen from 1.2 percent of gross national product (GNP) in 1965 to 2.9 percent in 1981–1984, the amount of cash aid has actually fallen as a percentage of GNP—from 1.1 percent to 1.0 percent—and is expected to fall even further. This allocation of transfers might have occurred because many voters are less concerned about poverty in general than about specific types of deprivation—lack of food, decent housing, and essential medical care. Voters may be generally satisfied with the highly unequal rewards handed out in the economic race, at least as rewards are measured by money incomes, but the public is unwilling to tolerate drastic penalties for those who fail. Starvation, homelessness, and lack of access to needed medical help are penalties that can be ruled out. Income poverty is complacently tolerated. The lack of sufficient income to secure a minimally comfortable life is viewed as a just desert for economic failure.

As mentioned, the fraction of national income distributed to the poor through means-tested programs has more than doubled since the early 1960s. Nonetheless, the fraction remains quite modest, has changed little since 1975, and is expected to decline slowly in the future. How efficient have these programs been in reducing poverty? Careful analysis of the income sources of American families has shown that a high fraction of means-tested benefits has been distributed to families whose pretransfer incomes were below the poverty line. For example, in examining 1974 means-tested transfers Robert Plotnick estimated that 84 percent of cash assistance and 73 percent of in-kind aid was received by people whose pretransfer incomes were in the poverty range (Plotnick, 1979, p. 284). Using more detailed monthly and quarterly statistics, Daniel Weinberg (1985) recently confirmed these estimates. In addition, he computed the percentage of payments that actually alleviated officially measured poverty by subtracting that portion of monthly benefits that raised a family's income above the poverty line. Weinberg's tabulations indicate that approximately three-quarters of cash welfare, food stamps, and housing assistance benefits directly contributed to reducing the poverty gap.

The target efficiency of means-tested transfers should hardly come as a surprise since, by definition, benefits are restricted to poor and near-poor families. The surprise in the statistics arises from the fact that poverty was reduced so little by means-tested transfers. Weinberg reports that only 23 percent of the April 1979 poverty gap was removed by income-conditioned transfers, including both cash and noncash benefits.[3] Since the monthly poverty gap was slightly less than $7 billion and monthly outlays on income-conditional transfers amounted to about $5.3 billion in fiscal year 1979, the amount of poverty reduction seems oddly small.

The modest impact of means-tested programs is attributable to a number of factors. Government outlays on assistance programs pay both for program administration and for benefits. Only the latter directly reduce poverty. Second, census surveys are plagued by underreporting of income, especially of means-tested income; for example, only 63 percent of AFDC benefits is reported on the census survey used in Weinberg's study. This situation diminishes the measured impact of transfers. Finally, the institutionalized population, mainly in nursing homes, receives an important fraction of means-tested benefits, particularly Medicaid.[4] That population is excluded in most census surveys, even though its well-being is substantially improved by income-conditioned transfers. Indeed, without Medicaid benefits many elderly poor could not afford to be institutionalized.

In spite of ample evidence that means-tested transfers are well targeted but nonetheless remain too small to eliminate poverty, many critics of aid to the needy claim that a high proportion of benefits is shamefully wasted on the nonpoor. Statistics in support of this view are not difficult to find and they appear to contradict the Weinberg findings just cited. The U.S. Office of Management and Budget (OMB) has published figures showing that benefits payments under means-tested programs far exceed the size of the poverty gap but that only half the gap is filled by these payments. For example, in calendar year 1982 the poverty gap was $54 billion; in the same year means-tested benefit payments reached almost $79 billion—46 percent more than the size of the poverty gap. Yet the gap was reduced by only $27 billion as a result of those income-conditioned payments, implying that two-thirds of payments went to the nonpoor (Stockman, 1984, pp. 247, 295).

One might infer from these statistics that our society is generous to a fault in attempting to reduce poverty but unaccountably careless in permitting benefits to be siphoned off by the affluent. The OMB statistics, however, reflect a different definition of the nonpoor than the one used in the analysis cited earlier. Rather than computing the fraction of benefits going to the pretransfer poor, OMB calculated benefits received by the *prewelfare* poor. Thus, the poverty gap is computed by taking account of the value of social insurance payments and the insurance value of Medicare benefits. Both the poverty gap and the number of poor are obviously much smaller under that definition. According to the OMB definition, society is wasting a large fraction of the Medicaid benefits that go to individuals whose well-being is brought near or slightly above the poverty line by Social Security and Medicare. I suspect that this view is shared by only a small minority of people with elderly relatives helped by the Medicaid program.

A reasonable assessment of the target efficiency of means-tested transfers lies somewhere between the two views just described but is probably much closer to Weinberg's view than to the OMB view. A very high fraction of all means-tested benefits goes to people whose incomes, without government help, would fall below the poverty line. Virtually all of the remainder goes to people with incomes close to the poverty threshold. But many people receiving means-tested transfers also receive government help in another form—social insurance. The combined total of social insurance and means-tested transfers raises the well-being of some assisted families, particularly elderly families, comfortably above the poverty threshold, but it leaves the well-being of many others, especially single-parent and single-person families, below the poverty line.

It would be simple, but politically unpopular, to raise the target efficiency of means-tested transfers. Most if not all forms of means-tested assistance could be combined into a single cash transfer in which there is a confiscatory marginal tax rate both on earnings and social insurance benefits. If the cash transfer were noncategorical, some groups presently suffering severe poverty, such as single-member families, would receive more generous treatment than they do under the existing transfer system. Uniting presently separate programs into a single cash grant would eliminate the possibility that transfer recipients receive multiple program benefits whose combined value substantially exceeds the poverty level. A confiscatory tax rate would ensure that benefits are paid only to the poor, not to the near-poor. The political unpopularity of this type of reform springs from voters' preference for selectively ensuring access to minimal housing, nutrition, and medical care rather than universally guaranteeing a minimum level of money income.[5] Moreover, voters have revealed a preference for imposing low marginal tax rates in medical care, housing, and nutrition assistance programs. One consequence of their preferences is that means-tested programs are less target efficient than they might be. Nonetheless, means-tested transfers are the nation's least costly mechanism for reducing the gap between market-provided incomes and the resources required for a standard of living above the poverty level.

SOCIAL INSURANCE

Social Security, Medicare, and unemployment insurance are the major social insurance programs available in the United States. Social Security Old Age and Survivors Insurance and federally supported unemployment insurance were first introduced during the New Deal. The population covered by these programs has been expanded repeatedly since that time and now includes all but a small fraction of the work force. Social Security Disability Insurance was added in 1956. Medicare—or hospital insurance—was begun in 1965 as a natural extension of the basic Social Security program.

None of the social insurance programs was specifically designed to eliminate poverty. The cash social insurance programs were intended to insure workers and their dependents against earnings losses arising from the retirement, death, disability, or temporary unemployment of a breadwinner. Medicare protects the elderly and disabled against extraordinary outlays for hospital and medical services. Obviously, social insurance provides protection against several important causes of poverty, but other sources of poverty were ignored in the design of the social insurance programs. A worker or new labor market entrant in a situation of long-term unemployment can expect to receive little help under our social insurance system. Workers who are steadily employed but at very low wage rates can also expect scant aid for their families until they reach age sixty-two, become disabled, or expire. Clearly, large classes of the poor receive little help from social insurance programs.

By contrast, nearly all middle-class and affluent workers can expect to receive social insurance benefits sometime during their lives. The level of benefits for middle-class workers has turned out to be quite generous. For current Social Security and Medicare beneficiaries, the amount of benefits received has far exceeded the amount of taxes paid. Because Social Security benefit levels are scaled to the level of past wages, it is actually possible that the difference between benefits and past taxes is larger for affluent retirees than for poorer retirees (Hurd and Shoven, 1983). As the system matures, such windfall gains for very affluent workers will become much less common.

There are good empirical and theoretical reasons for the perception that social insurance provides income protection primarily for the middle class. Nonetheless, these programs are far more important than means-tested transfers in raising families out of poverty. In the study mentioned earlier, Weinberg estimates that 64 percent of Social Security and Medicare benefits have been received by families and individuals whose pretransfer incomes were below the poverty line. More than one-third of Social Security and Medicare benefits have gone toward reducing the poverty gap,[6] and one-half of the pretransfer poverty gap was eliminated by Social Security and Medicare benefits (Weinberg, 1985). Among families headed by someone over sixty-five, Social Security and Medicare alone reduced the pretransfer poverty rate by 51 percentage points, from 68 percent before transfers to 17 percent after Social Security and Medicare benefits were counted. These two social insurance programs eliminated nearly 90 percent of the pretransfer poverty gap for elderly families (Weinberg, 1985).

As suggested earlier, Social Security and Medicare are much less redistributive if viewed in a lifetime perspective. Since the beneficiary population includes virtually the entire population over age sixty-five, it must be the case that a majority of recipients had moderate or high incomes before their retirement. In addition, the pretransfer poverty rate of the elderly overstates the hardship of their situation in the absence of Social Security. If social insurance had never been invented, many of the elderly would have worked longer, would have accumulated savings to finance a larger share of postretirement consumption, or would have chosen to live out their lives in the households of more affluent relatives, especially their children. Although it is difficult to estimate the precise effect of Social Security and Medicare on the earnings, savings, and living arrangements of the elderly, it is likely that the total impact has been important (Danziger, Haveman, and Plotnick, 1981).

Notwithstanding the behavioral response to Social Security and Medicare and the high preretirement incomes of Social Security and Medicare recipients, it is certain that these two transfer programs have significantly reduced poverty among the elderly and disabled. This can be seen in the very sharp declines in poverty among the aged that have occurred as real benefits have been raised. In 1959 the income poverty rate of the elderly was 35 percent, while the rate for the remainder of the population was only 22 percent. By 1983 the income poverty rate for the elderly had fallen to 14 percent, while for the nonelderly it was more than 15 percent. If one takes account of in-kind income sources—including Medicare—the poverty rate for the elderly was less than 10 percent in 1983. A large share of the decline in poverty among the elderly has been due to the rise in real Social Security and Medicare benefits since 1960.

Unemployment insurance (UI) is less effective as an antipoverty program than either Social Security or Medicare. A higher proportion of jobless benefits is received by families whose annual incomes would be above the poverty line in the absence of social insurance payments. To be insured under UI an unemployed worker must have a recent and fairly stable work history. This eligibility criterion precludes benefit receipt for important classes of the poor—the nonemployed, the erratically employed, and the chronically underemployed. In spite of this, the program is significantly redistributive. Among husband-wife families with two earners, the average UI benefit for poor households is nearly five times the average benefit received by families with annual incomes more than 400 percent of the poverty threshold. (Nonrecipients as well as UI recipients are counted in computing the average benefit.) Among husband-wife families with only a single earner, the average benefit for poverty-level households is nearly 25 times greater than that for families whose incomes are more than 400 percent of the poverty line (Burtless, 1984, p. 125). Unemployment insurance appears even more redistributive when evaluated according to a weekly or monthly accounting period. Although only 18 percent of UI recipients were below the poverty level before they became unemployed, the percentage in poverty rose to 61 percent once earnings ceased (Burtless, 1984, p. 126).

One of the main differences between UI and Social Security is that unemployment is a temporary phenomenon while retirement and disability can last indefinitely. Unemployed workers typically find jobs after only brief spells of unemployment; hence their annual incomes may put them well above the poverty line. Retired and disabled workers usually do not engage in paid employment at all; consequently, their annual earned incomes are well below the poverty line. But for both groups of workers—the temporarily unemployed, on the one hand, and the retired and disabled, on the other—social insurance is vital for maintaining income during a period in which earnings are absent.

The notion that unemployment insurance, Medicare, and especially Social Security are middle-class programs is at once a political strength and an ideological weakness. Because benefits are so broadly distributed, because they indisputably provide a critical source of support for millions of families, and because taxpayers can reasonably expect to receive similar benefits at some future date, social insurance is by far the most popular vehicle of income redistribution (see Chapter 13). But the vast size of the target population prompts both conservative and neoliberal criticism. If the program simply redistributes income from one phase of a worker's life to another, conservatives argue, why is government intervention required at all? Workers on their own could surely devise a redistribution scheme superior to the one imposed by the government. The neoliberal questions the logic of social insurance programs as a means of redistribution: Why should poor wage earners be heavily taxed in order to pay for benefits received by the middle class and affluent elderly?

The question posed by the neoliberal rests on the presumption that social insurance is not redistributive enough. As shown above, however, the pretransfer poor receive a high proportion of social insurance benefits.[7] A large share of the remainder is paid out to families not very far above the poverty line. Further, because a recipient of Social Security appears securely ensconced in the middle class, it does not follow that he or she would remain there if Social Security payments ceased. Payments made to the very affluent elderly, like payments to the less affluent, are regarded as a right earned by virtue of prior tax contributions. The link between benefits and tax contributions makes the program more palatable to taxpayers and makes benefit payments acceptable as a form of government aid to recipients. It is doubtful that the immense amount of redistribution carried out through Social Security would be long continued if the link between taxes and benefits were severed.

Liberal and conservative analysts have both felt growing disquiet about social insurance programs. Economists in particular have devoted increasing attention to the undesirable side effects of retirement and disability insurance, jobless benefits, and third-party payment of medical bills. The recent concern about social insurance is a natural consequence of the rapid growth in these programs over the past quarter-century. Unlike means-tested programs, in which the rate of growth in real outlays fell after 1975, real outlays for the major social insurance programs have continued to rise rapidly. Since 1975 means-tested outlays have risen at an annual rate of only 3.0 percent, while social insurance spending has been increasing—on top of a much higher base—at a 4.9-percent rate. In fact, since the mid-1970s annual spending on Social Security, Medicare, unemployment insurance, and black lung benefits has *risen* by an amount exceeding total outlays for all means-tested programs. After remaining relatively constant in the early 1960s, social insurance outlays as a percentage of GNP rose from 3.3 percent in 1966 to 7.1 percent in 1984.[8]

Real outlays for other social insurance programs have climbed much more rapidly over the past twenty-five years (Figure 2.2). Expenditures on Old Age and Survivors Insurance (OASI) have risen by more than 350 percent since 1960. Outlays grew especially rapidly between 1968 and 1973, rising at an annual rate of 10 percent. This rise occurred because of the maturation of the OASI program—new beneficiaries were receiving much higher benefits than older ones—and because of the 20-percent rise in real

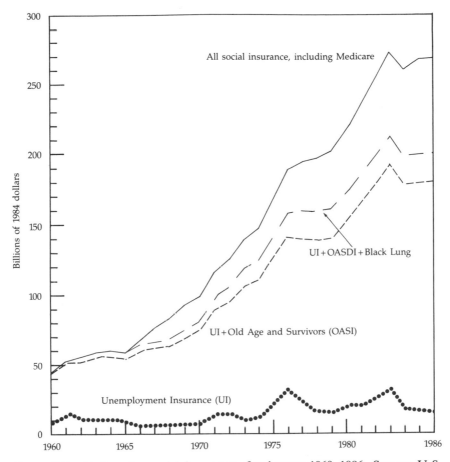

Figure 2.2. Outlays for social insurance, fiscal years 1960–1986. Source: U.S. Office of Management and Budget, *Budget of the U.S. Government,* various years.

basic benefit levels implemented between 1970 and 1973. Since 1973 OASI outlays have grown more slowly, averaging about 4.9 percent per year, and the future growth rate is expected to fall further, to about 2.1 percent per year between 1983 and 1987. The declining growth derives partly from the elimination of unintended double indexing of benefits, effective in 1979, and from the delay in cost-of-living adjustments, voted in 1983.

The pattern of disability insurance (DI) outlays has been broadly similar to the OASI experience. Real program expenditures rose more than eleven-fold between 1960 and 1981, although they have fallen since that year. Outlays grew especially quickly from 1968 to 1977, rising at a compound annual rate of nearly 14 percent. Part of the rise was due to the 20-percent real benefit increase mentioned earlier, but most of it was attributable to a doubling in the number of recipients.[9] The number of applications for benefits rose sharply in that period, and the standards for program eligibility may have loosened. But the number of beneficiaries has fallen by one-fifth since 1977, and real outlays have risen only slightly. The explosion in DI outlays is over.

The same cannot be said of Medicare expenditures. Although the rapid rise in Medicare outlays in the late 1960s was predictable—the program was introduced only in 1965—the increase in spending since 1973 was largely unexpected. Medicare expenditures measured in constant dollars more than tripled in the eleven years after 1973. Thus, outlays grew at a compound annual growth rate of more than 11 percent. The number of persons enrolled in Medicare has risen by less than one-quarter of that rate.[10] Most of the rise in outlays has been due to rising utilization of medical services by enrollees and to medical care inflation that has outstripped general price inflation.[11] Thus, compared with the Medicare-covered population in the late 1960s and early 1970s, the covered population today is obtaining more medical services and treatment that is far more costly. As in the case of Medicaid, the program has generated measurable health benefits for the elderly (see Chapter 5), but it is doubtful that the eligible population would be willing to pay for this level of improved health care if the program were converted from insurance protection to cash grants costing taxpayers the same amount of money. In improving the health status of the aged and disabled, Medicare has achieved some real gains, but as a method of raising the post-transfer well-being of the poor and near-poor aged, it is extremely costly.

In terms of both outlays and effects, social insurance programs dwarf means-tested assistance programs by a substantial margin. A great deal more money is spent on them, and they keep a far greater number of low-income families out of poverty. The relative size of social insurance and means-tested programs might have been difficult to foresee as recently as thirty-five years ago. In June 1950 more old people were receiving government aid through the Old Age Assistance (OAA) program than under Old Age Insurance (2.8 million as opposed to 2.1 million). The average OAA payment in 1949 was 70 percent higher than the average primary insurance amount under OAI. Assistance rolls were rising steadily and at a pace fast enough to remain ahead of the insurance rolls (Derthick, 1979, p. 273). Disability insurance and Medicare had not yet been invented. The disabled received cash aid under public assistance programs, and the aged and disabled received government help in paying medical bills through means-tested programs.

The development of disability insurance and Medicare, the maturation of the Old Age Insurance program, legislated increases in real cash benefit levels, and the extension of Social Security, Medicare, and unemployment insurance coverage to nearly all classes of workers have dramatically increased the scope of social insurance in the United States. For low- and average-wage workers who succeed in becoming insured, social insurance programs frequently make the difference between a life in want and life of comfortable subsistence when a breadwinner is faced with unemployment, disability, or forced early retirement. But other groups continue to experience high poverty rates in spite of the rise in spending on social insurance and means-tested aid. More than one-fifth of all children under eighteen and one-quarter of children under six live in families with money incomes below the poverty line (U.S. Bureau of Census, 1984d, p. 25). For the most part the families of these children are poor as a result of circumstances that are not covered by the nation's social insurance programs. Means-tested assistance by itself is simply not sufficiently generous to eliminate the poverty of these families.

INVESTMENT IN EDUCATION AND TRAINING

When the War on Poverty was launched in 1964, the Johnson Administration asserted that its strategy to reduce poverty would raise the earnings of poor people rather than increase transfers. In outlining the administration's proposed policies, the 1964 *Economic Report of the President* was conspicuous in omitting any mention of cash aid to the nonaged, nondisabled poor. According to the report, "Americans want to *earn* the American standard of living by their own efforts and contributions. It would be far better, even if more difficult, to equip and to permit the poor of the Nation to produce and to earn the . . . $11 billion [required to eliminate poverty]" (U.S. Council of Economic Advisers, 1964, p. 77). Among other elements, the strategy outlined in the 1964 *Economic Report* called for improved labor market exchange, expansion of educational opportunity, and added job counseling and training for poor teenagers and adults.

The authors of the 1964 report had a powerful faith in the ameliorative effects of education and training. One of the most frequently quoted statements in the report is the assertion that "if children of poor families can be given skills and motivation, they will not become poor adults" (U.S.

Council of Economic Advisers, 1964, p. 75). To be fair, this view was widely shared at the time by members of both the public and the social science professions. It derived from the well-documented association between educational attainment, on the one hand, and social status and income, on the other. Since those on the top of the earnings distribution had more education than those on the bottom, it was believed that by raising the quality and amount of training received by workers on the bottom inequality of income could be reduced. A scientific model to rationalize this faith was introduced in the early 1960s when the theory of human capital investment was first propounded.[12] This belief led to a variety of program initiatives.

Space does not permit a review of all of the education and training programs introduced during or after the War on Poverty. Their number is too large, their target populations too numerous, their aims too diverse, and their funding levels too small to justify such a discussion. In Figure 2.3 I show the trend in real federal outlays for targeted human capital programs over the past quarter-century. Outlays are divided into two general categories. The first category includes expenditures on education programs, primarily for economically disadvantaged students in nursery, elementary, and secondary schools and in college. Since it is unclear whether the guaranteed student loan (GSL) program can strictly be considered "targeted," outlays for that program are shown separately. The second category of spending includes federal expenditures for manpower training, work experience, and public service employment (PSE).[13] Like GSL, PSE is an ambiguous item: The program was not always carefully targeted on the low-income population, although most jobs went to the economically disadvantaged, especially in the late 1970s; neither was the main purpose of the program to enhance the human capital of participants. For those reasons, PSE spending has been separately tabulated.[14]

Federal spending on targeted human capital programs rose very quickly after 1964. The rise of educational outlays, particularly for Head Start and Title I of the Education Act, was especially rapid. From 1965 to 1967 annual expenditures increased from less than $1 billion to slightly more than $6 billion in constant 1984 dollars. Spending on manpower programs rose somewhat more slowly but nevertheless tripled between 1965 and 1967 and rose to nearly $4 billion by 1968. In spite of these impressive rates of gain, in 1968 federal spending on human capital programs was less than half the level of federal spending on means-tested assistance programs and less than one-third of combined federal, state, and local spending on public assistance programs. In fact, the absolute rise in spending on targeted

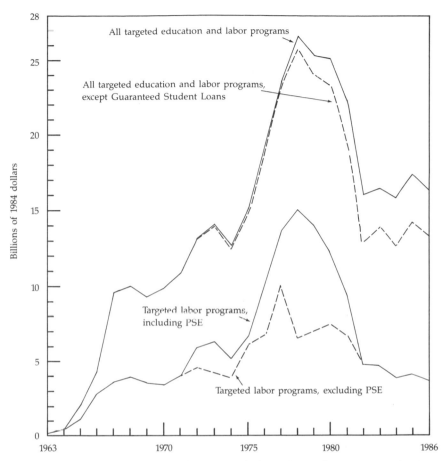

Figure 2.3. Outlays for targeted human capital programs, fiscal years 1963–1986.
Source: U.S. Office of Management and Budget, *Budget of the U.S. Government*,
various years.

human capital programs was somewhat smaller than the rise in combined
outlays for means-tested transfers. To be sure, only a small part of the rise
in means-tested benefits during the Johnson administration was in the form
of cash assistance; most of the increase was in in-kind aid. Nonetheless,
there was a wide gap between the trend in government spending and the
President's 1964 promise to restrain assistance outlays by increasing public
investment in education and training.

Education and manpower spending rose much more slowly under President Nixon than under Johnson. From 1968 to 1975 real spending grew
slightly faster than 6 percent per year, even including outlays for the new

GSL and PSE programs. The main action during those years was in the means-tested assistance programs, outlays for which were growing more than 12 percent a year (on a much higher base). During the Ford and early Carter administrations, however, spending on targeted human capital programs spurted once again, rising more than 75 percent between 1975 and 1978. The majority of this rise was due to increased spending on the PSE program, which rose from $0.6 billion to $8.6 billion, and on the GSL program, which rose from $0.2 billion to $0.8 billion. Spending on other education and training programs continued to rise at about the same pace as during the Nixon administration.

When the PSE program was trimmed and then eliminated between 1979 and 1983, real outlays for human capital programs began to fall substantially. Spending on the main targeted human capital programs fell in the latter part of the Carter administration and then dropped much more sharply after President Reagan's election. Between 1978 and 1983 outlays for programs other than PSE and GSL fell by one-fifth. Including the PSE and GSL reductions, outlays fell by almost two-fifths. The Reagan administration expects continued spending decreases in the future, although the declines will occur at a slower rate than in the recent past.

Federal programs to educate and train low-income children and adults represent the only large category of programs for the poor in which spending patterns have broadly conformed to widely held perceptions about the recent history of social welfare outlays. The programs were inconsequential prior to the Kennedy administration, expanded very rapidly in the four years after President Johnson declared war on poverty in 1964, grew more slowly during the administrations of Nixon, Ford, and Carter, and then shrank substantially after the inauguration of President Reagan. By contrast, real outlays for both means-tested and social insurance transfers have risen regardless of the political party in office and continue to rise, although at a much more moderate pace, under President Reagan. Presidents can exercise a greater degree of budgetary control over grant-in-aid programs than over entitlement programs, particularly entitlement programs indexed to inflation such as Social Security, Medicaid, and food stamps. When prices rise sharply, as they did during President Carter's term, or joblessness increases, as it did under Presidents Ford and Reagan, spending on indexed entitlement programs will automatically increase. By contrast, there is no direct connection between prices or unemployment and federal spending on human capital investment. For that reason, spending on targeted human capital programs provides a more direct reflection of the in-

cumbent president's views on the desirable size and composition of
government spending for the poor.

Even if a president wishes to trim poverty spending, the amount devoted
to human capital programs is simply too small for changes in outlays to
have a major impact on trends in total poverty spending. This point is
illustrated in Figure 2.4, which shows trends in poverty and social insurance
spending since 1960. Measured as a percentage of GNP, outlays for targeted
human capital programs and PSE rose from virtually nothing to 0.85 percent in 1978 and since then have fallen to less than 0.45 percent. Although
the drop in human capital spending since 1978 has been significant, it has

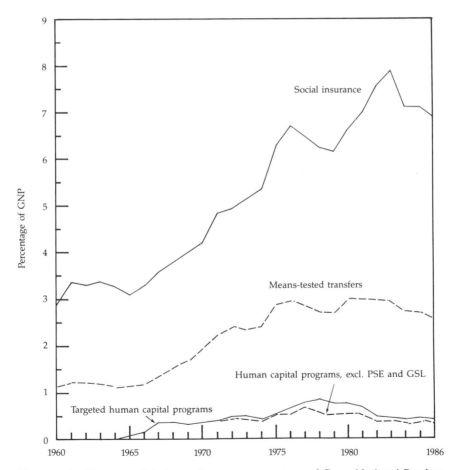

Figure 2.4.   Poverty-related spending as a percentage of Gross National Product,
fiscal years 1960–1986. Sources: See Figures 2.1–2.3.

been offset by movements in means-tested transfers, which rose 0.2 percentage points of GNP between 1978 and 1983, and in social insurance, which rose 1.7 percentage points. The rise in Medicaid expenditures alone has been enough to compensate for most of the decline in human capital outlays.

Although outlays for targeted education and training programs have been comparatively small, it is nonetheless important to consider whether this spending has been effective in reducing poverty. The question requires more careful analysis than I can give it here. The evaluation literature on targeted education and training programs is enormous, is highly varied in quality, and includes some studies showing nil or even negative program effects on cognition, achievement, school attainment, and postprogram earnings. I am most familiar with the literature on manpower training and therefore shall concentrate on the manpower programs.[15]

Manpower training should have a more immediate impact on poverty reduction than education programs, since the former is generally provided to teenagers about to enter the labor force and to adults of working age and is supposed to be directly relevant to employment. Education assistance, by contrast, is not specifically aimed at improving job skills and is provided to young students who may be years away from earning a living. The consensus among manpower analysts is that the main training programs have been beneficial in raising many participants' earnings, at least in the short run.[16] Classroom training, on-the-job training, and work experience under the Comprehensive Employment and Training Act (CETA) have been especially beneficial for adult women and less helpful or not helpful at all for adult men and teenagers. The Job Corps, which provides a comprehensive set of health, basic education, and vocational services to young people, has also been helpful in raising postprogram earnings. (But much of the net social benefit of this program arises from reductions in criminal activity during and after a youngster's participation. The reduction in crime represents a gain to potential criminal victims but does not directly affect poverty.) Public service employment jobs have directly provided income to otherwise unemployed disadvantaged workers but apparently have achieved only a minor degree of success in raising postprogram earnings.

On a microeconomic level the gains from some programs have been impressive. The Congressional Budget Office estimates that adult women participating in CETA-sponsored classroom training, on-the-job training, and work experience programs raised their annual real wages by $1,000 to $1,640 (1984 dollars) as a result of participation. This represents a gain of 25 to 75 percent of average earnings before enrollment, a substantial improvement by any standard (U.S. Congressional Budget Office and National Commission for Employment Policy, 1982, pp. 19, A-42). In view of the costs of these programs, the earnings gains by adult women are high enough so that taxpayers might reasonably prefer to spend money on training rather than direct transfer payments.[17] One dollar spent on training ultimately raises the incomes of recipients by more than one dollar. Effective training not only redistributes the economic pie from the nonpoor to the poor but increases the size of the pie.

We should not judge an antipoverty strategy solely by its successes, however. Many individual women and the great majority of adult men and teenagers are not helped by most of the low-cost training strategies our nation has tried. Manpower training remains a highly uncertain mechanism for raising the incomes of any *individual* breadwinner and is only modestly effective in raising the *aggregate* income of trainees, including men, women, and teenagers. I suspect that the earnings impact of education programs targeted on younger students is even more tenuous (also see Chapter 7). The lesson to be drawn is not that targeted education and training are valueless; they are modestly useful. But unfortunately they are unlikely to make a crucial difference in the lives of most people who participate in them.

Economic Limits to Poverty Spending

Social insurance and other poverty-related expenditures have increased tremendously in the past two-and-a-half decades, both absolutely and as a percentage of national output (see Table 2.1). They have risen in the context of generally rising government outlays, but they have also become a much larger fraction of government spending. In the two decades after 1960, social insurance and poverty spending increased from 16 percent to 30 percent of government outlays and have stabilized at that level over the past several years.

Between 1960 and 1984 overall federal spending as a share of GNP rose 5 percentage points. All of the rise was concentrated in the three categories of spending considered above—means-tested transfers, social insurance, and targeted human capital programs. The rise in other federal nondefense spending as a share of GNP was just about offset by a decline in defense spending. Meanwhile, state and local outlays have grown as a fraction of national output, although in recent years they have been declining. Total federal, state, and local spending rose from 27 percent to 34 percent of

Table 2.1. Poverty spending and other government spending as a percentage of GNP, fiscal years 1960–1984

Type of spending	1960	1965	1970	1975	1980	1984
Means-tested transfers[a]	1.1	1.2	1.9	2.9	3.0	2.8
Social insurance[b]	2.9	3.1	4.2	6.3	6.6	7.1
Targeted education and training	—	0.1	0.4	0.5	0.8	0.4
Defense	9.1	7.7	8.4	5.8	5.2	6.4
Other federal[c]	5.8	6.5	6.7	8.3	9.2	8.4
Total federal	18.5	18.0	20.2	21.9	22.4	23.3
Other state and local[d]	8.0	8.7	10.0	10.3	9.3	8.6
Total government	26.9	27.1	30.8	33.1	32.5	33.6

Sources: Figures 2.1–2.4. Statistics for "other state and local spending" based on reports in U.S. Department of Commerce (various years).
  a. Sum of federal, state, and local outlays on means-tested transfers.
  b. Outlays on OASDI, Medicare, unemployment insurance, and black lung benefits.
  c. Excludes outlays on means-tested transfers, social insurance, targeted education and training, and national defense.
  d. State and local expenditures minus outlays on means-tested transfers and excluding spending financed with federal grants-in-aid.

GNP between 1960 and 1984. More than three-quarters of this rise is accounted for by the rise in means-tested transfers, social insurance, and targeted education and training.

How much poverty reduction has the nation purchased with these outlays? Disturbingly little, according to official statistics. Census tabulations show that the percentage of all persons in poverty was 22.4 percent in 1959, fell by half to 11.1 percent in 1973, and has risen since then to 15.2 percent.[18] Much of the reduction was concentrated among the elderly and disabled. Single women with children, as well as some other groups, continue to suffer very high poverty rates.

However, only cash transfers are counted by the Census Bureau in measuring family incomes. Census statistics, therefore, mask the full extent of poverty reduction because they exclude the consumption gains that resulted from in-kind transfers. Because the growth in means-tested transfers has been overwhelmingly concentrated in in-kind programs, the official series provides an especially defective yardstick for measuring long-term progress against poverty. The Census Bureau estimates that the number of poor in 1983 may be overstated by 17 to 49 percent, depending on the way in which noncash assistance is valued (U.S. Bureau of Census, 1984e). The overstatement of the poverty population was presumably much smaller in 1960 when in-kind benefits were substantially lower. But even with in-kind trans-

fers accounted for, the fraction of population that is poor has risen substantially in recent years and remains unacceptably high, ranging from 10.2
to 13.0 percent of the population, depending on the method used to count
noncash benefits.

A number of authors have attempted to explain why poverty has declined
so little when transfers have risen so much.[19] As suggested above, the goal
of the most expensive transfer programs is not primarily to reduce income
poverty. Social insurance programs protect family incomes when wages
have been lost because of unemployment, retirement, death, or disability.
In-kind assistance programs are designed to ensure the provision of certain
merit goods—food, housing, and medical care. In addition to reducing the
level of want among the pretransfer poor, these social insurance and in-
kind transfers also provide benefits to the nonpoor and to the pretransfer
poor whose incomes have already been raised by other transfers above the
income poverty line. Also, despite the immense sums spent on transfers,
some of the pretransfer poor are eligible for no cash aid and only a small
amount of in-kind assistance.

Can the nation afford to increase the share of national income devoted
to reducing poverty? Here we should distinguish between poverty spending
that represents a genuine claim on society's resources and spending that
consists of simple redistribution among U.S. households. The former reduces the resources available for other worthwhile consumption and investment. The capital and labor that are used in education and training
programs and in administering public transfer programs have potential
alternative uses in both the public and private sectors. For example, by
devoting real resources to aiding the poor, society is foregoing the opportunity to invest those resources in better roads, houses, or capital plant
and equipment. (It is also passing up the opportunity to consume more
video recorders, restaurant meals, and trips to Disneyland.) But an overwhelming fraction of poverty spending consists of transfers rather than
direct government purchases of goods and services. Those transfers neither
add nor subtract from national income; they merely redistribute it among
the households.

So long as the nation is willing to levy the taxes necessary to finance
poverty spending and the taxes do not substantially impair incentives to
work and save (see below), there is no macroeconomic reason to limit
outlays to their current level. By and large the nation has shown itself
willing to pay for added transfers through added taxes. Social insurance is
financed with very visible earmarked taxes, and those taxes have roughly
kept pace with social insurance outlays. Means-tested transfers and targeted

education and training programs are another story. Those programs are financed out of general revenues, the same source of funds used to finance nearly all other government activities. Since 1981 the federal government has been unwilling to finance its obligations—including targeted transfers, education, and training—with tax revenues, relying instead on borrowed resources to pay for current activities. In one respect, this situation is hardly unusual; all but one of the federal budgets after 1960 have been in deficit (as the deficit is usually measured). What is unusual about the budget situation in 1985 is the magnitude of the discrepancy between revenues and outlays and the expectation that large deficits will persist indefinitely.

The macroeconomic problems arising from deficits are not caused by the level of poverty spending per se or indeed by the level of spending on any other particular category of government activity. They are caused by the tendency of the deficits to absorb a large fraction of domestic saving, thereby reducing domestic investment in capital formation. As noted by the Council of Economic Advisers, "Federal borrowing to finance a budget deficit of 5 percent of GNP would absorb about two-thirds of all the net domestic saving that would otherwise be available to finance investment in plant and equipment and in housing" (U.S. Council of Economic Advisers, 1984, p. 37).

There is little doubt that the federal budget situation in the mid-1980s provides an effective political check on added poverty spending. The prospect of large and growing federal deficits places pressure on the Congress and President to reduce government spending. But this check on spending is essentially political rather than economic in nature. While federal deficits do indeed have important economic consequences, fear of those consequences has not deterred the Congress or President from substantially raising spending on other federal activities—for example, national defense, aid to agriculture, and support of biomedical research. Nor has it spurred the government to take the most obvious corrective action to reduce deficits, namely, raise taxes. In the long run, to be economically defensible the level of poverty spending must be based on the degee to which society is willing to tax itself in order to pay for that spending. If our underlying willingness to tax is high, the current budget situation represents only a temporary political check rather than a permanent economic limit to outlays for means-tested transfers and targeted education and training.

If poverty expenditures are financed by an appropriate level of government revenues, the main objection to increased spending is a microeconomic one. Both the taxes raised to support poverty spending and the spending itself induce distortions in microeconomic incentives. These distortions may reduce national income and aggregate welfare even as the added poverty spending is raising the incomes and welfare levels of the poor. Two distortions have received special attention from economists—distortions of labor supply incentives and of saving incentives.[20]

Considerable uncertainty exists both about the detailed micro-level effects and the general equilibrium effects on labor supply of specific tax and transfer provisions. The range of uncertainty about individual labor supply is certainly far smaller than it was a decade ago, but it nonetheless remains important (see Killingsworth, 1984).

Some of the most precise estimates of the impact of transfer programs on work incentives for the poor were obtained in the negative income tax (NIT) experiments (Moffitt and Kehrer, 1981). Although it would be difficult to infer from the experiments the aggregate labor supply effects of all current welfare programs, the experimental results can be used to predict the impact of increases or decreases in current programs. The most elaborate predictions of response are based on estimates from the Seattle and Denver NIT experiments (SRI International, 1983). Those predictions show the effect in 1975 of replacing the existing AFDC and food stamp programs with a variety of NIT plans. Here I will describe the effect of an NIT that would eliminate poverty among husband-wife families and single-parent families containing children. The plan would offer a basic payment level equal to the poverty line and would tax earnings at a 70-percent rate and unearned income at a 100-percent rate. (The hypothetical NIT plan also reimburses income and payroll taxes for families with incomes below the plan breakeven.) To give an idea of the generosity of this plan, SRI estimated that it would cost $11.9 billion (1984 dollars) in added transfers, even in the *absence* of any labor supply response. In comparison, the approximate cost of AFDC and food stamps in 1975 was $23 billion.

The labor supply response to the simulated NIT would raise the cost of the plan by $3.9 billion, bringing total outlays for the program to $15.7 billion more than the cost of the existing welfare and food stamp programs. For two-parent families with initial incomes less than $13,500, the NIT plan would cause reductions in work effort of 7.5 percent for men and 18 percent for their wives. Among single-parent families with initial incomes less than $13,500, the plan would reduce work effort by 6 percent. (The reduction is smaller among single-parent than two-parent families because the former are more generously treated under the existing welfare system.) Ignoring the labor supply responses of nonrecipient families, who presumably would be required to pay higher income taxes to finance the NIT, SRI estimates that the population response to the NIT would imply a 1-

percent reduction in work effort among all husbands and wives in two-parent families and a 5-percent increase in labor supply among women heading single-parent families. (Single-parent families raise their work effort because about half of all current welfare recipients would receive lower payments under the NIT plan than they do under the existing welfare system.) As mentioned, the NIT plan would cost approximately $15.7 billion more than the existing welfare system, but the net income of recipients would be only $12.2 billion higher. The reason for the discrepancy is the reduction in earnings among recipient families, which accounts for more than a fifth of the added cost of the NIT (SRI International, 1983, pp. 177–187). To use Arthur Okun's analogy of a leaky bucket, it is apparent that the NIT is not a leak-proof redistributive bucket. In carrying money from affluent taxpayers to poor transfer recipients, more than one dollar in five is lost in transit. Is this loss unacceptably high? The answer to that question must derive from an ethical, not an economic, judgment.

The literature on detailed labor supply effects of individual antipoverty programs on recipient populations is too vast to summarize briefly. It is valuable, however, to distinguish between the effects of broad classes of programs. First, the effects of transfer programs should be clearly distinguished from those of wage subsidy and education and training programs. The former provide income support to families who might otherwise be forced to earn more wages on their own. Some forms of transfers—such as AFDC—impose high marginal tax rates on wage earnings and hence reduce even further the incentive to work. By contrast, successful wage subsidy programs and education and training programs should *raise* the earnings of participants; if they succeed, these programs contribute to economic efficiency and growth. There is an equally important difference between social insurance benefits and means-tested transfers. The former are largely paid for by eventual recipients.[21] Workers covered by social insurance may expect that their current tax contributions will eventually be returned to them as unemployment or retirement benefits. Viewed in this light, social insurance is simply a form of delayed compensation and should cause no more labor supply distortion than other forms of nonwage compensation, for example, private health or pension benefits.[22] Hence, there are good reasons to believe that social insurance taxes should cause less labor supply distortion than an equivalent amount of income taxes raised for the purpose of paying means-tested benefits. In spite of this distinction between social insurance and means-tested transfers, nearly all interested analysts would agree that an increase in the present level of either type of program would reduce the level of self-support of affected low-income breadwinners.

Another objection to transfers is that they distort the incentive to save and consequently reduce the amount of aggregate saving and investment. This objection was raised and ostensibly proved in the case of Social Security by Martin Feldstein (1974). Although the original research supporting this view was marred by a serious data error, the argument continues to be accepted by many economists. I believe that this objection to transfers is far less serious than the claim that transfers reduce aggregate labor supply. First, personal saving shows no particular trend over the past several decades: if it is too low now as a result of generous Social Security payments, it was also too low when Social Security benefits were lower. Second, as Henry Aaron (1982, pp. 51–52) has sensibly pointed out, if the objective of policy is to increase net savings and investment, there are far more direct methods of accomplishing this than by reducing transfers. For example, if the federal government ran budget surpluses rather than deficits, a larger fraction of domestic savings would be available for private investment.

The microeconomic literature on incentives does not provide a strong message to the policymaker who contemplates general increases in poverty spending. The efficiency costs of an overall increase may be large or small, depending on the microeconomic specialist consulted. The uncertainty is reduced once attention is focused on particular reforms or benefit increases, but even then the statistical evidence may be too weak or contradictory to support strong conclusions about losses in earnings or savings. In summarizing the literature on incentive effects a few years ago, three economists concluded that "research findings are too varied, too uncertain, and themselves too colored with judgment to serve as more than a rough guide to policy choices" (Danziger, Haveman, and Plotnick, 1981, p. 1020). There is no reason to modify that conclusion today. An economist might reasonably suggest reforms to reduce poverty at lower expense or with less distortionary economic effects than present policies, but current knowledge does not permit an economist unequivocally to predict the total efficiency gains or losses that would arise from a particular policy. While the direction of effect may be known with tolerable accuracy, the magnitude of change is often uncertain.

Macroeconomic theory and microeconomic evidence have only limited usefulness in establishing the terms of trade-off between poverty spending and economic prosperity. Economists are a long way from being able to say what price is paid for marginal increases in overall spending and even further from knowing the total penalty paid by the United States for its current level of spending. However, some international comparisons can shed light on the latter issue. The United States spends a smaller share of national income on redistribution than do most other Western industrialized nations. Not surprisingly, by devoting fewer resources to redistribution the United States also accomplishes less redistribution, leaving a greater degree of income inequality than found in other countries (Saunders, 1984).

International statistics do not prove that generous redistribution has a high cost in terms of slower economic growth. The United States spends comparatively little on redistribution, yet its rate of economic growth has not been outstanding in comparison to that of other advanced industrialized nations. Germany redistributes an unusually high fraction of national output, yet its growth has not been conspicuously slow. Table 2.2 presents OECD statistics on social welfare spending, per capita national output, and rates of growth of real output in the six largest advanced capitalist nations. The first two columns in the table show the percentage of gross domestic product (GDP) devoted to social spending (except education) in 1960 and in 1981. The OECD definition of social expenditures includes public outlays for education, health, pensions, and other income maintenance programs. I have excluded the education component in my series because only a minor fraction of educational outlays is specifically redistributive. The third column shows per capita GDP in 1981 as measured using 1981 prices and exchange ratios; these figures provide rough indi-

Table 2.2. Social expenditure and economic growth in six OECD countries, 1960–1981

| Country | Social expenditure as percentage of GDP[a] | | GDP per capita, 1981 | Annual growth in GDP per capita, 1960–1981 |
	1960	1981		
Germany	18.0	26.5	$11,080	3.1%
France	13.4	23.8	10,550	3.6
Italy	12.7	22.7	6,120	3.6
United Kingdom	10.3	18.9	8,880	1.8
United States	7.3	14.9	12,650	2.1
Japan	4.0	13.8	9,610	6.4

Sources: OECD (1983, 1984a, 1984b).
a. Government outlays on pensions, health care, and other income maintenance.

cators of average well-being in the six countries, although they are subject to substantial year-to-year movement because of exchange rate fluctuations. The last column shows the average annual growth rate of real per capita GDP over the period from 1960 through 1981.

If there is a strong association between fast economic growth and low spending on redistribution it is not evident in Table 2.2. Japan has the smallest share of GDP devoted to social expenditures and has enjoyed the highest growth rate since 1960; but the U.S. expenditure share was only slightly above that of Japan in 1981 while its economic growth rate through 1981 was only modestly ahead of that of the United Kingdom, which had the lowest growth rate. Interestingly, social expenditures surged much faster in Japan than in the United States after 1960, rising from only 4 percent to nearly 14 percent of GDP. Social expenditures also grew faster in Germany, France, and Italy from a higher base, and each of these countries has enjoyed faster per capita economic growth than the United States.

In sum, there is no evidence that the United States has enjoyed a growth dividend as a consequence of limiting redistributional outlays. Other advanced nations have done as well or even better since 1960, even though they have redistributed a larger share of income in the tax-transfer reshuffle. Of course, it would be incorrect to conclude that there is *no* economic penalty arising from activist redistributional policy. Special factors have affected growth in each of the advanced nations. The high level of U.S. income in 1960 may have made it much more difficult to achieve high growth rates since that year. Also, tax-transfer policies may be less distortionary abroad than in the United States, either because policies are more efficient or because the taxpayer and recipient populations are less responsive to tax and transfer incentives. The fact remains, however, that substantial government redistribution has not prevented rapid economic growth in other nations.

The choice of redistribution policy is ultimately political rather than purely economic. The United States has not chosen modest levels of redistribution because its tax-transfer policies are less efficient than similar policies abroad. Nor has it chosen less redistribution because Americans are more responsive to the baleful effects of taxes and transfers than are Europeans or Japanese. Economists know next to nothing about the comparative economic efficiency of policies in different advanced nations and nothing at all about the relative responsiveness of different populations to identical tax-transfer policies. Even if economists possessed such knowledge, it could not be used, by itself, to determine the amount of national treasure that governments ought to divert to the poor; of equal importance in deciding this issue would be the taste of society for redistribution. Voters with a strong preference for equality may be willing to sacrifice two dollars in national output in order to divert one additional dollar to society's poorest member. Conversely, voters with a weak taste for equality may not wish to give up even one penny of their own income in order to raise the net incomes of the poor by one dollar.

Prospects for the Future

In the absence of good working knowledge about the terms of the trade-off between national output and income equality, redistributional policies are determined by a political process that largely depends on voter tastes. I am referring here not just to an abstract taste for equality but also to voter preference or aversion for particular mechanisms of distribution. Americans may in fact have a more intense taste than Europeans for strict equality in the distribution of political and judicial rights, but the preference for equality does not extend to the economic sphere. Greater economic equality in the United States would require that a highly prized distribution mechanism—the market—be replaced by a more controversial one—government interference. The market enjoys far higher prestige in the United States than in nearly any other country. Therefore, the rewards it confers are sanctified in a way that is probably unknown in less market-oriented societies. To quote Arthur Okun, "The market has been sold to a mass market" (Okun, 1983, p. 624). The widespread belief is that so long as legal remedies are enforced to ensure that the market race is fair, the rich and the poor will get what they deserve.

In view of Americans' deep-seated beliefs, there are scant grounds for optimism that the lot of this nation's poor will soon be radically improved. The steep rise in social welfare spending between 1960 and 1980 substantially raised the well-being of many poor families, and these improvements ought not be lightly dismissed. But much of the increased spending was concentrated on the lucky poor insured by our social insurance programs— the aged, the infirm, and the insured unemployed. Most of the remainder was devoted to in-kind benefits that raised specific forms of consumption, but not the money incomes, of the poor. In the recent past, government initiative to reduce poverty has come to a halt and may even have been reversed.

For economists and policy makers seriously interested in the fate of the poor, the main hope for future improvements lies in the market or in marginal improvements in the effectiveness of existing policies. While I doubt that there is much chance that either markets or minor policy changes will be especially effective in reducing poverty, I am even more skeptical that we soon will see a revolution in American tastes for redistribution. Yet if American poverty is to be reduced to the levels now observed in northern Europe, I suspect that such a revolution is required.

3   Antipoverty Policy: Effects on the Poor and the Nonpoor

Sheldon H. Danziger
Robert H. Haveman
Robert D. Plotnick

IN THIS CHAPTER we analyze trends in poverty and antipoverty policy over the 1965–1983 period and conclude that although poverty has declined, a significant problem remains. Economic growth has helped to reduce poverty directly by creating jobs and raising earnings and will continue to do so if it is sustained. Income transfers have played a major role as well and remain an essential tool of comprehensive antipoverty policy. The income transfer system creates some disincentives, but their modest size poses no serious threat to economic growth. We conclude by outlining an antipoverty policy that has the potential of reducing both poverty and dependence on government payments. In so doing, we seek to maintain the gains against poverty and financial uncertainty that have been achieved by public policy while reducing the losses associated with it.

Federal Policy Toward the Poor: A Brief History

The initial strategy of the War on Poverty, outlined in the 1964 *Economic Report of the President,* consisted of a broad range of interventions. Job training, education, citizen participation, and community development were major components. Income transfers were not a central feature because the problem of low labor market productivity dominated strategic thinking. (For a detailed discussion, see Introduction in Haveman, 1977; and Lynn, 1977.) Poverty was high because the poor did not work enough or because their skills were insufficient even if they worked hard. Lagging economic growth, the characteristics of the poor themselves, and discrimination by those who controlled access to jobs or goods and services all were fundamental problems. Since more generous income transfer programs for the poor would not alter these structural deficiencies, the federal govern ment had to improve the performance of the economy, the productivity characteristics of the poor, and the attitudes (or at least the behavior) of those who hired or sold to the poor.

Revitalization of the nation's economy received high priority. Unwilling to concede that the poor desired to work less than the nonpoor, policy planners viewed high unemployment and low labor force participation of the poor as macroeconomic problems. Accelerated economic growth was to be a key weapon—hence the tax cut of 1964 (Heller, 1966).

Stimulating aggregate demand would not, by itself, be sufficient. The gap in work skills between poor and nonpoor needed correction. Manpower training—both institutional and on-the-job—was required. Hence, Job Corps, Neighborhood Youth Corps, the Manpower Development and Training Act (MDTA), and other programs were either established or expanded. In addition to a lack of skills, the poor generally had less ed-ucation than the nonpoor. As a result, Head Start, Upward Bound, Follow Through, Teacher Corps, and Title I of the Elementary and Secondary Education Act were launched. In the belief that deficiencies in diet con-tributed to low performance in school and on the job, food assistance was expanded and a school lunch program was established. Similarly, the de-bilitating effects of illness and disability on job performance would be reduced by providing the poor with subsidized or publicly provided medi-cal care through Medicaid and neighborhood health centers. Finally, the Community Action and Legal Service programs sought to restructure the social institutions by which the poor gained access to jobs and goods and services.

Most observers agree that the announcement of the War on Poverty served as the catalyst for additional policy initiatives that could be justified on antipoverty grounds. Some of these were within the Office of Economic Opportunity; others were associated with the Great Society; others were seemingly unrelated to a major initiative (Friedman, 1977; Patterson, 1981; Brauer, 1982). No government agency and no Congressional committee escaped the persistent query about policies under their jurisdiction: "What does it do for the poor?" (Lampman, 1974). During the next decade a wide range of social programs were enacted and expanded (see Chap-ter 2 and Garfinkel and Haveman, 1983). Nixon's Family Assistance Plan, which sought both to extend cash welfare to all needy families with chil-dren and to establish a federal floor on benefits, did not become law, however.

The sources of this growth in cash and in-kind transfers were complex.

They included increased leniency by welfare administrators, expanded rights and entitlements stemming from legislation (often promoted by organized groups of recipients and legal rights activists), more liberal court interpretations of beneficiary rights and entitlements, the raising of state benefit levels, and reduced stigma attached to being on welfare. Because transfers grew so large relative to other antipoverty programs, they became the focus of much of the analytical and popular reactions to antipoverty policy.

Whatever the source, federal spending on social programs grew very rapidly through the mid-1970s. Their average annual real growth rates were 7.9 percent during the Kennedy-Johnson years and 9.7 percent during the Nixon-Ford years (Palmer and Sawhill, 1984, p. 350). By the late 1970s real growth slowed, primarily because benefits that were not statutorily linked to consumer prices lagged as inflation surged. Real federal social welfare spending grew less than 4 percent per year during the Carter administration, and only one program to aid low-income people, the Low Income Energy Assistance program, was established.

A major shift in social welfare policy occurred with the first Reagan administration. The real growth rate of social programs fell to about 1.5 percent per year, and major structural changes designed to reduce all programs save Social Security retirement and some basic benefits for those unable to work were undertaken.

The changes in AFDC contained in the Omnibus Budget Reconciliation Act of 1981 exemplify the shift in antipoverty policy under the Reagan presidency (see Glazer, 1984b). The administration argued that the break-even level for welfare benefits had grown so high in some states because of work incentive provisions in the program that many who were not needy received benefits and remained dependent. Work effort was best provided by work requirements (proposed by the President, but not enacted), not work incentives. The program changes—higher benefit reduction rates on recipients' earnings and more restrictive income limits for participation— were to change welfare from a system encouraging simultaneous receipt of wages and welfare to a safety net, providing cash assistance only for those unable to secure jobs.

Despite this shift in philosophy, income transfers today remain well above their pre-1965 levels (see Chapter 2). Most programs that were initiated or expanded during the past twenty years are still in place, although the provision of public service jobs under the Comprehensive Employment and Training Act has been ended.

The Trend in Poverty Since 1965

To evaluate the effects of the policies described above, this section documents changes in the poverty problem in a variety of ways. We begin with the official definition of poverty—an absolute measure relying on after–transfer money income. Then we adjust this definition by adding the value of major in-kind benefits. Additional comparisons are made by presenting measures of pretransfer and prewelfare poverty and poverty based on a relative rather than an absolute definition.

OFFICIALLY MEASURED POVERTY

The official measure of poverty specifies a set of income thresholds adjusted for household size, the age of the head of the household, and the number of children under age 18.[1] The thresholds are updated yearly to maintain their purchasing power based on changes in the Consumer Price Index. Because the thresholds represent the same purchasing power each year, they are absolute poverty lines that do not vary with average household income. In 1983 the official poverty line ranged from $4,775 for a single person over 65 years of age, to $10,178 for a family of four, to $20,310 for a family of nine or more.

The official income concept, current money income, includes cash income received during the calendar year from all public and private sources, except capital gains. It takes no account of government or private in-kind benefits (food stamps, Medicare, imputed rent, employer-provided health insurance), nor does it subtract taxes. Yet all of these factors affect a household's level of economic well-being.

The past twenty years are marked by numerous debates on whether the official income concept and poverty thresholds are conceptually sound and relevant to policy choices (see U.S. Department of Health, Education, and Welfare, 1976; Birdsall, 1984). Despite these controversies, the official measure of poverty remains an important social indicator, symbolizing the country's concern with the standard of living of its poorest citizens.

By the official measure, 19 percent of the population was poor when the War on Poverty was declared in 1964 (see Table 3.1, column 1). The level of poverty declined quickly in the 1960s during the robust expansion attributable in part to the Vietnam war. During the early 1970s it continued edging downward to a low of 11.1 percent in 1973; for the balance of the 1970s it fluctuated around 11.5 percent. With the major recession beginning in 1980, the poverty rate rose sharply to 15.0 percent in 1982, then to 15.2

Table 3.1. Percentage of persons in poverty, 1964–1986, by six measures of poverty

Year	Official measure (1)	Adjusted for in-kind transfers underreporting, and taxes (2)	Adjusted for in-kind transfers only (3)	Pretransfer poverty (4)	Prewelfare poverty (5)	Relative poverty (6)
1964	19.0	—	—	—	—	—
1965	17.3	13.4	16.8	21.3	16.3[a]	—
1966	14.7	—	—	—	—	—
1967	14.2	—	—	19.4	15.0	—
1968	12.8	9.9	—	18.2	13.6	14.6
1969	12.1	—	—	17.7	13.3	—
1970	12.6	9.3	—	18.8	13.9	—
1971	12.5	—	—	19.6	13.8	—
1972	11.9	6.2	—	19.2	13.1	15.7
1973	11.1	—	—	19.0	12.4	—
1974	11.2	7.2	—	20.3	13.1	14.9
1975	12.3	—	—	22.0	13.7	—
1976	11.8	6.7	—	21.0	13.1	15.4
1977	11.6	—	—	21.0	13.0	—
1978	11.4	—	—	20.2	12.6	15.5
1979	11.7	6.1	9.0	20.5	12.9	15.7
1980	13.0	—	10.4	21.9	14.2	16.0
1981	14.0	—	11.7	23.1	15.1	16.9
1982	15.0	—	12.7	24.0	15.9	17.8
1983	15.2	—	13.1	24.2	16.1	18.6
1984	14.4	—	12.2	22.9	15.3	18.7
1985	14.0	—	11.8	22.4	14.9	18.0
1986[b]	13.9	—	—	—	—	—

Sources: Column 1: for 1964, U.S. Bureau of the Census (1969); for 1965–1985, U.S. Bureau of the Census (1986a); for 1986, Danziger and Gottschalk (1985).

Column 2: for 1968–1979, Smeeding (1982), recipient value. For 1965 Smeeding shows 12.1 percent in contrast to an official level of 15.6 percent. That official level was computed from the Survey of Economic Opportunity (SEO), which obtained more complete income reporting than the corresponding Current Population Survey (CPS); the latter produced the estimate of 17.3 percent in column 1. To maintain consistency with column 1, we reduced 17.3 percent by the ratio of 12.1/15.6 to derive the 13.4-percent value. In-kind transfers include food stamps, school lunch, public housing, Medicare, and Medicaid.

Column 3: for 1979–1985, U.S. Bureau of the Census (1986b), recipient value. For 1965, when food stamps, public housing, and medical assistance cost less than $1 billion, we roughly estimated that they would reduce the official poverty rate by only 3 percent.

Columns 4, 5, and 6: for 1965, computations from 1966 SEO data tape. For 1967–1985, computations from annual March CPS data tapes.

a. Note that this figure is *less than* the official measure in column 1 and the adjusted one in column 3, even though prewelfare poverty excludes welfare and in-kind income in determining poverty status. This anomaly reflects the fact that for 1965, column 5 is derived from the SEO whereas columns 1 and 3 are derived from the CPS.

b. Projected.

percent in 1983, the highest level since 1965. The current economic recovery will produce a lower level of poverty, but projections for 1984–1986 suggest that it is unlikely to return to the 11 or 12 percent range during that period (Danziger and Gottschalk, 1985).

> If one accepts the official definition, poverty has never faded to insignificance in the years since the War was declared. Currently, about one in seven Americans is poor.

ADJUSTED OFFICIAL POVERTY

The most frequent criticism of the official poverty measure is its omission from income of in-kind, government-provided benefits (Anderson, 1978; Paglin, 1980). Since these benefits increase household consumption, their exclusion understates the true access of families to resources and hence overestimates poverty. Because these benefits have grown more rapidly than money income, their exclusion also affects estimates of the trend in poverty.

Since 1980 the Bureau of the Census has gathered data on in-kind transfer income and used three alternative procedures to value it.[2] The Bureau has issued "exploratory" estimates of the poverty population for 1979–1983 based on these procedures. For selected years between 1965 and 1976 academic analysts have prepared similar but not directly comparable estimates (Smeeding, 1975 and 1982; Paglin, 1980). Smeeding, for example, also adjusted for the underreporting of cash income in census surveys and subtracted the payment of federal personal income and payroll taxes.[3] Columns 2 and 3 in Table 3.1 show both the Smeeding and census adjusted poverty series. Because of their differences, the patterns in the series must be interpreted carefully.

By definition, the adjusted statistics indicate a lower poverty rate than the official ones in each year. They also show a decline in poverty between 1965 and 1972 of more than 50 percent. In the years after 1972 the trend in adjusted poverty mirrors the official one—no progress in the mid-1970s, then a large increase after 1979.[4]

If an official poverty rate of 19 percent in 1964 serves to indicate the size of the problem that was to be solved by the War on Poverty, we are but halfway there after twenty years, even when noncash benefits are counted.

Table 3.2 provides a different perspective on progress against poverty for selected (but not mutually exclusive) demographic groups. To provide

Table 3.2. Percentage of persons in poverty, by demographic group, 1964–1983

Demographic group[a]	Official measure 1964 (1)	Official measure 1983 (2)	Adjusted for in-kind transfers at market value 1983 (3)	Percentage difference between columns 3 and 1[b] (4)
All	19.0	15.2	10.2	−46.3
White	14.9	12.1	8.6	−42.3
Black	49.6	35.7	21.2	−57.3
Hispanic[c]	—	28.4	20.2	—
Living with female householder, no husband present	45.9	40.2	24.7	−46.2
Elderly (65 +)	28.5[d]	14.1	3.3	−88.4
Children under 18	20.7[d]	22.2	15.6	−24.6

Sources: Columns 1 and 2: U.S. Bureau of the Census (1969, 1984d); column 3: U.S. Bureau of the Census (1984e), p. xiii.

a. Owing to constraints in the published data, these groups are not mutually exclusive. For example, the category "white" includes all persons living in a household whose head is white. Those whites who are, for example, elderly female household heads will also be included in the other two groups.

b. Defined as ((adjusted rate 1983 − official rate 1964)/official rate 1964) × 100.

c. Hispanics may be of any race.

d. Figures are for 1966 since none were published for 1964 or 1965.

an upper-bound estimate of the declines in poverty from 1964 to 1983, we compare adjusted official figures (obtained by valuing noncash benefits at market value) for 1983 and the official rate as a proxy for the 1964 adjusted official rate.[5] For the elderly the percentage decline has been about twice that of all persons: nearly 30 percent of older people were poor in the mid-1960s; the poverty rate of the elderly now stands at less than 4 percent.[6] Poverty levels for whites, blacks, and persons living in female-headed families all dropped by about 40 to 50 percent over this period. The smallest decline is for children, primarily because of the rapid increase in the percentage of children living in female-headed households.

This focus on progress against poverty should not obscure the very high levels of poverty remaining among certain groups. By 1983 the adjusted poverty rate among persons in households with black, Hispanic, or female heads still exceeded 20 percent, which is higher than the rate for all persons prior to the War on Poverty. Hence, while real progress against poverty has been made for the elderly and those living in homes headed by white males, high poverty rates persist among nonaged nonwhites and female-headed households. Indeed, approximately 15 percent of the population lives in a major demographic group with an incidence of adjusted official poverty in 1982 that exceeded the aggregate poverty incidence in 1964.[7]

Those who suggest that the War on Poverty is largely won have overlooked the high poverty rates among the nonaged, nonwhite, and female-headed households.

PRETRANSFER AND PREWELFARE POVERTY

Adjusting the data for in-kind transfers addresses one problem of the official measure. Yet neither the adjusted nor official measure distinguishes market and private transfer income sources from government sources. As such, they do not separate the private economy's antipoverty performance from the performance of the entire society, including government transfer programs. Households that do not receive enough money income from private sources to escape poverty are referred to as *pretransfer poor*.[8] Information on pretransfer poverty is essential for analyzing the "trickle-down" effects of economic growth, the number and kinds of persons needing assistance in the labor market, and the extent to which public transfer programs reduce poverty.[9]

A related concept is *prewelfare poverty*. While pretransfer income does not count any money income from government programs, prewelfare income includes all money income except that from cash public assistance (welfare) programs. Prewelfare income does count social insurance benefits. Because such benefits are determined by past earnings and tax contributions, they may be regarded as in some sense "earned." A family that is pretransfer poor but is moved over the poverty line by social insurance income would not generally be viewed as economically dependent. Prewelfare poverty provides a measure of those who are economically dependent and allows us to assess the antipoverty impact of welfare programs.[10]

In 1965 the pretransfer poverty rate (Table 3.1, column 4) was 21.3 percent.[11] It declined to 18.2 percent by 1968 and hit its lowest level, 17.7 percent, in 1969. After the mild recession in 1970–71 and during the slower growth of the 1970s, pretransfer poverty edged up to between 19 and 22 percent. In the early 1980s it jumped rapidly and reached 24.2 percent in 1983, the highest value observed. The pretransfer rate for the nonaged has generally been about 5 percentage points lower than the rate for all persons, but it has followed the same pattern.

Prewelfare poverty (Table 3.1, column 5) also fell during the late 1960s.

It attained its lowest level (12.4 percent) in 1973, fluctuated around the 13 percent level during the remainder of the 1970s, then increased to 16.1 percent by 1983. The prewelfare rate for the nonaged is similar in both level and trend.

The recent increase in the pretransfer and prewelfare poverty rates will probably be reversed by the current recovery. In the mid-1980s, though, these rates will remain above the levels of the early 1970s.

> If solving the poverty problem means eliminating reliance on any income support program to obtain nonpoverty incomes, no progress toward a solution is evident.

> If solving the poverty problem means eliminating the need for public assistance to achieve above-poverty incomes, a solution still eludes us.

THE POVERTY GAP

The poverty gap shows the dollar amount needed to bring all poor households up to the poverty line. As such, it is an indicator of the degree of poverty. Data on poverty gaps (expressed in 1982 dollars) reinforce the conclusions based on incidence statistics. For several years after 1965 the gap based on the official poverty definition fell in absolute terms (Table 3.3, column 1). Beginning in 1979, it increased; the 1983 gap of $45.6 billion is much larger than the 1965 gap in real terms, although as a percentage of personal income it is slightly smaller (1.7 as opposed to 1.9 percent). The gap derived using adjusted statistics (columns 2, 3, 4) is, of course, smaller in each year but shows a similar trend. The pretransfer poverty gap (column 5) has risen in real terms almost every year and exceeded $116 billion in 1983. As a percentage of personal income it declined from 4.1 percent in 1965, varied between 3.6 and 3.9 percent in the 1970s, then rose to its largest value, 4.4 percent, in 1983.

RELATIVE POVERTY

The measures we have discussed are based on different income concepts and convey different information about the level and trend in poverty. All, however, use the official poverty thresholds, which remain fixed in real terms. Critics have charged that such absolute thresholds do not adequately reflect poverty in a society with an increasing average standard of living and that the poverty lines should be tied to the average income level. To

Table 3.3. Total poverty gap, 1965–1983 (billions of 1982 dollars)

Year	Official measure (1)	Adjusted measures			Pretransfer measure (5)
		(2)ᵃ	(3)ᵇ	(4)ᶜ	
1965	31.8	—	—	—	67.6
1968	27.1	19.2	—	—	65.1
1970	28.5	18.2	—	—	72.0
1972	27.9	12.3	—	—	78.3
1974	27.7	18.0	—	—	86.2
1976	28.3	—	—	—	92.9
1978	28.8	—	—	—	91.2
1979	30.8	—	22.1	17.9	92.1
1980	35.4	—	24.9	20.2	102.2
1981	40.1	—	29.1	23.7	108.4
1982	43.9	—	31.7	25.9	113.2
1983	45.6	—	—	—	116.2

Sources: Columns 1 and 5: computations from 1966 Survey of Economic Opportunity and 1967–1984 March Current Population Survey (CPS) data tapes. Columns 2–4: for 1968, 1970, 1972, Smeeding (1975); for 1974, March 1975 CPS data tape (modified by Smeeding to add in-kind transfers, subtract taxes, and adjust for underreporting); for 1979–1982, U.S. Bureau of the Census (1984e).

a. Based on recipient value of in-kind benefits but also corrected for underreporting and taxes.

b. Based on recipient value of in-kind benefits.

c. Based on market value of in-kind benefits.

reflect this concern about inequality at the lower end of the income distribution, we use a 1965 relative poverty line that equals the official one for that year. For later years the relative line varies directly with the median income.[12]

The official poverty line has fallen since 1965 relative to median family income—for a family of four, this ratio was .46 in 1965, .38 in 1979, and .41 in 1983. As a result, the relative line exceeds the official one in each successive year, and relative poverty (Table 3.1, column 6) is higher than official poverty. Relative poverty did not decline very much in the 1960s or early 1970s. Because average income was stagnant or falling in the late 1970s and early 1980s, relative poverty did not rise as sharply as absolute poverty during this period. By 1983 relative poverty was 18.6 percent, about 20 percent higher than its level at the outset of the War on Poverty.

TRENDS IN THE COMPOSITION OF THE POOR

At the outset of the War on Poverty, analysts thought that poverty could be eliminated by 1980 if the economy could be kept on a stable growth path and if additional opportunities could be made available to the poor. Poverty obviously has not been eliminated. Income transfers to the poor have grown more rapidly than expected, but the economy has not grown steadily. What then does the poverty population look like today?

Table 3.4 classifies pretransfer and post-transfer poor household heads in 1967 and 1983 in a way that highlights their policy-relevant characteristics (see Stockman, 1983, for a similar disaggregation). Any household head falling into more than one category is classified in the highest one in the table. This hierarchical classification begins with those least likely to be expected to work (or least able to escape pretransfer poverty in the labor market) and moves toward those who are generally expected to earn their way out of poverty. As one moves down the hierarchy, transfers become less appropriate and labor market policies more appropriate.

Table 3.4 Composition of households with incomes below the official poverty line, 1967 and 1983

	1967		1983	
Demographic group	Pretransfer poor (1)	Post-transfer poor (2)	Pretransfer poor (3)	Post-transfer poor (4)
Over age 65	50.56%	40.43%	42.79%	21.32%
Female, with children under age 6	5.48	6.97	7.60	12.45
Student	4.05	5.54	4.21	6.87
Disabled	9.36	10.00	10.08	10.72
Person working full time, full year	14.74	19.11	9.10	14.38
Single, working less than full time, full year	6.25	7.59	10.77	15.16
Male family head, working less than full time, full year	5.47	6.18	10.10	11.49
Female family head, no children under age 6, working less than full time, full year	4.10	4.18	5.35	7.60
Number of households (in millions)	15.5	10.8	25.9	14.7

Sources: Computations from March 1968 and 1984 Current Population Survey data tapes.
Note: Classification is mutually exclusive and hierarchical: any household head who fits more than one category has been classified only in the one closest to the top of the table.

The largest group among the pretransfer poor is the aged. The most significant policy success of the 1965–1982 period has been their rapidly declining poverty rate. As a result, they fell from about two-fifths to about one-fifth of the post-transfer poor. Social Security retirement and survivors benefits and Supplemental Security Income, together with food stamps and Medicare, now provide sufficient income to remove almost all the aged from poverty. To the extent that any aged remain poor (and their measured poverty is not simply a result of underreported income), the appropriate policy seems to be outreach programs to increase participation rates.

Society is willing to accept the pretransfer poverty of the aged because they are not expected to work. Societal expectations of female household heads with young children have changed, however. Twenty years ago most people were comfortable with the view that mothers should stay home and care for their children, but as more married women have entered the labor market, similar expectations have been applied to unmarried mothers. These women have a very high incidence of poverty and make up an increasing share of both the pre- and post-transfer poor.

Students who are household heads are frequently counted among the income poor, partly because census data do not completely record transfers received from their parents or student financial assistance. Their poverty may be best perceived as a measurement rather than a policy problem, since many currently poor are not likely to be poor when they graduate.

The definition of the disabled in the Current Population Survey (CPS) includes only those who self-report that their disability keeps them from working full-time. Thus, most of them are unlikely to escape poverty through the regular labor market. For those who are least disabled, subsidized employment (for example, sheltered workshops) may be a substitute for income transfers.

Those already working full-time full-year are poor because they have low skills and earn low wages or have large families. Together with the three remaining groups—able-bodied male and female heads and single persons who work less than full-time full-year—they composed about one-third of the pretransfer and about one-half of the post-transfer poor in 1983. They are the least likely among the pretransfer poor to receive income transfers and the most likely to be aided by economic growth.

Explaining the Trend in Poverty

In simple accounting terms the changes in post-1965 official and adjusted poverty depend on two factors—changes in pretransfer poverty, which largely reflect macroeconomic conditions, and changes in the level of public transfers and the extent to which they are targeted on the poor. The accounting story runs as follows:

> Between 1965 and 1969 poverty rapidly declined as the economy flourished and the antipoverty impact of transfers increased. From 1969 to 1975, while pretransfer poverty rose substantially, transfers became more effective at taking people out of poverty. These two forces roughly balanced out, and post-transfer poverty remained steady.

> From 1975 to 1978 pretransfer poverty edged down, the antipoverty effect of transfers stayed nearly constant, and consequently post-transfer poverty fell slightly. During 1978–1983 a decline in transfers' antipoverty impact and a substantial rise in pretransfer poverty due to the recession both contributed to the increase in official and adjusted poverty.

In what follows, we describe the impacts of economic conditions and income transfer policies on the trend in poverty. In addition, because shifts in the population toward demographic groups with higher (lower) than average levels of poverty tend to increase (decrease) the overall level of poverty, we review the effect on measured poverty of demographic change and the extent to which federal policy may have induced such change. We divide the analysis into two periods—the 1965–1978 period of declining and then roughly stable levels of poverty, and the 1978–1983 period of rising poverty. Because of data availability, the poverty indicators used are the absolute measures of pretransfer and official poverty. Using measures adjusted for in-kind transfers or the disincentive effects of all transfers would change the magnitudes of the reported effects, but not the trends.

PRETRANSFER POVERTY: THE ROLE OF ECONOMIC CONDITIONS AND
BEHAVIORAL AND DEMOGRAPHIC CHANGE

Between 1965 and 1978 overall pretransfer poverty declined from 21.3 to 20.2 percent. This small reduction masks significant declines for some demographic groups. As Table 3.5 shows, the declines for persons in male-headed families with children were large, irrespective of race. For whites real earnings growth among men and an increase in the fraction of families with two earners were important. The dramatic reduction in pretransfer poverty from 41.2 to 17.9 percent for nonwhite male-headed families re-

Table 3.5. Percentage of the population in pretransfer poverty, by demographic group of household head and presence of children, 1965–1983

Demographic group	1965	1978	1983
Under age 65			
White male, with children	10.6%	7.9%	13.1%
Nonwhite male, with children	41.2	17.9	23.8
White female, with children	48.5	45.7	50.1
Nonwhite female, with children	80.0	70.3	68.8
White, unrelated individuals and childless families	11.4	11.6	13.5
Nonwhite, unrelated individuals and childless families	27.4	22.4	28.0
Age 65 or more			
White	57.6	54.3	52.5
Nonwhite	72.3	69.8	72.3
All persons in pretransfer poverty	21.3	20.2	24.2

Sources: Tabulations from 1966 Survey of Economic Opportunity and March 1979 and 1984 Current Population Survey data tapes.

flects the steady improvement during those years of the educational levels of black workers and a decline in labor market discrimination.

Pretransfer poverty among nonaged female-headed families with children remained high throughout the period. Among whites it declined slightly from 48.5 to 45.7 percent. For nonwhites the decline from 80.0 to 70.3 percent was greater, but the level far exceeded that of any other nonaged category. The reasons for this poorer record are unclear, although labor supply responses may have played some role, especially for whites. While nonwhite women faced the same work disincentives from welfare, their pretransfer poverty rate declined, even during the years of rising real welfare benefits.

Among households headed by an aged person, pretransfer poverty showed little change during the years 1965–1978. For aged nonwhites it fluctuated between 69 and 75 percent; for whites, between 54 and 58 percent. Any reductions in earnings induced by rising Social Security and welfare benefits during this period (SSI began in 1974) were offset by higher and more extensive private pension incomes, greater property income, and higher wages for those who continued working.

While several of the groups in Table 3.5 showed sizable decreases in pretransfer poverty, the aggregate incidence fell only 1.1 percentage points (or 5 percent). Population shifts toward groups with higher than average levels of pretransfer poverty (the elderly and single-parent families) largely counteracted the declines in groups with lower rates. If demographic composition had remained at its 1965 level, changes in the group-specific rates would have lowered aggregate pretransfer poverty in 1978 to 17.0 percent, 4.3 percentage points (20 percent) below the 1965 value of 21.3 percent.

Between 1978 and 1983 pretransfer poverty rose from 20.2 percent to 24.2 percent, and six of the eight demographic groups experienced an increase. Given the decline in the real value of transfers during these years, it would be difficult to argue that greater work disincentives contributed to these increases. Instead, deteriorating economic conditions appear to be the major factor.

For persons in white nonaged male-headed families with children, a group very sensitive to cyclical changes, the pretransfer poverty rate climbed from 7.9 to 13.1 percent. For the corresponding nonwhite group, the increase was from 17.9 to 23.8 percent. Nonaged childless couples and unrelated individuals also experienced large increases. For both nonaged women with children and the elderly, groups whose incomes are less affected by macroeconomic conditions, pretransfer poverty either rose slightly or remained essentially steady.

Within this five-year period demographic shifts that reduced the relative size of groups with low levels of pretransfer poverty continued to exert upward pressure on the overall pretransfer poverty rate. If demographic composition had stayed at its 1978 configuration, pretransfer poverty in 1983 would have been 23.5 instead of the actual level of 24.2 percent. Even without this demographic change, then, a significant rise in pretransfer poverty would have occurred.

POST-TRANSFER POVERTY: THE ROLE OF PUBLIC TRANSFERS

Between 1965 and 1978 the growth in real expenditures on cash and in-kind transfers per recipient household far exceeded the real increase in per household income. This growth in transfers accounts for much of the observed decline in poverty. Table 3.6 measures the antipoverty impact of transfers by the percentage of pretransfer poor persons who are removed from poverty by transfers.

During the 1965–1978 period public transfers became increasingly effective in reducing poverty. The fraction of pretransfer poor households

Table 3.6.   Percentage of all pretransfer poor persons removed from poverty by various transfers, 1965–1983

Year	Cash social insurance[a]	Cash public assistance[b]	All cash transfers	In-kind transfers[c]	All transfers
1965[d]	—	—	18.8	18.3	37.0
1968	25.3	4.4	29.7	15.9	45.6
1972	31.8	6.3	38.1	29.7	67.7
1976	37.6	6.2	43.8	24.3	68.1
1978	37.6	5.9	43.6	—	—
1979	37.1	5.9	43.0	13.2	56.1
1980	35.2	5.5	40.7	11.9	52.5
1981	34.6	4.8	39.4	10.0	49.4
1982	33.8	3.6	37.5	9.6	47.1
1983	33.7	3.4	37.1	9.2	46.3

Sources: Tabulations from 1966 Survey of Economic Opportunity (SEO) and March 1979 and 1984 Current Population Survey (CPS) data tapes.

a. Includes Social Security, railroad retirement, unemployment insurance, workers' compensation, government employees' pensions, and veterans' pensions and compensation.

b. Includes AFDC, SSI (Old Age Assistance, Aid to the Permanently and Totally Disabled, and Aid to the Blind before 1976), and general assistance.

c. Includes Medicare, Medicaid, food stamps, school lunch, and public housing. For 1965–1976, this column also includes the effect of income underreporting and direct federal taxes on poverty, while data prepared by the Bureau of the Census for 1979–1983 do not. Hence, results in the last two columns before 1978 cannot be directly compared with those for 1979–1983. The 1965 figures for columns 4 and 5 that would be directly comparable to the 1979–1983 series are 2.3 and 21.1 percent. The effects of in-kind transfers are evaluated by the recipient value method since the 1965–1976 figures were computed in this manner.

d. Columns 1 and 2 are blank because the 1965 level of prewelfare poverty, which is needed to compute these columns, is lower than the official post-transfer poverty level; using those statistics would yield meaningless results for columns 1 and 2. This problem arises because the prewelfare poverty figure is derived from the SEO, while the post-transfer poverty figure is derived from the published official poverty data calculated from the March 1966 CPS. Column 3 is computed on the basis of the pretransfer poverty level derived from the SEO and official postcash transfer poverty derived from the CPS. In previous work we have used the SEO's official poverty incidence (15.6 percent) instead of that from the CPS (17.3 percent) to compute the antipoverty impact of transfers in 1965 and thus have shown a greater impact.

Note: The numbers here are derived from more detailed data than those used in Table 3.1 and thus may differ from calculations based on it.

receiving a cash transfer rose from less than 70 percent in 1965 to more than 80 percent in 1978, and the real value of the typical transfer also increased. As a result, while transfers moved about 37 percent of the pretransfer poor over the poverty line in 1965, 68 percent were shifted over the line in 1972, in 1976, and probably in 1978 as well.[13]

After 1978 the growth of real cash and in-kind transfers per household virtually halted, while pretransfer poverty increased. Consequently, the percentage of pretransfer poor persons taken out of poverty by all transfers declined from 56.1 percent in 1979 to 46.3 percent in 1983.[14] Cash social insurance, cash public assistance, and in-kind transfers all became less effective at reducing poverty.

Cash social insurance transfers removed more persons from poverty in all years than cash public assistance transfers because a greater portion of the pretransfer poor received them and because the average social insurance payment was higher. In-kind transfers—which include benefits from both social insurance and public assistance programs—had a smaller antipoverty impact than cash social insurance and a larger impact than cash public assistance transfers.

The poverty-reduction impacts of cash transfers for particular demographic groups have, by and large, followed the aggregate trend—increased effectiveness between 1965 and 1978, then declines (Table 3.7).[15] The antipoverty effectiveness of transfers varies widely by group.[16] For example, 12.3 percent of the pretransfer poor in families headed by white males with children escaped poverty via transfers in 1965, and 26.6 percent did so in 1978; but by 1983 only 20.6 percent escaped. Similarly, for the white and nonwhite elderly, the antipoverty effects improved from 57.3 and 25.7

Table 3.7. Percentage of pretransfer poor persons removed from poverty by cash transfers, by demographic group of household head and presence of children, 1965–1983

Demographic group	1965	1978	1983
Under age 65			
White male, with children	12.3	26.6	20.6
Nonwhite male, with children	7.0	22.9	13.3
White female, with children	30.1	21.8	13.8
Nonwhite female, with children	10.5	13.3	8.0
White, unrelated individuals and childless families	27.2	41.3	36.3
Nonwhite, unrelated individuals and childless families	11.7	28.1	24.5
Age 65 or more			
White	57.3	78.5	78.0
Nonwhite	25.7	55.3	50.2
All persons in pretransfer poverty	26.8	43.6	37.1

Sources: Tabulations from 1966 Survey of Economic Opportunity and March 1979 and 1984 Current Population Survey data tapes.

percent, respectively, in 1965 to 78.5 and 55.3 percent by 1978, then declined slightly by 1983.

An unexpected pattern appears for pretransfer poor persons in families headed by single women with children: for whites cash transfers removed a smaller percentage from poverty in 1978 than in 1965. By 1983 the antipoverty impact had fallen to less than half of its 1965 level. For nonwhites cash transfers removed 10.5 percent from poverty in 1965 and 13.3 percent in 1978, but by 1983 they, too, were less effective than in 1965, removing only 8.0 percent.

The reason for this pattern lies in the declining real value of nonindexed welfare transfers after the early 1970s and the retrenchment in welfare policy after 1981. As a result, while persons in nonaged female-headed families were more likely than their male counterparts to escape pretransfer poverty in 1965, by 1983 they were much less likely to do so. The combination of persistently high rates of pretransfer poverty for female household heads, the sharply diminished antipoverty effectiveness of the transfers they receive, and rapid growth in their numbers has produced the widely noted "feminization of poverty."

Although the large and increasing expenditures on income maintenance programs have been a topic of great concern, less attention has been focused on the gaps in coverage in the present system—the holes in the safety net: although virtually all of the aged pretransfer poor are transfer recipients, almost 40 percent of nonaged pretransfer poor households receive no income transfers, and many of those who do receive them do not obtain enough to lift their households above the poverty line.

Our estimates of the poverty-reduction impacts of transfers ignore the labor supply and demographic changes induced by transfers, both of which tend to increase pretransfer poverty. While there exist numerous analyses of the role of transfers as they affect labor supply and household structure, evidence on the poverty-increasing effects of these responses is scarce. Public assistance increases somewhat the number of single women with children who head their own households, but the resulting effect on poverty is rather small (Danziger et al., 1982; Ellwood and Bane, 1984). Among the aged the shift to living independently of their children was largely completed by the mid-sixties and perhaps had been accelerated by increasing Social Security benefits during the 1950–1965 period. But the trend since 1965 in pretransfer poverty among the elderly—and, thus, of the antipoverty impact of transfers—seems largely unaffected.

The problem is somewhat more serious in the case of labor supply. A simulation for 1974 (Plotnick, 1984) shows that after adjusting for reductions in earnings that are induced by transfers, the net decline in poverty resulting from transfers for prime-age families would have been 8 percent instead of the calculated 18 percent. Because a significant proportion of the decline in aged male labor force participation may have been due to Social Security retirement benefits (Danziger, Haveman, and Plotnick, 1981), we expect the true antipoverty effect of transfers for the aged to be below the calculated effects as well. Thus, for any year the net overall effect of transfers on poverty may be up to 50 percent less than the accounting calculations we reported. However, because transfers lead to net increases in income, their true impact on poverty would still have increased from 1965 to 1978, although at a slower pace than suggested by Tables 3.6 and 3.7. For the same reasons the reported decline in antipoverty effectiveness after 1978 is likely to be overstated as well.

A DECOMPOSITION EXERCISE

While recognizing the upward bias in the calculated effects of transfers on poverty reduction, we nevertheless provide for each time period a statistical decomposition to identify the impact on the trend in post-transfer poverty of each of its three primary components: the trend in pretransfer poverty, changes in the transfer system's antipoverty effectiveness, and demographic changes—aging, divorce, independent living. We compute what the level of post-transfer poverty would have been in 1978 if one of the three components had remained at its 1965 level, while the other two components had been at their 1978 levels. Then we compare this hypothetical incidence with the actual 1978 incidence. If the hypothetical incidence exceeds (is less than) the actual one, we conclude that the change in the component between 1965 and 1978 contributed to a fall (rise) in post-transfer poverty. The same procedure is followed for the 1978–1983 period.

Between 1965 and 1978 observed post-transfer poverty declined from 15.6 to 11.4 percent, or 4.2 percentage points.[17] If the incidence of pretransfer poverty for each demographic group had been constant at the 1965 levels but the antipoverty effectiveness of transfers and the distribution of persons among demographic groups had been at their 1978 levels, then post-transfer poverty would have been 14.2 instead of 11.4 percent. Thus, largely because of aggregate economic conditions, decreases in pretransfer poverty led to a post-transfer decline of 2.8 percentage points. Similarly, because post-transfer poverty would have been 14.4 percent if the antipoverty effectiveness of the transfer system had not improved, the increased coverage and generosity of public transfers contributed 3.0 points to the decline. However, demographic changes contributed to a 2.1-point increase in official poverty. By definition, the residual was −0.5 points.[18]

For the 1978–1983 period post-transfer poverty rose by 3.8 percentage points to 15.2 percent. Each of the three factors contributed to this increase—changes in economic conditions reflected in pretransfer poverty rates for the groups, 2.3 points; declines in the effects of transfers, 1.2 points; demographic change, 0.6 points. The residual was −0.3 points. For the full 1965–1983 period the small decline in poverty (0.4 points) was produced by the net balance of demographic shifts that increased poverty (2.6 points), an expanding transfer system which reduced poverty (−2.5 points), and slight downward pressure from within-group changes in pretransfer poverty (−0.6 points).[19]

The Effects on the Nonpoor of the War on Poverty

We have traced the post-1965 trends in poverty and discussed the contribution of public transfers to those trends. Other chapters in this volume identify impacts of federal antipoverty policy on the poor. Little attention, however, has been paid to the impacts of antipoverty policy on the nonpoor. In a political context it is these effects that determine the viability of antipoverty policies.

To make such an assessment is fraught with difficulty. One can usually trace the impacts of policy measures on transfer recipients, but the costs of these measures to the nonpoor are largely borne through taxes, with no direct assignment possible. In this section we identify some of these effects. While our estimates are crude, they provide some notion of how the nontargeted majority has been affected by policies targeted on the poor.

Antipoverty policies may affect the pretransfer nonpoor through many channels.[20] A catalog of major effects is as follows:

> Because of the policy changes motivated by concerns reflected in the War on Poverty and Great Society, public expenditures and hence taxes are higher than they would otherwise have been. The bulk of the increase in taxes is borne by the nonpoor.

> The reduction in labor supply and savings resulting from the higher taxes increases the availability of these resources for other uses. In the labor supply case there is increased time for home produc-

tion activities and leisure, which partially offsets the reduced earnings.

Some portion of the growth in public expenditures on cash and in-kind benefits that is attributable to policy changes provides benefits directly to the nonpoor, since most programs do not terminate eligibility at the poverty line.

To the extent that human capital investment policies—education, employment, and training—are successful, there will be increased productivity of the low-income working population and hence increased competition for jobs, reduced wage rates, and, perhaps, earnings losses of those displaced by the competition. The burden of these shifts will be borne largely by the nonpoor.

The increases in productivity resulting from the improvements in education, training, and economic security attributable to social policies will, to the extent that these increased productivities are utilized, increase GNP. This economic growth will be shared by both the poor and the nonpoor.

Because of policies motivated by concern for the poor, there will be a reduction in the extent of hunger, poor health, poor education, and poor housing, and a decrease in the insecurity that poor persons bear because of income loss or irregular and extraordinary expenditure. To the extent that nonpoor individuals value these improvements in the lot of the poor, their own economic well-being increases.

The increase in social welfare spending is likely to lead to increased macroeconomic stability to the extent that the expenditures are countercyclical (for example, unemployment compensation).

The increase in effective income guarantees provides a better safety net protecting the nonpoor from the full consequences of unexpected income losses or extraordinary expenditures that might affect them. The nonpoor would be willing to pay some amount for this increase in their own economic security.

In this analysis we consider two counterfactuals:

Scenario A: Without the impetus provided by War on Poverty–Great Society policies, *total social welfare expenditures (SWE) would have grown at a rate equal to the growth rate of GNP,* implying a constant ratio of SWE to GNP from 1965 to 1980.

Scenario B: Without the impetus provided by War on Poverty–Great Society policies, *total SWE would have grown at a rate equal to the growth rate of SWE relative to GNP in the 1950–1965 period.*

Aggregate SWE in 1980 would have totaled about $372 billion per year under scenario B and $287 billion under counterfactual A. The actual level of expenditures was about $493 billion. Thus, in 1980 actual SWE were from $121 billion to $206 billion greater than they would have been.

Table 3.8 shows the various components of the gains and losses to the nonpoor population of this additional social welfare spending.[21] Assuming a long-run balanced budget, aggregate federal, state, and local taxes in 1980 were $121 billion to $206 billion greater than they would have otherwise been. While it is impossible to know exactly how this added revenue was financed, we assume that 95 percent was paid by the nonpoor. These estimates—$115 and $195 billion—appear as item 1.

Not all of the increased social spending went to assist the pretransfer poor. Plotnick and Skidmore (1975) and Plotnick (1979) found that the pretransfer poor received 41 to 43 percent of all SWE in the 1965–1972 period and about 45 percent in 1974. For 1980 we estimate that about 45 percent of total spending went to the pretransfer poor. Conversely, the 55 percent benefiting the nonpoor represents gains of $63 and $107 billion (item 2).

Both the increased taxes and the increased benefits are likely to decrease labor supply. Haveman's (1984) simulation method, developed for a similar tax and spending change, results in an overall "guesstimate" of about a 2.5- to 3.5-percent decrease in labor supply. This leads to earnings losses of $27 and $37 billion (item 3).

This loss of work time and earnings is compensated at least in part by an increase in nonmarketed uses of time such as home production, schooling, or leisure. In the face of existing taxes, the net wage rate at the margin will be less than the gross wage rate. It is the former rate at which increments of nonmarket time are valued. Assuming a wedge between the gross and net rate of 25 percent, the benefit of the increase in nonmarket time of the nonpoor is about $28 billion for scenario A and $20 billion for scenario B (item 4).

A rough estimate for item 5 completes the list of quantifiable items. Education and training expenditures in 1980 were $120.6 billion. If these expenditures had maintained a constant ratio with GNP over this period, they would have been about 15 percent lower. Summing the additional

Table 3.8. Annual gains and losses to pretransfer nonpoor population in 1980 as result of antipoverty policy efforts (billions of 1980 dollars)

	Gains		Losses	
Gains or losses	Scenario A	Scenario B	Scenario A	Scenario B
1. Increased taxes required to finance increase in SWE	—	—	195	115
2. Spillover of transfer income and education, training, and medical care services from increases in SWE	107	63	—	—
3. Reduction in labor earnings from reduced labor supply as a result of higher taxes paid by and benefits received by nonpoor	—	—	37	27
4. Increase in leisure and home production outputs as a result of reduction in labor supply of nonpoor (see 3)	28	20	—	—
5. Share of increased growth in incomes as a result of higher productivity of low-income workers	8	8	—	—
6. Reduced wages and job losses of nonpoor as a result of increased job competition from better trained and educated disadvantaged workers	—	—	X	X
7. Increased satisfaction as a result of reduction in poverty, inequality, and insecurity of poor	X	X	—	—
8. Share in increased production as a result of more stable macroeconomic performance	X	X	—	—
9. Increased security from unexpected job or income loss or extraordinary expenses as a result of better safety net	X	X	—	—
Total	$143 plus items 7–9	$91	$232 plus item 6	$142

spending over the entire 1965–1980 period yields an increase in education and training expenditures—an increment in human capital investment— of $125.7 billion. Assuming that foregone student (trainee) income is about equal to these direct expenditures and assuming a real rate of return of 5 percent on this increased human capital stock of $251.4 billion suggests an increase in 1980 GNP of $12.6 billion. This translates into an increase in personal income of about $10.4 billion. We assume that 80 percent is retained by the nonpoor and enter $8 billion for both scenarios.

Item 6 concerns the effects of increased training and education on the structure of wage rates and hours worked. The increment in human capital that was concentrated on low-skilled disadvantaged workers enabled them to compete better with higher-skilled workers for available jobs. This tends to reduce wages for all higher-skilled workers. Similarly, the associated reduction in the supply of lower-skilled workers tends to raise their wage rates and earnings. We cannot quantify item 6, but place it in the loss column, since more-skilled nonpoor workers would probably be adversely affected.

Items 7, 8, and 9 are also unquantifiable. The nonpoor's psychic gains from reduced poverty, inequality, and insecurity may be large or small but are surely positive. Since the aggregate level of insecurity is reduced by the increased social spending, all citizens are more insulated from the effects of unexpected income losses or expenditure increases or the business cycle.

We identify a total quantifiable loss to the nonpoor of from $142 billion to $232 billion in 1980. This is offset by a total quantifiable gain of from $91 billion to $143 billion plus the nonquantifiable benefits. Assuming that the losses associated with item 6 are negligible, the $51 to $89 billion of net costs to the nonpoor represent from 2 to 3 percent of personal income in 1980.[22] One year's increment to personal income would seem a small price for the nonpoor to pay for the gains accruing to them from items 7–9.

Reflections on Antipoverty Policy, Past and Future

The 1960s saw a nation ready to undertake bold initiatives in social policy, optimistic that poverty could be reduced, racial inequalities diminished, and worthwhile investments in human productivity made. Now, twenty years later, disappointment with past efforts, a desire to scale back existing programs, and a reluctance to embrace new social initiatives characterize the mood.

As we have documented, public income transfers have grown rapidly since 1965, and most of this growth is attributable to the initiatives of the War on Poverty and Great Society. Because of this growth, a sizable reduction in poverty occurred, at least up to 1980. Yet progress against poverty generally stalled after the early 1970s, and almost no progress has been made against relative poverty.

Even this progress against absolute poverty, however, has been bitter-sweet. The growth in transfers has had some negative side effects in the form of reductions in labor supply and savings and perhaps has affected family structure, all of which are often perceived to be more serious than research indicates they actually are. Moreover, an income-transfer strategy is inconsistent with societal preferences for aiding the able-bodied poor. The lack of success of the preferred strategy—increased earnings and self-sufficiency—is reflected in the failure to reduce pretransfer poverty for many of the able-bodied.

We conclude that the War on Poverty and Great Society initiatives have imposed relatively small quantifiable net losses on the nonpoor who paid for the programs undertaken. These initiatives also yielded a variety of nonquantifiable gains to the nonpoor which may even offset the net losses.

Our review prompts us to draw a few lessons, lessons that are clearly a blend of the research evidence and our interpretations. The first lesson is that the income support strategy of the past two decades has worked. Providing cash and in-kind transfers has reduced the extent of both poverty and income disparities across age and racial groups. While large budgetary costs are involved, rather modest efficiency losses have resulted.

A second lesson concerns the palliative as opposed to the curative nature of the income support strategy. Although both the definition and measurement of dependence are far from settled, the growth of transfers in the post-1965 period has probably increased its extent. A policy that cannot reduce pretransfer or prewelfare poverty among the able-bodied and put people to work in a society that prides itself collectively and individually on being independent will never be considered successful. However, because rising incomes generated by robust labor markets largely bypass important groups such as the aged, the disabled, and women heading families with young children, a continuing commitment to transfers is essential if the gains that have been made are to be preserved and enlarged.

Third, economic prosperity and reductions in poverty go hand in hand.

Higher productivity and economic growth create more jobs and increase wages, thereby directly reducing the extent of pretransfer poverty.[23] Recession and slow growth, conversely, exert profoundly negative effects. Moreover, the recent historical record suggests that expansion of antipoverty policies is more feasible during periods of economic growth.

A fourth lesson from both the policies implemented and the social experiments or demonstrations undertaken is that economic disparities based on race, sex, and family headship are extremely difficult to reduce. Securing full participation of the poor in economic life requires a long-run effort and involves improving their employability and expanding educational opportunities for their children, changes in labor markets, the provision of social and job-related services, the provision of transitional income, employment, and in-kind support, and a growing economy. No simple formula—no single isolated policy measure or approach— is likely to make a substantial dent in the extent of the problem.

Fifth, nonintensive short-duration interventions are unlikely to have lasting effects. Programs that attempt to change the economic performance of individuals lacking basic skills by providing a few months of training, counseling, or placement services may or may not demonstrate positive and statistically significant impacts on work or earnings; but even in cases where benefits exceed costs (Job Corps, Supported Work), the gains were small in relation to the initial deficiencies (Gottschalk, 1983; Burtless and Haveman, 1984).

Finally, incentives matter. The poor, just like the nonpoor, respond to incentives—they work less in the face of high income guarantees and benefit reduction rates. Although the evidence is less clear, they may also change living arrangements and reduce investments in themselves in response to public programs.

These lessons suggest a reorientation of antipoverty policy to reduce both poverty and dependence on transfers (see Rivlin, 1984, for some related proposals). Because no single policy measure can be a cure-all (lesson 4), our strategy has several components.

Income support benefits for those not expected to work should not be reduced (lesson 1). Poverty has decreased because these benefits increased—especially for the aged. Because the official poverty lines are adjusted for increases in the consumer price index, transfers to those who are not expected to work must also be indexed, or poverty will rise.[24] Women who head households with young children face one of the most serious poverty problems. A national minimum, indexed AFDC benefit should be introduced. This would have a particularly large impact in the South, where benefits were low originally and have eroded the most in recent years.

Because income support is not curative (lesson 2), the second component attempts to increase employment and reduce pretransfer poverty for both those expected to work and those who wish to work in spite of other income support options. Development of carefully designed employment subsidies warrants priority. For example, the New Jobs Tax Credit subsidized employers who expanded their work rolls; it stimulated employment while restraining price increases (Bishop and Haveman, 1979). A targeted employment program that allows recipients to mix work and welfare, such as the Supported Work Demonstration project (Hollister, Kemper, and Maynard, 1984), is also attractive. Such a program could both increase work effort and reduce dependence on welfare and poverty (Danziger and Jakubson, 1982).

Third, the Earned Income Tax Credit (EITC), which currently subsidizes the earnings of low-income workers with children, should be extended to all workers and the credit could be increased and indexed. This would enhance work incentives for the working poor (lesson 6) and offset recent increases in their tax burden.[25]

These reforms increase public spending or lower revenues. Our last two suggestions should reduce the need for additional public funds. The fourth component of our strategy is a social child-support program under which all adults who care for a child and do not live with the child's other parent would be eligible for a support payment that would be financed by a percentage-of-earnings tax on the absent parent. If the tax on the absent parent fell below a fixed minimum level because the parent's earnings were too low, the support payment would be supplemented up to that level by government funds. Even if total AFDC expenditures were cut somewhat, the program could reduce post-transfer poverty because of the additional revenue raised from absent parents (Oellerich and Garfinkel, 1983). It would also reduce dependence on welfare.

Our fifth component links tax simplification and welfare reform. In place of the current food stamp program and the personal income tax, a credit income tax with a modest income guarantee would be adopted. Per capita tax credits would replace both the personal exemptions in the current income tax and the food stamp program and would be paid in monthly installments to all persons in the manner of children's allowances in other countries. To keep the tax rate required to finance the credits from becoming too high, the tax base would be broadened by eliminating most itemized deductions in addition to the personal exemption and by making income from all sources (except the credits themselves) taxable. The tax rate would be identical on all incomes except the very highest, which would pay surtaxes. The broader tax base and constant marginal tax rate (for most of the population) would increase total tax payments for upper-income families while decreasing their marginal tax rates. This suggestion complements the current debate on tax simplification.

While current prospects for the adoption of these or similar suggestions are not high, they might improve in the mid-1980s if the economy remains strong. Tighter labor markets encourage employers to hire low-skill workers and induce transfer recipients to seek employment. Both of these responses reduce the target population for our reforms. Higher real per capita income eases the financial burden and political tensions of increased spending for the needy. If economic growth falters, however, countercyclical transfers will rise, and prospects for reform will diminish even further.

While some argue that expansion of antipoverty policy is inconsistent with the objective of sustaining economic growth, our reading of the evidence on the efficiency costs of such policies is not so pessimistic (Danziger, Haveman, and Plotnick, 1981). Modest additional spending on transfers targeted on those not expected to work will have minor effects on work effort and savings, and the labor market programs we suggest would reduce reliance on transfers and mitigate efficiency losses.

This reorientation protects benefits for the truly needy who are not expected to work and promotes employment for those who can work by subsidizing private employers and employees. It also emphasizes parental responsibility for children and lowers marginal tax rates for the nonpoor. An antipoverty agenda containing these features is consistent with both economic growth and some social policy objectives that have been recently pursued, and it would produce a lower rate of poverty than would a continuation of current policy.

4   Poverty in America: Is Welfare the Answer or the Problem?

David T. Ellwood
Lawrence H. Summers

POVERTY IN THE UNITED STATES is not now an active policy issue. Following the cutbacks achieved in the first two Reagan administration budgets, there are few proponents of further major reductions of antipoverty spending. At the same time, in an era of huge budget deficits, there is little support for new major initiatives to combat poverty. The negative income tax, perhaps the only major policy proposal of any type ever to command the enthusiastic support of a wide spectrum of economists ranging from Milton Friedman to James Tobin, has slipped entirely off the policy agenda. The policies that are discussed represent incremental changes in existing programs. Little attention is devoted to radical reforms.

The lack of discussion of major reform proposals in no way indicates widespread satisfaction with either the intellectual underpinnings or the results of current policies. Indeed, almost no one is satisfied with current efforts. The sources of dissatisfaction are well illustrated in two recent tracts on the poverty problem: Charles Murray's *Losing Ground* (1984) and Michael Harrington's *New American Poverty* (1984). Murray notes that poverty has increased in the past fifteen years in concert with increases in federal social spending. He argues for a poverty Laffer curve: attempts to improve poverty actually made things worse. Harrington sees the problem of rising poverty as caused by government inaction rather than action. He asserts that the War on Poverty was never really declared and argues that without a far more massive effort, there is no real chance of combating poverty. Nor have more moderate voices been satisfied with the current outcomes. The picture painted by Alice Rivlin in a recent speech is illustrative: she described poverty as one of those truly hard problems, like the arms race, that urgently need solution but for which we currently have few good ideas.

The poverty issue is gridlocked. No one is satisfied with current policy, but no conceived alternative to the contours of existing policy can generate much support. In this chapter we review existing policies and our record in reducing poverty. Despite the haphazard evolution of these policies and their seeming lack of coherence, we find much to recommend them. Given the resources devoted to fighting poverty, we have done about as well as we could have hoped. There is a logic to the broad outlines of the current "safety net": using categorical programs, we have provided financial support to the needy and probably have not caused an appreciable share of the current problems. But current transfer policies do relatively little to help the poor achieve self-sufficiency or to ameliorate some of the serious social problems attending poverty.

We begin by reviewing trends in poverty, poverty spending, and economic performance. It is immediately apparent that economic performance is the dominant determinant of the poverty rate. Essentially all of the variation in the poverty of the nonelderly is explained by movements in the ratio of the poverty line to median family income. Some might have expected that in the aftermath of the Great Society programs, poverty rates would have fallen by more than can be explained by movements in median family income, but such expectations are unrealistic. Expenditures on cash assistance programs to the nonelderly represented less than 1 percent of the gross national product in 1980. Despite widespread perceptions to the contrary, there has been no prodigious increase in antipoverty spending over the past ten years on programs that provide cash to the poor. Real benefits in the Aid to Families with Dependent Children program actually declined between 1970 and 1980, and the number of children on the program changed little, in spite of dramatic increases in the number of children in single-parent families. The large increases in social spending that did take place between 1970 and 1980 were primarily for in-kind programs like Medicaid and food stamps, which do not affect measured poverty because they are not counted as income when poverty rates are calculated, and in social insurance programs, which are aimed at the middle class.

We then focus on three disadvantaged groups that have been the subject of considerable discussion in recent years: disabled workers, female family heads with children, and unemployed black youth. Government is frequently blamed for causing the problems of these groups: disability insurance has been alleged to reduce the labor supply of older men; AFDC benefits have been implicated in the dramatic changes in family structure, particularly among blacks; and welfare is occasionally blamed for the employment problems of black youth. In all three cases we find the actual damage done by government transfer policies to be far less serious than is often supposed. It is clear from the discussion, though, that the problems faced by the groups are very different. More important, the potential dangers of expanding welfare benefits also differ. In the case of unemployed youth, for example, an expanded welfare system could do significant damage.

We conclude by discussing the implications of an examination of the evidence for current transfer policy. We are led to reject out of hand the increasingly fashionable view that poverty programs are the source of poverty problems. Yet we do not advocate a move away from the problem-specific and heavily categorical approach of the past. Both logic and empirical evidence suggest the desirability of a complex categorical welfare system of the type we now have, and we suspect that the broad outlines of the current system are sensible; major reform appears both infeasible and undesirable. But our analysis does suggest that some scope exists for carefully designed benefit increases that would reduce suffering without adverse side effects. It also underscores the importance of the much more difficult tasks of achieving sustained prosperity and economic growth and of devising policies directed at helping the poor become more self-sufficient.

Trends in Poverty and in Antipoverty Spending

Any discussion of trends in poverty must rely on some measure of the incidence of poverty, and any single poverty measure is bound to be misleading. We concentrate here on trends in the officially defined poverty rate—the fraction of population living in families with incomes below the poverty line. It is important to understand that the poverty line is a fixed level of real income (which varies by family size) thought to be sufficient to provide a minimally adequate standard of living. It is adjusted each year only for changes in the cost of living. Changes in the poverty rate thus provide an indicator of society's success in alleviating income hardship among those with relatively low incomes; they do not necessarily indicate changes in income inequality. It is also important to recognize that cash payments are the only benefits treated as part of family income in the official poverty measure. In-kind benefits such as medical care, food stamps, and housing assistance are not counted at all.

Figure 4.1 depicts the trends since 1959 in the poverty rate, defined as the percentage of all persons living in families with cash income below the

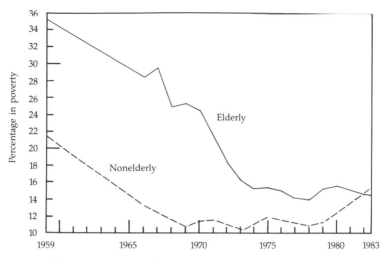

Figure 4.1.   Official poverty rates for the elderly and nonelderly, 1959–1983. Source: Official poverty statistics published annually by the U.S. Bureau of the Census (Current Population Reports, ser. P–60).

poverty line. We have separated the figures for the elderly and nonelderly. For those over 65 there was dramatic and relatively continual progress up to 1974, some modest progress through 1978, and a relatively flat poverty level since that time. For the nonelderly there was a dramatic decline in the poverty rate between 1959 and 1969. Then progress largely halted. The rate moved up and down throughout the 1970s, finally turning up rather sharply in the 1980s. The fact that the dramatic halt to progress in reducing the poverty rate for the nonelderly seemed to coincide with the onset of the Great Society programs has sparked the current discouragement with our antipoverty efforts. In this chapter we shall focus primarily on the nonelderly, since there appears to be less concern that our efforts at helping senior citizens were ineffectual or counterproductive.

POVERTY AMONG THE NONELDERLY IN RELATION TO ECONOMIC CHANGE

How much of the poverty rate can be explained by general economic developments? Figure 4.2 plots the nonelderly poverty rate along with the poverty threshold expressed as a fraction of median income. It is apparent that the curves dovetail almost perfectly. Almost all of the variation in the poverty rate is tracked by movements in median family income.[1]

One does see a slight divergence of the trends in the eighties. This apparent fall in the relative position of the poor has been widely discussed

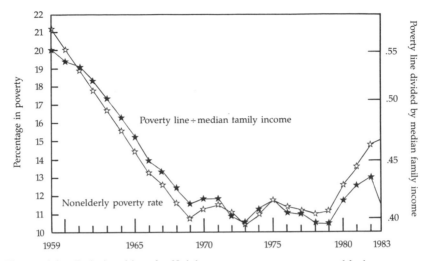

Figure 4.2. Relationship of official poverty rate among nonelderly persons to poverty line as a fraction of median family income, 1959–1983. Source: See Figure 4.1; median family income from U.S. House of Representatives (1983, p. 64).

elsewhere, although there is no agreement on the actual reasons for the divergence.[2] Even here, it should be noted, the poverty rate is basically tracking the performance of the economy. In real terms median family income in 1980 was no higher than it was in 1969. In the recession of 1982 it actually fell 5 percent below the 1969 level. Since average families have no more than they did almost fifteen years ago, it should not come as a great surprise that poor families are not much better off either. It seems reasonable that the same factors account for the stagnation in the fortunes of both the poor and the nonpoor.

The reasons for the lack of growth in median family income are not entirely clear. Real per capita disposable income did rise by 27.5 percent. Some of the explanation must therefore lie in demographic changes, which were affecting both the poor and the nonpoor: There was a large increase in the number of female-headed families, and average family size declined from 3.6 to 3.3; the share of income going to unrelated individuals also increased substantially. But demographic changes are not the entire story. Median income of full-year, full-time male workers also declined between 1970 and 1980. Much of the blame must be placed on the productivity slowdown, which reduced the annual rate of growth of productivity to 0.8 percent in the 1970s after nearly two and one-half decades of growth at almost 3 percent per year.

Whatever the reasons for the decline, it would be absurd to attribute it to social welfare program mistakes. Making the poor better or worse off does not affect median income because the middle family in the income distribution is not directly affected. Nor can attitudinal changes sometimes traced to welfare be blamed for our economic problems. The market valuation of corporate physical capital, which is presumably free from attitudinal problems, has declined by more than 50 percent since the late 1960s.

A brief consideration of the relevant magnitudes demonstrates why movements in average family incomes are a dominant determinant of the fortunes of the poor. The bottom fifth of all families gets about 6 percent of total personal income. This figure has been remarkably stable for most of the past twenty years. In 1982 disposable personal income was $2,172 billion. A 10-percent increase in disposable personal income would raise the amount of income flowing to the poor by $13 billion. A 25-percent increase, which was achieved between 1961 and 1966, would increase the income to the bottom fifth by more than the total cost of all means-tested cash assistance programs plus food stamps. These calculations probably understate the power of a strong economy in reducing poverty because they neglect the cyclicality of the share of income going to the bottom fifth of the population (see Chapter 8).

There is an alternative way of seeing that the performance of the economy is a dominant determinant of the economic condition of the poor. A majority of the poor are in male-headed families. For this group at least 75 percent of income results from earnings. Even among poor female-headed families with children, 40 percent of all income comes from working. The fraction is much greater for families near the poverty line—the ones who will be drawn into or out of poverty as the economy swings (U.S. House of Representatives, 1983, p. 34).

THE ROLE OF ANTIPOVERTY PROGRAMS

Still, it is troubling that poverty rates have tracked median family income so closely. Expenditures on social welfare programs increased enormously during the late 1960s and early 1970s. These transfers from the government should have pushed more people across the poverty line, yet no improvement in poverty was recorded. This lack of progress seems to have fueled the current perception that the antipoverty programs were a failure. Murray even argues that the growth in government programs induced the poor to stop relying on private sources of income and start relying on public sources, thus reducing the prospects for eventual self-sufficiency. Let us examine these charges.

It is customary to divide social welfare expenditures into three categories: social insurance, cash assistance, and in-kind benefits. The social insurance system is clearly geared to the middle class, designed to protect those who retire or who suffer some calamity such as total disability, unemployment, or work injury and therefore are unable to earn money. Medicare, which covers much of the medical care needs of the aged and totally disabled who receive Social Security, is usually classified as a social insurance program, even though it provides in-kind benefits. Most workers are covered by these programs as long as they have worked a reasonable period. Far from being income tested, these programs tend to give higher benefits to those who had higher earnings before retirement, disability, or unemployment. Thus, these programs do protect some families from poverty, but they really were designed to protect middle-class incomes.

Cash assistance is offered to certain low-income groups. In most areas only three groups qualify for significant cash assistance: the aged, the totally disabled, and persons in single-parent families. Supplemental Security Income covers the first two groups, while AFDC covers the third. There is some assistance available for others. Most states offer a very modest general assistance (GA) program, often for people who are partially disabled. Further, some states also offer an AFDC-Unemployed Parent (AFDC-UP) program for two-parent families with an unemployed parent, but there are stringent restrictions on eligibility, and the program is extremely small— less than 5 percent of the total AFDC program. The cash transfer programs are explicitly income tested, and benefits decline as income rises.

Finally, a variety of in-kind benefits are available. Food stamps provide modest benefits per person in the form of vouchers, which are available, on a scale that varies by income, to all poor persons (except students and strikers). Medicaid provides medical benefits to the poor, but only to those who are aged, permanently disabled, or in single-parent families.[3] There are housing assistance programs and a number of other modest in-kind benefits, like Low Income Home Energy Assistance.

Table 4.1 shows the magnitude and growth of these various programs. Expenditures are divided by major beneficiary group: the elderly, the totally disabled, and all others. Certainly the most prominent fact demonstrated by the table is that the bulk of all expenditures and of dollar growth has been in programs for the elderly. We would certainly expect to see, as we have seen, a very dramatic reduction in poverty among this group, even in the seventies when growth was rather flat. Let us examine expenditures for the nonelderly, exploring separately expenditures on cash assistance, in-kind benefits, and social insurance.

Table 4.1.   Costs of major public assistance and social insurance programs for the elderly, totally disabled, and all others, 1960–1980 (billions of constant 1980 dollars)

Program	1960	1970	1980
Programs for the elderly			
Social insurance			
Social Security Old Age and			
Survivors	29.2	60.7	104.7
Public employee and railroad			
retirement	9.7	21.9	44.3
Medicare[a]	0.0	16.8	29.1
Cash assistance			
Supplemental Security Income			
(and Old Age Assistance)	4.5	4.0	2.7
In-kind benefits			
Medicaid[a]	0.0	4.1	8.7
Food stamps	0.0	0.2	0.5
Housing[b]	0.1	0.5	2.5
Programs for the totally disabled			
Social insurance			
Social Security Disability[c]	1.6	6.5	15.4
Medicare[d]	0.0	0.0	4.5
Cash assistance			
Supplemental Security Income			
(and Aid to the Disabled)	0.7	2.1	5.0
In-kind benefits			
Medicaid[a]	0.0	2.2	7.0
Programs for others			
Social insurance			
Unemployment insurance	8.4	9.3	18.9
Workers' compensation	3.6	6.5	13.6
Cash assistance			
Aid to Families with			
Dependent Children			
(AFDC)	2.8	10.3	12.5
General assistance (GA)	0.9	1.3	1.4
In-kind benefits			
Medicaid[a]	0.0	3.7	7.5
Food stamps	0.0	1.1	8.6
Housing[b]	0.4	1.0	4.7

Sources: U.S. Department of Health and Human Services, Social Security Administration (1983), tables 2, 18, 19, 154, 155, 160, 172, 192, 200; U.S. Bureau of the Census (1978c), table 549, and (1983d), tables 640, 643.

a. Began in 1966.

b. Estimates based on fraction of persons receiving housing assistance who are elderly (see U.S. Bureau of the Census, 1982d).

c. Began in 1956.

d. Extended to the disabled in 1974.

Cash Assistance. In spite of considerable growth in the late sixties, means-tested cash assistance programs for the nonelderly remain very small. Total benefits have grown only modestly since 1970, and most of that growth has been in the disability program.

Taken together, all of the cash assistance programs for the nonelderly totaled less than $20 billion in 1982. That figure is a considerable increase over expenditures for 1960, when benefits were less than $5 billion (in 1980 dollars), but it still represents much less than 1 percent of GNP. Federal expenditures for these programs are less than 2 percent of the federal budget.

These expenditures are too small to have very much effect on measured poverty. Cash assistance moves only 5 percent of poor persons out of poverty.[4] Spreading the $20 billion spent on cash assistance across 30.6 million poor persons yields an average cash benefit of slightly more than $50 per poor person per month. Benefits are concentrated on those persons who are single parents or disabled. But for single parents benefits average only $100 monthly per person; for the disabled they average roughly $220. These amounts are not sufficient to have an appreciable effect on poverty.

Perhaps even more important, over the period when poverty rates were stable, there were only modest changes in expenditures for these programs. Between 1970 and 1980 cash assistance expenditures rose from $13.7 billion to $18.9 billion. Over the entire decade *annual* real expenditures per non-elderly poor person rose just $93. Such an increase would have little effect on poverty statistics. Even that figure overstates the significance of the increase, since nearly all of the growth was in the disability program, which reaches only two million persons.

Expenditures for the AFDC program, the only cash assistance program for the nonelderly nondisabled, had essentially no growth over the seventies. In fact, expenditures have been falling sharply in real terms since 1976. Fewer persons were in the program in 1980 (before the Reagan budget cuts) than in 1972, in spite of a dramatic increase in the number of people living in single-parent families. The reason for the paradox is quite simple: Between 1972 and 1980 real benefit levels were cut by close to 30 percent; even though single-parent families were increasing, a smaller number were qualifying for AFDC.

In-Kind Benefits. Programs that provide in-kind benefits, such as food stamps, housing assistance and medical care, did grow considerably over the 1970s, but these are not counted as income for purposes of defining poverty. Thus, expenditures for these programs do not reduce measured poverty, although they clearly reduce hardship.

The food stamp program comes closest to offering cash assistance, and such benefits should surely be counted as income in calculating poverty. Unlike almost every other major social program, food stamps are available to all poor families regardless of their characteristics. The program was established nationally in the early 1970s, and benefit levels have been fixed in real terms since 1971. Costs have grown rapidly as participation increased, reaching $9 billion in 1980 and more than $11 billion in 1985. Some twenty million nonelderly persons are in families receiving food stamps, but average benefits are relatively low—less than $40 per month per person. Thus, the program would not have a significant effect on poverty statistics even if its benefits were included as measured income. If food stamps were treated as income in 1982, the number of nonelderly poor would have fallen from 30.6 million to 29.1 millon.[5] Housing assistance is also available—in 1980 $4 billion was spent on the nonelderly—as well as a variety of child welfare, child nutrition, social services, and other programs. We do not have an exact total for these for the nonelderly, but it is probably between $5 and $10 billion.

Persons who are in single-parent families or who are totally disabled and a few others qualify for Medicaid. In 1980 the cost for single parents was $7.5 billion; for the disabled, $7.0 billion. Medical care falls into a special category. It cannot be thought of in the same way as cash assistance and food stamps because the poor never bought much health insurance prior to the start of the Medicaid program in 1967 and provision for medical care was not counted in determining the poverty level. Care was provided, if at all, on a charity basis in government-financed county hospitals.

Because these in-kind benefits are not counted as income, they do not reduce officially measured poverty. But there are indications that these programs have been at least partially successful in achieving their specific goals. Life expectancy in the United States rose more during the 1970s than during the 1950s and 1960s. Perhaps more significantly, life expectancy rose more for nonwhites than whites: 4.2 years versus 2.7 years. Similarly, the nonwhite infant mortality rate declined almost twice as much in absolute terms as the white rate. Both caloric intake and protein consumption of the poor increased relative to the middle class. "Nutritional inequality" declined noticeably (U.S. Bureau of the Census, 1983d, Tables 101, 104, 203).

Social Insurance Programs. The really large growth in social benefits for the nonelderly came in the social insurance programs—the programs for the middle class. Unemployment Insurance (UI), Workers' Compensation (WC), Social Security Disability Insurance (DI), and Medicare for the disabled together cost $52 billion in 1980, up from $22 billion just a decade earlier.

These programs are not generally perceived by the public as being anti-poverty programs, and rightly so. Their benefits go largely to the middle class. Only one-quarter of UI and WC funds are distributed to persons who would otherwise be poor. Nonetheless, their significance in aiding the poor should not be understated. Three-fourths of those formerly poor persons lucky enough to receive UI or WC benefits are pushed out of poverty by this income. Indeed in some respects these programs probably do more to reduce poverty among the nonelderly than cash assistance programs do. If UI and WC did not exist, at least three million more nonelderly people would be poor.[6] (We have no comparable figures for the DI program.)

IN SUM, it is not very surprising that measured poverty improved little during the 1970s. The single most important correlate with poverty—median family income—did not change. On government's side of the ledger, expenditures for cash assistance directed to the poor started small and hardly increased at all. In-kind benefits increased much more dramatically, but they are not counted as income and thus have no impact on measured poverty. The really dramatic growth came in the social insurance programs aimed at the middle class. Some of those benefits did reach people who would otherwise have been poor, but most went elsewhere.

Whether or not government transfers were large enough to have a significant effect on poverty, an additional concern is that government may actually be contributing to the poverty problem by discouraging work and encouraging single-parent family formation. Three groups enter prominently in any discussion of the disadvantaged in America: the disabled, those in single-parent families, and unemployed black youth. The first two are afforded the bulk of cash assistance, and existing policies have been indicted as having important counterproductive influences. Black youth have at times been cited as associated victims of the current welfare system. Should transfer policies bear significant responsibility for the problems faced by these groups?

The Disabled

The disability insurance portion of Social Security has been increasingly seen as a complement to the antipoverty strategy of other cash assistance programs. While eligibility and benefits are based in large part on previous earnings, its focus on the permanently and totally disabled suggests that it offers protection to a group who would suffer a sizable income loss without it. In addition, Supplemental Security Income provides benefits for those who are disabled and poor.

As we have seen, these programs grew enormously during the 1970s—both more than doubled during the decade. The combined cost of social insurance, cash assistance, and in-kind benefits for the disabled totaled nearly $33 billion in 1980. Naturally one wonders whether the money is being well spent. But a more serious question has arisen: some believe that the program has actually reduced labor force participation of middle-aged men. The charge is serious, since the program is intended solely for those who cannot work.

The program's growth has coincided with a significant decrease in labor force participation among some men: In 1960 only about 4 percent of men aged forty-five to fifty-four were out of the labor force; by 1980 the figure had reached almost 9 percent. For black men the increase was even more dramatic: from 7 percent up to 16 percent. Motivated by these statistics, a need to cut budgets, and a host of anecdotes indicating abuse of the program, the Reagan administration undertook a major tightening of DI eligibility rules in the early 1980s, cutting several hundred thousand people and making eligibility more difficult to obtain. These policy developments coincided with increasing criticism of the program within academic circles. For example, Donald Parsons (1980) concluded that the recent increase in nonparticipation in the labor force of prime-aged men can be largely explained by the increased generosity of social welfare transfers.

The significance of DI's effects goes far beyond its relatively small size. If a program with complex and hard-to-satisfy eligibility requirements (66 percent of applicants were denied benefits in 1980) has major perverse incentive effects, the prospects that broader-gauged redistributive measures could be efficacious would be bleak. Alternatively, if the program succeeds in reaching people who are too disabled to work, it provides at least one example of a successful targeted antipoverty effort.

DISABILITY AND WORK

The magnitude of the incentive effects of the DI program is the subject of considerable dispute. Leonard (1979) reaches conclusions similar to those of Parsons, using similar econometric techniques. Haveman and Wolfe (1984), using different data and alternative estimation techniques directed at selection biases, dissent from these conclusions, finding small effects of

DI on participation. The econometric literature taken as a whole is inconclusive on the effects of DI. This situation derives from the inherent difficulty of such analyses. The extrapolation of cross-sectional results to explain time series trends is problematic, as evidence on other problems ranging from fertility to investment behavior demonstrates. Moreover, the key variable in such an analysis—an individual's true capacity to work—is not observable, considerably complicating the inference problem.[7]

An alternative way to explore the employability of those who received disability insurance is to look at the earnings patterns of those who applied but were denied.[8] Certainly those who were denied assistance are on average considerably more employable than those granted benefits. Unfortunately, there are few data from recent years on the subsequent earnings of those denied disability benefits. However, the Social Security Administration (SSA) examined the subsequent earnings experience of those denied benefits in 1967 and 1970: in the late 1960s virtually all of those who were rejected by the disability insurance program did little work in subsequent years. In assessing this evidence, it is important to recall that the fraction of disability applicants denied eligibility has risen steadily through time, from 49 percent in 1965 to 52 percent in 1975 to 66 percent in 1980. Thus, rejections are even more common now than during that study period.

A SSA staff paper summarized the 1967 survey results by noting, "A large proportion of the denied applicants never returned to competitive employment despite many years of work prior to their disability and an administrative decision in 1967 that they were still able to do so." Further, "four-fifths of these claimants who were initially denied in 1967 did not return to sustained competitive employment in the following five years" (Tretel, 1976, pp. 22, 25). Similar results were obtained in the 1970 survey: of all those denied benefits at the initial hearing in 1970, 72.3 percent had no earnings in 1975, and only 10.7 percent earned as much as $6,000.[9]

Preliminary work in Bound (1985) suggests that these basic conclusions hold even in recent years and even if one looks across the entire age distribution of persons under sixty applying for disability benefits. More than half do not return to sustained work, and those who do so suffer earnings losses of nearly 50 percent.

One possible implication from these data is that the DI eligibility determination process is essentially capricious. However, mortality data demonstrate that this is not true. The 1970 survey found large differences between the mortality rates of those denied benefits and those found eligible: among those declared eligible who were under sixty, 25.6 percent died in the following five years, while among those found ineligible only 6.9 percent died. It is clear that, despite the many horror stories about the eligibility process, it does much better than a random process in sorting out those with health problems.

Since 1970 the DI program has doubled in size. Some of the increase is undoubtedly due to increased knowledge of the program and some may be a result of increased benefit levels and relaxation in standards. But even if the program now were taking people equivalent to the least employable *four-fifths* of those rejected in 1970, it still would include a group that would have done no sustained work whether or not they were accepted. And we doubt that standards have been relaxed to anything like that degree. Recall that in 1980, prior to the recently increased restrictions, 66 percent of applicants were denied entry to a program designed for the totally disabled. Those who apply are unlikely to be very healthy. Note also that medical expenditures for the disabled are very large and have continued to grow even out of proportion to the number of new beneficiaries and the growth in medical costs. The recent disastrous experiment of removing those thought least disabled from the disability rolls would seem to confirm these inferences.

IMPLICATIONS FOR TRANSFER POLICY

Disability insurance appears to be an example of a carefully targeted program that can provide generous benefits without generating large adverse incentive effects. But the program succeeds largely because benefits are based on a relatively objective and difficult-to-alter set of physical conditions. The disabled are generally out of the labor force for life. It would be no surprise to find that many would live in a state of perpetual poverty in the absence of government transfers. Moreover, the program has severe work disincentives. Effectively, if you begin working you prove that you are not totally disabled and you are no longer eligible to receive benefits. Benefits are reduced far more than dollar for dollar of earnings; they are reduced completely for any sizable sustained earnings.

Yet there is little concern about a "culture of poverty" or welfare dependence for this group. Nor is there an outcry about the lack of work incentives. There is some discussion about these issues to be sure, but it generates little energy. Attempts to cut the program result in considerable outrage.

The reasons are quite simple. In a program where the eligibility criteria call for recipients to be totally disabled, it seems unlikely that those who slip in "inappropriately" will be very healthy individuals unworthy of compassion or financial support. Moreover, it is almost unthinkable that otherwise healthy people would inflict damage on themselves in order to become eligible. The success of the disability program in targeting resources on a very needy group with little efficiency loss and broad-based public support is in large part a function of the narrowness of its purpose.

Poverty among Single Mothers

The mounting number of children being raised in single-parent households is commanding increased national attention. The apparent "crisis of the family" is noted most acutely with respect to black households, but the trend seems to extend to all racial and economic groups. The numbers are stark: by the time today's children turn eighteen, 45 percent of whites and a remarkable 85 percent of blacks are expected to have lived for some part of their lives in single-parent households (Bane and Ellwood, 1984a). At a minimum those who live in single-parent households face financial hardship; some worry that other negative consequences are likely as well.

Government welfare programs are frequently blamed for exacerbating this problem. By providing an alternative to reliance on a husband, government support is said to encourage family break-up and childbearing among the unmarried and to discourage remarriage and reconciliations. By providing an alternative to work, welfare is also said to discourage work and promote long-term dependence.

WELFARE AND FAMILY FORMATION

Certainly the most troubling and potentially most damning accusation leveled against the current welfare system is the charge that it encourages the formation and perpetuation of single-parent families. The specifics of the charges have changed over time but not the basic message. Originally, it was suggested that we had developed a welfare system that rewarded single-parent families by denying benefits to families with two parents. More recently, in the wake of the negative income tax experiments, it is alleged that by relieving a family of the necessity of relying on two parents for income, welfare facilitates marital disruption.

We believe that the impacts of welfare on family structure are very modest. Comparisons of changes in family structures over time with changes in the welfare system and of differences in family structures across states to differences in welfare benefits across states both suggest that welfare has minimal effects on family structure.

Time Trends in Welfare and Family Structure. Many different kinds of decisions influence family structures—divorce and separation, remarriage, and births to unmarried women. Probably the simplest measure of overall family structure is the fraction of all children living in a female-headed household. Also, there are many ways to analyze changes in welfare over time; one of the most straightforward is to examine the fraction of all children who receive AFDC. Figure 4.3 plots these two trends.

The fraction of all children living in a female-headed household started rising much faster in the late 1960s, at precisely the time when the number of children on AFDC rose sharply. But then the trends diverge—dramatically so. Since 1972 the fraction of all children living in a female-headed household rose from 14 percent to almost 20 percent. During that same period the fraction of all children in homes collecting AFDC held almost constant, at 12 percent The figures are even more dramatic for blacks: Between 1972 and 1980 the number of black children in female-headed families rose nearly 20 percent; the number of black children on AFDC

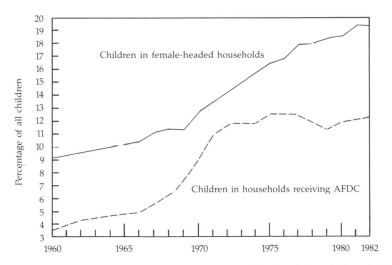

Figure 4.3. Comparative percentages of children in female-headed and AFDC households, 1960–1982. Source: U.S. Bureau of the Census, Current Population Reports, ser. P–20, *Household and Family Characteristics,* various years; *Social Security Bulletin, Annual Statistical Supplement,* various years.

actually fell by 5 percent. If AFDC were pulling families apart and encouraging the formation of single-parent families, it is hard to understand why the number of children on the program would remain constant throughout a period in our history when family structures changed the most.

These figures seem hard to believe, but they are easy to understand in light of the fact that real AFDC levels fell by almost 30 percent between 1970 and 1980 in the median state. Even in some comparatively liberal states, benefits plummeted: in New York City benefits dropped 33 percent in real terms over this period. Food stamps mitigated the declines somewhat, but between 1971 and 1983 combined food stamp and AFDC benefits fell by 22 percent in real terms in the median state (U.S. House of Representatives, 1983, figure 7, p. 82). A smaller and smaller fraction of children in single-parent families were receiving AFDC for a very simple reason: benefit levels, and therefore eligibility, were being sharply cut back.

Perhaps the impact of AFDC benefits was delayed, or perhaps once a threshold is reached, people do not react to changes in benefit levels. These explanations could explain why family structures continued to change even as benefits fell. But we can think of no argument crediting AFDC with a very large part in inducing changed family structures that is consistent with a falling absolute number of children on the program.

What about the sharp rise in the fraction of all black births to unmarried women? The birth rate to unmarried black women *fell* 13 percent between 1970 and 1980, but the birth rate to married black women fell even more— by 38 percent; thus, the fraction of births to unmarried women rose. During the same period the unmarried birth rate to whites *rose* by 27 percent. It seems difficult to argue that AFDC was a major influence in unmarried births when there was simultaneously a rise in the birth rate to unmarried whites and a fall in the rate for blacks.[10]

Probably the most important lesson of the time-series analysis is that family structure changes do not seem to mirror benefit level changes. We have already made rather draconian cuts in benefit levels and family structure changes have not slowed appreciably. It seems unlikely that further cuts would do much to hold families together.

Comparisons of Welfare and Family Structure across States. This country has been conducting a natural experiment for many decades: it has allowed states to set benefit levels for AFDC at whatever levels they choose. As a result benefits vary widely. In Mississippi in 1980 a single-parent family of four could get a maximum of $120 per month in AFDC benefits, and that amount had been raised from $60 per month only a few years earlier.

In California and New York the same family would be eligible for more than $500 in benefits. We find such variations extremely hard to justify on equity or efficiency grounds, but they do provide a powerful way to test for the impact of AFDC benefits.

The gaps between states are not quite as large as they might seem. Food stamps, as a federal program with uniform benefit levels nationally, narrows the gaps in benefits between states. But even including food stamps, benefits vary by a factor of two to three. Since food stamps are available whether or not one is in a single-parent family, their impact on family formation choices is unclear.

The obvious experiment is to compare the fraction of children living in female-headed households, or the divorce rate, or the birth rate to unmarried women, with benefit levels across states. Figure 4.4 provides such a comparison for 1980. There is no obvious relationship between the fraction of children not living in two-parent families and AFDC benefit levels across states. The same holds for almost every other measure of family structure as well, including divorce rates and out-of-wedlock birth rates. More sophisticated regression techniques, which control for differing socioeconomic characteristics across states, typically also show little or no relationship.

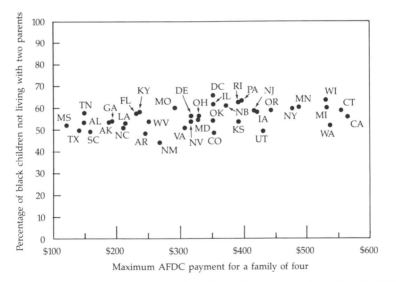

Figure 4.4. Relation of state AFDC benefit levels to proportion of black children in single-parent households, 1980. Sources: State volumes of the 1980 census; AFDC benefit amounts from U.S. House of Representatives (1983, p. 83).

Ellwood and Bane (1984) looked at changes in patterns of divorce and childbearing across states over time, comparing groups likely to collect AFDC with groups who were not. They found very small effects of AFDC on family structures.

Our conclusion is that AFDC has had far less effect on changes in family structures than has been alleged. We suspect that these changes are more likely to have resulted from changing attitudes toward welfare and heightened independence brought about by a host of forces that seemed to culminate in the late sixties. In the black community family structure changes may relate more to the changing fortunes of black men than to the availability of AFDC.

AFDC, Reduced Work, and Dependency. A wide variety of studies have dealt with the impact of welfare on work of female household heads. Danziger, Haveman, and Plotnick (1981) indicate that estimates of the effect of current programs vary widely. Generally, studies suggest that AFDC has had a modest effect in reducing work. Welfare mothers do not seem to be very sensitive to work incentives. Most recently, changes have been made in the AFDC program that essentially eliminate all work incentives: after four months benefits are reduced by at least one dollar for each dollar the woman earns over $30. Yet there apparently has been little change in the work of single mothers (see, for example, Research Triangle Institute, 1983).

Concerns about AFDC run deeper than just a fear that short-term work incentives are distorted. There is a sense that long-term dependency has developed, that people have come to rely on it to meet needs that they could and would meet on their own if they had no alternative. Except for the case studies of sociologists, we know of no definitive work on the extent to which pathological dependency exists or on the role that AFDC has had in creating such dependency.

Information on the duration of AFDC receipt does shed some light on this issue. The evidence, as analyzed by Bane and Ellwood (1983a), for example, suggests two sides of the AFDC population. Most people who receive AFDC benefits stay on the program a relatively short time: at least 50 percent leave within two years, and 85 percent leave within eight. Thus, most AFDC recipients do not seem to get trapped by it. At the same time, the minority who do stay on the program a long time accumulate and thus ultimately receive most of the benefits that are paid out. They also represent a large fraction of people on the program at any one point in time. The 15 percent of recipients who stay eight years or more on the program collect more than 50 percent of the benefits paid out. Further, certain women are at particular risk of long-term dependency: unmarried mothers, high school dropouts, and nonwhites all tend to have much longer stays than others.

Thus, the program does provide short-term relief to the majority of the people it reaches, but the bulk of its expenditures go to a group that is in fact dependent on welfare for an extended period. This dependent group is a legitimate source of concern. There is no good evidence that they are trapped by welfare per se; we only know that they rely on it for at least part of their support. Such dependence is easily explained: there are just two routes to self-sufficiency for single mothers, work and marriage, and both of these can be hampered by the presence of young children. Still, the fact that many women are in this state of dependence seems undesirable.

IMPLICATIONS FOR TRANSFER POLICY

Knowingly or unknowingly, we have been engaged in an experiment over the past ten years. This experiment has been carried out at the expense of single mothers, and its results can be judged a failure. We have cut back AFDC benefits considerably. There has been no noticeable effect on family structure or work. We can be sure, however, that its impact on the well-being of single mothers was noticed by the families. We have also conducted an experiment in allowing benefits to vary across states for years. Here, too, there is little evidence that these differences had any noticeable effect on work or family structure.

We see no reason to continue with these experiments. The complete elimination of aid to such families would surely have some effect on both work and family structure but at great cost. There is very little justification for low AFDC benefits or for the enormous variations across states. Female-headed families with children face enormous problems both at home and in the labor market. Even after AFDC is counted, half of these families live in poverty. One-quarter have incomes less than half the figure established as the poverty line. Without compelling evidence of damage caused by the programs, such stinginess seems mean-spirited and pointless.

Yet there are sources of concern. Although there is little evidence that the current system causes large changes in family structure, massive widening of welfare benefits to other groups could have more serious disruptive effects. The negative income tax experiments, a system that allowed husband and wife to split up and each collect benefits independently, seemed to increase marital splits among low-income families by as much as 40 percent, according to Groeneveld, Hannan, and Tuma (1983).[11] The results of this study, while not definitive (splits did not increase in one site, racial patterns differed across sites), do serve as a warning that major changes in incentives could have important consequences, at least for marital stability.

Also, dependency is a problem for some AFDC recipients, at least if dependency is defined as long-term welfare receipt. We find such dependency troubling, particularly since it seems to be greatest among groups that have considerable disadvantages to begin with. Our current welfare policies may have some influence on this dependence. One would hope that government could do something to help these women become self-sufficient, but government has not yet shown much capacity to improve the situation very much. We know of no serious policy that encourages family formation. Various programs (particularly Supported Work) have had some success in helping long-term recipients and poor women generally, but gains have been quite modest in comparison to the problems. It seems essential to continue to pursue ways to improve the ability of single women to support themselves, but few who have tried to design such programs have grandiose expectations.

The peculiar nature of the welfare problem for single mothers is the fact that society generally encourages mothers to stay home and care for children, but it also sees self-sufficiency as a virtue and is increasingly unwilling to accept welfare dependence among single mothers in the way that it accepts it among the disabled. Thus, a program of high benefits and no work incentives, as is offered the disabled, is unacceptable. More complex regulations about work and child care are necessary. Diverse services must be offered, and some argue for work requirements. Pure transfer policies seem undesirable.

Unemployment of Black Youth

By every conceivable measure the labor market situation for young blacks is bad and getting worse. Figure 4.5 shows the unemployment rate among black and white youth aged sixteen to nineteen from 1954 to 1980. While the rate for white youth was relatively steady throughout the period, the rate for blacks rose almost continually, and during the 1970s the gap widened considerably. If we look at the sexes separately, we see similar patterns for young men and women. The situation becomes somewhat

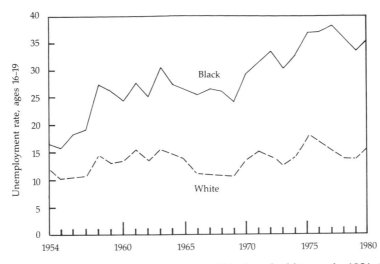

Figure 4.5. Unemployment among teenaged black and white youth, 1954–1980. Source: U.S. Bureau of Labor Statistics (1984b).

better as the youth enter their twenties, but the gap between the races has been widening for those aged twenty to twenty-four as well. The magnitude of the problem cannot be overstated: in 1980, before the recession exerted a major effect, only one out-of-school black youth in three had any job.

This widening gap is all the more perplexing because it has taken place at a time when developments were occurring that might have been expected to narrow the racial differential. Civil rights legislation passed in the 1960s reduced overt discrimination in the workplace. The educational patterns of the races have been converging: similar proportions of blacks and whites now complete high school, and college is almost as common for nonwhites as whites. Blacks are also narrowing the racial gap in the more highly paid professions.

The fear of many conservatives is that the social forces that culminated in the late 1960s, particularly the rise of social welfare programs, led to a destruction of traditional values and the expectation that hard work pays off in the long run. We are not competent to judge the entire sociological impact of public policy generally or to evaluate changing values in America's ghettos, but we can explore the logic of the assertion that the expansion of social welfare programs played a major role in the decline of work among black youth.

WELFARE POLICY AND BLACK YOUTH

To avoid the problems associated with the childbearing decisions of young women, we will concentrate on employment of black male youth and examine the plausibility of the contention that social welfare policies have caused a severe decline in work among this group. We believe that it is not plausible that such policies have removed incentives to work.

Single men are eligible for very little in the way of federally sponsored welfare benefits. A youth living alone is eligible only for food stamps. In 1982 his benefits would have been $70 per month, hardly enough to live on. For the first $85 the youth earns, benefits are not reduced at all; then for every dollar earned these benefits are reduced by only 25 cents. If he found a full-time minimum wage job, he would earn $560 per month in gross earnings and at least $450 net of taxes and expenses. It certainly seems hard to believe that the food stamp program would be a major disincentive to work.

If the youth instead lives at home (as most do), the picture hardly changes. If he lives in a poor two-parent household, his family is likely to be collecting food stamps. His presence in the home increases the monthly stamp allotment by roughly $60 per month. This allotment is diminished by the same formula as above if he works. Contrary to popular belief, the situation is no different if the youth is in a single-parent family that collects AFDC. A child eighteen years old or over who is not in school cannot now and never could be counted as a part of an AFDC unit. That means the family's benefits do not depend on whether the youth lives with the family or not, and benefits will not be reduced if he earns more.

Thus it is extremely unlikely that the direct effects of welfare programs have robbed young black men of an incentive to work. But there is a broader concern: perhaps the whole structure of welfare has created a culture of nonwork and dependence. Such a possibility is very hard to test, but several facts seem to contradict this hypothesis. Employment rates for young men living in two-parent families are not very different from those of youngsters living with one parent. In 1975 23 percent of young men living with two parents and 21 percent of those living with one parent had jobs. For whites the figures are closer to 50 percent for both family types.[12] One would generally expect to find a difference by family type simply because youth jobs are typically found through informal networks, and one would anticipate that those in fatherless homes would have less access to such networks. Moreover, although unemployment does fall among blacks as family income rises, the differential between whites and blacks is largely unchanged.

Black youth living in central cities do not seem to fare much worse than those living outside the ghettos. According to the 1980 census, 32 percent of out-of-school black youth in central cities had jobs, whereas 38 percent of those living in the suburbs were employed.[13] Similarly, only 35 percent of out-of-school nonwhites living in nonfarm rural areas were working.

While the figures above differ slightly, they are all vastly lower than the 62-percent figure for whites. If black youth unemployment were concentrated in the ghettos, it would be easier to accept the culture of poverty hypothesis. The fact that black/white youth unemployment differentials seem to persist for all geographic locations, for all family types, and for all income groups clearly suggests that the cause is something more fundamental than the growth of welfare programs, which amount to less than 1 percent of GNP.

IMPLICATIONS FOR WELFARE POLICY

Among researchers who have looked at the problem, no consensus has evolved about what is happening. The simple theories do not account for all of the widening differential between blacks and whites. There is considerable evidence of a job shortage for black youth (see, for example, Clark and Summers, 1981; Freeman and Holzer, 1985), but this explanation is only part of the story. Macroeconomic conditions did worsen over the 1970s, but not enough to explain so large a differential, and the racial gap widened somewhat even during the extraordinarily strong economy of the late 1960s. There are fewer jobs in the ghettos, but nonghetto youth seem to fare just as badly as ghetto youth (see Ellwood, forthcoming). Nearly all researchers agree that the minimum wage lowers black youth employment, but the differential continued to widen even during periods when the minimum wage did not change. Women entered the labor force in large numbers in the 1970s, but their entrance did not seem to hurt white youth. Taken together, the various explanations might account for half or more of the widening differential, but one gets the sense of a more fundamental cause. Moreover, the explanation of job shortages begs the question of why jobs are not being offered to young blacks when they are being offered to young whites.

Just as black youth joblessness defies easy explanation, it defies easy solution. Most careful experiments have shown disappointing long-term results. Public service employment increases youth employment, but when the public jobs end, employment rates seem to fall back to their previous levels. There just are not any good answers at the current time.

This is not the appropriate place to discuss what might be done to help such youth, but one thing is very clear: it would be extremely undesirable to expand welfare benefits to this group. The negative income tax experiments showed that when income was afforded to youth aged sixteen to twenty-one, there was a 40-percent reduction in the already low employment rate (see Venti and Wise, 1984). It is hard to imagine a policy with more deleterious effects on the long-run well-being of black youth.

The employment problems of black youth then cannot be blamed on current welfare policies, in large part because we have avoided offering welfare to young people. While there is surely some financial suffering as a result, the fact that extending benefits to these persons would so dramatically reduce work troubles us even more.

The Role of Government in Combating Poverty

The analysis in this chapter suggests three main conclusions. First, growth in the economy is a powerful tool for raising the incomes of the poor. A restoration of the rapid productivity growth enjoyed by the American economy after World War II through the 1960s would do more to alleviate poverty than any plausible policy initiative. This observation, while important, provides relatively little policy guidance, since reductions in poverty are only one of many reasons for favoring rapid economic growth. The problem is that we do not really know how to restore rapid growth.

Second, government transfer policies do not seem to be responsible for a large part of the problems of the disadvantaged: We found no support for the hypothesis that disability policies had seriously distorted the work patterns of older men; we found no evidence that AFDC was a major cause of family structure changes; and we saw no indication that the problems of black youth were linked to current welfare policies.

Finally, because the problems of the three groups are so different and the consequences of aid vary so greatly, continued reliance on a categorical approach to offering aid to the disadvantaged seems appropriate. For the disabled there is little concern with dependence or work incentives; this allows for liberal benefits and forces no compromises on work incentive. For single mothers the need is quite real, and there is little evidence that we have been overly generous in our benefits, but some long-term dependency has resulted. A complex policy is required to balance the needs of children, the rights of mothers to care for their children, and the desire of society (and the mothers themselves) for recipients to become self-sufficient. For youth, the reduced work that would apparently accompany an extension of benefits to that group makes us extremely wary of expansion of welfare in that direction.

The question naturally arises whether our current categories are the appropriate ones. We suspect that the broad outlines of current policy are in fact reasonable. Current policy focuses on helping those groups who are thought least able to help themselves. As we have seen, the lion's share of antipoverty money goes to the disabled and to one-parent families. Other assistance goes to those who have demonstrated their willingness to work but who have suffered injury or involuntary unemployment. All of this is backstopped by food stamps, which is essentially a negative income tax with a very low guarantee and tax rate.

We believe that it can be defended on both economic efficiency and philosophical grounds. Certainly for the three groups we looked at, the broad outlines of current policy seemed quite successful in balancing our desire to help with our desire to avoid encouraging adverse behavior. The finding that current policy cannot be blamed for creating much poverty does not suggest that incentive effects are always unimportant. The present system may have had few adverse consequences because it was well targeted. We have seen that for youth at least an expansion of benefits could be quite destructive.

The categorical nature of current welfare policy works to reduce potential adverse incentive effects. We are most generous where incentive effects are least worrisome—in the case of the disabled. We are not generous at all in cases, such as that of young people, where incentive effects are most troubling. While current welfare programs do not have large incentive effects, they do funnel a significant amount of money to some poor people. In this limited sense of redistributing income to those in need without creating undue economic distortions, current policy is economically efficient.

More fundamentally, general economic principles suggest the desirability of a complex welfare system with different rules for different groups and partial reliance on in-kind benefits. The basic problem of welfare policy is to transfer income to those truly in need without sizable adverse incentive effects and without diverting significant resources to those who are not truly in need. Seen in this light, prominent features of our current welfare system seem easily explainable. Efficiency in redistribution can be increased if payments are based on available indicators of true earning power.

Particularly desirable are indicators that are not easily altered, such as disability and perhaps family status. Moreover, the use of any type of assistance that will help the truly poor but be relatively unattractive to the nonpoor will raise the amount that can be redistributed with a minimum of distortion. Thus one can justify substantial reliance on some types of in-kind programs. People not in need are less likely to try to appear poor in order to qualify for public housing than they are to qualify for cash assistance. Some administrative burdens on welfare recipients might also be defended, in that such documentation can increase the government's ability to separate those in serious need and thereby facilitate redistribution.

Current policy may also be defended on philosophical grounds. It reflects the value that society places on self-reliance: we expect those who can to help themselves. Benefits are provided only to those able to provide some evidence of their inability to support themselves. Most Americans regard the reasons for indigency as sharply influencing their willingness to offer aid. The disabled, single parents and those injured or laid off from work can offer some evidence that their financial straits are not caused by an unwillingness to work.

The observation that the broad contours of current policy seem appropriate is not meant to imply that the exact policies in effect today are optimal. While we see reason for concern about the effects of reducing eligibility restrictions, we believe that raising benefit levels under current programs would be desirable. Restoring real AFDC benefits to the levels of a decade ago and reducing or eliminating regional disparities would do a great deal for people in need without much disincentive effect on work. Certainly working poor families deserve consideration for aid beyond food stamps.

We believe that the primary notion of categorical and differential treatment has much to recommend it, in spite of the large apparent income inequities it can create. In any case, the current outlines seem unlikely to change much in the near future. We do think that it is worth remembering that some of the basis for a categorical approach is that groups differ both in current need and in prospect of need. Ultimately the hope for government policy ought to be that it can do more than just provide targeted aid. It should help people become self-supporting. Unfortunately, we have tried massive short-term jobs programs and discovered once again that the problem is complex. Although government intervention does not appear to have exacerbated the problem, neither has it contributed much to a long-term solution. Yet the occasional successes (such as Supported Work) offer the hope that programs that are carefully tested and implemented may offer movement toward self-support. It would be tragic if narrow budgetary concerns or discouragement about the poverty problem eliminated our experiments with promoting self-sufficiency.

5   Health Care for the Poor:
The Past Twenty Years

Paul Starr

A FEW FUNDAMENTAL FACTS stand out about the past two decades' national experience in providing health care for the poor: First, we have vastly enlarged our commitment of public expenditures; second, the health of the poor, as of Americans generally, has significantly improved; and third, despite increased expenditure, we have failed to provide public or private health coverage for between one-tenth and one-sixth of all Americans, including roughly one-quarter of those below the poverty line.

Over the same period the share of antipoverty expenditures going for medical care has increased to about 40 percent (see chapter 2), and government programs—notably Medicaid—have displayed a strong institutional bias: hospitals and nursing homes have received far more money than have ambulatory and community health services. The medicalization of the antipoverty budget and the institutional bias of welfare medical care raise difficult questions about the allocation of scarce financial and political resources. Antipoverty programs—indeed, the entire array of Social Security and means-tested welfare programs—appear to be subject to an historic expenditure drift toward medical care (and, one might add, benefits for the aged) that potentially jeopardizes their support and success in producing improvements in well-being.

In the mid-1970s, when Karen Davis reviewed health programs as part of a ten-year review of antipoverty efforts sponsored by the Institute for Research on Poverty, the great question was whether the previous decade's programmatic innovations had done any measurable good. She thought they had (Davis, 1977). Most of those programs still exist today, as do the questions about their effects, but the intervening years have thrown up new issues and the political and economic environment now is radically different. Instead of asking, "Has more health care helped?" researchers ask, "Has less hurt?" and "Would still less hurt more?" Moreover, a diminished political willingness to spend has been accompanied by an increased political willingness to experiment with structural change in both health programs and the health care industry. How that altered—and as yet still unsettled—system affects the poor needs assessing.

This new setting in the mid-eighties requires us to look at somewhat different questions from those of the mid-seventies. Instead of reviewing efforts in health care program by program—as Davis (1977) did in her ten-year appraisal, which seems to me not to be in need of fundamental revision—I want to consider, first, the basic forces that have shaped the growth and limits of health care for the poor; and second, the implications for the poor of emerging structural changes in public programs and the private health care industry. In the process I will review the evidence about the effects of public policy on health and access to health care.

The Growth and Limits of Health Care for the Poor

SOME ENCUMBRANCES OF HISTORY

In all Western societies three principal frameworks have developed for state intervention in health care: public health, social insurance, and public assistance. The relative importance of each varies from one country to another. In the United States public health agencies were blocked from providing direct medical services or assuming a role in their financing or coordination (Starr, 1982). And when social insurance finally won acceptance in the New Deal, it was limited to income protection in unemployment and old age. Health care for the poor, insofar as it became a governmental function, remained within the third framework—public assistance.

Encumbrance 1: the welfare piggyback. The antipoverty programs of the sixties were characterized by continuities as well as breaks with earlier thought and practice. For Medicaid, the largest health program for the poor, the continuity is deep and the root of much trouble.

Only through a gradual process did the federal government in the twentieth century become involved in supporting local welfare medicine. Before the 1930s health care for the poor was entirely a local responsibility. To a great extent it was also a private responsibility—a function of voluntary hospitals, dispensaries, and philanthropy—but some local governments maintained public hospitals and contributed to private ones. During the Depression two related changes took place: the federal government became involved in relief efforts (ostensibly on a temporary basis because of the national emergency), and local public welfare agencies began to recognize medical care as an "essential relief need" and to pay for needed services. Voluntary hospitals, therefore, began to bill welfare agencies for care previously rendered free, so that the locality could shift part of the cost to the federal government. A function that had been mostly private and entirely local became increasingly public and partly federal—at first as an expedient and then on a more permanent basis (Stevens and Stevens, 1974; Starr, 1982). The Social Security Act of 1935, while omitting health insurance, provided some matching support to the states for maternal and infant care, rehabilitation of handicapped children, and aid for dependent children. In 1950 Congress extended the practice, supporting local governments' purchases of medical care for those on cash assistance. A decade later the Kerr-Mills Act increased the level of federal support and expanded eligibility for federally subsidized medical care to the medically needy aged who did not qualify for welfare.

In 1965, while Medicare shifted health care for the aged into the framework of social insurance, Medicaid kept health care for the poor within the framework of public assistance. The former brought universality; the latter, means-testing and the limitation of benefits to those categories of the poor thought to be helpless and deserving: the blind and disabled, the aged (insofar as Medicare did not protect them), and single mothers with dependent children. The categorical limitations generally bar from Medicaid most two-parent families and single adults unless they are aged or disabled. Moreover, the criteria for means-testing are set by the states, and many states set eligibility cutoffs well below the poverty line. As a result many of the poor—roughly 60 percent today—have been ineligible for Medicaid (Davis and Rowland, 1983).

The histories of Medicare and Medicaid have been largely governed by this original choice—I am tempted to call it the original sin of American health policy—to piggyback Medicare on Social Security and Medicaid on the welfare system. Medicare enjoys the political protection created by a span of eligibility that includes the middle class; Medicaid suffers from the political vulnerability created by identification with welfare and the poor. The hospital benefits of Medicare are additionally protected by financing that comes from an earmarked payroll tax, whereas Medicaid must compete for general revenues—at not only the federal but also the state level. That Medicaid is a federal-state program leads also to its greater regional variations and inequities. We have no reason to be surprised about Medicaid's sundry omissions, inequities, and vulnerabilities to cutbacks: they were all there from the beginning.

Encumbrance 2: fiscal asymmetry. In recent years the total cost to the federal government of the tax exemption of employer contributions to health insurance has actually exceeded the federal contribution to Medicaid. The tax subsidy is highly regressive as a result of three factors: the higher one's income, (1) the more likely one receives health insurance via employment, (2) the more generous those benefits, and (3) the greater the value of any tax exemption. But while the politics of the budgetary process at both the state and national levels continually reminds the public of the cost of Medicaid, the tax subsidy is generally free from public understanding, much less scrutiny. Appropriations for Medicaid must be made every year; the tax subsidy grows without any action to increase it. Medicaid and Medicare are considered "uncontrollables" in the budget because they are entitlement programs, but the tax subsidy is actually far less controllable, an entitlement of the employed. Moreover, Medicaid has been cut back, but the Reagan administration's laudable 1983 proposal to cap the tax exemption of employers' contributions to health insurance has met a vast array of interest group opposition.

Encumbrance 3: adverse selective perception. Private insurance plans carry the risk of adverse selection; public programs have another problem. Parts of social programs or certain groups of beneficiaries stand for the whole and influence the perception of the entire undertaking. Medicaid benefits are perceived as flowing to black AFDC families. In fact, two-thirds of Medicaid expenditures go to the aged and disabled (much of it for nursing homes), and the majority of AFDC families are white, but these beneficiaries do not figure prominently in popular awareness. The Veterans Administration, on the other hand, is perceived as treating veterans' war injuries. In fact, three-fourths of admissions to VA hospitals are for nonservice-connected conditions, but it is the war-related activity that imparts legitimacy to the VA.

Encumbrance 4: the legacy of political accommodation. In suggesting that fiscal illusions and political misperceptions adversely affect health programs for the poor and work to the advantage of employee health plans, I do not mean to minimize the concern that arises from objective causes: the rise in real expenditures. But the growth in expenditures for Medicaid and Medicare is also partly a burden of politics past: the aftermath of legislative and executive accommodation to the demands of the health care industry. The years of struggle with the AMA over national health insurance and Medicare had left their advocates wary of further antagonizing the profession. It was hard enough to win any legislation; they did not have the strength to fight about reimbursement provisions. So, in what now seems an extraordinary concession, the Medicare legislation stated explicitly: "nothing in this title shall be construed to authorize any federal officer . . . to exercise any supervision or control over the . . . compensation of any institution . . . or person providing health services" (Public Law No. 89–97, Sec. 102A). Medicare would have no fee schedules; the government would pay according to what was usual, customary, and reasonable in a particular community. Doctors would not be obligated to take what Medicare paid; they could charge more. (Medicaid was different, of course: states could and did restrict physicians' fees, and the beneficiaries' access to physicians was restricted accordingly.) Both Medicare and Medicaid agreed to pay hospitals on the basis of their costs. Why? Because, says Wilbur Cohen simply, that is the way the American Hospital Association wanted it (W. J. Cohen, 1984). Actually, the programs displayed no commitment to the control of hospital costs in part because the designers of the legislation thought more money ought to be spent on hospitals. They were also anxious to secure cooperation from hospitals and doctors (Starr, 1982). But appeasement in health policy has its costs in battles that have to be fought later—and we have been living through them since.

CUTTING AND GROWING, GROWING AND CUTTING

Concern about the poor in the sixties affected national health policy in multiple ways. After the Second World War federal programs had principally sought to expand the nation's medical resources. The Hill-Burton program subsidized hospital construction, and the National Institutes of Health supported medical research centers. Although Hill-Burton stipulated that hospitals receiving aid provide the poor a reasonable amount of free care, the requirement was not defined or enforced for two decades. In the 1960s and 1970s the federal government shifted toward more directly redistributive objectives not only in the new programs it established but also in the old ones it redirected. Aid to medical schools was recast to encourage them to turn out more doctors to alleviate reported shortages and, in later measures, to promote training in primary care. To provide medical professionals to underserved areas, Congress in 1970 created the National Health Service Corps. Originally a tiny program, the NHSC was enlarged in the mid-seventies when scholarship funds for medical students began to be distributed in return for commitments of service in the corps.

As a result of litigation by legal services attorneys, the free care requirements of Hill-Burton were explicitly defined. These redirections of earlier
federal programs illustrate the general tendency to ask of all government
policy, "What does it do for the poor?" (Lampman, 1974).

The major new health care programs of the War on Poverty and Great
Society may be divided roughly into two types: (1) those that provided
services directly to the poor (and were intended to strengthen communities
and to provide job and leadership opportunities as well as to improve
health), and (2) those that provided financing for health care (and were
intended to bring the aged and the poor into the mainstream of American
medicine). The former emphasized public and community organization;
the latter, public payment for private service. From an ideological standpoint, the service programs such as the community health centers were the
key initiatives. From a budgetary standpoint, the core efforts were the
programs that financed private services. Medicaid and Medicare coincided
with the War on Poverty, but their design does not reflect the distinctive
participatory ideals of the period.

In 1967 the Department of Health, Education, and Welfare drew up
plans for 1,000 community health centers to serve 25 million enrollees by
1973. The program never reached those dimensions in part because the
restrictions on Medicaid eligibility and the restricted scope of services financed by both Medicaid and Medicare meant that health centers could
recover only a small portion of their costs from those programs. For a
time, Congress also restricted the centers from enrolling large numbers of
paying patients. Hence the centers needed large direct subsidies, which
were not forthcoming. By 1977 there were only 125 health centers, serving
1.5 million people. Under the Carter administration, however, the centers
did grow; their number reached 800, and their enrollment more than 4
million (Davis and Schoen, 1978; Starr, 1982; Geiger, 1984). The National
Health Service Corps helped to supply them with medical staff (Mullan,
1984). In 1981 Congress refused to collapse their funding into a block
grant. But their budgetary position, like that of all discretionary domestic
programs, has been tenuous because of the growth of the entitlement
programs and the overwhelming pressures of the federal deficit.

The community health centers have enjoyed a decidedly positive record.
A series of evaluations find a significant impact on the health of their
communities (Davis and Schoen, 1978); moreover, Medicaid beneficiaries
enrolled in health centers have substantially lower rates of hospitalization
and lower overall costs than beneficiaries who receive care elsewhere (Klein,
Roghmann, and Woodward, 1973; Zwick, 1974). Better health at lower

cost—and yet the health centers have never received the acclaim or policy support given to health maintenance organizations (HMOs), the other great success in health care innovation. The answer is clearly ideological. If health centers exemplify the ideological distinctiveness of the War on Poverty, the failure to capitalize on their achievements illustrates the ideological repudiation of the War on Poverty.

Although handicapped from its inception, Medicaid did represent an advance over earlier federal grants-in-aid to the states for health care for the poor. It provided a generous federal match for state spending (from a minimum of 50 percent of total expenditures to a maximum of 77 percent, the proportion of federal support varying inversely with state per capita income). Medicaid also introduced somewhat more specific requirements for states, if they chose to participate—and nearly all did within a few years. Congress created a zone of necessity and a zone of flexibility for the states in each of three separate areas: the determination of eligibility, scope of benefits, and payment to providers.

The determination of eligibility. In the zone of necessity Congress put the "categorically eligible": states had to include recipients of AFDC and the blind, disabled, and aged on Supplemental Security Income. In the zone of flexibility it put the "optionally categorically eligible," principally the medically needy (those who meet the categorical limitations but who have incomes no more than one-third above the cutoffs for cash assistance or who have "spent down" their assets in the face of overwhelming medical bills). If the states covered the latter, they received federal matching funds. They could cover still other groups entirely at their own expense.

Benefits. Medicaid required the states to cover inpatient hospital care, physicians' services, laboratory tests, and other items. However, it did not specify the amount of services to be covered, and it classified thirty-two other services as optional. Originally, whatever coverage was provided to one group of eligibles had to be provided to another. Once determined to be eligible, a recipient had the right of free choice among providers—a freedom for both recipients and providers that represented an important constraint upon the states (Rowland and Gaus, 1983).

Payment to providers. Medicaid specified that hospitals be reimbursed on the basis of their costs, but allowed states discretion in the payment of physicians, except that payments could not be so low as to deny recipients their rights under the program.

Originally, Medicaid called on states to adopt plans for providing comprehensive medical care to beneficiaries by 1975. But almost immediately, the more ambitious state Medicaid programs, such as those in New York and California, experienced exploding costs and were cut back. Amendments passed by Congress in 1967, 1969, and 1972 gave the states more flexibility to make cutbacks to control costs and withdrew the requirement for comprehensive care. Nonetheless, Medicaid expenditures grew rapidly, from $2.5 billion in 1967 to $9 billion in 1973 and about $30 billion in 1982.

Although the growth in Medicaid expenditures continued unabated, its sources changed. In the program's first years, while welfare rolls were expanding, increases in expenditures came mainly from the rising number of beneficiaries, which hit a peak in 1976 of about 23.5 million people. After 1973 some of the increase came from expanded benefits, especially a rise in use of intermediate care facilities (aimed at reducing even more expensive skilled nursing care costs). By the mid-seventies, however, most of the expenditure growth was coming from higher unit prices, particularly in hospitals and nursing homes. Between 1974 and 1979, a period when Medicaid expenditures doubled to $20.5 billion, 48.6 percent of the jump came from increased expenditures on nursing homes, 29.5 percent from hospitals, and only 4.7 percent from physicians' services. At the end of that period, the number of eligibles had actually fallen by two million from the peak three years earlier (Rowland and Gaus, 1983). Much of the reduction came in AFDC and fell upon children. In Medicaid, the expenditure drift toward hospitals and nursing homes has effectively taken money away from primary and preventive health care, the kind of services provided by community health centers and received by poor female-headed households.

The overall rise in Medicaid expenditures reflects the general trend in medical care. Medicaid's cost increases are no worse than the increases for private health spending (Bovbjerg and Holahan, 1982). However, after 1975, with all medical costs rising rapidly, Medicaid's burgeoning demands outstripped increases in state revenues because of slower economic growth, state revenue restrictions, and the emerging tax revolt and "welfare backlash."

States have responded by cutting back Medicaid in different ways. Some tend to restrict eligibility and the scope of service coverage but are generous in paying providers for the services covered, whereas others are generous in coverage but restrictive in payment (Bovbjerg and Holahan, 1982). Even states with a history of broad eligibility, however, have come under pressure to restrict it in the past decade. They have done so by (1) reducing or eliminating eligibility for optional groups, such as unemployed parents or the medical needy; or (2) reducing the numbers "categorically eligible" under AFDC by not raising income cutoffs during a period of inflation, a kind of welfare "bracket creep" (Moloney, 1982). Some states have introduced arbitrary limits on the lengths of hospital stays or number of annual physicians' visits. Although the federal requirement for cost-based reimbursement to hospitals and nursing homes limited the retrenchment in institutional payment, many states kept physician payment at extremely low levels—a choice that intensified the institutional bias of the program since it led many physicians not to participate in Medicaid and many beneficiaries to use hospital emergency rooms and outpatient departments. These measures thus undercut the original aim of Medicaid to bring the poor into the mainstream of medical care.

Surprisingly, despite the repeated cutbacks especially during recessions, "almost no state has significantly retreated from the scope of its original Medicaid program" (Bovbjerg and Holahan, 1982, p. 20). Cutbacks are partly restrained because a large share of expenditures goes to the elderly and the disabled, many of them in institutions. Cutbacks in Medicaid also shift some costs to local and state governments, denying them federal matching money and thereby sometimes aggravating their fiscal problems. The original structure of the program—the mixture of federal requirements, options, and matching funds—succeeded in setting up an equilibrating system that tends to restrict program expansion and retrenchment beyond certain limits.

Immediately upon coming into office, the Reagan administration moved to change some fundamental features of this system, particularly the open-ended nature of federal liabilities, by capping federal support for Medicaid and giving the states greater operational flexibility. Congress rejected the cap, but in the 1981 Omnibus Budget Reconciliation Act (OBRA) it took a number of steps to reduce costs, including a series of small staggered reductions in the share of federal support. OBRA cut cash public assistance for the working poor, which disqualified about half a million people from Medicaid (by 1985 other changes brought the total disqualified to a million). Congress also gave the states more flexibility in determining eligibility and limiting the scope of coverage for different categories of recipients.

According to Urban Institute studies, the annual rate of increase in Medicaid spending dropped from 17.3 percent in 1979–1981 to about 6.4 percent in 1981–1982 (Bovbjerg and Holahan, 1982; J. Cohen, 1984; Holahan, 1984). Because these cutbacks occurred while the poverty rate was rising, Medicaid now covers a smaller proportion of the poor. The ratio of Medicaid recipients to the population below the poverty line—which is *not* the percentage of the poor on Medicaid, since some recipients are above the poverty line, but it is nonetheless a useful indicator—dropped from .59 in 1970 to .53 in 1979 and to .45 in 1982 (Bovbjerg and Holahan, 1982; Cohen and Holahan, 1984).

These data suggest that the population of the uninsured poor has grown significantly in recent years, particularly since there was no offsetting expansion of private insurance. However, we lack a data series for the past two decades to delineate secular and cyclical trends in rates of "uninsurance." Furthermore, we cannot simply add up private insurance policies, Medicare, and Medicaid enrollments, since many people are covered by more than one insurance policy, more than one public program, or combinations of both. Also, various household surveys that ask questions about health insurance probably suffer from significant underreporting: many people (new workers, workers whose insurance contributions are automatically deducted, dependents of workers, Medicaid "categorical" eligibles) do not know what their coverage is.

But we do have some estimates of the overall numbers and composition of the uninsured population. Drawing on both the Survey of Income and Education and administrative sources, one study found that about 5 to 8 percent of Americans were uninsured as of 1976 (U.S. Congressional Budget Office, 1979). From the 1977 National Medical Care Expenditure Survey (NMCES) comes an estimate that at any one time twenty-five million were uninsured, but as many as thirty-four million were uninsured at some point during the year. Of poor families with incomes below 125 percent of the poverty line, 27 percent were uninsured. Low-income people were twice as likely to be uninsured as middle-income and three times as likely as those in upper-income groups. Counting only people under sixty-five, blacks in the South have a 30-percent rate of uninsurance; whites, 20 percent (Davis and Rowland, 1983).

A 1982 Harris survey found that 25 percent of those below the poverty line, 29 percent of the unemployed, and 9 percent of all persons were without coverage. Among families without insurance, two-fifths were poor and 24 percent of individuals reported themselves in poor or fair health (compared to 18 percent overall) (Louis Harris and Associates, 1982).

Since 1979 the March supplement of the Current Population Survey has included a question about health insurance. According to Katherine Swartz (1984) of the Urban Institute, the CPS data indicate that the number of people under age sixty-five who report themselves as uninsured rose in 1982 to 32.7 million (16 percent of the population), up from 28.7 million in 1979—a 15-percent increase. (The percentage increase is more meaningful than the percentage of the population reported to be uninsured because of likely underreporting of coverage.) Swartz finds that income best predicts insurance status. In 1982 11.6 million people without insurance had incomes below the poverty level, and another 9.6 million had incomes between 100 and 200 percent of poverty—together accounting for almost two-thirds of the uninsured (Swartz, 1984).

Without regular monitoring, studies of "uninsurance" often appear long after the data are collected. In one case the results may have seriously misled policy makers. The 1981–82 recession saw legislative movement toward expanding health insurance opportunities for the unemployed, but the effort was dealt a serious blow by the release of a study, based on the 1977 NMCES data, showing that most of the unemployed did not lose their coverage. However, according to Swartz, since the nation's economy was recovering in 1977, those unemployed tended to be secondary workers covered by their spouses' insurance, but in 1981–82 many primary earners lost their health insurance when they lost their jobs (Swartz, 1984). The 1981–82 recession disproportionately hit industries with high levels of health insurance; many who lost jobs still remain unemployed, while others now work in service businesses where health coverage is less common and less generous. These secular changes, like the retrenchment in Medicaid, may, therefore, be raising the number of the uninsured.

Assessing the Impact

CHANGES IN ACCESS

In the mid-1970s much talk and some evidence suggested that (1) access of the poor and nonpoor to health care had been substantially equalized; and (2) increased health care expenditures were having no impact on health. Together, these conclusions took much of the urgency out of any reforms other than cost containment. Important findings since then, however, show that substantial inequities of access remain, and medical care expenditures probably do positively affect health. But both questions remain controversial.

Discussions of changing patterns of access always begin with the simple point that before 1965 the poor saw physicians less frequently than the nonpoor, but in years after Medicare and Medicaid the poor saw physicians more often (U.S. Department of Health and Human Services, Public Health Service, 1983). The rate of hospitalization of the poor—previously about the same as that of the nonpoor—grew to be significantly higher than that of the nonpoor by 1970. Other indicators tell a similar story (Davis and

Schoen, 1978). That this represents an important change everyone agrees, but most analysts also agree that it does not establish equality of access since illness and disability are more prevalent among the poor. Using data from the National Health Interview Survey (NHIS) of 1969, Davis and Reynolds (1976) showed that, once adjusted for differences in health status, rates of physician visits were, in fact, lower among the poor. However, a study by Aday, Andersen, and Fleming (1980), drawing on a 1976 survey carried out by the Center for Health Administration Studies (CHAS) at the University of Chicago, also adjusted for variations in need and found differences in use of medical services by the poor and nonpoor to be small. This finding led some to declare that problems of unequal access to health care had been fundamentally resolved. But the conclusions of the CHAS study have been subject to sustained attack from two principal directions: (1) that other sources of data and different methods tell the opposite story; and (2) that other kinds of comparisons, particularly between the insured and uninsured populations, demonstrate the persistence of dramatic inequalities.

Different data, different story. In response to Aday et al. (1980), Kleinman and his colleagues at the National Center for Health Statistics, using data from the center's National Health Interview Survey conducted between 1976 and 1978, found that sharp disparities between poor and nonpoor remained (Kleinman, Gold, and Makuc, 1981). There were several key differences between the CHAS and NHIS data. The CHAS low-income definition had no adjustment for family size and included one-third of the population; the NHIS criteria followed the official poverty level and included only one-sixth of the population. CHAS asked respondents to recall physician visits over the previous year; NHIS, over the previous two weeks. CHAS excluded telephone consultations; NHIS included them. Most significantly, the studies employed different strategies for adjusting for differences in need. Aday et al. created a use-disability ratio—a ratio of health care utilization to disability days (days unable to perform one's normal work or responsibilities, an indicator that does not vary much by income). Kleinman et al. used two methods of adjustment: First, they stratified the population into groups according to their self-assessed health; and second, they computed a ratio of physician visits to bed-disability days rather than disability days (on the grounds that the former better represent conditions requiring medical attention). In the Kleinman study the poor show significantly lower levels of physician use at comparable levels of health and disability, and the age-adjusted number of physician visits per hundred bed-disability days proved to be 80 percent higher among high-income whites than among whites below the poverty level. Other studies corroborate these findings (Davis, Gold, and Makuc, 1981).

Comparing the insured and uninsured. The uninsured have decidedly lower rates of use of health care than the insured. Using the 1977 NMCES data and defining as uninsured only those always uninsured for the year, Davis and Rowland (1983) found that the insured made 54 percent more visits to physicians and received 90 percent more hospital care than the uninsured. In the South insured whites made two-and-a-half times as many physician visits a year as uninsured blacks, 3.7 visits compared to 1.5 (while insured blacks saw physicians an average of 2.8 times a year). These differentials could not entirely be explained as overutilization or self-selection by the insured, or as the result of better health among the uninsured. According to self-assessments, the uninsured were in worse health than the insured. Among those who rated their health as poor, the insured saw a physician 70 percent more often than the uninsured.

Different data, a still more complex story. The 1982 Harris survey (Louis Harris and Associates, 1982) gives a somewhat more positive picture but still shows inequities. Seven percent of all families, 11 percent of families below the poverty line, and 13 percent of families without insurance reported that they did not receive all the medical care they felt they needed in the previous year. Four percent of the poor families said a member had been refused care because of inadequate insurance or inability to pay. Harris estimated that 7.8 million adults experienced reductions in health insurance coverage the previous year (1.6 million losing coverage entirely), 2.2 million of those whose coverage was lost or reduced put off getting some medical care, and 850,000 were unable to obtain medical care as a result of the changes in coverage. But nearly all Americans reported they had a usual source of medical care.

How to balance these findings? If we take as an indicator of official judgment the 1983 report on access to health care of the President's Commission for the Study of Ethical Problems in Medicine and Biomedical and Behavioral Research, we get a clear reading of the evidence as showing serious inequities that need to be corrected (U.S. President's Commission, 1983). But if we take the silence that greeted the commission's report as an indication of public concern, we get the clear impression that Americans don't much care, either.

HEALTH EFFECTS

Disenchantment with medical care in the mid-seventies had numerous sources; it reflected more general doubts that rational action of any kind, particularly by government, could make any positive difference. But there was also a historical influence that no one at the time could appreciate. Public health data available in the early seventies seemed to show no significant increase in life expectancy or reduction in mortality rates since the mid-1950s, despite the great increase in national spending for health care. A spate of new econometric studies purported to show no association between medical expenditures and health (Benham and Benham, 1975; Fuchs, 1979).

The evidence looks different today, partly because the facts are different. Although life expectancy failed to increase in the decade before 1965, it began to improve around 1968—and by 1980 average life expectancy at birth grew by four years. Age-adjusted mortality rates fell by 20 percent (U.S. Department of Health and Human Services, Public Health Service, 1983). These improvements, while conceivably unrelated to national health expenditures, do change the tenor of questions being asked about medical care. In the early seventies, reflecting on the apparent inability to improve health, it was natural to wonder, What explains this failure? If nothing was working, medical care was part of that nothing. Now the question is a happier one, What explains our success?

No one as yet has, to my knowledge, successfully decomposed the contribution to recent improvements in health from reductions in smoking, the control of environmental pollutants, safety measures for automobile driving, consumer products, and the workplace, improvements in nutrition from public programs and greater cultural awareness of dietary effects on health, more physical exercise and other changes in "lifestyle," as well as medical care. The one recent econometric study of the health impact of medical expenditures found a significant marginal effect (Hadley, 1982). A number of other facts argue for the same conclusion. First, the diagnostic categories and populations in which mortality rates have fallen are categories in which medical care has demonstrable effects and populations on whom considerable resources have been invested. Dramatic reductions in mortality have been recorded in ten of the fifteen major causes of death in the United States, notably in diseases in which therapeutic remedies are effective (Davis and Schoen, 1978).

Infant mortality rates are a particularly instructive case: they were virtually unchanged in the decade before 1965 but were reduced by half between 1968 and 1980. Because we do not have good data on mortality rates by income, the experience of the poor is not precisely known. But if we take blacks' experience as a proxy, we see parallel declines in infant mortality rates, although the racial differences remain (U.S. Department of Health and Human Services, 1983). The reduction in infant mortality comes not from increases in birthweights (a strong predictor of complications) but rather from the improved survival of infants born at low birthweight. If improvements in nutrition or other social and economic factors were the chief cause of lower infant mortality, they would have done so by improving birthweights. But average birthweights have scarcely changed; the cause for greater survival is medical intervention—specifically, such innovations as the improved treatment of respiratory distress syndrome in premature infants, the development of neonatal intensive care units, and the surgical repair of birth defects. In this area public spending for both medical research and medical care has unquestionably paid off.

This is not to say that nutrition programs have been ineffective. On the contrary, some evidence suggests that the Special Supplemental Food Program for Women, Infants and Children (WIC) has had a positive impact on infant survival (Kotelchuck et al., 1984). This finding is contested (Rush, 1984), and in general the evidence on the health effects of nutrition programs, such as food stamps, is ambiguous (see Graham, 1985). But even if one accepts the positive findings for WIC—as Congress has (Rauch, 1984)—the reductions in infant mortality still seem to be explained more by medical than by nutritional advances (Fuchs, 1983). WIC itself provides entry into the health care system as well as food supplements. However, further progress in reducing infant mortality probably will require improvements in birthweights (McCormick, 1985), and recent slowdowns in the rate of progress in reducing infant deaths may well be due to cutbacks in maternal and child health programs (Mundinger, 1985).

Other evidence supports a more generous view of the effectiveness of medical care. Studies of the impact of programs such as health centers, whose effects are concentrated in specific communities, have borne out the proposition that medical care makes a difference. In her ten-year appraisal Davis (1977) cited this evidence as one of the grounds for concluding that medical care is effective; another such study has since appeared (Goldman and Grossman, 1982). Furthermore, Hadley's study (1982) showing a significant marginal contribution to health from medical expenditures supports the view of Davis and Schoen (1978), who disputed the earlier econometric findings on methodological grounds. The irony is that the changing evidence has so little effect on public policy. In the 1960s and 1970s, while we were expanding health coverage, the evidence suggested that it was making no difference; now that we have evidence it does, we are cutting back. Of course, not all medical care does improve health and well-being, and there are good theoretical and empirical reasons to believe that much of the growth in health care spending has had no health benefit.

From a theoretical standpoint, it is clear that the underlying incentives of health care finance have inflated expenditures; and on an empirical basis— for example, comparisons among different regions of the country and between standard insurance plans and HMOs—it seems likely that the health care system could withstand expenditure reductions of perhaps 20 percent without harm to Americans' health or welfare.[1] But bringing about such changes poses an immense political challenge.

The Changing Environment of Poor People's Health Care

STRUCTURAL REFORM IN PUBLIC PROGRAMS

While barring any major extension of health coverage to the uninsured, the fiscal crisis of the past decade has opened up Medicare and Medicaid to organizational reform. And this development is likely to bring long-lasting changes in health care for the poor.

The principles of payment to doctors and hospitals originally adopted for Medicare and Medicaid were an extraordinary fetter on prudent management of the public purse. Both programs reimbursed hospitals according to their costs, paid doctors by fee-for-service, and guaranteed beneficiaries the right to choose freely among providers of health care. In other words, if a recipient—or more likely, the recipient's doctor—chose an inefficient hospital whose costs for an operation were twice those of another institution nearby, so much the worse for the Medicare trust fund or the state. They had no means to encourage use of the least-cost suppliers. Since Medicare approved fees according to what was "usual, customary, and reasonable" in a community, the program paid more for doctors who charged higher fees, thereby encouraging doctors to do so and providing greater subsidies to beneficiaries who visited more expensive physicians. Retrospective cost-based reimbursement to hospitals and "usual, customary, and reasonable" payment to doctors directed more funds to areas higher in hospital costs and physician charges. In fact, Medicare Part B (coverage of physicians' services) actually redistributed money from poorer to wealthier areas, since the cost of premiums was uniform nationally while the value of benefits varied with the level of physician fees (Davis and Shoen, 1978).

The recoil from the politics of accommodation began in the 1970s with the development of regulatory programs to oversee capital investment by hospitals and to review medical utilization under public financing programs. The change was also evident in the adoption of the HMO Act in 1973 and actions by the Federal Trade Commission to stimulate competition in the health care industry. Since they failed to address the basic financing mechanisms under both public and private insurance, the new apparatus of planning and regulation and the relatively marginal efforts to promote competition had little effect. Only in the past few years has reform hit the main avenues of health care finance.

The biggest change has come in the financing of hospitals. In 1981 OBRA released the states from cost-based reimbursement to hospitals under Medicaid. In 1983, in a largely undebated provision of the Social Security salvage legislation, Congress threw out cost-based reimbursement from Medicare and introduced prospective payment to hospitals by diagnosis-related groups (DRGs)—a fee-per-case system as opposed to fee-for-service, aimed at giving hospitals an incentive to reduce costs per admission. The new system gradually phases in a national rate, thereby ending higher subsidies to high-cost regions. The DRGs are widely perceived as the most radical step in reforming Medicare since its passage.

The initial evidence about the impact of prospective payment on costs is favorable, although possibly fortuitous and transitory. The average length of hospital stays for Medicare has fallen. Hospital admission rates have dropped slightly, too—a paradoxical result, since the new payment system actually offers an incentive for overadmitting. However, prospective payment has arrived at a time when overall hospital utilization is declining significantly for the entire population. In fact, admissions rates have fallen faster for people under sixty-five, and it is unclear what has caused the general decline. If Medicare's new payment system has had a positive effect, so may other changes: increased cost-sharing in employee benefit plans; the growth of ambulatory surgery, home health care, HMOs and other alternatives aimed at reducing hospital utilization; and perhaps epidemiological trends and simultaneous but unrelated changes in physician practice patterns. Some of the decline may be due to loss of insurance coverage.

The new payment method has some features that suggest long-run dangers. It encourages "revenue maximization" strategies by hospitals, including the manipulation of diagnostic coding—so-called DRG creep—to put patients into high-yield categories. It encourages hospitals to view their activities as a series of product lines with varying rates of return, depending on the relative DRG prices, and leads their managers to adopt marketing strategies to keep and attract doctors who bring in the high-paying cases. A recent study suggests that the DRGs for surgical cases are by far the most profitable (Omenn and Conrad, 1984). Thus the new system continues the long-standing bias in favor of invasive, hospital-oriented therapeutic approaches. The longer hospital managers have to master the rules of the new payment game, the more sophisticated they are likely to become in maximizing revenues. However, under the principle of "revenue neutrality," the federal government can hold down annual adjustments for inflation to keep the hospital trust fund from being soaked—a response that protects its solvency but does not prevent perverse effects as hospitals individually seek to maximize their shares within a zero-sum environment.

The new payment regime creates some potential hazards specifically for the poor, who tend to have longer lengths of stay in hospitals, probably because their health status is worse and they suffer from more overlapping conditions. DRGs do not fully reflect differences in severity and the presence of multiple problems. Therefore, the system may encourage hospitals to shun the elderly poor, just as they generally have an incentive to shun more complicated and expensive cases that are money-losers under DRG payment. Insofar as the new reimbursement system makes cream-skimming profitable, it will make the poor unattractive as patients, even when covered by Medicare.

Some states have introduced DRGs into their Medicaid programs. But in releasing states from cost-based reimbursement, OBRA permitted them to experiment, and as of mid-1984 thirty-seven state Medicaid programs had dropped Medicare's cost-based approach in favor of one or another alternative employing incentives and standards (Abt Associates, 1984). Congress also modified the requirement that Medicaid allow free choice of provider, giving states permission to "lock in" overutilizing recipients (requiring them to use a specific provider) and to "lock out" overprescribing or low-quality providers. Congress also made it easier for states to obtain waivers to use alternatives such as HMOs or case-management systems. Under these arrangements, recipients may initially choose a plan or primary care doctor but then are restricted to services that the plan or doctor advises. Such alternatives call for capitation payment (that is, a flat payment per recipient) and put the provider at risk for the costs of service. As of mid-1984, twenty-eight states had undertaken demonstration projects or other efforts to begin moving Medicaid from fee-for-service to one of various alternatives involving at-risk contracting, capitation, or case management (Iglehart, 1984). However, only two states—California and Arizona—have made such reforms statewide. In 1982 California introduced a system of selective contracting for hospital care that uses competitive bidding, confidential negotiations, and flat per diem contracts to drive down the rates paid by the state and to put the hospitals at risk for the cost of services to Medicaid beneficiaries. That same year, Arizona—the last state without Medicaid—introduced its program on an entirely novel basis: competitive bidding by capitation plans (that is, HMOs) for physician as well as inpatient care.

The 1982 California reforms involved a series of measures from which the state achieved, according to its own estimates, a saving of $470 million in its roughly $4 billion Medicaid program (Koetting and Olinger, 1984; Bergthold, 1984; Iglehart, 1984). In addition to setting up a special office to negotiate aggressively with hospitals about Medicaid rates, the legislature narrowed the definition of "medical necessity" in its coverage of services and terminated the eligibility of "medically indigent adults," a group that had never received any federal matching funds. Responsibility for their care was returned to the counties. However, over the previous two decades some California counties had sold off their public hospitals to the private sector and now, because of restricted tax revenues, had limited ability to purchase care. As a result, many medically indigent adults lost access to medical services. A six-month follow-up study of terminated beneficiaries found that their health, compared with controls, had indeed worsened (Lurie et al., 1984). This is one of the few studies available that measures the health impact of recent Medicaid cutbacks.

In a related step the California legislature in 1982 also gave private insurance companies authority for selective contracting—that is, authority to establish preferred provider organizations (PPOs). PPOs contract selectively with doctors and hospitals, and enrollees are given a list of providers preferred and covered by the plan; if they use other sources of care, they must pay a larger share or all of the bill. By negotiating aggressively with hospitals, the PPOs can prevent hospitals from shifting to their subscribers the costs of uncompensated service to the uninsured poor. The more hospital patients covered by HMOs, PPOs, and selective state contracting, the smaller the number remaining whom hospitals can "tax" to finance the costs of the uninsured. Although still in its early stages, the development of PPOs, according to most observers, is likely to make hospitals more allergic to serving the poor. "We are being forced to become more sophisticated in our dumping of indigents," says one hospital administrator of the impact of PPOs (Koetting and Olinger, 1984).

In sharp contrast to the California approach is the kind of hospital rate-setting for "all payers" introduced in such states as Massachusetts and New Jersey. Under waivers from the federal government, these states have sought not only to regulate rates charged by hospitals to all payers, private and public, but also to spread the cost of uncompensated care across all payers, including Medicaid and Medicare. The advocates of this approach argue that, unlike the California approach, it offers "strong support for the social mission of hospitals" (Kinzer, 1983). However, the local press in Boston reports an increase of patient dumping into the public sector, and analyses of the Massachusetts regulatory system indicate that such transfers do benefit private hospitals (Knox, 1984). But patient dumping may be much worse in states without any program to spread the hospital costs of the uninsured.

The all-payer systems, like Medicare's DRGs and California's selective contracting, emphasize changes in hospital payment—logically enough, it would seem, since hospitals absorb about 40 cents out of every dollar spent on health care. But these various reforms generally concentrate on cutting costs per hospital stay; they are unlikely to bring about the deep reductions in total volume of hospital activity that have yielded large and well-verified savings in health maintenance organizations (Luft, 1981; Manning et al., 1984).

The prospect of substantial reductions in hospital costs—and hence some correction of the institutional bias of Medicaid and Medicare—is the chief stimulus of interest in the use of capitation payment. HMOs and PPOs both provide medical care for a fixed, monthly fee to an enrolled population, but each can assume a variety of organizational forms. Other capitation plans include case-management systems and "primary care networks" (PCNs) that provide incentives for primary care physicians to manage prudently the entire range of health services. All of these use incentives for limiting rather than performing services and thereby raise concerns about possible underprovision of needed care. These concerns are reinforced by the record of a Medicaid experiment with HMOs in California in the early 1970s that proved a fiasco when it attracted some entrepreneurs who were unable to provide adequate medical care. However, established HMOs have good records, and even the AMA now concedes that there is no evidence they provide lower-quality care than the fee-for-service sector. Yet the development of such plans primarily for Medicaid beneficiaries inevitably raises suspicions, particularly among advocates of the poor, that savings will be achieved through underprovision. There is also worry about the increased role of for-profit companies in a system with strong incentives for withholding treatment. The primary care networks are perhaps especially subject to this criticism because of the direct linkage between more care and less money for the doctor. In a PCN the primary care doctor is given two accounts—one for his own services and another for specialty and hospital services. If underspent, the second account yields a profit to the doctor; if overspent, the doctor may be at risk for some percentage of the cost.

Besides fearing underprovision, critics of capitation payment for Medicaid are concerned that the suspension of the free-choice-of-physician rule denies the poor a freedom available to the middle class. The requirement for free choice in Medicaid, however, has been illusory and misleading. Most states have restricted Medicaid recipients' freedom to choose physicians by not paying doctors well enough to get most to accept Medicaid clients. Furthermore, free-choice-of-provider requirements in state health insurance laws and employee benefit plans as well as Medicaid have long obstructed the development of HMOs. Requiring free choice of physician denies consumers the right to choose health plans offering comprehensive services through their own panel of doctors. If every health insurance plan has to be open to all doctors, then no plan can compete by organizing or selecting a more efficient medical group. Thus, permitting some health plans that restrict coverage to their own physicians or facilities widens consumers' range of choice. New capitation options in Medicaid might also substantially expand the freedom of beneficiaries by achieving economies and thereby encouraging legislatures to broaden benefits. But there is no question that freedom of choice is narrowed if Medicaid beneficiaries are forced to accept a specific capitation plan solely to keep down state expenditures. That prospect has raised opposition from representatives of the poor, and in Massachusetts it blocked implementation of a major effort to reorganize Medicaid.[2]

Other factors also complicate the development of HMOs for the poor. The logic of prepayment depends on the ability of an HMO or other plan to budget in advance for a defined population. However, since Medicaid beneficiaries frequently go on and off welfare, their eligibility fluctuates, making it difficult for prepayment plans to enroll them. The scope of benefits in Medicaid is also typically narrower than in HMOs, which, therefore, have to create invidious distinctions among their members. To alleviate these problems, Congress in 1981 gave states the authority to guarantee HMOs that Medicaid enrollees would have a minimum of six months' continued eligibility. The law also gave HMOs the right to add services otherwise not covered by Medicaid, which can be used to make enrollment attractive. A variety of capitation experiments are now in progress. Arizona's attempt to base its entire Medicaid program on capitation payment has faced some highly publicized difficulties (including some apparent involvement of organized crime), but it is not clear that these problems arise from the fundamental structure of the program; other demonstrations show evidence of both economy and enrollee satisfaction (Sullivan and Gibson, 1983).

However, substantial economies from capitation payment seem far less likely in Medicaid than in Medicare because of Medicaid's generally low physician fees. If a state is paying $7 for a physician visit, it can scarcely expect to enroll Medicaid recipients in HMOs without paying more for doctors' services. Even significant economies in hospitalization may not be enough to offset the costs from expanded service coverage. Therefore, the argument for capitation in Medicaid is not to reduce state expenditures but to make better use of them in the interests of the poor.

Second, capitation is unlikely to make Medicaid less costly, because 70 percent of Medicaid expenditures are for the elderly and disabled. There have been some demonstration projects of social health maintenance organizations (SHMOs), but the problem of reducing the costs of long-term care is relatively intractable without an extension of social services and their integration under a single organization, which can then orchestrate home and community services and serve as gatekeeper to nursing homes. But this presumes major changes in financing, which are difficult to envision.

Medicare, on the other hand, offers considerable potential for the development of capitation plans. The DRG system divides up care by diagnosis, which is least suitable for the elderly because of the prevalence of overlapping chronic conditions. HMOs, on the other hand, are accustomed to providing comprehensive services and monitoring the relation between them. The elderly are also high users of physicians' services, for which HMOs can partially substitute the services of physicians' extenders. And, finally, the extremely high rates of hospitalization of the elderly are as susceptible to reduction as those of other age groups through more judicious supervision and the substitution of ambulatory and home health alternatives.

Nor are these savings entirely speculative. Some of the best early research comparing HMOs and fee-for-service involved Medicare beneficiaries and showed substantial savings by the HMOs (Gaus, Cooper, and Hirschman, 1976). Nonetheless, Medicare from its inception has offered HMOs extremely unattractive terms. Under the original law, hospitals were paid directly for HMO enrollees, and although the HMOs were paid prospectively for physicians' services, the payments were retrospectively adjusted to reflect actual costs. In other words, Medicare treated HMOs on the same cost basis it treated other providers; it had no room conceptually for an alternative. The law has since been reformed twice, each time with some

improvement, but it still imposes substantial barriers against HMO participation in Medicare (Bonanno and Wetle, 1984). As a result, fewer than
2 percent of Medicare beneficiaries (compared with roughly 7 percent of
all Americans) have been enrolled in HMOs. Now, however, after conducting several successful demonstration projects, Medicare is encouraging
capitation plans, and a significant rise in elderly enrollment in HMOs seems
possible.

PRIVATE COST CONTAINMENT, COMPETITION, AND THE POOR

The trend toward greater prudence in the purchasing of health care has
its parallels in the private sector. Employers have begun to reform their
health benefits and to form coalitions to contain costs. This is not the place
to review all of these efforts, but it is necessary to explain why they affect
the poor.

Financing for health services for the poor comes not only from public
sources and the out-of-pocket payments the poor make but also from cross-
subsidies within the health care system. Hospitals perform much uncompensated care—that is, charity care plus bad debts—whose cost is shifted
primarily to the privately insured. Furthermore, when government programs like Medicaid reimburse providers below their costs, the providers
also shift costs to other payers. The ability of providers to shift costs
depends on the absence of price competition in the system. Since hospitals
"market" their services primarily to doctors, they have not had to be
concerned about a price-sensitive buyer's reactions. Under extensive third-
party insurance, the patients as well are largely indifferent to hospital
charges inflated to reflect cross-subsidies.

The foundations of cost-shifting, however, are now eroding. Instead of
hospitals facing individual physicians indifferent to price, they are now
selling an increasing portion of their services to health plans, such as HMOs
and PPOs, which buy patient days in quantity and seek the best price.
Similarly, employers, especially if they have large concentrations of workers in specific communities, have been pressing hospitals for discounts in
return for channeling blocks of patients to particular institutions. This new
"aggregation of demand" means that the hospital can no longer count on
passing on the costs of the poor and the uninsured.

Furthermore, the hospital industry now faces intensified competition
because of long-range forces eroding demand. A variety of developments
are now shifting medical services into other settings. New technologies in
such fields as ophthalmology are facilitating ambulatory surgery and office-

based diagnostic work; and doctors, who themselves face greater competition as their own numbers rise, have an interest in performing tests and procedures in ambulatory surgery centers and group practice facilities, where they receive more of the profit. New specialized providers, such as rehabilitation centers and home health agencies, are offering lower-priced and attractive alternatives to the traditional general hospital. The HMOs are cutting hospital use severely where they have gained a major market share. These various competitive pressures make it harder for hospitals to subsidize care of the poor.

Recent studies confirm that the hospitals under the most financial stress are those with the "wrong" mix of patients: they have the most uninsured and Medicaid patients and the fewest with private insurance (Feder, Hadley, and Mullner, 1984a, 1984b). It is an entirely logical survival strategy for hospitals, therefore, to avoid service to the poor. "Dumping" such patients—putting them in a taxi and sending them across town to the public hospital, if there is one—is only the most overt response. Newspaper reports suggest that such practices have been increasing. In Washington, D.C., for example, patient dumping has increased three-fold in recent years (*Washington Post,* October 15, 1984). But in hospital finance as in public health, prevention is to be preferred. Hospitals can "de-market" the poor by making them feel unwelcome and out of place and by closing services such as emergency rooms that lead them to the hospital. The most effective form of prevention is simply to locate in an area where few poor people live, an approach favored by the proprietary hospital chains.

Proprietary chains own or manage a growing, although still minority, share of the hospital industry (roughly one-eighth to one-fifth). Their first objective is maintaining a high rate of return, and service to the poor has never been a highly regarded means of pursuing that goal. In defense of their small contribution of charitable care, the companies argue that they pay taxes and that public hospitals and public programs should assume responsibility for the poor. At nonprofit hospitals, there is also more talk about marketing product lines than about community service. Although it is difficult to evaluate its impact, there is little doubt that health care has seen a change in management culture. The professional backgrounds of hospital administrators are shifting from public health to business administration, the finance officers are increasingly influential within the organizations, and from Washington they are being urged to make—and some provisions of law make advantageous—a shift toward an entrepreneurial mode of operation. Under these circumstances, there is no cachet, much less any material reward, in serving the poor.

Thus, several separate developments in the private sector are simultaneously affecting the supply of free care: the increased vigilance of employers; the "aggregation of demand" for hospitals and the increasing competition in the hospital business; and the rise of for-profit hospitals and entrepreneurial managers. Competition drives out cross-subsidies, and the growing commercial ethos erodes whatever commitment to community service the hospitals once had. These developments in the private sector, combined with cutbacks in public programs, suggest that it may prove difficult even to sustain the degree of equity in health care we have achieved, much less to increase it.

Prospects for the Future

Let me bring together the various threads of the argument that suggest why the access to health care of the poor and the uninsured may diminish. First, their level of insurance protection seems to be dropping. Medicaid eligibles as a percent of the poor have fallen because poverty has risen while programs have been cut back. Likewise, there has been a drop in private insurance coverage, which may partly reflect the long-term trend of job losses in smokestack industries with high levels of insurance and job gains in service industries with less coverage. The related decline in unionized workers as a proportion of the labor force probably also contributes to the same result.

Reductions in other government programs besides Medicaid will have an impact in the late 1980s. For example, while the National Health Service Corps continues to place physicians in underserved areas because of commitments from earlier scholarship aid, its size will gradually diminish because of the termination of student assistance. Similarly, the free-care obligations of hospitals under Hill-Burton are expiring, and many hospitals that have provided some care to the poor will thereafter have no legal obligation to do so, except in emergencies.

On the other hand, the supply of doctors is growing rapidly, and community hospitals will have excess capacity. Some physicians may be driven into less affluent areas to practice, which would benefit low-income groups; and some hospitals may be willing to accept reduced payments from Medicaid or other sources as long as their variable costs can be covered. But, as I have suggested, competitive pressures and the changing structure of the industry should diminish the supply of care of the uninsured poor.

The view that the poor face increased barriers to medical care is not mine alone. The same opinion is widely voiced in the hospital industry, but it has received relatively little public discussion. The hospitals have succeeded in drawing some policy attention to the problem of "uncompensated care"—the phrase itself suggests how the problem is being understood—and there is a danger that if any measures are enacted, they will be measures chiefly to protect the institutions. All-payer rate-setting, a kind of legislative enforcement of the traditional cross-subsidies, suffers from the same institutional tilt that has aggravated medical inflation throughout the postwar era. Hill-Burton provided subsidies for hospital construction; private and then public insurance systems provided better coverage for hospital than for ambulatory care; the fees paid for physicians' services have been severely biased toward hospital over office activities and toward "procedural" over "cognitive" work—all of these factors led to overinvestment in hospitals, overcommitment of physicians to hospital-oriented specialties, the distortion of styles of medical practice, and severely inflated medical expenditures. State programs that redistribute hospital costs of the poor but not the cost of other services would simply repeat and extend the institutional bias we desperately need to correct.

In one of the few recent positive efforts to improve access of the poor, Florida enacted legislation to expand Medicaid coverage and tax hospital revenues. The proceeds from the tax are to be used for a number of redistributive purposes, including support for hospitals that provide an above-average rate of uncompensated care (Florida Task Force on Competition and Consumer Choices in Health Care, 1984). Florida, with one of the most limited Medicaid programs, also has one of the highest percentages of for-profit hospitals, and the measure seems to represent an effort to diminish the advantage proprietary hospitals have enjoyed by skimming the market and dumping the poor. Even some advocates of competitive market reform advocate similar proposals to distribute the burden of uncompensated care more evenly.

Under a regime of hidden cost-shifting—or even open cost-shifting under state law, as in the all-payer systems or the Florida initiative—the insured pay a tax for health care for the poor that they do not clearly see. Politically, these measures are easier to enact than any extension of health insurance coverage financed out of general tax revenues, but by just subsidizing providers, they buttress a costly and inadequate system.

The alternative to regulatory or fiscal subterfuge is increasing coverage of the uninsured tenth under arrangements that promise more prudent use of public finance than the open-ended, cost-based, fee-for-service reimbursement methods that the medical profession and the hospital industry originally extracted from the federal government in the design of Medicare and Medicaid. Through the development of HMOs, PPOs, and their various kin, we are seeing the emergence of an institutional base that can provide services to the beneficiaries of public programs at controlled cost. Structural reform is essential to make coverage of the uninsured tenth plausible and to reduce the expenditure drift of the welfare state toward medical care. Rather than "national health insurance," which suggests a program run from Washington, we can more plausibly expect a series of measures that chip away at the residual population of the uninsured—for example, by eliminating the categorical restrictions of Medicaid; by simultaneously requiring and subsidizing employers to provide health insurance to the working poor, particularly policies that include dependents; by establishing more effective insurance mechanisms for specific industries, such as agriculture and retail trade, in which insurance coverage is low; and by extending private coverage for employees and their families during periods of unemployment and/or allowing them to buy into Medicaid.

At this point, of course, few such efforts are being undertaken because of the 1981 tax reductions, the rise in defense spending, and the consequent structural deficit.[3] It may seem foolish to try to think beyond the close horizon that the deficit imposes on the political imagination. But the money required to cover the uninsured tenth is not that large. Since the uninsured are already receiving some medical and hospital care, providing them coverage would increase expenditures by less than 10 percent (less than the annual increase owing to inflation during the past decade). And since the potential savings from HMOs and other reforms are greater than 10 percent, the challenge is to use resources released from those reforms. To serve the uninsured, America needs no more doctors or hospitals; it needs to reallocate their services.

Many observers are deeply convinced that the United States cannot afford or agree upon any plan for universal health insurance protection, such as that of most major Western nations. Our world groans under many intractable problems, but I am convinced that this ought not to be one of them. Decent health care for the poor is not a fiscal impossibility, nor a political impossibility, unless we become utterly resigned to a kind of national incompetence in public policy.

6 The Effect of Direct Job Creation and Training Programs on Low-Skilled Workers

Laurie J. Bassi
Orley Ashenfelter

FOR MORE THAN TWO DECADES the federal government has been continuously involved in some type of active intervention in the labor market. The debate concerning the appropriate size and method of intervention has been long, emotional, and political. In some instances federally funded employment and training programs have clearly been used to appease special interest groups; others have been implemented because of their widespread political popularity. The central economic rationale for federally funded employment and training programs has often been lost against this political backdrop.

From an economic perspective, there are only three possible reasons for the government to intervene in the operation of the labor market. One rationale is to reduce frictional unemployment; the Employment Service has long been in business for exactly this purpose. The second rationale is to reduce cyclical unemployment; we would expect that programs that are countercyclical in nature would be turned on and off in response to changes in the unemployment rate. The final rationale is to alleviate structural unemployment—unemployment that is in some sense involuntary and persists over the course of the business cycle. Programs that are structural in nature should have targeting mechanisms to ensure that the individuals served are persistently unemployed or underemployed.

This chapter concentrates on what is known about the effectiveness of programs that are primarily structural in nature. As will become evident, however, it is not always possible to distinguish clearly between countercyclical and structural programs. We review the historical development of employment and training policy in the United States, examine how funding levels for these programs have changed over time, present the evidence on what is known about the effectiveness of these programs, and consider the costs of alternative types of programs. We also describe how the size of the programs and fiscal substitution rates affect the aggregate impact.

Federal Involvement in Employment and Training Programs

The history of federal involvement in employment and training programs can be divided into five phases. The first phase evolved out of the unemployment crisis of the Great Depression. The Works Progress Administration (WPA), created in 1935, was a massive direct job creation program. During 1936, the program's peak year, WPA employed more than three million of the nine million who were unemployed (Howard, 1943). At the same time, the Public Works Administration (PWA) concentrated on capital-intensive projects in the public sector on the assumption that this spending would generate increased private sector activity. These programs were phased out by 1943.

After this initial involvement in the labor market, there was a long period of no intervention. Only in the early 1960s did public employment programs once again receive widespread attention. This second phase had a much different emphasis (and life span) than did the first. It grew out of a concern for workers who had been displaced by technological advances as well as a concern about the employment bottlenecks that these advances generated. The Manpower Development and Training Act (MDTA), passed in 1962, was originally designed to provide vocational and on-the-job training for displaced workers. Initially the program served male heads of households with substantial previous labor market experience. However, the emphasis of the program quickly changed to meet the needs of more disadvantaged individuals, those with hard-core unemployment problems.

This shift in emphasis ushered in the third phase of federal involvement, coinciding with the implementation of Great Society programs and lasting through the early 1970s. Employment and training programs were increasingly targeted at minorities, welfare recipients, low-income youth, the elderly, and other hard-to-employ groups. The plethora of programs included Job Corps, Neighborhood Youth Corps, Operation Mainstream, New Careers, Concentrated Employment Program, Older Americans, Model Cities, Foster Grandparents, and the Work Incentive Program. These programs provided work experience and training (both on-the-job and classroom), with the intention of improving the long-term employability of participants and providing career ladders for moving from temporary public sector jobs to permanent jobs in the private sector. The emphasis was structural in nature.

With the recession of 1970–71 public attention began to shift from the long-term employability problems of the disadvantaged to the problems of the cyclically unemployed. Under the Emergency Employment Act (EEA) of 1971, the federal government provided $1 billion during fiscal year 1972 and $1.25 billion during 1973 for the purpose of direct job creation within state and local governments under the Public Employment Program (PEP). These funds were allocated in proportion to the number of unemployed within each area. The disadvantaged, however, were not completely forgotten: provisions were made for targeting a variety of groups including Vietnam veterans, youth, the elderly, migrants, non-English-speaking persons, and welfare recipients. In addition, a limited amount of money was made available for training. The passage of the Emergency Employment Act represents the beginning of the fourth phase of federal involvement in employment and training policy. This phase, which continued through 1978, was characterized by a mixed strategy that attempted to combat both cyclical and structural unemployment.

This strategy continued with the passage of the Comprehensive Employment and Training Act (CETA) of 1973, which consolidated many of the training programs of the late 1960s and early 1970s and also incorporated the Public Employment Program. When CETA passed, unemployment was well below its 1971 peak, and its original emphasis was clearly on training rather than employment. However, some provisions for public service employment (PSE) were made for high unemployment areas. The deep recession of 1974–75 resulted in a change of priorities under CETA, with countercyclical PSE occupying center stage. Very substantial countercyclical expenditures continued to be made through 1978 when CETA was reauthorized.

During this period employment and training programs were very well funded by historic standards, and considerable experimentation was undertaken. A wide variety of alternative policies were implemented on a trial basis. The first of these was the Supported Work Demonstration, one of the few employment/training programs that has been run as an experiment with a randomly selected control group. The demonstration tested the effects of a highly structured work experience on four disadvantaged target groups: long-term AFDC recipients, ex-addicts, ex-offenders, and young school dropouts. Supported Work was distinguished from other programs by its emphasis on gradually bringing individuals with extreme employment disabilities into the world of work by using peer group support, graduated stress, and close supervision as program techniques.

The second major development in this period was the Youth Employment and Demonstration Projects Act (YEDPA) passed in 1977, which funded a variety of programs specifically directed to the needs of youth. These programs were administered under the CETA umbrella and provided large budgets for research and evaluation. A third development was the use of the targeted Jobs Tax Credit to subsidize (and potentially increase) employment among certain disadvantaged groups.

The 1978 reauthorization of CETA represents the entrance of the phase of employment and training policy in which we currently find ourselves. During the CETA reauthorization, funding for countercyclical PSE was cut drastically, partly in response to a dramatic decline in unemployment and partly in response to widespread allegations of abuse and fraud under the PSE program. CETA once again became almost exclusively structural in nature.

In late 1982 CETA was replaced by the Job Training Partnership Act (JTPA), which emphasizes combating structural rather than cyclical unemployment. No funds were made available for any form of direct job creation despite the fact that the unemployment rate had reached double-digit levels while the JTPA legislation was being created. The Reagan administration opposed direct job creation in the public sector, believing strongly that the only federal responsibility is to provide training for disadvantaged individuals. This philosophy is reflected in the JTPA legislation.

We have now come full circle and returned to the types of programs we had in the mid-1960s. Our programs are structural in nature, providing training for the most disadvantaged members of the labor force. However, over the course of these two decades much has changed. Table 6.1 shows real per capita funding levels for countercyclical and structural programs and unemployment rates over the past two decades. These data indicate that funding levels for structural programs increased steadily from the early 1960s through 1979, when they dropped sharply, and funding levels for countercyclical programs have gyrated wildly through the 1970s. This table also indicates that changes in countercyclical funding have not been well timed in terms of changes in the unemployment rate.

The empirical relationships between funding levels and unemployment rates were examined using regression analysis.[1] An interesting result that emerged from this analysis is that funding levels for both structural and countercyclical programs were higher when the Democrats were in office.

Table 6.1   Real per capita funding levels for Department of Labor employment and training programs, 1963–1984

Year	Unemployment rate	Real per capita structural funding ($ 1972)	Real per capita countercyclical funding ($ 1972)
1963	5.48	.4	0
1964	5.31	1.0	0
1965	4.64	2.9	0
1966	3.84	4.2	0
1967	3.68	5.1	0
1968	3.61	4.8	0
1969	3.33	5.9	0
1970	4.17	7.6	0
1971	5.72	7.5	0
1972	5.67	8.3	4.6
1973	4.96	6.8	5.5
1974	4.94	7.6	1.1
1975	7.69	9.5	5.7
1976	7.75	9.7	7.9
1977	7.28	10.9	20.0
1978	6.23	15.4	6.6
1979	5.74	19.9	9.0
1980	6.57	17.5	4.1
1981	7.27	13.7	2.9
1982	8.77	9.5	.2
1983	9.25	8.9	0
1984	7.86	6.4	0

Sources: Unemployment rates and GNP price deflator for 1963–1983: U.S. Council of Economic Advisers, *Economic Report of the President* (Washington, D.C., annually); unemployment rate and GNP price deflator for 1984; U.S. Department of Commerce, *Business Conditions Digest* (Washington, D.C., January 1985); funding levels for 1963–1981: U.S. Department of Labor, *Employment and Training Report of the President* (Washington, D.C., annually); funding levels for 1982–1984: estimates by Demetra Nightingale of the Urban Institute.

Note: Obligations for the Public Employment Program and the Public Service Employment Program were defined as being countercyclical. All other obligations were considered to be structural.

The analysis also confirms that funding levels have, indeed, been very poorly coordinated with the unemployment rate.

While this finding is not too surprising for structural funding levels, since these programs are intended to combat structural rather than cyclical unemployment, it does indicate that the funding levels for countercyclical programs have not been very sensible from an economic perspective. In order to be effective from a macroeconomic perspective, it would be necessary for funding levels to be highly correlated with current unemployment. However, it is lagged unemployment, rather than current unemployment, that is a much better predictor of countercyclical funding.

Critics of countercyclical programs have frequently pointed to this phenomenon. The political system is unable to respond quickly enough for the programs to be timely. It could, in fact, be the case that such programs are actually counterproductive—turning on the faucet just when it needs to be turned off.

The poor timing of countercyclical programs was, no doubt, at least partially responsible for their ultimate demise. By the time the programs were in full swing, our concerns had usually switched from reducing countercyclical unemployment to combating structural unemployment. Inevitably, countercyclical programs have been judged by a criterion that would be more appropriate for evaluating the effectiveness of structural programs.

With this discussion as background, we turn now to an examination of that criterion—the extent to which employment and training programs have increased the earnings capacity of their participants. We remind the reader of our primary emphasis on structural programs, even though it may not be valid to judge countercyclical programs within this context.

The Effects of Employment and Training Policies on Low-Wage Workers

During the past two decades billions of dollars have been spent on employment and training programs, and millions have been spent on research, evaluation, and demonstrations. It would be a heroic task to summarize and integrate the results of all this work, and one that would probably not be tremendously fruitful. We concentrate on some of the major studies of two fundamental aspects in the evaluation of the effectiveness of employment and training programs: the estimation of the microeconomic impact of the programs, in particular, the employment and earnings impacts on participants, and the determination of the macroeconomic effect of the programs, that is, their net employment effect.

MICROECONOMIC EFFECTS

Primarily because almost no employment or training programs have been run on an experimental basis, much, if not most, of the analytic work in this area is woefully inadequate. Researchers have been forced either to create artificial comparison groups or to conduct their analysis without them. In the latter case, the impact of the program on participants' post-program employment and earnings experience is estimated simply by comparing their pre- and postprogram experience, with no regard for the effect of the passage of time or changing economic conditions.

Another problem that has plagued evaluations of employment and training programs is what has come to be known as the preprogram dip. It is generally the case that, immediately prior to program entry, participants experience a marked decline in employment and earnings. This is no doubt in large part because many of the programs have required, as a condition of eligibility, that participants be unemployed. Since it is impossible to know whether this dip in earnings is merely transitory or the beginning of a permanent decline, it is difficult to ascertain a participant's permanent earnings level prior to the program. Also, it is not easy to find comparison group members that experience the same decline in employment and earnings.

Even if it is possible to generate a comparison group that is comparable to the participants based on observable characteristics that affect earnings and employment, it is very likely that the comparison group members differ in other ways from the participants in a systematic but unobservable fashion. Participants, for instance, may be systematically more (or less) motivated than their comparison group counterparts. Since motivation is not observable, and it is likely to be an important determinant of earnings, it is unclear the extent to which postprogram earnings differentials between participants and comparisons result from program participation or differences in motivation. Consequently, in the absence of an experimental design that randomly assigns individuals to either a treatment or a control group, it is necessary to employ statistical techniques in an attempt to control for nonrandom assignment owing to unobservable characteristics.

Finally, researchers have been confronted with contamination of available comparison groups. Contamination occurs when members of the comparison groups are, or at some point have been, program participants. In general, there is no way to identify which members of the comparison groups have been contaminated. This introduces an errors-in-variable problem, since program participation is measured inaccurately for contaminated individuals.[2]

Very few evaluations of employment and training programs have had well-chosen comparison groups, adjusted for contamination and simultaneously controlled for nonrandom selection. In the review of the evaluation literature that follows, we confine our discussion to a few of the better evaluations, even though most of these have serious shortcomings. The review will proceed on a chronological basis.

Ashenfelter (1978) did one of the first evaluations of the MDTA program that attempts to meet most of the criteria specified above. Using a comparison group drawn from the Continuous Work History Sample, he estimated the effect of participation in classroom training for all participants who entered the MDTA program during the first three months of 1964. The outcome measure of program participation was annual Social Security earnings in the first five postprogram years.[3] Ashenfelter found that MDTA classroom training did have a positive and statistically significant effect on participants' earnings, ranging from $200 per annum for white males to about $550 for black females. In general, the effects were larger for women than for men—a finding that appears consistently. Ashenfelter also found some evidence of a decay in the earnings effect over time for men but not for women. He points out, however, that the decay effect (particularly for men) is sensitive to the estimation procedure. This sensitivity points to the central dilemma that confronts researchers: in the absence of experimental data, the estimated benefits of programs and the pattern of these benefits over time may vary dramatically, depending on the estimation strategy. The decay rate of these effects, or the lack thereof, has important implications for the cost-effectiveness of training programs.

Using different cohorts of MDTA participants and alternative comparison groups drawn from other samples, two other studies found widely differing earnings gains for men: Kiefer (1978) found large negative effects, while Cooley, McGuire, and Prescott (1979) found large positive effects. The estimated earnings gains for women, however, are much less sensitive to the choice of the cohort and the comparison group.

The next major employment/training program was the Public Employment Program, which was primarily countercyclical but also had some structural objectives. Because it is in some sense inappropriate to judge countercyclical programs, which have income maintenance goals, by criteria that are intended for structural programs, we should not be too surprised if they do not generate long-term employment and earnings gains.

Westat (1979) has done the only major analysis of the net earnings impact of the Public Employment Program. The Current Population Survey (CPS) was used with matched Social Security earnings files to generate comparison groups for PEP participants. Using both an autoregressive earnings model and a comparison of mean earnings between participants and comparisons, Westat came to conclusions similar to those of Ashenfelter. While in-program earnings gains were substantial for all race and sex groups, women generally experienced greater postprogram gains than did men; the gains were also larger for minorities than for whites. The estimated earnings gains for men were not significantly different from zero.

The availability of CPS data and matched Social Security files allows researchers to inexpensively generate a variety of comparison groups. In addition, the recently available Continuous Longitudinal Manpower Survey (CLMS) represents a major data development effort of the Department of Labor for evaluation of CETA-financed employment and training activities. The public-use tapes contain large representative samples of individuals who participated in the program during fiscal years 1975 through 1979.[4] For each of these individuals, the CLMS includes a four-year record of labor force experience beginning one year prior to CETA enrollment, the type of CETA program(s) in which the individual participated, basic demographic characteristics, a history of public benefits received by the individual and/or the individual's family, and family-related variables. Although the CLMS is the best available data base, it is still less than ideal; for example, variables that are often included in earnings equations, such as union status, geographic location, and work experience, are not included. However, the unique advantage of having both the CLMS and the CPS available with merged records from the Social Security Administration is that researchers can now generate a wide array of comparison groups, facilitating testing of the sensitivity of estimated program effects to the choice of the comparison group. And because longitudinal data are available, researchers have used autoregressive or fixed effects models to control for nonrandom selection.

Not surprisingly, this expanded ability to experiment with comparison groups and estimation techniques has led to a broad array of estimated program effects. Some consistent findings do emerge, however, from this growing literature. As was the case with evaluations of earlier programs, CETA evaluations have found with remarkable consistency that women benefit more from program participation than do men.[5] In fact, CETA appears to have generated no significant earnings gains for men whatsoever. It seems that participation in employment and training programs increases earnings primarily through an increase in hours worked rather than through an increase in wages (Bassi et al., 1984, and Levy, 1982). Since women generally work fewer hours than men, there is obviously more room for an impact on their hours of work than is the case for men.

Related findings indicate that the individuals who benefited most from CETA participation were among the most disadvantaged with the least amount of previous labor market experience. This suggests that CETA has been successful in preparing participants for entry level positions. This may represent a substantial improvement for many female participants, but it may leave many male participants no better off. Consistent with this hypothesis is Fraker, Maynard, and Nelson's (1984) finding that young men are the only subgroup of men who experience substantial postprogram employment and earnings gains.[6]

A final finding from the CETA evaluation literature is that the least effective method of increasing participants' postprogram employment and earnings is through work experience programs.[7] Four basic types of programs were available under the auspices of CETA: classroom training, on-the-job training, public service employment, and work experience. The work experience program seemed to be reserved for the most disadvantaged participants. Apparently, this activity involved a good deal of acclimation to the world of work and not much training or working at a real job. This was very different from the public service employment program where participants often worked side by side with regular civil service employees. This difference may account for the differential postprogram effects associated with these two alternative types of employment programs, but it is also possible that the difference merely reflects a selection bias.

Classroom training, on-the-job training, and public service employment all resulted in positive and significant postprogram employment and earning gains for women. There is, however, no clear agreement on which program activity was the most effective. In general, earnings gains for women in a two- to three-year period after the program were from $600 to $1,200, with most estimates in the upper end of this range. The gains show no sign of decay in the postprogram period, although few years of postprogram data are available. Since most researchers have not adjusted for contamination bias, these estimates are best considered as lower bounds and as very substantial in light of the average earnings levels of female participants (about $2,700 in the preprogram period).

None of the programs had a consistently significant effect on men. Occasionally, positive effects of on-the-job training were found for some subgroups of men, but because there appears to be significant "creaming" of participants into on-the-job training, the validity of this result is in serious question.

There is also an expanding research on programs addressing the employability problems of youth. Perhaps the best known and certainly the most enduring of these programs is the Job Corps. In continuous operation since 1965, the Job Corps serves limited numbers of the most disadvantaged youth aged sixteen to twenty-one. There are two types of Job Corps centers, residential and nonresidential. The program provides very intensive (and expensive) evaluations of each participant's barriers to employment and extensive services, including individual and group counseling, medical attention, remedial education, vocational training, graduate equivalence degree courses for high school dropouts, and courses in citizenship.

Two major evaluations of the Job Corps have been undertaken (Cain, 1968, and Mallar et al., 1980), and a third is now underway. Both studies found very significant increases in employment and earnings and reductions in welfare dependence, unemployment insurance usage, criminal activity, and out-of-wedlock births.[8] Cost-benefit calculations indicate that for fiscal year 1977 the value of the benefits generated by the Job Corps exceeded the costs of the program by almost 40 percent (Mallar et al., 1980).

These Job Corps studies, however, utilized comparison groups rather than control groups. The absence of a randomly assigned comparison group may be especially critical for studies of youth, since it is not possible to rely heavily on preprogram earnings levels—as is often done with adults—to generate comparison groups.

The findings now emerging from the Youth Employment and Demonstration Projects Act of 1977 are, however, largely consistent with the Job Corps findings. A variety of approaches were used under YEDPA, but the most effective seemed to be a combination of intensive remedial education and training along with training in job search techniques (Hahn and Lerman, 1984). Unfortunately, despite the fact that YEDPA was a demonstration, it was not run as an experiment. Consequently, even the most consistent findings are subject to the caveats mentioned above.

The National Supported Work Demonstration, run on an experimental basis, was designed to provide a highly structured and supportive work environment for four target groups: women with histories of long-term dependence on AFDC, ex-addicts, ex-offenders, and young school dropouts. Of these four groups, the program was the most effective in improving the postprogram (eighteen months to two years) employment and earnings of AFDC recipients, and it had a substantial impact on ex-addicts as well.

Only for the AFDC recipients and ex-addicts do the benefit-cost calculations show that the program paid for itself on purely economic grounds. For AFDC recipients substantial increases in both hours worked and hourly wage rates were found, with accompanying decreases in receipt of welfare benefits. For ex-addicts, however, there seemed to be only small earnings gains, with most of the societal benefits coming from reduced criminal activity. These findings are not very controversial, since they are based on an experimental design.

One of the unexpected benefits of the Supported Work Demonstration is that it has given us a capacity to check the estimated program impacts generated by nonexperimental methods against those of an experiment. In two separate analyses Lalonde (1984) and Fraker, Maynard, and Nelson (1984) generated comparison groups by methods similar to those used in other studies.[9] These comparison groups were used to generate estimates of the net earnings impact of the Supported Work Demonstration, which can be compared to the "true" impact generated by the experiment's control group.

The results of these analyses are disquieting because the estimated impacts based on the comparison groups generally differed dramatically from the true impacts. Further, the comparison group results became progressively less reliable as the postprogram period lengthened (Fraker, Maynard, and Nelson, 1984). Often the estimates based on the comparison group were statistically significant, while those based on the control group were not, and vice versa. In general, the comparison groups generated for youth were the least reliable, and those generated for adult women were the most reliable.

The good news from these two studies is the confirmation that the comparison groups generated for adult women were probably the best of the available comparison groups. Also, the finding that adult women benefit most from participation is confirmed by the Supported Work Demonstration. The bad news is that both the magnitude and the statistical reliability of even this best set of nonexperimental results may diverge widely from the true effects. Clearly, the importance of an experimental design cannot be overstated.

An alternative to using public sector employment and training (which is essentially a 100-percent subsidy to state and local governments) is to subsidize wage costs for private employers when they hire workers from a particular target group. Although this idea seems to have caught on in Europe, it has been used on a very limited basis in the United States. Consequently, our ability to analyze the effectiveness of such programs is extremely limited.

The most recent of several wage subsidy programs is the Targeted Jobs Tax Credit. Under this program companies can receive a tax credit on wages paid for certain groups of disadvantaged workers, including welfare recipients and youth from poor households. Employer participation in this program, as in its predecessor, the New Jobs Tax Credit, has been very limited. Many eligible individuals hold jobs with employers who do not claim the subsidy.

Why do firms and/or prospective employers fail to claim these tax credits? The results from a recent wage subsidy experiment suggest one possible explanation. In 1981 a Dayton, Ohio, manpower agency randomly divided able-bodied welfare recipients into three groups. Each member of the first group was given a tax credit voucher informing prospective employers that the applicant was eligible for the Targeted Jobs Tax Credit and outlining the precise nature of the credit. Members of the second group were given comparable wage subsidy vouchers that provided reimbursement through a cash payment rather than a tax credit. The purpose of this was to test whether the low response rate was created by a fear of a possible tax audit associated with the credit. All participants were encouraged to show the vouchers when they applied for jobs. The third group was not given any voucher.

In a recent analysis of the Dayton experiment, Burtless (1985) found that 21 percent of the unvouchered group found jobs within an eight-week job search period, but only 13 percent of the vouchered groups found jobs. No significant differences between the two types of vouchers were found. Of the vouchered job finders, only one-quarter of their employers bothered to apply for the subsidy. This suggests that tax credit schemes may identify and stigmatize job applicants as being from a disadvantaged group.

This phenomenon of low response rates by employers (and perhaps prospective employees, as well) represents one of the most fundamental limitations of using the private sector to promote employment and training among very disadvantaged individuals. Although private sector programs may be much less expensive than public sector programs, they appear able to at best play a very limited role.[10]

RELATIVE COST-EFFECTIVENESS OF ALTERNATIVE PROGRAMS

Given what appear to be the relatively modest effects of employment and training programs, it is fair to ask whether such programs for the disadvantaged represent a worthwhile expenditure of scarce resources. Do they generate more benefits either to the participants or to society as a whole than they cost?

Unfortunately, our inability to estimate reliably the benefits of employment and training programs makes any attempt to generate benefit-cost ratios extremely hazardous. Probably the most exhaustive benefit-cost ratios have been developed for the Job Corps and the Supported Work Demonstration.[11] Although the Job Corps is a very expensive program, it appears to almost pay for itself from the taxpayer's perspective—the program produces benefits of 96 cents for every dollar invested (Mallar et al., 1980). From a societal perspective (which includes both participants and taxpayers) the benefits are $1.45 for every dollar invested. The benefits to taxpayers come in the form of in-program output, increased tax payments on postprogram income, reduced transfer payments, reduced criminal activity, and reduced use of other federally provided services. If these estimates are accurate, very large benefits accrue to Job Corps participants at the cost of a very small income redistribution from taxpayers.

The results from the Supported Work Demonstration, however, indicate that social benefit-cost rations for youth are well below 1. Yet it is impossible to know if the estimated difference is due to the difference in treatments or methodologies. Since the Supported Work results are based on an experimental design, it is difficult to dismiss them lightly. The results from Supported Work are, however, more positive for the AFDC target group, whose estimated benefit-cost ratios are well in excess of 2, while those for ex-addicts are 1.87.

Benefit-cost calculations are always subject to criticism and controversy because of the heroic assumptions made to derive them. These calculations for the Job Corps program and the Supported Work Demonstration have, however, been redone under a variety of assumptions and the basic conclusions stand. These results indicate that intensive training and employability development, like that found in these two programs, could be wise investments from society's point of view. Supported Work's benefit-cost ratios for ex-addicts and young school dropouts indicate that there is, however, no guarantee that such an investment will pay off for all disadvantaged groups and/or all types of programs.

There is much less evidence available on the societal benefit-cost ratios for more traditional (and less comprehensive) forms of employment and training such as those that existed under MDTA and CETA. However, a comparison of only the long-run increase in earnings resulting from various programs relative to their costs suggests that training programs are a more cost-effective method of increasing disadvantaged participants' postprogram earnings than are employment programs. This result is not surprising since the objective of many employment programs has been merely to provide temporary employment. However, employment programs (with perhaps the exception of work experience programs) have probably been at least as effective as training programs in increasing postprogram earnings. Employment programs, however, are much more expensive since participants are generally paid at least the minimum wage, while training programs offer at most only a small stipend.

From a benefit-cost point of view, in-program transfers to participants do not affect the societal calculations, since the cost of the transfer to taxpayers is a benefit to participants. However, from the taxpayer's point of view, training programs are clearly preferable if they generate comparable earnings increases as do employment programs but at a lower cost.[12] Also, programs will be most cost effective if they are tightly targeted on those groups that experience the largest earnings gains from participation.

FISCAL SUBSTITUTION AND THE NET EFFECTS OF EMPLOYMENT AND TRAINING PROGRAMS

The extent to which employment and training programs ultimately affect aggregate employment and earnings levels is determined by a number of factors including the number of individuals who participate and the impact of the programs both on participants and on individuals who do not participate.[13]

As Table 6.1 indicates, funding for programs grew steadily through the 1970s and then fell dramatically after 1979. Even at its peak, "average enrollments in CETA training components represented one-twentieth of the unemployed, less than a tenth of the low-income persons in the work force full-year and predominantly full-time but with earnings below the poverty level, and only half a percent of the labor force" (Taggart, 1981, p. viii). Clearly, with the drastic reduction in funding of structural programs since that time, even these numbers have declined dramatically.

As the previous discussion demonstrates, employment and training programs have not been a panacea for disadvantaged workers. The long-run earnings gains that they generate seem to be at best fairly modest. These moderate earnings gains in combination with the low levels of funding indicate that programs that grew out of the War on Poverty certainly have not eliminated and probably have not substantially reduced unemployment and poverty among the working age population.

But a complete evaluation of program effects must also consider the potential displacement effects that they generate. If the estimated employment and earnings gains that accrue to participants are associated with a comparable loss to those individuals who did not participate in the programs, the net macroeconomic effect of such programs would be zero.

Unfortunately, no formal analysis of this issue has been undertaken.

Such an analysis would require a shift from the partial equilibrium frameworks used to evaluate the microeconomic impacts of the programs to a general equilibrium framework that identifies economy-wide effects. Given the enormous difficulties that have been encountered with efforts to derive defensible estimates of the microeconomic impacts, we seem a very long way from achieving this next step.

Some indirect evidence can, however, be elicited. A number of studies estimated the fiscal substitution rate within the public sector. In this context, the term *fiscal substitution* refers to the extent to which state and local governments use funds from the federal government to finance expenditures on employment that would have been self-financed in the absence of the federal funding.[14] The available estimates of fiscal substitution are based almost entirely on the public service employment component of CETA.

Estimation of the fiscal substitution rate under PSE proved to be a difficult task, because the program underwent several major legislative changes. It became increasingly targeted on economically disadvantaged individuals over time, making it less countercyclical in emphasis. It seems reasonable to expect that the more targeted the program, the lower will be the fiscal substitution rate associated with that program. On the other hand, we would expect the fiscal substitution rate to have risen over time, since state and local governments had an opportunity to replace regular civil servants with PSE employees.

These two confounding effects have made it impossible to estimate a general substitution rate. Indeed, substitution rates vary by time periods and depend on the nature of the program (structural or countercyclical). By looking at all of the fiscal substitution studies, however, we can discern a pattern.[15] Fiscal substitution seems to be lower in structural programs than in countercyclical programs, and it tends to rise over time in both types of programs.

A major shortcoming of these studies is that they only measure substitution within the public sector and do not attempt to measure any offsetting employment effects created in the private sector. Also, these studies estimate only the potential displacement effects of employment programs; they are silent about displacement resulting from training.

Despite the shortcomings of the fiscal substitution literature, one useful result emerges: employment and earnings effects will be overstated to the extent that the gains that accrue to participants represent losses for nonparticipants. The evidence suggests that this displacement (at least within the public sector) is likely to be less severe for structural programs than for countercyclical programs. An ironic implication is that structural programs may well generate larger employment effects than do countercyclical programs.

However, programs within the public sector that have low displacement/ substitution effects may not be politically viable (Nathan et al., 1981). To the extent that local governments are not able to engage in fiscal substitution (since they typically hire very few low-skilled workers), they are not particularly interested in participating in the program. However, programs that have high substitution rates (and are, therefore, popular with local governments) are unpopular with unions. The elimination of PSE under the Reagan administration was not a difficult task since the program, by then, had very little political support.

If this analysis of the effectiveness of large-scale employment programs is correct, it seems unlikely that they can be counted on as a permanent method for increasing the employment and earnings capacities of the disadvantaged. Training programs are likely to be a more viable political alternative. They are also likely to be a more cost-effective vehicle for increasing earnings than are employment programs.

To judge from the evidence of the past, it is women and the economically disadvantaged who have benefited most from employment and training programs. In most cases the resulting employment and earnings gains even to these groups have been modest, in part because it is not easy to solve the employment difficulties of the hard-to-employ and in part because the resources devoted to any one individual are fairly modest. There is some indication that programs providing intensive (and expensive) investment in each participant, such as the Job Corps and the Supported Work Demonstration, have, at least for some groups of the disadvantaged, more than paid for themselves from a society-wide point of view.

These findings suggest that employment and training programs have been neither an overwhelming success nor a complete failure in terms of their ability to increase the long-term employment and earnings of disadvantaged workers. Our ability to improve the lot of any given participant and the collective economic well-being of the disadvantaged has been modest—as has been the level of resources devoted to this endeavor.

These lessons have implications for the likely success of the Job Training Partnership Act, which is still too new to be evaluated. JTPA has been targeted on the most disadvantaged which, according to the evidence from the past, is the most effective targeting device for allocating scarce employment and training dollars. Because the program does not allow for any stipends to be paid to recipients and is simultaneously designed to serve only the most disadvantaged, it is likely that only those on welfare will be able to "afford" to participate in the program. This essentially limits the program to welfare mothers, precisely the group that is most likely to benefit from the program.

Unfortunately, the level of support that is available to any given participant remains limited as no stipends are available and maximum length of program participation is limited. Given the severe employment barriers that many participants face, we may be making a mistake that we have made before—investing too little and hoping for too much.

Despite nearly twenty years of continuous federal involvement, we still have to do a good deal of guesswork about what will work and for whom. We have had substantial and on-going difficulties in identifying what works, for whom, and why. This has been, in large part, because of an unwillingness on the part of Congress and policymakers to allow for adequate experimentation in the delivery of employment and training services. As long as analysts are forced to use comparison groups instead of true control groups, there will always be debate and controversy over the effectiveness of such programs.

Two decades of nonexperimental program evaluation in the employment and training field have taught a lesson about which there can be little disagreement: convincing program evaluation is going to require continued use of randomized clinical trials. We wish to emphasize that this is not simply a statement that randomization is a preferable methodological approach regardless of the field of study. Instead, we believe the evidence in the study of employment and training programs overwhelmingly indicates that *randomization is essential in program evaluation in the employment and training field.* The difficulty seems to be that the earnings determination processes of workers and the selection methods of current programs interact to make it nearly impossible to produce reliable estimates of workers' potential earnings in the absence of a program. The evidence to support this finding comes from both experimental and nonexperimental studies. The nonexperimental studies indicate that minor changes in methods, for which there is no empirical justification, produce large swings in estimated program effects. The study of experimental findings indicates that perfectly plausible nonexperimental methods may lead to dramatic errors in inferences about program effects.

This basic finding raises a fundamental question: What is the proper reaction of policymakers? In our view the appropriate reaction is for policymakers to begin the development of a credible research and development effort using randomized clinical trials in a wide variety of study areas.

It is even possible that enough may be learned from this approach in a decade or two of experience that nonexperimental analyses will be able to play a larger role. We wish to emphasize, however, that it will take at least a decade before the full fruits of the effort will be in evidence. The successful use of randomized clinical trials in the National Supported Work Demonstration indicates that, like the great progress at the Food and Drug Administration and the Federal Trade Commission in the use of statistical methods, randomized clinical trials is an entirely practical and ethical way to deal with model uncertainty in the employment and training area.

We believe that experimentation will naturally proceed in two ways, and whether one or the other is favored will no doubt depend in part on the political environment. One kind of experiment continually tests and evaluates on-going programs; the other investigates prototypes for new programs. Building up a treatment and control comparison in the longitudinal analysis of the Job Training Partnership Act is an example of the former. There is no doubt that a similar approach could be applied to the Job Corps, the Neighborhood Youth Corps, or any of the other large-scale employment and training programs that now exist.

More challenging in some ways is the use of experimentation in the design of new programs and in the modification of continuing programs, such as the unemployment insurance system, the disability income system, and other welfare programs. Here small-scale modifications can be tested by randomized clinical trials in selected sites. Likewise, new programs can be tested in selected sites before being implemented on a national scale.

Not until we have accumulated evidence from this type of experimentation can even the most consistent finding from the evaluation literature—that women benefit most from program participation—be accepted without doubt. There is always the possibility that women participants appear to be more successful in the postprogram period because those women who have chosen to enter or re-enter the labor force self-select into employment and training programs, and those women who have chosen to remain out of the labor force are over-represented in the comparison groups. Of course, to the extent that these programs facilitate entry or re-entry, the estimated program impacts are "real." But to the extent that the programs simply are a vehicle for entry for those who would have entered even without the program, the estimated program effect will be overstated. No selection bias adjustment mechanism can promise to eliminate the effects of this type of nonrandom assignment.

7   Education and Training Programs and Poverty

Nathan Glazer

In 1974, at a conference sponsored by the Institute for Research on Poverty, Henry Levin analyzed "A Decade of Policy Developments in Improving Education and Training for Low-Income Populations" (Levin, 1977, pp. 123–188). A great many programs were described and knowledge of their effectiveness discussed: Head Start, Title I of the Elementary and Secondary Education Act of 1965, Upward Bound, School Lunch Program, School Breakfast Program, Vocational Education, Teachers Corps, Neighborhood Youth Corps, Job Corps, Educational Opportunity Grants, Guaranteed Student Loans, Work Study, Talent Search, Adult Education Act of 1966, Migrant Workers, Work Experience, Job Opportunities in the Business Sector, Manpower Development Training Act. Even so, Levin was hardly exhaustive.

The judgment, not Levin's alone, as to the effectiveness of such programs in combating poverty was gloomy: "there are few who would deny the basic failure of existing approaches toward education and training for alleviating poverty" (Levin, 1977, p. 179). The general position was that schooling did not improve achievement, achievement did not improve economic circumstances.

What I am describing, of course, is the common wisdom of the mid-1970s. *Equality of Educational Opportunity* had appeared in 1966, at a time of great ferment in programs addressed to poverty, but its impact on the academic community was expanded by the reanalyses of its data in Mosteller and Moynihan (1972). Also, Jencks's *Inequality* appeared in 1972. While it would be unfair to summarize the message of these major works as "nothing worked," that is certainly how the message came across. And indeed sophisticated analyses of the effects of intelligence or educational skills or schooling, isolated from other factors, on inequality or earnings came closer to sending that message than any other. The narrower evaluations of specific programs available during the first decade after the War on Poverty confirmed the verdict: nothing that one did in education worked. If one wanted to redistribute income or reduce poverty, one should redistribute income directly.

Two highly qualified discussants did not contradict Levin's findings. Burton Weisbrod pondered the assertions in the 1964 *Economic Report of the President,* one of the opening guns in the War on Poverty, that "universal education has been the greatest single force contributing both to social mobility and to general economic growth" and that "if children of poor families can be given skills and motivation, they will not become poor adults." Can we still believe that, he asks. He does not dispute the findings on the weak relationship between learning, as measured, and earnings. But he is definitely uncomfortable and suggests a variety of hypotheses that might mitigate this disastrous lack of connection: Perhaps education does teach people more, but they do not use it to increase earnings; perhaps certain types of education do not work with the poor but others would; perhaps we may not be measuring the correct variables (years of schooling may not equal amount of education). "Our measures may be bad, our theories may be bad, our specification of relationships may be bad." Finally, he points out that even if education did not make a difference, the American people would prefer educating or training people out of poverty to simply redistributing income (Weisbrod, 1977, pp. 193–196).

The second discussant, Wilbur J. Cohen (1977), makes the point more resoundingly: "The evidence shown by these papers is that there is no concrete way to prove that money spent on these educational programs leads to specific IQ, cognitive, or affective improvement" (p. 191).

Does Education Matter?

The American people have not changed their minds since the mid-seventies—certainly not on direct income redistribution, if we take the results of the 1980 and 1984 elections seriously, and certainly not on the efficacy of education for some things, if we take their continued and extraordinary interest in educational reform seriously. But something else has happened: the findings of evaluations have begun to change. Evaluations are technically better and bigger. They are less ambitious in assuming any direct link between education and poverty. We find a more sober assessment of what is possible—and therefore less disappointment than in 1974—but, more important, some evidence as to real effects and changes, although limited and only doubtfully owing to direct policy efforts.

This chapter does not address the effects on poverty of any improvement in education or the effectiveness of work training to improve job prospects. As we know, the distribution of income in 1984 is as unequal as in 1974 or 1964 (in fact it may have increased somewhat in recent years—see Pechman and Mazur, 1984; Jencks, 1984; Moon and Sawhill, 1984). The poverty rate stopped declining in 1973 and has increased since (Gottschalk and Danziger, 1984, pp. 188–189). The modest signs of change in the educational achievement of the poor that I will discuss may or may not have effects on inequality or on poverty. Even if one accepts the model that achievement improves economic well-being, it is possible for a narrowing of differences in achievement between poor and nonpoor to have no influence on poverty or inequality: one can envisage a system of queuing for good positions such that each group maintains its previous position, with the educational achievement that once qualified a person for a certain kind of job now discounted and only used to admit one to a lesser paying job (Thurow, 1972; Boudon, 1974). (Indeed, it is possible to argue that even directly redistributing income to the poor, the alternative that Jencks and Levin once favored, does not improve their relative economic position—see Murray, 1984.)

Instead of trying to trace the economic effects of improvements in the educational achievement of the poor, I will simply take for granted the common wisdom that was so battered during the 1970s: improvements in educational achievement and in the amounts of schooling will help poor children. That is what their parents believe, what the neighbors believe, what the children believe, what Congress believes, and what beleaguered educationists believe. I am convinced of the merit of that position when I read that large numbers of unemployed high school graduates and dropouts cannot distinguish between doors marked "cafeteria," "library," "nurse," and "principal," when asked "which door would you go in for lunch?" It was on the basis of such questions, asked by the National Assessment of Educational Progress in 1978, that 13 percent of seventeen-year-olds—and 56 percent of blacks, 44 percent of Hispanics—were judged functionally illiterate (Hahn and Lerman, 1984, p. 7). I believe, along with all the nonauthorities mentioned above, that it would be desirable for them to be able to answer the question, and feel that is reason enough to explore educational effects.

Without trying to assert any specific connection with occupation and earnings, Christopher Jencks, most notorious among educationists for having argued that "nothing works," points out in a work subsequent to *Inequality* that "the best readily observable predictor of a young man's eventual status or earnings is the amount of schooling he has had. This could be because schooling is an arbitrary rationing device for allocating scarce jobs; or because schooling imparts skills, knowledge, or attitudes that employers value; or because schooling alters man's aspirations" (Jencks et al., 1979). That view has seemed good enough for most people and most policymakers. It is true that there is a "substantial reduction in the apparent effect of schooling when we control causally prior traits [which] suggests only part of the association between schooling and success can be due to what students actually learn from year to year in school" (Jencks et al., 1979, p. 230). Perhaps one reason for the common wisdom is that it has appeared to be easier to change schooling than the causally prior factors.

The perspective from 1984 is thus somewhat different from that of 1974. The difference is created not only by new studies and new results but also by a shift in opinion, in which the once simple and thus desirable approach to overcoming poverty by redistribution and transfer payments has run into great opposition, and even into some considerable argument as to its effectiveness in reaching simple redistribution objectives, owing to its effects on work effort and family composition. Thus, we see a return to the common man's view: education is the best single available route to overcoming poverty.

Evaluations That Show Gains

Stephen P. Mullin and Anita A. Summers (1983) conducted a major review of evaluations of the effectiveness of spending on compensatory education. Most of these evaluations are of programs established under Title I of the Elementary and Secondary Education Act of 1965, the largest effort to provide federal assistance for the education of poor children. The mechanism that was devised (and that has been constantly fiddled with) consisted of first selecting educational districts that had high proportions of children in poverty and then identifying within districts target schools on the basis of children who did poorly educationally. Just what was to be done for these children was left up to local school districts and schools. Targeted for sharp reductions by the first Reagan administration, it survived fairly well; its support in Congress and in the local school districts was strong, and in the 1985 budget the program continued to receive a fairly steady level of support (O'Neill and Simms, 1982, pp. 335–342; *Major Themes and Additional Budget Data, FY 1985,* 1984, p. 199). Retitled Chapter I of the Educational Consolidation and Improvement Act of 1981, it spent $3.376 billion in 1984; this figure is scheduled to rise to more than $4 billion by 1989. Fourteen thousand school districts get some funds and almost five million children receive services that provide supplements to their education at a cost of about $700 per child.

With what effects? In a field in which so many evaluations are conducted, to select a group for meta-evaluation is no simple task. In the Mullin-Summers review forty-two studies, some of which were themselves aggregations of a substantial group of primary evaluations, were selected. The major conclusions are as follows:

> The programs have a positive, though small, effect on the achievement of disadvantaged students.
>
> The results of most studies are overstated because of the upward biases inherent in several statistical procedures.
>
> The gains appear to be greater in earlier years, and the evidence is fairly strong that early gains are not sustained.
>
> No significant association exists between dollars spent and achievement gains.
>
> No approach or program characteristic was consistently found to be effective.   (Mullin and Summers, 1983, p. 339)

This cautious and hard-headed summary suggests that something can be done. It seems to me to understate the actual achievement. One notes that the more recent studies—and, one suspects, the better ones—seem to show results, while the earlier ones do not. The average year of publication of fifteen studies that show no result—evaluations were being conducted a few years before publication generally—was 1973; the average year for the thirty-two studies that showed some result was 1975. Some of these studies are substantially more comprehensive and better designed than others; two important evaluations of the effects of educational intervention are described below.

In a study entitled "Lasting Effects After Preschool," researchers selected subjects and control groups who had participated in various preschool intervention programs in the early 1960s and followed up these children in 1976 and 1977, ten years after the programs had been completed.

The investigators discovered some interesting differences between exper-
imentals and controls. There were no lasting differences of significance in
IQ or achievement test scores, but substantial differences were found in
the degree to which the children who had participated in special programs
were "retained in grade"—held back—or were assigned to special education classes. (One of these studies, conducted in Ypsilanti, has recently
received considerable publicity.) The median rate of failure (that is, failing
a grade or being assigned to special education) was 45 percent for the
controls, 24 percent for the experimental subjects (Darlington et al., 1980;
Lazar, 1981). The subjects were from low-income families and disadvantaged; 92 percent were black, and 40 percent had no father at home. The
methods used in the preschool programs varied substantially: traditional
nursery preschool, emphasis on language development, cognitive development and self-concept, work at home with mothers of children along
with center attendance by children, different kinds of Head Start curri-
cula—indeed the whole gamut of ideas of the 1960s. The period in which
children were involved ranged from one to five years. In contrast to the
view that nothing works, this research indicates that everything works, to
some extent, if one uses the measure of not failing a grade and not being
required to attend special classes.

Clearly this study will not satisfy purists. Each of the original enterprises
was based on the faith that something would help these children do better
educationally. One suspects that each involved the kinds of teachers and
child workers drawn to academic and experimental enterprises, whose
quality is probably higher than the quality of those who would be available
if an effort were made to make preschool opportunities universal. But a
number of features of this study warrant attention: one is that it seems to
coincide with the judgment of increasing numbers of Americans about
what is good for their children, as evidenced by the rising numbers of
children now attending preschool from middle-class families. (Enrollment
of three- and four-year-olds in preprimary education increased between
1968 and 1980 from 15.7 percent to 36.7 percent; enrollment of five-year-
olds is almost universal, with an increase from 66 percent in 1968 to 84.7
percent in 1980 [National Center for Education Statistics, 1982, p. 12].) It
coincides with the consistently positive evaluation of Head Start both by
those who participate in it and by policymakers, who refused to accept the
no-effects results of the early Westinghouse study (Skerry, 1983).

The programs examined in this study, despite their experimental character and the involvement of academic social scientists in designing and
evaluating them, seem very similar, in their variety and type, to the pre-

school programs that Head Start makes possible. Head Start remains the most popular of the efforts launched under the poverty program. It sustains more than any other a substantial degree of parent and local community involvement. Of the social programs that the Reagan administration hoped to cut, it was the least threatened and survived best. In 1984 430,000 children were included in it, and it spent almost $1 billion (U.S. Office of Management and Budget, 1984, p. 240).

I begin with this study, modest as its conclusions are, for a number of reasons. First, it permits us to begin at the beginning—the earliest time that we may expect public efforts in education and training to have an effect is in preschool education. It suggests both that something can be done, and, at a time when little more in the way of effort is being proposed, what more may be done: the expansion of preschool education in recent decades still leaves large numbers of children from poor families unaffected. It also demonstrates sharply the difference in evaluations by econometricians—who are not overly impressed—and members of the softer social sciences and educationists, who are.

There is also harder evidence relating to early school effects. The largest evaluation ever conducted of Title I, known as the Sustaining Effects Study of Compensatory and Elementary Education, was funded by the Department of Education under a mandate from Congress in 1975. It had many objectives, the most important being to conduct a three-year longitudinal study of children receiving Title I services and those who did not. As is inevitable with a massive study in real school districts and schools, the controls in this research do not satisfy strict methodological requirements but are poor children ("needy") not receiving Title I services. The process involved in the distribution of Title I funds to final recipients of services ensures that there will be many such. No less than 120,000 students were tested, in a representative sample of more than 300 schools, drawn from a survey of principals of more than 5,000 schools.

Such a comprehensive undertaking also made it possible to determine the effectiveness of complex formulas and regulations and intradistrict and intraschool decisions in targeting the Title I funds on poor and low-achieving children. The results display the difficulty of distributing federal funds to 14,000 districts, under the guidelines set by a Congress determined that each congressman's district not be short-changed: It appears that 60 percent of economically poor children, using the Orshansky Index, receive Title I services; 40 percent do not. In 1976–77, of 2,923,000 children receiving Title I services, a minority, 1,230,000, were poor. Among low-achieving students (one or more years behind grade level), only a minority—46 percent—received Title I services; 19 percent of children who were not low-achieving received them. The children receiving such services, compared to all poor or low-achieving, were disproportionately Hispanic and black, living in large cities and rural areas.

In such a large study even small effects are convincing: "Statistical analysis showed significant gains for Title I students, relative to needy students [who qualified for but did not receive Title I services], for the Mathematics section of the Comprehensive Tests of Basic Skills. This was true for grades 1 to 6. For the reading section . . . significant reading gains were found for grades 1 to 3, but not for grades 4, 5, and 6" (Carter, 1984, p. 8). The overall results for mathematics are demonstrated in Figure 7.1.

The largest relative gains are in first grade. But the rate of gain for title I students in all three grades is at least equal to that of regular students, while gains of those without Title I services are less. The other major finding is that students who receive these services for one year do better than those who receive them for all three years. The explanation is that the first were not so far behind, extra teaching was effective for them, and they thus "graduated" from Title I eligibility. Those who were far behind

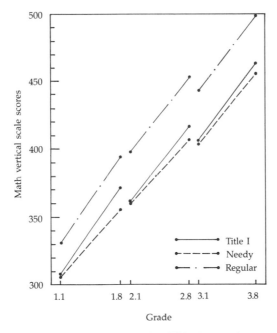

Figure 7.1. Math vertical scale scores for Title I, regular needy, and regular students in Grades 1, 2, and 3. Source: Carter (1984, p. 7).

to begin with, and who qualified for Title I each year, showed no improvement.

Gains are not lost over the summer, but by the time the students had reached junior high, no sustained or delayed effects were observed, and Title I students took more remedial courses in junior high than others. Fifty-five high-poverty schools were studied in depth to find "successful practices": the results are too complex for easy reproduction or dissemination. No programs that were particularly effective with disadvantaged students were found.

The study considers the problem with which we began: do schools have effects on the achievement of children independently of background? Path diagrams relate background, school characteristics, and initial achievement to a school composite measure and final achievement. Since students were followed for three years and cohorts were initially selected from grades one to four, it was possible to study the effects of these interactions among children of different ages. The results are sobering. The path coefficients between school learning experiences and final achievement decline from the first cohort to the fourth: "These figures are very important. They imply that in the beginning grades, School Learning Experiences are almost as effective as Initial Achievement and perhaps as important as Background. But as grade progresses, the influence of School Learning Experiences decreases . . . [and then by the sixth grade it exerts] little influence on Final Achievement" (Carter, 1984, p. 11).

These results are confirmed more generally by the surveys of the National Assessment of Educational Progress (NAEP). The NAEP tests large samples at ages nine, thirteen, and seventeen every few years. Progress has been noted in early grades, less progress or decline has been evident for junior high school and high school students. Black nine-year-olds and thirteen-year-olds showed a better rate of improvement than whites on reading performance between 1971 and 1980. Black seventeen-year-olds showed slight improvement, whites a decline. On mathematics, between 1973 and 1978 there was a decline for white nine-year-olds and an improvement for black; a more modest improvement was recorded for black thirteen-year-olds, and a white decline for the same age grade. For seventeen-year-olds, declines were recorded for both groups, somewhat less for blacks than for whites (National Center for Education Statistics, 1982, pp. 184, 188).

A full analysis for all areas in which tests have been given twice (writing, science, and social studies, in addition to reading and mathematics) for nine- and thirteen-year-olds shows a remarkably steady rate of reduction of the black-white disparity for all fields and for both cohorts, which means for all students regardless of year of birth back to 1956. But this same analysis does not include the seventeen-year-old results because, as it points out, by this year dropouts mean a much less complete coverage of the population. However, as we have seen, the data for seventeen-year-olds are not positive. Trying to reach the dropouts for testing will hardly improve matters. Indeed, they might make the seventeen-year-old showing even worse, for since the 1970s there has been a steady decline in the percentage of youth, particularly males, finishing high school (Burton and Jones, 1982, pp. 23, 27).

Which Target: Poor, Black, Minorities?

We have described improvements for low-income students in the lower grades that were related to Title I compensatory education expenditures, and improvements for black students in the lower grades that were not related to specific expenditures for compensatory education. But we know that Title I expenditures manage to reach, although somewhat erratically, substantial numbers of low-income and black students. The pattern of improvement in both the Sustaining Effects Study and the NAEP assessments is consistent: more in the earlier grades, extending into later elementary grades for mathematics but not for reading.

Some of the evidence above relates to groups defined by income, some to groups defined by minority, specifically black, status. I would argue that educational failure, insofar as it is a problem of public consciousness, of politics, of social policy, and of the attainment of social harmony, is predominantly a problem of failure with and among blacks. It is incorrect to say that it is an issue affecting minorities: some of the most rapidly growing minorities, such as Asians, show no general problem of educational (or for that matter, economic) backwardness, despite substantial differences from group to group and in income and other features within groups. Note, for example, dropout rates for 1980 high school sophomores by the spring of 1982: the white non-Hispanic rate was 12.2 percent, the black non-Hispanic rate was 17.0 percent, the Hispanic rate was 18 percent, the Asian rate was 3.0 percent (National Center for Education Statistics, 1984, Table 5.1). The low achievement of Hispanics and of the low-income group (other figures in the same source indicate that the dropout rate for the low-income group is 17.4 percent, the same as that for blacks) should be a matter of great concern. But as a *political* issue blacks dominate the discussion of poverty because they are by far the largest minority, because they are the most politically active and effective of the deprived minorities, and because no additional complications relating to language problems, recency of immigration, or legal status in this country can be brought forward to explain or excuse the situation. In this country low-income or working-class status as such has not been a force in the effort to improve education as a means of overcoming poverty: it is well known, for example, that low-income whites in urban high schools have been on the whole content with their achievement and their prospects and have not been active in urging greater expenditure on education. Indeed, when such expenditure has been conditioned on integration with blacks, it has often been opposed vigorously. It is not low-income or working-class groups as such that are the main force demanding educational improvement.

Despite the increase in numbers of Hispanics and in the degree to which they are becoming politically mobilized, I believe that the problem of poor education as a barrier to economic advancement influences them less than blacks—and thus affects public policy less than the parallel problem among blacks. One reason is that substantial numbers are recent immigrants and have language problems, and it is taken for granted among Americans in general—and perhaps among the group in question, if not its leaders— that these factors understandably take time to overcome and offer plausible explanations for educational backwardness. A second factor is that some Hispanic groups do not have special problems in education that mark them out as a group requiring long-term and serious concern. This is certainly true of Cubans and may well be true of recent immigrants from Central America and countries of South America, who may come as immigrants primarily to take advantage of educational opportunities in the United States or to enable their children to take advantage of such opportunities. Finally, the special problem we have noted for blacks, that of the increasing ineffectiveness of educational programs with advancing grade in school, may not be a problem of the same severity for Hispanics. Thus, in comparisons of reading performance, nine-year-old Hispanics made the same progress as blacks (and thus more than whites) between 1975 and 1980; thirteen-year-olds made somewhat less progress than blacks, but more than whites; and for the key seventeen-year-old group, the Hispanics showed progress, when the blacks showed none, and the whites retrogression (National Center for Education Statistics, 1983, p. 54). On mathematics test scores of high shool seniors related to number of years of mathematics taken, Hispanics regularly perform slightly better than blacks, far worse than whites (who perform worse than Asians). Where we have data for American Indians, we also find better performance than blacks, if lower than whites (National Center for Education Statistics, 1983, pp. 194, 196). This pattern was evident at the time of publication of *Equality of Educational Opportunity* and has not changed.

We have problems in education across the board, as the movement for educational reform indicates. And if we consider how education is related to income, we must be concerned with the fairly regular decline in achievement with declining income. The problem of black achievement in education is more than this, however. It is first, analytically, more than a matter of low income: controlling for poverty reduces the relationship between minority status and achievement, but it still remains substantial (Hoepfner, Zagorski, and Wellisch, 1977, pp. 97–104). We must be concerned as a matter of social policy and politics, because it is here that the demand for improvement is concentrated, where the moral and constitutional commitment is greatest, and where the results of failure are most serious.

Problems of Improving Achievement in Higher Grades

Can we understand the successes in improving educational achievement in the lower grades and does it lead to any hope for the upper grades or any course for policy? Compensatory education under Title I in the mid-1970s was a concentrated effort. Class sizes were small, averaging nine students in reading and twelve in mathematics, compared with twenty-seven in homeroom classes. Students spent an average of five-and-one-half hours a week in special instruction, which amounted to 29 percent of total instruction time for students in reading and 29 percent of total instruction time in mathematics. Forty-six percent of the students in Title I were minority, despite the difficulty under the formula, regulations, and local practices of ensuring that poor students and educationally disadvantaged students were the only ones to receive services. The services were almost entirely devoted to elementary school students—more than 99 percent—even though there was no such limitation in the legislation (National Institute of Education, 1977, pp. 1–3). Under these circumstances it would have been discouraging indeed if the result was no effect—or, as a more complex cost-benefit analysis might well conclude, insufficient effect.

The consensus on the educational changes of the 1970s and early 1980s offers modest encouragement for those who believe that something can be done, but it raises serious questions when we try to define what more can be done, particularly for those students whose preparation for the transition to work or college is being completed, where we have been so unsuccessful. First, according to a number of analysts the improvement at lower grade levels and the narrowing of the white-black gap seem to indicate that it is easier in principle to improve achievement when a minimal mechanical ability in reading and mathematics is being attempted (Brown, 1983, p. 40). Also, Jeanne Chall, one of our wisest scholars of reading, suggests that some of the improvement at the earliest ages can be attributed to a change in methods of instruction of reading in the early years and that the younger cohorts tested benefited from this change. But she also questions whether we can expect improvement among older cohorts who have received better early reading instruction. She notes that reading changes its character after fourth grade; it is there that the influence of differential family background becomes effective: "Pre-Grade 4 reading can be said to represent the oral tradition, in that text rarely goes beyond the language and knowledge that the reader already has through listening, direct experience, TV, and so forth. We can view reading beyond Grade 4 as comprising the literary tradition . . . the reading of texts that are ever more complicated, literary, abstract, and technical" (Chall, 1983, p. 6).

An education journalist, cautioning against overinterpreting the increased improvement on tests in large cities, in addition to pointing out problems associated with reuse of the same tests, quotes other authorities to the same effect: "Some education professors who have followed testing trends argue that the narrow focus on the basics in the elementary grades causes an increase in the scores at the lower grades but then results in a decrease in scores at the upper grades. 'To read for comprehension and inference, you need broad, general knowledge,' says Harry Singer, an education professor at the University of California at Riverside. 'Schools have narrowed their curriculum to fit the tests. But they have ignored the general knowledge that makes you a good reader' " (Savage, 1984).

There may be other explanations for the failure of improvement at the lower grades to be maintained in higher grades. Richard Murnane points out important changes in the quality of teachers, owing to the decline in numbers of children and thus reduced opportunity for jobs and to the decline in the real wages of teachers. One could expect this decline in quality to be greatest for math and science teachers, since those trained in these fields in college face a wide gap between what they can earn in teaching and in other occupations (Murnane, 1984). I think that we must combine this explanation with the insights of educators as to the difficulties involved in moving from respectable minimal achievement in the lower grades to an improvement at the high school level.

Desegregation, Bilingual Education, and Special Education

A full analysis of the relationship between low socioeconomic status and educational achievement must deal with three other policies of the 1970s, two highly controversial, the other less controversial but much more expensive. One was the substantial effort to bring black and white children into the same schools and classrooms. The educational effects of integration per se have been much disputed. Authorities agree that it has not hurt black achievement and has modestly increased skills by a fraction of one standard deviation, amounting to between two and six weeks of gain; the more optimistic (or liberal), looking at longer-range effects and particularly those on children all of whose education has taken place in integrated settings, argue for a more substantial effect, amounting to a third of a standard deviation, which is not insignificant (Cook et al., 1984, pp. 9, 85). Desegregation was accompanied by federal expenditures for low-income students, expenditures that were greatest in the South, where desegregation went furthest. Although the gap between the Southeast and the rest of the country in educational achievement closed considerably during the 1970s, we would be hard put to separate the effects of federal programs targeted on low-income groups from those of desegregation.

The educational achievement effects of another controversial program of the 1970s, bilingual education, have also been much disputed. There is not even the minimal agreement one finds for the effects of desegregation. Its costs were modest at the federal and state level; the current consensus, political if not educational, is that it should allow a greater measure of teaching in English for the children from homes in which a language other than English is spoken (*Education Week,* February 22, 1984).

The third major program with particular impact on children from low-income families and black children was special education. The cost of the great expansion of special education for the handicapped, driven by court decisions, state legislation, and federal legislation, has been enormous: an informed observer asserts that "an educated guess would be that it has been, after inflation, the most important factor in school budget increases between 1973 and 1980" (Pittenger and Kuriloff, 1982, p. 92). Only a fraction of this was covered by the federal budget, despite a federal commitment on the basis of the Education for All Handicapped Children Act to reimburse a substantial part of the costs to states. A 1982 appropriation of $874 million was 10 percent of state and local expenditures (Pittenger and Kuriloff, 1982). The federal appropriation of $1.3 billion in 1985 would cover only 8 percent of the additional educational costs of a handicapped child (U.S. Office of Management and Budget, 1984, p. 211). This implies additional local and state costs for special education of $16 billion. The mandates—legislative and judicial—that require it have been attacked strongly by Mayor Koch of New York City (Koch, 1980).

At the same time, the numbers of such children—the "learning re-tarded," the mentally retarded, and the emotionally disturbed—have grown rapidly to include in 1982–83 4.3 million children, or almost 10 percent of all. Any full analysis of the effects of governmental intervention on the education of the poor should consider this program. However, one cannot expect, despite great expenditures, substantial improvement by the tests of graduating from high school or getting a stable job. While I have seen no evaluations from this point of view, it is taken for granted that the best hope for most of these children is that they may eventually enter regular classes, generally at low achieving levels—in other words, become like the students whose achievement we have been discussing above.

Concentrating on Black Youth

It is convenient to distinguish between education and training for obvious reasons, such as the institutions that are at work in both and the ages of those affected. The fact is that the connection is unbreakably close: if more students managed to graduate from high school, if they did better at the skills taught in school, the problems of employment and jobs would be much reduced. I realize this may be disputed (the number of good jobs may not increase). But consider only the problem of the black minority: even if the number of good jobs did not increase, a group that numbers only 12 percent of high school youth could see its economic status im-prove considerably if it did better at these educational tasks, with only a moderate reduction for all the rest. Unemployment declines and wages rise as young people move to higher and higher steps in the educational ladder.

Our system of work training is in very large part devoted to making up for educational failure. Its chief clients are high-school dropouts. There has been, against all expectations, a steady drop overall in the numbers of youths who got high school diplomas over the past dozen years. Between 1972 and 1982 for the country as a whole the graduation rate, according to a set of figures compiled by the Secretary of Education, declined from 77.2 to 72.8 percent, a drop of 4.4 percentage points. The decline was sharpest in some big industrial states: California, 11 percent; New York, 8.4 percent; Michigan, 8.3 percent; Pennsylvania, 6.2 percent (*Education Week,* January 18, 1984). It appears that the decline has been concentrated among white males, with a small decline among white females, and an actual decrease of high-school dropouts among black males and females (Rumberger, 1983, p. 202).[1]

The most serious employment problems of youth are disproportionately concentrated among dropouts, and among them, minority youth. If young blacks are doing better at completing high school education, they are doing much worse at gaining employment. In the past two decades we have seen a disturbing increase in unemployment among minority youth. In 1954 the percentage of black and white teenagers unemployed was about the same. By 1964 the disparity had increased considerably, and by 1983 it had increased much more. These unemployment rates understate the situation, because they are based on numbers looking for work. When we consider the percentage of the population employed, the situation is even worse (see Table 7.1). In 1983, 31 percent of black eighteen- and nineteen-year-olds were employed, compared with 58 percent of white eighteen- and nineteen-year-olds. Disproportionate school attendance does not explain this: 32 percent of black and other youths aged sixteen to twenty-four are neither in school nor employed compared to 18 percent of whites. That discrimination exists cannot be denied; that it can explain such a change goes against all reason. A National Bureau of Economic Research Survey, concentrating on inner-city black males in Boston, Philadelphia, and Chi-

Table 7.1. Employment and unemployment rates, 1954–1983

	Black and other					White				
	1954	1964	1969	1977	1983	1954	1964	1969	1977	1983
Percentage of population employed										
Age 16–17	40.4	27.6	28.4	18.9	13.7	40.6	36.5	42.7	44.3	36.2
Age 18–19	66.5	51.8	51.1	36.9	31.3	61.3	57.7	61.8	65.2	58.0
Age 20–24	75.9	78.1	77.3	61.2	57.2	77.9	79.3	78.8	80.5	74.2
Percentage of labor force unemployed										
Age 16–17	13.4	25.9	24.7	38.7	47.3	14.0	16.1	12.5	17.6	22.6
Age 18–19	14.7	23.1	19.0	36.1	43.8	13.0	13.4	7.9	13.0	18.7
Age 20–24	16.9	12.6	8.4	21.7	27.2	9.8	7.4	4.6	9.3	13.8

Source: Freeman and Holzer (1985); data from U.S. Department of Labor, *Employment and Training Report of the President, 1982: Employment and Earnings* (Washington, D.C., 1984).

cago (Freeman and Holzer, 1985) throws some light on the situation. These youths are, of course, worse off than all black youth—fewer are in the labor force (80 against 90 percent), more are unemployed (41 to 33 percent), only 28 percent come from a household with a man in it as against 51 percent for all black youth, 45 percent are from families on welfare, and 32 percent live in public housing.

Many explanations of the decline in black youth employment do not hold up in their analysis. It would be hard to maintain that discrimination has gotten worse. Unemployment rates for black youth have increased both in good times and bad, so an overall poorer economic performance does not explain it. Nor is the matter explained by the entry of more women and immigrants into the labor force or, surprisingly, by inaccessibility of jobs in the suburbs—big city areas with easy access to suburban jobs do as badly as areas without suburban opportunities. On the "supply side," one of the most striking helpful factors in black youth employment is attending church; staying in school longer and getting better grades also help. One of the most harmful factors is involvement with the welfare system: "Youths from welfare homes, with the same family income and the same other attributes as from non-welfare homes, do much worse in the job market. Youth living in public housing also do less well than youths living in private housing" (Freeman and Holzer, 1985).

Another analysis of these data reports an even more surprising finding. There should be an incentive for young persons on welfare to work and attend school since benefits are not reduced for the earnings of dependent children who are students and not holding a full-time job. Further, owing to variations in the definition of a household, in many states until 1981 eighteen- to twenty-one-year-old children were not included in estimating household benefits, and their earned income was therefore not deducted from the welfare grant. Despite this apparent incentive, fewer youth in welfare families worked (Lerman, 1984).

It is also worth noting how the transition from school to work is managed by young minority females. The situation here is particularly disastrous because so many bear children at a young age. A study of reasons why high-school dropouts, aged fourteen to twenty-one, left school shows that 41 percent of black females, 15 percent of Hispanics, and 14 percent of whites left because of pregnancy (Rumberger, 1983, p. 201). Substantial efforts are now made to keep pregnant girls in school, mainstreamed, or in special classes adapted to their situation, to reduce the number of dropouts.

The Training Record

After dropping out, one must count on work-training programs, and major efforts of the post-1964 policy explosion were directed to creating new types of work training and education outside formal school settings.[2] Since, it was argued, the school did not seem to know what to do with sixteen- and seventeen-year-olds who were not interested in the standard curriculum, something new was needed. The policy thrust of the past twenty years seems to have been to accept the fact that school will fail to prepare many for work and to create new institutions for the purpose. Unfortunately, we have not made up for the failure in schooling by developing successful work programs, although we have certainly tried.

When it comes to what works in work training for the inadequately educated, the despairing, dulled, drugged, or vicious, or those frustrated by their own absent but crucially necessary minimal skills, the situation is far more complicated than that described for the education of the children of the poor and of minorities in the lower grades. In the latter case the objective is simpler. Despite the substantial differences among schools, programs, teachers, there is surprising uniformity in American schooling. If we say that this works but that does not, we have a sense of what is happening in schools and what can continue to happen if we do the right thing: spend more time on reading or arithmetic, use a phonic instead of a whole-word approach, or whatever. Just as the difficulty of achieving better results increases in high school with a more differentiated curriculum and the need to develop more abstract skills and higher processes of reasoning and inference, so we find an additional quantum jump of complexity associated with programs designed for the high-school dropout or the high-school graduate of minimal skills. The objective is more difficult and ambitious: not only to improve very often minimal academic skills (reading, calculating) but also to teach work skills related to a specific occupation and social forms related to work (dress, appearance, speech, demeanor). The approaches to achieving this goal are also far more varied than in the elementary and secondary school: counseling; classroom training, part-time or full-time, long term or short; training on the job; residential training; various mixes of all the above; with stipends for support or without; with different kinds of reward and punishment mechanisms or none at all.

It is understandable that it should be very hard to reach any conclusions. We could say nothing in 1974, and we can say little more in 1984 despite a great expansion in the scale and sophistication of evaluations of work-training programs. The most extensive effort to evaluate the evaluations by an advocate of the programs who is also a social scientist and an administrator communicates a sense of the difficulty of the task, and the near-despair that must overwhelm the person who tries to make sense of what has been done. The mere roll call of the initials of different programs, each of which has had its own evaluations in number, reduces one to dumbness: ARA, MDTA, JC, NYC, WIN, JOBS, CEP, PEP, CETA, PSE, STIP, HIRE, YEDPA, PSIP, PICs, YCCIP, YIEPP. They all stand for something that is substantial and of some consequence or that once excited enthusiasm, but very little emerges that can be asserted with confidence.

Robert Taggart comes to the following conclusions after reviewing the evaluations:

> Income maintenance should be deemphasized. Allowances and wages in training and subsidized jobs are in some cases more than is justified by need or productivity; they attract and hold some participants who have limited interest in improving employability. Reduced allowances and wages would encourage transition into subsidized employment and would leave room for incentives to reward participant performance.
>
> More intensive investments are needed. A second tier should be built on the short-duration training and remediation efforts which now predominate . . . Sorting the performers from nonperformers among participants should be an objective rather than a taboo, as long as remediation and training is focussed on those who need it most. The "winners" among the disadvantaged can be rewarded without punishing the "losers" . . . Training for the disadvantaged should utilize mainstream institutions wherever possible, providing participants with greater choice and applying stricter standards of individual performance.   (Taggart, 1981, p. ix)

To sum up: We do not pay youth to go to school, and we should not pay them to attend the training and remediation programs that are required by their failure. Programs that do not work should be dropped. Some intensive programs have good records (Job Corps), others poor (Supported Work), as applied to youths. Yet even a "good" record is not very good. The Job Corps deals with the hardest of the hard core. The 1980 cost per service (cost for a person for one year) was $13,193, as against $8,046 for classroom training and $6,088 for on-the-job training. Its cost-benefit ratios are best, but would seem very modest to those not yet battered by the sad story of remedial attempts with the hard core. Nineteen seventy-seven "corps members were employed two-fifths of the weeks in the first post-termination year. Just half were employed 18 months after termination and only a fourth were employed full-time . . . Because less than a third of entrants completed training, while only a proportion of these found employment and a small proportion found training-related jobs, just one in seven entrants completed a full vocational program and was subsequently employed in a training-related job" (Taggart, 1981, p. 28).

One important reason why the Job Corps comes out well in cost-benefit analyses despite this record is primarily because of reduced criminal activity and therefore reduced criminal justice system costs, personal injury costs, and stolen property costs. This is not insignificant, but even so the taxpayer gets back, in one analysis, 96 cents for every dollar. The corpsmember does much better, $1.45 for every dollar of his costs (Taggart, 1981, p. 60). Though one wonders what that means.

One of Taggart's conclusions reflects his belief that training programs should be more like school, "failing" some students and "promoting" others. While he would have services for all, there should be some mechanism in these programs for rewarding success. He favors the model and the reality of schooling as the means by which to achieve the objectives of work training. Educationists will be pleased by the positive assessment of some of the aspects of schooling by an analyst who has been immersed in the hard-headed and hard-objectives world of work training. Yet it is startling to discover that this massive evaluation of work-training programs has identified something in school—which failed these youths to begin with—that the enormous and in large measure *ad hoc* and free-standing work-training system we have created might emulate.

It was therefore not surprising that during the Carter administration one of the largest experimental efforts ever undertaken in work-training tried to use the provision of guaranteed work as an incentive to maintain attendance in school. A high-school diploma, for whatever reason, does more to help in getting and keeping a job than expensive and carefully designed work-training programs. The Youth Incentive Entitlement Pilot Projects offered "16- to 19-year-old youths from low-income or welfare households who had not yet graduated from high school . . . minimum-wage jobs, part-time during the school year and full-time during the summer, on the condition that they remain in high school (or its equivalent) and meet academic and job standards" (Gueron, 1984, p. 1).

The cost of keeping a participant in the program for one year averaged $4,382. On the basis of the response, a national program would bring in almost a million youths at a cost of $1,501 million in 1980. And what would one get for it? One would eliminate the gap between black and white youth unemployment, while the program was in effect, demonstrating that black youth will work at the minimum rate. But during the brief postprogram period this advantage was greatly reduced. There was a large percentage increase in earnings among youth participating, compared to those in the control cities. This advantage declined but was still substantial in the year after the program. As for the school, not many dropouts were brought back into school or kept there by the job offer. There was no effect in reducing dropouts or increasing school attendance or graduation rates. By the time the participants were nineteen, in the fall of 1981, only half had graduated and almost two-fifths were dropouts.

There have been more optimistic evaluations of this program than mine, based on the greater earnings of the program participants. But one does not have the impression much had been done to make a long-range difference.

Modest Findings, Modest Proposals

One does not expect that another review of what we have learned from schooling and training as means to overcome the disadvantages of poor and black youth would give us the answer or the answers. We know a bit more, far from enough. We know enough, I would hazard, to suggest that greater resources would be most usefully spent in preschools and elementary schools. There we have evidence that improvement is possible. That improvement, if broadened and sustained, suggests that more poor minority youth will be able to get through high school. It is likely that it is the still inadequate educational base laid down in elementary school that makes so many so unreachable by so much of the high school curriculum, leading to high dropout rates and poor job prospects. (Of course, it may be the curriculum itself, but there are limits to which that can be modified without making it a travesty, signalling to employers that a high school diploma does not mean what they think it means.) If this is the case, much in the present spate of reform, which emphasizes the use of competency tests for exit from high school and stiffer academic requirements in high school and for college entry, is, I believe, irrelevant to the problems of poor and black youth. Not being able to meet present standards, they certainly cannot be expected to reach higher ones (Glazer, 1984a). It is not easy to deal with this educational failure by means of remedial work-training and education programs specially designed for the failures: few manage to get much from these programs, as the Job Corps experience demonstrates. We cannot induce these children to stay in school with a job offer, and it is doubtful that the job experience combined with the requirement to stay in school will have more than very minimal effects in improving their prospects. There is sufficient evidence that the welfare culture itself (or, if one is to be noninvidious, the experience of living in poor female-headed families on income transfers and in concentrations of such people) serves independently to damage the children in these settings. This much we have learned. It is a sober and minimal level from which to continue.

Comment by Christopher Jencks

Nathan Glazer is certainly right that evaluations of compensatory education reach more positive conclusions today than they did a decade ago. To some extent this change in tone reflects a change in investigators' judgments about compensatory programs' actual effects on students' test performance and noncognitive characteristics. In large part, however, the change in tone reflects a revolution of declining expectations about what compensatory programs should be expected to accomplish.

The change in our empirical assessment of compensatory education is clearly a step in the right direction. A decade ago most evaluators believed that compensatory education had no effect on academic achievement, even in the short run. They believed this because most evaluations of compensatory education set out to test the "null hypothesis" that the programs did not work. This meant that even when the programs had positive short-term effects, as they usually did, investigators came to negative conclusions if there was more than one chance in twenty that the positive effect could have been due to random sampling error. Early in 1974, for example, Urie Bronfenbrenner wrote a paper about the effect of preschool programs on cognitive development for the Office of Child Development. Bronfenbrenner could only locate five preschool programs that had had a pretest, a control group, and a follow-up test at least two years after the end of the program. All five studies were very small: the mean number of children in the "experimental" groups was 18. Largely as a result, the difference between the experimental and the control group was statistically insignificant by conventional standards in all five studies. Bronfenbrenner therefore concluded that the programs were ineffective.

But while the difference between the experimental and the control group was insignificant in Bronfenbrenner's five studies, it was also positive in all five studies. Furthermore, if we calculate the difference between the experimental and the control group in each study and then average across all five studies, the preschoolers typically score half a standard deviation above the controls. This difference is highly significant for the pooled sample ($p < .001$).

The implication is clear. By looking only at controlled studies with long-term follow-ups, evaluators like Bronfenbrenner inevitably restricted themselves to small samples. If they then emphasized statistical significance—which is, after all, simply a measure of uncertainty—and calculated it on a study-by-study basis, they usually reached negative conclusions, even if the program was quite effective. To avoid this recurrent bias, analysts had to abandon the crutch of a null hypothesis, look at the average effect of the program in question, and then live with uncertainty about the "true" effect.

Averaging effects from many studies—commonly known as meta-analysis—became increasingly common in the late 1970s. This strategy allowed investigators to pool an immense amount of data on compensatory education. In many cases the samples became so large that virtually all effects were statistically significant. This encouraged investigators to emphasize the absolute magnitude of program effects rather than statistical significance and made it obvious that the typical compensatory program had some positive impact in the short run, even though the impact was not always reliably different from zero in particular studies. The upbeat mood of today's scholarly literature owes a lot to this development.

The use of more diverse dependent variables has also contributed to the change in our view of compensatory education. Although graduates of Bronfenbrenner's five experimental preschool programs had substantially higher IQ scores than the control groups two years after preschool ended, for example, subsequent work showed that the difference declined sharply by the end of elementary school (Lazar and Darlington, 1978). A decade ago this would have led most investigators to conclude that preschools had no long-term effect. Yet today these same preschool programs are widely viewed as a success. The reason is that their graduates did better on a variety of *other* long-term outcome measures, such as being promoted to the next grade rather than being held back, and not being placed in special education classes (Darlington et al., 1980).

While both meta-analysis and noncognitive outcome measures have helped us develop a more realistic empirical understanding of what compensatory programs actually accomplish, they do not suffice to account for the upbeat mood of Glazer's paper. To understand the change in mood we must also consider the revolution of declining expectations. This revolution has taken three forms: (1) abandonment of the idea that compensatory programs can reasonably be expected to raise poor children's achievement to middle-class levels, (2) shorter time horizons for evaluating test score gains, and (3) reduced attention to the question of whether test score gains translate into improved adult life chances.

The most important reason why people were gloomy about compensatory education a decade ago was that they were asking whether it could *eliminate* disparities in academic achievement between poor and middle-class children. It could not. Today we are content if it can *reduce* the gap. Since any compensatory program that does more good than harm will reduce the gap if it is directed at students with low scores, it has become much easier to declare such programs "successful."

A second reason why people were gloomy about compensatory education a decade ago was that even when these programs produced statistically significant gains in the short run, the gains seemed to "wash out" if students were followed up a year or two later. This pattern still holds, but we no longer find it as disturbing as we did a decade ago. Thus, while Glazer quotes Mullin and Summers's (1983) conclusion that "the evidence is fairly strong that early gains are not sustained," he still finds grounds of optimism in their report. To me, this finding is still as depressing as it was a few years ago.

Why aren't the gains from compensatory education sustained? An analogy from higher education may help answer the question. For many years conventional wisdom among Ivy League admissions officers has held that while private school applicants do better as freshmen than public school applicants with similar SAT scores, the difference disappears by the time the two groups reach their senior year. Private schools evidently teach a variety of skills that are extremely helpful in college, but public school students can and do acquire these skills once they reach college. As a result, public and private school students eventually perform at levels dictated by their native ability, their motivation, and the quality of their college experience, not by their secondary school experience. Among students who attend Ivy League colleges, in other words, private schools merely *accelerate* the mastery of certain skills rather than raising students' *ultimate* level of mastery. Needless to say, the story might be quite different if we looked at students who did not attend college.

Compensatory programs at the elementary level seem to work in much the same way. They accelerate the rate at which students master certain skills, but they do not increase ultimate levels of competence. The reason,

I suspect, is that the elementary school curriculum contains a lot of repetition and review. As a result, students have many opportunities to acquire the skills these schools teach. Consider multiplication. It is easy to accelerate the rate at which children learn to multiply, simply by devoting more time to it earlier in school. But students who do not learn it one year have a chance to learn it the next year and again the following year. Because all children have so many chances to master multiplication, no one-year program is likely to make a permanent difference.

None of this means poor children cannot learn more than they now learn. As Glazer emphasizes, they certainly learn more in elementary school today than they did in the 1960s. The National Assessment of Educational Progress shows that reading and arithmetic skills have been rising among nine-year-olds and that they have risen more among black nine-year-olds than among whites. But there is no evidence that this improvement is traceable to Title I.

Such evidence as we have suggests that school desegregation has reduced the black-white gap more than Title I. As Glazer notes, studies of school desegregation generally show that it has quite small effects on black students' achievement. But these studies usually cover only the *first year* of desegregation. If the first-year effects reported by Cook et al. (1984)—a gain of about 0.1 standard deviation in the typical study—were to recur year after year, their cumulative effect would be to eliminate the black-white gap entirely. We know from various "natural experiments" that this does not happen (Jencks et al., 1972; Jencks and Brown, 1975). But the evidence from these natural experiments suggests a cumulative gain of perhaps 0.2 standard deviations for black students. This is, I believe, more than Head Start or Title I can claim.

The third—and most disturbing—element in the revolution of declining expectations is that we no longer worry much about whether compensatory programs will get children out of poverty. Glazer explicitly sets aside the question of whether cognitive gains can appreciably reduce poverty in the next generation. He seems to argue that since the public still believes that educational success is the key to worldly success, we can afford to ignore social science research showing that poor test performance actually plays a fairly modest role in the transmission of poverty from one generation to the next. I find this position unsettling. When Mary Corcoran and I (1979) analyzed a number of different surveys, we found that when children from differing socioeconomic backgrounds did equally well on standardized tests, this only reduced the difference in their adult earnings by a third. Two-thirds of the impact of socioeconomic background thus operates in ways that are independent of school achievement. This tells me that we ought to be devoting at least as much effort to identifying and eliminating these noncognitive sources of unequal opportunity as to remedial reading and math programs. It also tells me that while the public may find it reassuring to believe that poor children will enjoy the same economic prospects as everyone else if only they learn to read and do their sums, this reassuring belief is wrong.

The fact that raising poor students' reading and math scores will not suffice to equalize economic opportunity does not, of course, imply that we should abandon such efforts. There are plenty of noneconomic justifications for such efforts—*if* they work. Those who do well in school are less likely to get in trouble with the law, for example, and are probably more likely to engage in effective contraception. If we cumulate all such benefits, the value of an 0.1 standard deviation test score gain is obviously greater than if we look at earnings alone. Cognitive skills also bring intrinsic rewards even when they do not keep you out of poverty. AFDC recipients who can read a magazine while they wait in line at the welfare office presumably have a better time than those who can only stare at the wall. But these arguments are only relevant to the debate about compensatory education if it has long-term as well as short-term effects on cognitive skills. Glazer cites no evidence that compensatory education has long-term effects on students' cognitive skills, and I know of none.

One of Glazer's major empirical findings is that programs for young children produce larger cognitive gains than programs for older children. There is no question that if you measure the impact of interventions using "standardized" scores, as meta-analysts these days almost always do, interventions aimed at young children usually have larger effects than interventions aimed at older children. But standardized scores are an elastic yardstick. If students' initial scores are normally distributed, a program that moves the typical student from the 50th to the 84th percentile of the initial distribution will produce a one standard deviation gain, regardless of how variable or uniform the initial distribution is. If students at the 50th and 84th percentiles are very similar in absolute terms, a one standard deviation gain is of little absolute importance. If you give entering first graders a multiplication test, for example, very few of them can do any of the items correctly. This means that you do not have to teach much multiplication to produce a one standard deviation gain. It also means that if Mrs. Smith teaches multiplication twice as effectively as Mrs. Jones, the difference between Mrs. Smith's students and Mrs. Jones's students may also be a full standard deviation. It does not necessarily follow that Mrs. Smith's students really know much more than Mrs. Jones's.

Sixth graders' skills are far more variable. Some sixth graders can multiply as well as adults. Others cannot multiply at all. One standard deviation now represents a huge difference in proficiency. Using this metric, therefore, it is almost impossible to produce a one standard deviation gain in a single year. As a result, even if Mrs. Smith still teaches twice as much multiplication as Mrs. Jones in sixth grade, her students' advantage now looks smaller on a standardized scale. Unfortunately, we cannot say whether their advantage is smaller in an absolute sense unless we devise a way of comparing what is typically learned in first grade to what is typically learned in sixth grade. This might be possible in principle, but existing tests do not allow us to do it.

Glazer also concludes that future interventions should focus on the elementary school years. Again he may be right, but the evidence he cites does not convince me. Not only does this evidence involve comparisons between standardized scores for children of different ages, it also involves short-term rather than long-term effects. We know that the short-run gains attributable to compensatory programs—and, indeed, to almost all interventions—tend to diminish over time. We do not know whether this tendency is as strong at the secondary level as at the elementary level, but there are plausible reasons for supposing that it might not be. I argued earlier that the initial advantage conferred by compensatory education at the elementary level tended to fade over time because the control group in elementary school usually had additional chances in later years to learn whatever the experimental group had learned in its compensatory program. This is less likely to be true in secondary school. If you cannot read by age fifteen, a remedial program designed to teach you is likely to be your last chance. If you do not learn to read at fifteen, you probably never will. Thus, it might well turn out that compensatory programs could have larger permanent effects at the secondary than at the elementary level.

As these observations suggest, the gaps in our understanding of the effects of compensatory education remain enormous. We now know that compensatory programs have some positive short-term effect on preschool and elementary school test performance. We do not know to what extent these effects persist over the long run, but the bulk of the evidence suggests that students who do not get compensatory education in any given year eventually catch up with those who do. We do not know how to compare the short-term benefits of compensatory programs for children of varying ages. We do know how to compare the long-term effects of such programs, namely by looking at adult test performance, but we have no data of this kind. We know that preschools can have important long-term effects on noncognitive success, but we do not know how large or consistent these effects are, or whether they also occur in elementary and secondary school compensatory programs.

All in all, the cumulative record of twenty years of research on these issues is not terribly impressive, primarily because federal agencies have seldom sponsored the kinds of long-term studies we would need to answer such questions. But progress has also been retarded by social scientists' obsession with statistical significance, by our failure to use curriculum-specific tests to measure the impact of curricular change, and by our naiveté in interpreting the results of the standardized tests that we do use. We have made some progress on all these fronts in recent years, but we have a long way to go.

8   Macroeconomics, Income Distribution, and Poverty

Rebecca M. Blank
Alan S. Blinder

THE PLIGHT OF THE POOR is often invoked in discussions of national economic policy. Those who take a hard line against inflation often justify their position by claiming that inflation, "the cruelest tax," victimizes the poor more than others. Similarly, those more concerned about unemployment assert that the poor bear a disproportionate share of the burden when high unemployment is used to wring inflation out of the system. It is unlikely that both groups can be right.

In this chapter we summarize the existing evidence on how macroeconomic activity affects the poor, add new evidence where appropriate, and examine some of the channels through which these effects work.[1]

The Business Cycle and Distribution of Income

MACROECONOMIC ACTIVITY AND POVERTY

During the 1960s the percentage of people living below the poverty line fell rapidly and continuously—from about 22 percent in 1961 to about 12 percent in 1969. Poverty declined particularly rapidly during the boom years of 1965, 1966, and 1968 (which, of course, were also the years in which the Great Society programs were getting started) and then rose slightly during the mild recession of 1969–70. When expansion resumed in 1971–73, the poverty rate ratcheted down another notch—to 11.1 percent, its historic low; the deep recession of 1973–75 pushed poverty back to 12.3 percent; the 1976–78 expansion trimmed the poverty rate once again; and back-to-back recessions in 1980 and 1981–82 raised poverty from 11.7 percent in 1979 to 15 percent in 1982. In 1982 and 1983 real

GNP fell and then rose, the average unemployment rate was constant, and poverty crept upward to 15.2 percent.

All in all, there seems to be a consistently negative correlation between real economic growth and poverty. In fact, Murray (1982) has noted that between 1950 and 1980 the simple correlation between changes in real GNP per household and changes in the percentage of the population below the poverty line was $-.69$. Events since 1980 seem to reinforce this correlation.

However, the poor are not a homogeneous population. Poverty rates differ significantly by race, sex, and age of household head. Focusing on the change in aggregate poverty numbers over the business cycle may disguise quite different cyclical experiences among various demographic subgroups.

Numerous researchers have attempted to measure the extent to which poverty rates among different groups respond to changes in overall economic growth, including Anderson (1964); Perl and Solnick (1971); Thornton, Agnello, and Link (1978, 1980); and Hirsch (1980). Most utilized simple regressions of changes in annual poverty rates by demographic group against changes in GNP, in government transfers, and in a few additional cyclical indicators (such as unemployment rates). These articles uniformly show that certain households—in particular, those headed by elderly people and by women—seem largely unaffected by changes in economic growth. The results for other types of households appear quite sensitive to the equation specification. Only among white male-headed households do clear effects emerge.

However, these studies provide only a very aggregate answer to the question "How do business fluctuations affect poverty?" Economic growth raises mean income and decreases the percentage of people below any absolute poverty line.[2] But changes in the *shape* of the distribution may also influence poverty in ways that mean income does not capture. For instance, if the distribution of income spreads out during boom times, incomes of as many or more people may be below the poverty line even though the poverty line falls to a lower point in the distribution.

Recognizing these complications, Gottschalk and Danziger (1984) implemented a more sophisticated approach, relating poverty to general macroeconomic conditions, with findings that are potentially disturbing for proponents of "trickle down." They found that changes in transfers had consistently negative effects on the poverty rate since 1967 (although this effect diminished in recent years). As expected, increases in mean income on average reduced poverty—an effect that reversed in years when real incomes declined. But they found that changes in the *shape* of the distribution largely served to *increase* poverty. Only the growth of the mean of the distribution, combined with the growth of transfer programs aimed at lower-income households, offset this change in shape and led to generally lower poverty rates.

MACROECONOMIC ACTIVITY AND INCOME DISTRIBUTION

It is obvious that any official poverty line is arbitrary—little economic difference exists between a family with an annual income $100 below the poverty line and another with income $100 above.

Part of the negative relationship between GNP growth and poverty follows arithmetically from the way in which the official poverty line is defined. The poverty line was first set in 1965, based on a calculation of need levels among various types of families. Since that time it has been automatically increased each year by the percent change in the Consumer Price Index. If the distribution of income remains unchanged, the percentage of the population below the poverty line will remain constant from year to year. However, if real incomes grow, shifting the distribution of income to the right without changing its shape, the percentage below the poverty line must shrink. Because of increases in real incomes, the poverty line fell from 50 percent to 33 percent of mean income from 1959 to 1973. However, the slowdown in economic growth in the past decade has kept the line at about 34 percent of mean income since 1973.

Because an absolute poverty line produces a falling poverty count in times of economic growth, many social scientists eschew the narrow focus on poverty and look more broadly at the problem of income inequality. Even if one is interested only in poverty, a case can be made that the share of income received by the lowest 20 percent of families (or some similar measure) is at least as good an index of progress against poverty as the official poverty rate (Blinder, 1980, pp. 455–456). For this reason we shall review the evidence on the effects of macroeconomic activity on income inequality rather than on poverty rates.

A series of articles published in the late 1960s and early 1970s examined the way in which the U.S. income distribution changed over the business cycle (Metcalf, 1969; Thurow, 1970; Mirer, 1973a, 1973b; Beach, 1977). Though their methods differed significantly, the authors reached similar qualitative conclusions: the income distribution widens when the economy shrinks and narrows when it expands, implying that the poor gain relative to the rich during cyclical upturns. Blank (1985) has recently shown that large differences exist in the cyclicality of different components of household income among various income and demographic groups. The primary channels by which low-income households "catch up" in periods of growth are very large procyclical movements in the labor income of the household head: real wages, hours of work, and labor force participation all increase among the poor during an expansion. The effect is so strong that it overcomes the fact that labor income is a relatively low percentage of total income (35.3 percent) for poor households.[3]

The general conclusion of these studies is that the bottom part of the income distribution loses in relative terms in a recession and gains in an upswing. We shall investigate the relationship between the macroeconomy and the income distribution in more detail by examining the various economic changes that take place during business cycles. We focus on fluctuations rather than on general economic growth for two simple reasons. First, while a permanent increase in the growth rate of per capita income would be welcome and would probably do wonderful things for the poor, no one has any idea how to achieve it. In contrast, at least some economists (including us) believe that policy has substantial influence over the business cycle. Second, since the long-run growth rate of per capita GNP has been remarkably constant in the United States for as long as we have data, statistical analysis can tell us little about the distributional effects of a permanent acceleration of growth. On the other hand, cyclical variations in the growth rate are frequent and sizable.

Inflation, Unemployment, and the Poor

WHICH IS THE CRUELEST TAX?

The postwar history of U.S. economic fluctuations can be summarized by looking at the behavior of two variables: the rates of inflation and of unemployment. Despite many denunciations of inflation as the cruelest tax, there is little doubt that unemployment, not inflation, actually bears most heavily on the poor.

We have already seen that the poverty rate increases in economic downturns, implying a strong positive relationship between unemployment and poverty. This correlation was predictable, since when times are bad, less productive workers with lower skills are likely to be laid off first.

But what about inflation and poverty? The poverty rate fell during the low-inflation years 1961–1965, but fell even faster from 1965 to 1969 as inflation accelerated. Inflation declined from 1970 to 1972 (assisted by price controls), and poverty fell again. But poverty also declined as infla- tion accelerated in 1973. The two most inflationary years of the postwar record were 1974 and 1979; in each of these years the poverty rate crept upward. But during the disinflation of the 1980s poverty increased even faster.

Despite frequent assertions that inflation weighs most heavily on the poor, no correlation has been demonstrated between poverty and inflation. Of course, the issue cannot be settled by looking at one variable at a time. Unemployment and inflation are correlated in the data, there are time lags, and inflation displays a strong upward trend in the postwar United States. It is possible that, once time and unemployment are statistically controlled for in a multiple regression, a meaningful relationship between inflation and poverty would emerge. But the statistical analysis described below confirms the apparent simple relationships: unemployment, not inflation, has the strongest bearing on the well-being of the poor.

NEW ECONOMETRIC EVIDENCE

Blinder and Esaki (1978) investigated the relative effects of inflation versus unemployment on the income distribution. Using annual data, they esti- mated the equation

$$S_{it} = a + bt + cU_t + dI_t + e_t, \tag{8.1}$$

where t is time, S_{it} is the income share of the ith quintile at time t, U_t is the national civilian unemployment rate, and I_t is the inflation rate (based on the GNP deflator).

They found that the lower quintiles systematically lose from unemploy- ment and gain (relatively) from inflation. Specifically, a 1-percentage-point rise in unemployment decreased the income share of the lowest quintile by .13 of a percentage point while a 1-point rise in the inflation rate in- creased their share by a scant .03 of a percentage point. Other quintiles followed a fairly consistent pattern: Unemployment is a regressive tax; inflation is a progressive one. More specifically, high unemployment re- distributes income away from the bottom two quintiles and toward the top quintile. Inflation redistributes away from the fourth quintile toward the lowest quintile.

These findings are broadly consistent with the literature reviewed in the preceding section, which showed that income distribution widened in economic downturns. Recent updating of the results for the bottom quintile by Asher (1983) shows similar effects.

We estimated a new set of regressions, differing in four respects from equation (8.1):

1. We adopted a quadratic specification on unemployment, including both U and U^2.[4]

2. The economic literature on the redistributive effects of inflation points to unanticipated inflation as the primary (perhaps the only) source of income redistribution. We separated inflation into anticipated and unanticipated components, using a simple autoregressive model to generate expectations.[5]

3. We used the prime-age male unemployment rate, U^*, rather than the overall unemployment rate, U, as a better indicator of labor market conditions since it is insensitive to the substantial demographic changes that have taken place over this period.

4. To allow income shares to adjust to macroeconomic conditions with a lag, we adopted a simple geometric distributed lag model of the form

$$S_{it} - S_{it-1} = (1 - g)(S^*_{it} - S_{it-1}), \tag{8.2}$$

where S^* is the equilibrium share of group i. This required that we include a lagged dependent variable in the regression.

After all these alterations, our final specification is:

$$S_{it} = a + bt + c_1U^*_t + c_2U^{*2}_t + d_1I^a_t + d_2I^u_t + gS_{it-1} + e_t, \tag{8.3}$$

where I^a is anticipated and I^u is unanticipated inflation. Estimation was by ordinary least squares and the sample period was 1948–1983.[6] Results are presented at the top of Table 8.1. From the estimated coefficients, we derived the equilibrium effects of inflation and unemployment (evaluated at the sample mean) on income shares; these are also shown in Table 8.1.

The results are about as expected. High unemployment has significant and systematically regressive effects on the distribution of income: the poorer the group, the worse it fares when unemployment rises. In only one of the five quintiles does unemployment show a significant nonlinear effect. In general, even with an additional nine years of data and a revised specification, our estimates are strikingly similar to those of Blinder and Esaki.

By contrast, few significant effects of inflation were found. First, we tested the hypothesis that the coefficients of anticipated and unanticipated

Table 8.1. Effects of inflation and unemployment on income shares and poverty rates (standard errors in parentheses)

Quintile income share, 1948–1983[a]

	Unemployment	Unemployment squared	Inflation	Lagged dependent variable	R^2	Durbin h-statistic[b]	Steady-state effect of 1-point rise in—	
							Unemployment	Inflation
Lowest quintile	-.100[c] (.023)	—[d]	.008 (.010)	.463[c] (.117)	.865	.973	-.185	.015
Second quintile	-.238[c] (-.050)	.019[c] (.005)	.021[c] (.008)	.404[c] (.095)	.946	-.774	-.160	.035
Third quintile	-.33[e] (.016)	—[d]	.010 (.009)	—[d]	.778	1.78	-.033	.010
Fourth quintile	.030[e] (.016)	—[d]	-.006 (.008)	.434[c] (.139)	.836	-1.33	.053	-.011
Fifth quintile	.198 (.046)	—[d]	-.016 (.023)	.314[e] (.131)	.818	-1.12	.289	-.023

Poverty rate, 1959–1983[a]

	Unemployment	Inflation	Transfers/ GNP	Poverty line/ mean income	Lagged dependent variable	R^2	Durbin h-statistic	Steady-state effect of 1-point rise in—	
								Unemployment	Inflation
All persons	.687c	.094e	−.280	.395c	.369c	.990	.115	1.089	.149
	(.281)	(.049)	(.279)	(.091)	(.118)				
All families	.603c	.077e	−.242	.324c	.376c	.991	.238	.966	.123
	(.227)	(.040)	(.225)	(.076)	(.113)				

a. Not shown are coefficients for intercept and time trends. Complete regression results available from authors on request.
b. Except in the third quintile calculations the presence of a lagged dependent variable requires use of Durbin h-statistic rather than Durbin-Watson.
c. Significant at 1-percent level.
d. Variable omitted from final regression due to insignificance.
e. Significant at 5-percent level.
f. Not shown are coefficients on intercepts. Unemployment squared was insignificant in both regressions and was therefore omitted from the model.

inflation were equal. Contrary to theory, this hypothesis could never be rejected. So we combined the two variables into actual inflation, which proved to be significant only for the second (from the bottom) quintile. Although mostly insignificant, the point estimates suggest that inflation is a somewhat progressive tax.

The lagged dependent variable was highly significant, except for the middle quintile. Estimated adjustment speeds for the other four quintiles ranged between 69 and 54 percent per year.[7]

We also tested to see if the poverty rate varies in the same way as the share of the bottom quintile. The same specification would not be appropriate for the official poverty rate because, unlike the shares data, it displays a pronounced downward trend until about 1973 (and no trend thereafter). Rather than include a linear time trend, we included two economic variables to explain this time pattern. The first is a measure of government transfers, whose expansion since the mid-1960s has significantly reduced the poverty rate (Gottschalk and Danziger, 1984); our measure of this effect is the ratio of total government transfers to persons, divided by GNP.[8] The second is a measure of where the poverty line is drawn in the income distribution. As noted above, the official poverty line falls relative to mean income in times of real growth, an effect that almost by definition will decrease poverty. To measure this effect we include the ratio of the poverty line for a family of four to mean household income.

The bottom of Table 8.1 shows the estimated equations explaining poverty rates among all persons and all families. The period of estimation starts in 1959, since that is when official poverty data were first recorded. The inclusion of the additional variables in these regressions provides a very close fit. (The R-squared statistics indicate that we are able to fit the poverty rate equations far better than the quintile share equations.) When a time trend is added to these regressions, it is insignificant. Because the results are so similar for both regressions, we discuss only the equation for all persons.

According to these estimates, a 1-point rise in prime-age male unemployment raises the poverty rate by 0.7 points in the same year. If the rise in unemployment were sustained, the final net effect would be a 1.1-point rise in the poverty rate.[9]

Here inflation is found to hurt the poor. But the effect of a 1-point rise in inflation is only one-seventh as large as that of a 1-point rise in unemployment. Our contention that unemployment, not inflation, is the cruelest tax is supported.

As expected, increases in transfers decrease poverty, although the coefficient is not significant. Decreases in the ratio of the poverty line to mean income do significantly reduce poverty.

Our results indicate that low-income households should be more concerned with rising rates of unemployment than with rising rates of inflation, but for high-income households the opposite is true. This conclusion is subject to at least one qualification, however. High unemployment is, presumably, a transitory phenomenon whereas the reduction of inflation that it "buys" is presumably permanent. Hence the poor should balance the large but temporary losses from high unemployment against the small but permanent gains from lower inflation. Clearly, with a low enough discount rate, even the poor will favor using unemployment to fight inflation. However, the economic behavior of poor people strongly suggests that the discount rates they use are extremely high. If the poor have reason to be more averse to unemployment and less averse to inflation than the rich, this promises clear conflicts among various groups in the struggle to determine national macroeconomic policy (see Hibbs, 1976, and Gramlich and Laren, 1984a).

DIFFERENTIAL RESPONSES TO A GENERAL INCREASE IN UNEMPLOYMENT

In order to investigate whether the unemployment rates of disadvantaged groups rise more than the national unemployment rate during recessions, we measured the sensitivity of unemployment rates of various labor market groups to changes in the aggregate unemployment rate and inflation by estimating simple regressions of the form:

$$U_{it} = a + bt + c_1 I^a_t + c_2 I^u_t + d_1 U^*_t + d_2 U^{*2}_t + f(P_{it}/P_t)$$
$$+ gU_{it-1} + e_t. \tag{8.4}$$

Here, as before, I^a and I^u denote anticipated and unanticipated inflation,[10] t represents time, U_{it} is the monthly unemployment rate of group i in time t,[11] U^*_t is the unemployment rate of prime-age *white* males (which we will refer to as "base-level" unemployment), P_{it}/P_t is the ratio of the population of group i to the total population, and U_{it-1} is the lagged dependent variable.[12] This regression is estimated using monthly data from January 1955 to May 1984 for thirty-two groups[13]: eight age categories (all ages, 16–19, 20–24, 25–34, 35–44, 45–54, 55–64, and 65+) and four race/sex categories (white males, white females, nonwhite males, and nonwhite females).[14]

The top part of Table 8.2 shows the sensitivity of each group's unemployment rate to a one-point rise in base-level unemployment.[15] The "all"

Table 8.2. Sensitivity of age-specific unemployment rates to monthly 1-point changes in base-level unemployment and in anticipated inflation, January 1955–May 1984

Age group	All	White males	White females	Nonwhite males	Nonwhite females
Sensitivity to 1-point change in base-level unemployment[a]					
All ages	1.096	1.096	.766	2.464	1.238
16–19	1.993	2.214	1.506	2.835	1.684
20–24	1.877	2.028	1.179	3.226	2.389
25–34	1.276	1.178	1.002	2.561	1.213
35–44	.917	.821	.708	1.914	1.176
45–54	.894	.871	.769	1.904	.790
55–64	.778	.772	.650	1.623	.671
65+	.569	.504	.373	1.941	.741
Sensitivity to 1-point change in anticipated inflation[b]					
All ages	.520[c]	.418[c]	.664	.698	− .563
16–19	− .786	.096	− 1.461	− 2.062	− 6.944[c]
20–24	.513[d]	1.629[c]	− .258	1.294	.134
25–34	.532[c]	.538[c]	1.155[c]	.382	− 1.898[c]
35–44	− .270[c]	− .154[d]	− .684[c]	.304	− 1.131
45–54	− .023	− .064	.383	− .074	− 1.504[c]
55–64	− .304	− .421	− .047	− .902	.561
65+	.085	− .877	.137	.264	− .080

a. Base-level unemployment is the unemployment rate for white males, age 25–54. The coefficient shown here is the marginal effect of a change in base-level unemployment on the group-specific unemployment rate. See note 15 for the exact definition. The underlying unemployment coefficients are all significant at the 1-percent level. See equation (8.4) for full regression specification. Monthly unemployment data from the Bureau of Labor Statistics.
b. In terms of equation (8.4), the coefficient is $c_i/(1 - g)$. Calculation of anticipated inflation data is described in note 10.
c. Significant at the 1-percent level.
d. Significant at the 5-percent level.

column (column 1) shows that the sensitivity of group-specific unemployment rates to the base-level unemployment rate decreases monotonically as age rises. During recessions unemployment rates among teens rise almost twice as fast as the base rate; those for the elderly rise about half as fast.

The patterns by race and sex reveal some striking differences. Nonwhite males are clearly the hardest hit by recessions. Unemployment rates for twenty- to twenty-four-year-old nonwhite males rise over three times more than base-level unemployment rates. Even the lowest sensitivity among nonwhite males (among fifty-five- to sixty-four-year-old workers) exceeds 1.5. In contrast, white female unemployment is least affected by changes in the general unemployment rate. This finding almost surely reflects the "discouraged worker" effect among women—a high propensity to drop out of the labor market in response to increases in unemployment. White males have higher sensitivities than white females but are considerably less sensitive than nonwhite males. Nonwhite females present a mixed picture: Teens and older workers tend to be less sensitive than men of either race; middle-aged groups are more sensitive than white men but quite a bit less sensitive than nonwhite men.

The patterns in these regression coefficients confirm that the burden of unemployment is distributed unequally across age, race, and sex groups. In particular, nonwhite and young workers are more severely affected. On the other hand, female and older workers (especially those over sixty-five)—who are also typically low-wage workers—are not as sensitive to changes in general unemployment levels. This probably reflects the availability of other income sources for these workers—either transfers or earnings of other family members—that make job search less mandatory, allowing them to drop out of the labor market more easily in times of high unemployment. In addition, it might also reflect the comparative cyclicality of the occupations and industries in which women tend to work relative to men.

The bottom panel of Table 8.2 shows the sensitivity of each group's unemployment rate to a one-point rise in the *anticipated* inflation rate,[16] since the coefficient on unanticipated inflation was usually insignificant and always small. The effect of anticipated inflation is typically significant but quite a bit smaller than that of base-level unemployment.

Inflation effects for all persons by age are shown in column 1. The effect is negative for teens, positive for workers twenty to thirty-four years and negative for those thirty-five to sixty-four. But this pattern varies between different race and sex groups (see the last four columns of the bottom panel of Table 8.2).

Why does anticipated inflation affect group-specific unemployment rates, given the national unemployment rate? It appears that workers in their twenties and thirties either respond differently to high expected inflation rates (perhaps they are more willing to quit and look for better jobs when demand is expected to be high) or are employed in a mix of occupations and industries that have been negatively affected by high inflation rates over this time period.

However, the main conclusion of this analysis is clear: the business cycle is not neutral in spreading the burden of unemployment. Certain workers experience much larger increases in unemployment when the general economy turns down than others.

DIFFERENTIAL PROTECTION AGAINST INCOME LOSSES FROM
UNEMPLOYMENT

The fact that certain groups experience higher unemployment than others
does not in itself mean that those groups are disproportionately harmed.
A variety of government and private programs are explicitly designed to
cushion the impact of unemployment on incomes. Unemployment insurance is available to all workers in covered industries who have worked a
certain length of time and who are involuntarily terminated. The percentage of jobs covered by UI expanded steadily from 58 percent in 1950 to
93 percent in 1980.

However, many of the unemployed are new entrants or re-entrants who
are not eligible for UI. Others do not draw benefits because they quit
rather than being fired or because their unemployment spell lasts longer
than their eligibility for benefits. The ratio of unemployed people receiving
UI to the total number of unemployed hovered between 45 and 55 percent
through the 1950s and 1960s, climbed to a peak of 78 percent in 1975, but
fell to 43 percent by 1982. The recent decrease in UI recipiency appears
to be due to legislative changes in both the eligibility rules for extended
benefits in times of high unemployment and the length of time extended
benefits are available (Smeeding, 1984; Burtless, 1983). For example, the
maximum duration of UI in 1976 was sixty-five weeks, but in 1983 it was
only thirty-four to fifty-five weeks (depending on the state).

Although unemployment compensation provides help to many unemployed persons, it is less frequently available to the poor or low-income
workers. Because of the eligibility requirements, low-wage workers with
unstable employment records—those who are most likely to experience
unemployment—are least likely to receive UI. The distribution of unemployment benefits in 1979 by race, sex, and age is presented in Table
8.3 and compared to the distribution of total unemployment. It is clear
that unemployment benefits were disproportionately received by whites,
males, and prime-aged workers.[17] The chi-squared statistics in Table 8.3
reject (at the 95-percent level) the null hypothesis that these numbers were
chosen from the same distribution for all three categories.

Private forms of unemployment protection are also available, primarily
to unionized workers. Many union contracts either contain provisions for
supplemental unemployment benefit funds, available to laid-off workers
as a supplement to UI, or provide for severance pay on the part of the
employer. In 1980 47.7 percent of union contracts had some such provision,
covering 65.2 percent of unionized workers (U.S. Department of Labor,
1980a). Unfortunately, this protection is also less likely to help lower-wage

Table 8.3. Distribution of insured unemployed and total unemployed by race, sex, and age, March 1979 (state-run programs only)

	Insured unemployed (%)	Total unemployed (%)	Chi-squared statistic
By race			
White	85.9	77.7	3.88
Nonwhite	14.1	22.3	
By sex			
Male	64.4	54.1	4.27
Female	35.6	45.9	
By age			
Under 25	20.8	46.8	29.08
25–54	63.0	44.8	
Over 54	16.2	8.4	

Sources: U.S. Department of Labor, BLS, *Employment and Earnings,* various issues; U.S. Department of Labor (1979, tables 32C and 33C). A similar table showing data for the mid-1970s is found in Hamermesh (1977), p. 22.

workers, primarily because low-wage jobs are less likely to be unionized. In 1980, 37 percent of the workforce earned less than $200 per week on their primary jobs (approximately $10,000 per year for a full-time worker); only 15.2 percent of all unionized workers were in this earnings category (U.S. Department of Labor, 1980b).

Although many poor or near-poor workers are not covered by explicit unemployment protection schemes, a variety of transfer programs are available to help low-income households, including food stamps and AFDC. The eligibility requirements for these programs guarantee that only very-low-income households qualify. For example, to be eligible for food stamps, a household can have no more than $1,500 in assets (other than a house and car), and its gross income must be no more than 130 percent of the poverty line. In addition, some programs are simply unavailable to certain households; for example, only half the states allowed AFDC payments to intact two-parent families in 1983.

Gramlich and Laren (1984a) investigated the extent to which tax and transfer systems cushion income loss resulting from unemployment. For poor white male-headed households they found that a 1-percentage-point rise in the unemployment rate produces a 6-percent income loss, 56 percent of which is replaced by tax and transfer changes. For poor nonwhite male-headed households, the loss is slightly larger (6.2 percent) and the replacement rate is smaller (40 percent). For poor female-headed households, the loss is much smaller (only 2.3 percent—as before, this group is less affected by unemployment changes), but the replacement rate is also much lower (just 27 percent).

THE EFFECT OF UNEMPLOYMENT ON THOSE REMAINING EMPLOYED

Unemployment can differentially affect poor and nonpoor workers in another way: beyond the loss experienced by those who are directly unemployed, changes in unemployment rates may also affect the relative earnings of those workers who remain employed. Are there some workers who gain or lose relative wages during business cycles?

To answer this question, we collected annual data on median earnings of full-time, full-year workers, by race and sex. We regressed earnings ratios between these groups on the same set of cyclical economic variables that were used above. The equation is

$$E_{it}/E_{jt} = a + bt + c_1 I^a_t + c_2 I^u_t + d_1 U^*_t + d_2 U^{*2}_t + f(U_{it}/U_{jt}) \\ + g(E_{it-1}/E_{jt-1}) + e_t, \tag{8.5}$$

where E_{it} is the earnings of group i (a lower income group) in time t, E_{jt} is the earnings of a comparison (higher income) group j, U_{it}/U_{jt} is the relevant unemployment ratio for groups i and j, and the other variables are defined as before. The results from estimating this equation by ordinary least squares using annual data from 1955 to 1983 are shown in Table 8.4.

The time trends show that significant shifts have occurred in relative median earnings among groups: nonwhites have improved relative to whites, and nonwhite women have improved relative to all other groups. But the business cycle seems to have had little effect on the relative earnings of most of the groups examined here.

The relative earnings of nonwhite women versus nonwhite men are unaffected by inflation or unemployment over this time period. The same is true for nonwhite versus white men. Increases in base-level unemployment do appear to raise the earnings of white women relative to white men, but the magnitude of the effect is small. In contrast, the cyclical variables have a significant effect on the earnings of nonwhite versus white women: nonwhite women lose wages relative to white women when base-level unemployment rises, and they gain a (small) amount relative to white women when anticipated inflation rises. This is also the only regression in which the group-specific unemployment ratio matters. Its negative coefficient and the significance of other economic variables perhaps indicate that these

Table 8.4. Cyclical effects on relative median annual earnings of race and sex groups 1955–1983 (standard errors in parentheses)[a]

Independent variables[b]	White women/ white men	Nonwhite women/ nonwhite men	Nonwhite men/ white men	Nonwhite women/ white women
Anticipated inflation	.0001 (.0008)	−.0002 (.0028)	.003 (.002)	.003[c] (.002)
Unanticipated inflation	.0003 (.0015)	.001 (.005)	.005 (.004)	−.0006 (.0035)
Base-level unemployment	.007[c] (.004)	−.009 (.014)	.007 (.005)	−.012[d] (.004)
Unemployment ratio	.026 (.024)	−.046 (.072)	−.025 (.030)	−.185[d] (.035)
Lagged dependent variable	.721[d] (.168)	.387[c] (.214)	−.055 (.241)	.520[d] (.120)
Time	−.0004 (.0006)	.005[c] (.003)	.005[d] (.001)	.008[d] (.002)
Constant	.107 (.119)	.490[d] (.203)	.741[d] (.173)	.752[d] (.138)
R^2	.794	.839	.863	.984
Durbin h-statistic	−2.23	1.92[e]	1.98[e]	−1.28

a. Median earnings are for full-time, full-year workers. (Source: annual Current Population Reports, Series P-60, U.S. Bureau of the Census.)
b. See text and equation (8.5) for description of variables.
c. Significant at 5-percent level.
d. Significant at 1-percent level.
e. These are Durbin-Watson statistics. Durbin h-statistics could not be computed.

two groups are closer substitutes in the labor market than men versus women or black men versus white men.

Thus, while the business cycle has clear distributional effects via unemployment, it appears to have less significant distributional effects on the relative earnings of many workers who remain employed.

INFLATION AND INCOMES OF THE POOR

For inflation to have negative effects on the relative position of the poor, either the incomes of the poor must rise more slowly than other incomes in inflationary times or the prices of commodities bought by the poor must rise faster than other prices. A significant component of income among the poor is government transfers. Money wages rise more or less proportionately with prices in the long run, but transfers may not. Inflation can hurt the poor (relatively) if transfers do not rise with inflation as quickly as average wages do. To some extent, this probably occurs—which may account for the positive coefficients of inflation in the poverty regressions.

A clear example is found in AFDC. The real value of the median state's maximum AFDC payment declined by 27 percent between 1970 and 1983. As Smeeding (1984) notes, much of this fall came during the high-inflation years of the mid-1970s, when states neglected to raise their benefit levels. The decrease has slowed in recent years.[18]

In contrast to AFDC, most other transfer benefits are indexed and therefore have not been eroded much by inflation. (However, legislative changes have reduced participation and real benefit levels in some programs.) SSI's federal minimum required benefit has been fully indexed, although state supplements have fallen in real value in many states. Similarly, food stamps were fully indexed to inflation up until 1981, when the Omnibus Budget Reconciliation Act reduced their indexing provisions, primarily by delaying the indexing procedures. Social Security has also been fully indexed (and in some ways overindexed) during this period.

Another way the poor could lose is if inflation tilts the relative wage structure, raising high wages faster than low wages. This is especially likely if unanticipated inflation occurs and high wages are indexed while low wages are not. We have no direct evidence on the relative indexation of high versus low wages. We do know, however, that union wages (about half of which are indexed) rose relative to non-union wages in the inflationary 1970s (Johnson, 1983). As noted above, low-wage workers are less likely to be union members, which indicates that they were probably on the losing side of this relative wage change.

The situation is better for low-wage workers who are unionized. Union contracts are typically indexed so that wages rise by a set number of "pennies per point" as inflation rises rather than by the same percentage as inflation. The effect of these contracts is to raise the wages of lower-paid union members by a higher relative percentage than that of their better-paid fellow members (Card, 1983).

Hamermesh (1983) found that higher unanticipated inflation *lowers* the variance of wages across industrial sectors, but the variance across sectors accounts for only a small portion of the variance of wages across individuals. If this finding holds true for the variance of *individual* wages, one would expect the poor to gain (relatively) from unanticipated inflation.

Among race and sex subgroups the regressions reported in Table 8.4 do not suggest that inflation, whether anticipated or unanticipated, tilts the relative wage structure very much. As noted above, the only group for whom inflation effects mattered were nonwhite versus white women, and in this case high anticipated inflation increased relative earnings for non-white females by a small amount.

In sum, inflation has *not* seriously lowered the relative incomes of the poor. The relative earnings of low-wage workers do not seem to have fallen with inflation. And although a few types of transfer income have lost real value, most programs have been adequately indexed.

RELATIVE PRICE CHANGES AND THE POOR

The poor could also be victimized by inflation if the prices of commodities they buy systematically rise faster than prices in general. This effect would not show up in our share regressions, which tacitly deflate the nominal incomes of every group by the same price index.[19] However, there does not seem to be any evidence that this is the case.

Hollister and Palmer (1972) found that a price index specific to poor people actually grew somewhat slower during the years 1947–1967 than the CPI. Mirer (1975) used the same technique for the period of the Nixon price controls (August 1971 to April 1974) and concluded that inflation for poor people was a little higher than average. Minarik (1980) showed that prices of necessities over the 1970–1979 period rose slightly less than the overall CPI. Michael (1979) calculated household-specific CPIs for each of several thousand consumer units and found no systematic relationship between inflation and income class during the 1967–1974 period. When Hagemann (1982) performed a similar analysis of the 1972–1982 period, he found some tendency for poorer households to experience higher inflation, but the differences among income classes were small and not persistent over different subperiods.

These studies suggest that if there is any systematic difference between inflation in prices paid by poor people and overall inflation, it is minuscule. In fact, it is probably the rich, not the poor, who are the chief victims of inflation, because after-tax income from property declines as inflation rises.[20]

Tax Policy and the Poor

Our analysis of general cyclical effects indicates that any expansionary policy that temporarily reduces unemployment at the expense of greater inflation transitorily raises the income share of the poor and probably reduces the poverty count. Contractionary policies have the opposite effects.

But cyclical effects are not the only way in which macroeconomic policy decisions affect the poor. In this section we abstract from any effects of policy variables on inflation and unemployment, which depend mainly on the *levels* of taxation and spending, and focus instead on how changes in the *structure* of taxation over the past thirty years have affected the poor. (We restrict our attention to taxes, rather than to spending programs, because the latter are covered in detail by other chapters in this volume.)

Naturally, complicated and controversial questions of tax incidence quickly arise. We cannot hope to resolve these issues here. All we can do is reveal our basic assumptions: (a) personal taxes (income and payroll) are not shifted much, and the employee bears both the employee and employer shares of the payroll tax; (b) corporate income taxes are borne by capital as a whole; (c) excise taxes are shared, but most of the burden is borne by consumers because long-run supply curves for most commodities are highly elastic.

THE CHANGING STRUCTURE OF FEDERAL TAXATION

Despite much oratory to the contrary, the overall burden of federal taxes has risen little over recent decades—from 17.3 percent of GNP in 1950 to 18.7 percent in 1983. But the structure of federal taxation has changed dramatically (see Table 8.5). Several developments are noteworthy.

First, the corporate income tax has fallen in importance from 34 percent of federal tax receipts in 1950 to only 7 percent in 1983, a process that was accelerated by the Reagan tax cuts of 1981. Roughly counterbalancing this decline has been a rise in the share of payroll taxes from 12 percent in 1950 to 38 percent in 1983. Replacing corporate income taxes (which are widely believed to be highly progressive with respect to total income) by payroll taxes has certainly shifted the tax burden toward the poor—particularly the working poor, for whom the payroll tax is often the most important tax.[21]

Less significantly, the share of excise taxes and customs duties has tumbled from 18 percent in 1950 to only 7 percent in 1983, probably increasing progressivity somewhat—but not by much because the particular items federally taxed are not a random sample of all consumption goods (Pechman, 1983, p. 192).

Finally, the share of personal income taxes increased substantially from 1950 to 1970 but declined slightly in recent years as a result of the Reagan tax cuts. The net increase in this share since 1960 is only 2.5 percentage points.

Table 8.5 The structure of federal taxation, 1950–1983

	1950	1960	1970	1980	1983
Overall distribution of federal tax receipts (percentages)					
Personal income tax	35.1	44.1	47.5	47.8	46.6
Corporate income tax[a]	34.1	21.7	14.5	11.2	7.4
Payroll taxes	11.9	18.6	26.4	33.2	37.7
Excises and duties	17.6	13.8	9.7	6.5	7.3
Estate and gift taxes	1.3	1.9	2.0	1.3	1.0
Key ratios					
Federal taxes/GNP	.17	.19	.19	.20	.19
Corporate tax/					
personal taxes	.97	.49	.31	.23	.16
Payroll taxes/personal					
taxes	.34	.42	.56	.69	.81
Evolution of the payroll tax					
Payroll tax rate[b]	3.00%	6.00%	9.60%	12.26%	13.40%
Ratio of maximum					
taxable earnings to					
average earnings[c]	1.13	1.19	1.30	2.10	2.54

Source: U.S. Department of Commerce, 1950–1983.
a. Excluding payments by Federal Reserve System to Treasury.
b. Sum of employee's and employer's shares.
c. Average earnings are average gross weekly earnings in the private nonagricultural economy times 50.

In a general way one can consider personal income, corporate income, and estate and gift taxes to be progressive taxes and excise, customs, and payroll taxes to be regressive taxes. Under this assumption the share of progressive taxes in total federal tax receipts is as follows:

1950	1960	1970	1980	1983
70.5%	67.7%	64.0%	60.3%	55.0%

A pronounced trend toward less reliance on progressive taxation is demonstrated.

CHANGES IN TAX PROVISIONS AFFECTING THE POOR

Numerous changes in the tax code have taken place since 1950.[22] Those relating to corporate income tax are basically irrelevant to the poor (except for general equilibrium reverberations). Likewise, the changes in the nature of federal excise taxes and customs duties are too disparate to permit any useful generalizations. Only two taxes have a direct effect on the poor: payroll taxes and personal income taxes.

The payroll tax. The payroll tax is viewed as highly regressive because it taxes only earnings, not property income, and because the marginal tax rate drops to zero once the maximum covered earnings base is reached. Since maximum taxable earnings have grown much faster than average earnings since 1950 (see Table 8.5), a larger and larger fraction of nonpoor workers have paid payroll tax on every dollar of earnings, thereby making the payroll tax less regressive. This offers little solace to the poor, however, since the payroll tax rate has more than quadrupled since 1950. There is little doubt that the burden of the payroll tax on the poor has increased dramatically during the past thirty-five years.

The personal income tax. The federal personal income tax is more complex. The provisions most relevant to the poor are the personal exemption, the standard deduction, the lowest bracket rates, and (since 1975) the earned income credit. Table 8.6 contains the pertinent data.[23]

The personal exemption remained at $600 from 1948 through 1969 and was steadily eroded by inflation. During the 1970s it was raised in stages to $1,000, where it has remained. Thus, the real value of the exemption fell by 1983 to about half what it was in 1955, reducing the progressivity of the tax at the low end.[24]

The lowest bracket rate was 17.4 percent in 1950 and rose to 22.2 percent

Table 8.6. Aspects of the federal personal income tax, 1955–1983

	1955	1965	1975	1980	1983
Personal exemption					
Nominal	$600	$600	$750[a]	$1,000	$1,000
Real ($ 1972)	$932	$777	$599	$ 559	$ 468
As percentage of median family income	13.6%	8.6%	5.5%	4.8%	4.1%
Lowest bracket rate	20%	14%	14%[b]	14%[b]	11%
Standard deduction	10% of AGI[c]	10% of AGI[c]	16% of AGI[c]	$3,400	$3,400

a. Plus $30 per capita tax credit.
b. Reduced further by earned income credit.
c. AGI = Adjusted gross income.

by 1952; since then it has mostly fallen and is now only 11 percent. This decline in the lowest bracket rate has helped reduce the burden of personal income taxation on poor families.

The standard deduction stood at 10 percent of adjusted gross income until 1969; then was gradually increased to $2,300 for an individual and $3,400 for a married couple in 1979, where it has remained. Inflation has reduced the real value of the standard deduction substantially since 1979. But this is a minor setback when set against the fact that the introduction of a large flat standard deduction in 1977 (called the "zero bracket amount") completely removed many poor and near-poor people from the income tax rolls.

We can amalgamate all these factors by constructing hypothetical but representative low-income families and comparing their income tax burdens under different tax structures. Table 8.7 considers three such cases.

The first case is one of abject poverty: a family of four whose 1983 income was $5,000 (about half the 1983 poverty line), and whose income in earlier years was the same in real terms. Such a family would never have been subject to income taxation; but starting in 1975 it would have received a 10-percent negative tax rate owing to the earned income credit. Over the entire period this family's total (income plus payroll) tax burden changed little.

Table 8.7. Average federal tax rates on earned income, 1955–1983 (percentages)

Income Level	1955	1965	1975	1980	1983
At 5,000 1983 dollars					
Personal income[a]	—	—	− 10.0	− 10.0	− 10.0
Personal income plus payroll	4.5	7.3	1.7	2.3	3.4
At poverty line					
Personal income[a]	0.4[b]	2.2	− 0.9	− 0.7	3.1
Personal income plus payroll	4.9[b]	9.4	10.8	11.6	16.5
At ½ median income					
Personal income[a]	—	2.9	3.9	4.3	4.9
Personal income plus payroll	4.5	10.2	15.6	16.6	18.3

a. For a family of four filing jointly and claiming the standard deduction.

b. We constructed a 1955 "poverty line" by adjusting the 1959 poverty line for the change in the CPI. Our thanks to Gordon Fischer for the suggestion.

The second family of four has earnings exactly equal to the poverty line. Its income tax burden was 2.2 percent of earnings in 1965, became negative owing to the earned income credit, but has lately risen to 3.1 percent. When coupled with the rising burden of the payroll tax, this family has paid an increasing share of its earnings in taxes since 1965 and by 1983 paid 16.5 percent of its earnings in federal taxes.

The third case is a family that earns half the median income—an amount suggested by some observers as a good definition of relative poverty (Fuchs, 1967). This income level ranges from $12,290 in 1983 to $2,209 in 1955 (all in nominal dollars). At this income level, normally about 20 to 25 percent above the poverty line, the average income tax rate has crept steadily upward from zero under the 1955 tax law to about 5 percent in 1983.[25] When the payroll tax is included, the overall tax burden on this hypothetical family has risen astronomically since 1955.

THE CHANGING STRUCTURE OF STATE AND LOCAL TAXATION

Between 1950 and 1970 state and local taxes grew much faster than GNP and federal taxes; their structure also changed dramatically (see Table 8.8). Personal income and payroll taxes are now much more important sources of revenue than they were in 1950. Sales taxes are slightly more important. The big shrinkage came in property taxes and miscellaneous "other taxes." A (very) rough summary of Table 8.8 is that the share of personal income

Table 8.8 Distribution of state and local tax receipts, 1950–1983 (percentages)[a]

Type of tax	1950	1960	1970	1980	1983
Personal income tax	4.3	6.3	11.0	16.4	17.3
Corporate income tax	4.3	3.1	3.5	5.6	4.7
Payroll taxes	6.4	8.5	9.1	11.4	11.5
Sales taxes	27.1	30.0	31.3	31.8	31.7
Estate and gift taxes	1.0	1.2	1.1	0.9	0.8
Property taxes	41.6	41.4	37.1	26.7	27.4
Other taxes	15.2	9.5	6.8	7.2	6.7
Addendum items					
State-local taxes/GNP	.06	.08	.10	.10	.10
State-local taxes/ federal taxes	.36	.43	.54	.50	.55

Source: U.S. Department of Commerce (1950–1983).
a. Includes only tax receipts. Grants from the federal government and nontax receipts, both of which are substantial sources of revenue, are excluded.

taxes increased by about as much as the share of property taxes decreased.

As late as 1960 only a few states had personal income taxes; now forty states plus the District of Columbia and a number of other large cities have them. With so many different taxes, we cannot profitably examine changes in tax provisions over time, as we did for the federal personal income tax. Most state income taxes have a progressive rate structure; top marginal rates are as high as 17.6 percent (the top rate in Minnesota). Most also have a substantial zero bracket amount, which effectively removes the very poor from the tax rolls. Thus, although the incidence of the property tax is highly controversial, it seems likely that the shift from property taxation to income taxation has decreased the overall regressivity of the state and local tax structure.[26]

Where the very poor are concerned, however, income taxes are basically irrelevant; only sales and payroll (and perhaps property) taxes matter. Over the 1950–1983 period the poor paid higher state and local sales taxes and higher state (and in some cases local) payroll taxes. Thus it seems likely that the state and local tax burden on the poor has increased.

IN SUM, where the poor are concerned, the main "event" in postwar tax history seems to have been the rapid and continuing growth of the payroll tax. Changes in personal income taxation have been minor for the very poor, as the earned income credit and the flat standard deduction more or less cancelled out the effects of a declining real personal exemption. But the not-so-poor have paid higher income taxes as well.

One crude way to summarize all this is to classify all state, local, and federal taxes (omitting "other" state and local taxes) as progressive or regressive, as we did for federal taxes. The uncertainty concerning the correct classification of the property tax leads us to calculate these numbers two ways:

	1950	1960	1970	1980	1983
Property tax progressive	68.2%	64.8%	61.5%	58.1%	53.2%
Property tax regressive	56.8%	52.0%	48.1%	49.0%	43.6%

Although the levels differ consistently, each calculation displays a roughly equivalent trend away from reliance on progressive taxes. These numbers summarize the conclusion that the tax burden on the poor has become greater in recent years.

Looking Back and Looking Ahead

The distribution of income has undeniably widened in the past decade. The shares of the bottom three quintiles have declined while those of the top two have risen (see columns 1 and 2 of Table 8.9).

Using the regression results reported in Table 8.1, we can estimate the extent to which inflation and unemployment have affected income shares and poverty rates between 1973 and 1983. We first calculate a noncyclical income share (or poverty rate) for 1983 by holding inflation and unemployment constant at 1973 levels. (For the poverty equation, we also re-move cyclical effects from transfers/GNP and from poverty line/mean income by trend-lining these variables between 1973 and 1983.) We then compare this noncyclical share to the observed income share to isolate the effects of cyclical conditions. Finally, we decompose this difference into the por-tions attributable to changes in unemployment and to changes in inflation over the decade.[27] The results are displayed in Table 8.9. Comparison of columns 1 and 4 indicates how the income distribution would have changed if no cyclical effects had occurred. The difference between columns 3 and 4 indicates the magnitude of the cyclical effects.

Before examining these results, we need to comment on the size of the effects we are discussing. A change of less than 1 percent in the income share of any group may appear to be rather small; but in a historical context even changes of this magnitude are unusual. For example, the postwar high and low for the share of the lowest quintile are respectively 5.6 percent in 1968 and 4.7 percent in 1983. Viewed against this background, the .8-percentage-point drop that has occurred within the past ten years is quite a dramatic change.

Columns 5 and 6 show the estimated effects of unemployment and in-flation on the share of each quintile from 1973 to 1983. Between these years the impact of inflation and unemployment (particularly unemploy-ment) widened the income distribution. The lowest quintile would have experienced a constant income share if no cyclical effects had occurred. However, the combined effects of unemployment and inflation lowered this by .96 points, which resulted in an observed income share of 4.7 percent in 1983. This same pattern occurred more strongly in the second quintile and less strongly in the third quintile but is reversed in the fourth and fifth quintiles. For the upper income groups, the net effect of inflation and unemployment is to raise the income share. Without these effects almost no change would have occurred. Note that unemployment consistently has a larger effect than inflation on all of these income share changes.

Table 8.9. Estimated effect of the business cycle on quintile income shares and the poverty rate, past (1973–1983) and projected (1989)

Income share	1973 actual (1)	1983 actual (2)	Regression predictions for 1983 (3)	1983 predicted noncyclical[b] (4)	Cyclical effects		Forecast (1989)[a]		
					Amount due to changes in unemployment (5)	Amount due to changes in inflation (6)	Non-cyclical (7)	Recession-recovery (8)	Pessimistic (9)
Lowest quintile	5.5	4.7	4.5	5.46	−.91	−.05	5.3	5.1	5.1
Second quintile	11.9	11.1	11.1	12.32	−1.08	−.14	10.9	10.7	10.8
Third quintile	17.5	17.1	17.2	17.44	−.19	−.05	17.2	17.1	17.1
Fourth quintile	24.0	24.4	24.5	24.17	.29	.04	24.4	24.5	24.4
Fifth quintile	41.1	42.7	42.9	41.26	1.54	.10	41.9	42.1	42.1
Poverty rate for individuals	11.1	15.2	15.2	10.70[c]	5.01	−.61	11.1	11.3	11.5

a. In all simulations the poverty line for a family of four is assumed to remain at 34 percent of mean family income. In the noncyclical simulation, transfers are assumed to remain at 12 percent of GNP even though the economy recovers. In the other simulations, transfers are adjusted to reflect the historical relationship between transfers and unemployment.

b. Holds inflation and unemployment at 1973 levels. Allows for effects of the time trend and the model's error structure over the decade.

c. Holds inflation and unemployment at 1973 levels. Also removes cyclical effects from poverty line/mean income and transfers/GNP. Allows for effects of trend-line growth in poverty line/mean income, in transfers/GNP and for the model's error structure over the decade. Cyclical effects in other variables (transfers/GNP and poverty line/mean income) add another .10 point to the poverty rate over this decade.

Finally, the effects of economic variables on the poverty rate are presented in the bottom of Table 8.9. Had no cyclical effects occurred over the decade, poverty would have fallen from 11.1 percent to 10.7 percent of the population. However, unemployment during this decade raised the rate by 5.01 percentage points. On the other hand, decreased inflation rates over the decade would have lowered the poverty rate by .61 points. Cyclical effects in the other variables had almost no effect on the poverty count. As the studies cited earlier have shown, the poverty population appears to have been particularly hard hit by the high unemployment rates during the past decade.

Predicting the future is more fun than examining the past; one is less constrained by the facts. We can use our poverty and income share equations, in conjunction with macroeconomic forecasts, to project the poverty rate and the quintile shares of the income distribution into the future. Since no one can foresee the timing of recessions well in advance, it is prudent to consider a range of possibilities. We therefore project the evolution of poverty and income distribution under three different scenarios.

Our noncyclical scenario is the August 1984 projection of the Congressional Budget Office (CBO) in which unemployment gradually declines to 6.3 percent and inflation remains in the 4- to 5-percent range.

Past history suggests, however, that it is most unlikely for the economy to grow steadily for seven years without a recession. Hence our second scenario (recession/recovery) reaches the same 6.3-percent unemployment rate by 1989 as the CBO projection but has the economy experience a moderate recession (in 1986–87) along the way. As a consequence, inflation falls to the 2- to 3-percent range in the later years of the projection.[28]

Our third scenario is pessimistic. It has the unemployment rate stall out at 7 percent in 1985 and remain there through 1989. Inflation is therefore intermediate between the other two scenarios.

Columns 7 through 9 in Table 8.9 show the projected poverty rate for all persons and the shares of each quintile under the three scenarios.[29] The share of the bottom quintile (which is now near its historic low) is projected to rise and the share of the top quintile (which is near its historic high) is projected to fall. The magnitudes are slightly larger under the noncyclical forecast than under either of the less sanguine alternatives. Under the CBO forecast the poor gain 0.6 of a percentage point and the rich lose 0.8 (compare column 9 to column 2). As noted previously, this would constitute a sizable redistribution by historical standards.

Projected movements in the poverty rate over the balance of the 1980s are also quite optimistic and not terribly sensitive to macroeconomic conditions (within the range considered). Under the noncyclical forecast the poverty rate falls to 11.1 percent (roughly its historic low) as the recovery continues. But if the pessimistic scenario is more accurate, the decline will be only to 11.5 percent. This difference is minor compared to the projected decline in poverty.

The basic reason is clear. The unemployment rate in 1989 in each of these forecasts is well below the 1983 rate. If this proves to be true, then, according to our regressions, the income distribution should become more equal and the poverty count should fall substantially. However, if bad luck (or bad policy) leads to much worse macroeconomic conditions, the poverty rate will not fall to that extent.

ACCORDING TO AN OLD CLICHE now enjoying a revival, a rising tide raises all boats. Our analysis confirms this view and indicates that the smallest boats get raised the most (relatively). Conversely, however, they also fall the most when the tide ebbs—a point to keep in mind when the unemployed are drafted to fight the war on inflation.

We find that both the poverty count and the share of the lowest quintile of income recipients move significantly over the business cycle. Our estimates in Table 8.1 suggest that a 2-point rise in prime-age male unemployment maintained for two years (a fairly typical recession) would subtract almost 0.3 of a percentage point from the share of the lowest quintile and add about 0.9 percentage points to the poverty rate for all persons. Our estimates in Table 8.9 suggest that the substandard economic performance of the 1973–1983 decade reduced the share of the lowest fifth by almost 1 percentage point and raised the poverty count by 4.5 percentage points. These are very large effects.

The effects of the business cycle are borne unevenly across demographic groups. Although the relative wage structure seems to be affected little by the cycle, group-specific unemployment rates are affected differentially. Specifically, unemployment among the old and among women appears to be less sensitive to overall economic conditions; unemployment among the young and nonwhites appears to be more sensitive. Low-wage workers also are less well protected by unemployment compensation than high-wage workers and so lose more when unemployment strikes.

In contrast, there is little or no evidence that inflation is the cruelest tax (that is, bears most heavily on the poor). The few effects of inflation that we found were the results of anticipated, not unanticipated, inflation. According to our estimates in Table 8.1, a rise in inflation has trivial effects on income shares but does increase the poverty count somewhat. We find few effects of inflation on either the relative wages received or the relative prices paid by low-income people. Although inflation has eroded the real value of AFDC benefits, other major transfer programs have been protected by indexing.

Over the postwar period the overall tax structure seems to have grown less progressive, primarily because of the increasing reliance on payroll taxes. The federal personal income tax has changed significantly, but the increased tax burden imposed on the poor by declining real exemptions was more or less offset by the earned income credit and the flat standard deduction.

WHAT THE FUTURE will bring in the way of tax changes and cyclical developments is, of course, anyone's guess. On the tax side, it is clear that payroll taxes will increase and that bracket indexing will halt the erosion of the zero bracket amount. But other policy changes are less predictable—especially with fundamental tax reform now high on the national agenda.

All in all, there is no strong reason to think that the future will look very different from the past. There is also no reason to think that poverty will be any less procyclical in the future than it has been in the past. In addition, if recent cuts in social welfare and unemployment programs are maintained, the income-cushioning role of government transfer programs will be reduced. The poor thus have good reason to fear the recessions that lie ahead.

9   Household Composition and Poverty

Mary Jo Bane

IT HAS BECOME COMMON KNOWLEDGE—whether true or not—that family structure is important in explaining contemporary poverty. "The feminization of poverty" has become conventional shorthand for the fact that women living alone or with their children are disproportionately represented among the poor. Over the past two decades the concentration of poverty among female-headed and single-person households has become more pronounced; at the same time, increased marital break-up, births to unmarried women, and independent living by elderly widows have become more common.

The publicity given to these changes might seem to imply that the bulk of contemporary poverty is a family structure phenomenon—that family structure changes "cause" most poverty, or that changes in family structure have led to current poverty rates that are much higher than they would have been if family composition had remained stable. In fact, previous research, including some reported in this volume, indicates that a rather small percentage of the changes in the poverty level over the past few decades can be attributed to demographic change. Gottschalk and Danziger (1984), for example, estimated that the poverty rate in 1982 was about 1.8 percentage points higher than it would have been if demographic composition had not changed since 1967. Danziger, Haveman, and Plotnick in this volume came to similar conclusions using different methods.

This chapter builds on that work. It begins with a description of the changes that have taken place in the composition of the population, and uses an accounting framework to assess the impact of these changes on overall poverty rates. An analysis of the composition of the poor demonstrates a dramatic increase in the proportion of the poor who are members of female-headed and single-person households, but also shows that the "feminization of poverty" is due at least as much (and more so among blacks) to changes in relative poverty rates of various household composition types as to changes in the family structure composition of the population.

This finding raises the interesting question of how much poverty follows family structure events and how much exists before the family structure change. Longitudinal data suggest that only about a quarter to a fifth of the poor in the late 1970s *became* poor when the family structure changed. The pattern, however, is quite different among whites and blacks: "event-driven" poverty is more common among whites, and "reshuffled" poverty much more common among blacks. The analyses point to several different trends:

> A general trend toward family split-ups and independent living. Among blacks there is less trend toward independent living but a much more pronounced trend toward female-headed families.
>
> An increasing proportion of poverty that is caused by family events— that is, the female family head or single individual was not poor before the split-up. Event-caused poverty is much more characteristic of whites than of blacks.
>
> A dramatic change in the family structure of poor blacks toward female-headed families. The members of these families are poor both before and after the family change that places them in female-headed or single-person households.

These empirical findings are developed in detail, and the chapter concludes with an assessment of the implications for policy of the different routes into poverty.

Household Composition and Poverty, 1960–1982

COMPOSITION OF THE POOR IN 1979

Table 9.1 shows the distribution of the total population and the distribution of poor persons by race and household type in 1979.[1] The definition of poverty is the standard definition used in published census reports; it includes as income the household's cash transfers but excludes noncash transfers.[2]

Table 9.1 Distribution of total population and poor population by race, 1979

	All races		Whites		Blacks	
	Total	Poor	Total	Poor	Total	Poor
Members of male-						
headed families	75.9	41.2	78.9	47.8	52.8	24.8
Children	(23.2)	(17.0)	(23.5)	(19.3)	(18.1)	(10.7)
Nonelderly adults	(46.2)	(19.7)	(48.5)	(23.2)	(30.7)	(11.3)
Elderly	(6.5)	(4.5)	(6.9)	(5.3)	(4.0)	(2.8)
Nonelderly adults						
living alone	8.3	13.4	8.1	15.2	9.7	9.6
Male	(4.5)	(6.0)	(4.4)	(6.6)	(5.7)	(4.7)
Female	(3.8)	(7.4)	(3.7)	(8.6)	(4.0)	(4.9)
Elderly living alone	3.6	9.0	3.8	11.1	2.6	5.0
Male	(0.8)	(1.7)	(0.8)	(1.9)	(0.8)	(1.2)
Female	(2.8)	(7.3)	(3.0)	(9.2)	(1.8)	(3.8)
Members of female-						
headed families	12.3	36.5	9.1	25.8	35.0	60.6
Children	(5.3)	(21.9)	(3.6)	(15.5)	(17.9)	(36.1)
Nonelderly adults	(6.1)	(13.7)	(4.7)	(9.6)	(15.7)	(23.1)
Elderly	(0.9)	(0.9)	(0.8)	(0.7)	(1.4)	(1.4)

Source: Calculated from U.S. Bureau of the Census (1981c).

The population is separated into four basic household categories, which will be used throughout the chapter: members of husband-wife and other male-headed families ("male-headed families," although sexist, is the traditional and briefer census terminology), of which about 96 percent are headed by married couples; members of female-headed families, no spouse present; nonelderly adults living alone; and elderly adults living alone. Persons in the two family categories are classified by age: children, nonelderly adults, and elderly. Note that not all female-headed families include children: in 1979, 31 percent were composed of adults only (U.S. Bureau of the Census, 1984b). Nor, of course, do all male-headed families: in 1979, 47 percent did not include children. Most of the elderly in male-headed families are elderly married couples, although a small proportion are elderly men and women living in the households of their children or other relatives. The two categories of single-person households are divided by sex.

The table shows that although three-quarters of the American population in 1979 lived in male-headed families, mostly husband-wife, only about 40 percent of the poor lived in such families. At that time 75.9 percent of the population lived in husband-wife and other male-headed families while 12.3 percent lived in female-headed families. Elderly living alone made up 3.6 percent of the population while nonelderly men and women living alone were 8.3 percent. In contrast, 36.5 percent of the poor were members of female-headed families, 13.4 percent of the poor were nonelderly men and women living alone and 9.0 percent of the poor were elderly living alone. Thus 58.9 percent of the poor were men and women living alone or members of female-headed families.

Blacks were much more likely than whites to be living in female-headed families in 1979, and these families were a much larger proportion of the black poor than the white poor. In 1979, 35.0 percent of all blacks lived in female-headed families, which made up 60.6 percent of the black poor. In contrast, 9.1 percent of whites lived in female-headed families, which were 25.8 percent of the white poor. Blacks and whites were about equally likely to live in single-person households, with 11.9 percent of the white population in 1979 living alone and 12.3 percent of the black population living alone.

These differences between the family structure of the poor and that of the population as a whole, and the differences between blacks and whites, hint that family structure may be implicated in causing or maintaining poverty. In 1983 15.2 percent of Americans were poor, 12.1 percent of whites and 35.7 percent of blacks. Might not those rates have been much lower if family structure were more stable—if married couples stayed together, if children lived at home until they could support themselves, and if families took care of their elderly relatives? And might not the differences between blacks and whites have been much less if black family structure were more similar to that of whites?

CHANGES IN FAMILY STRUCTURE AND POVERTY

Those questions can be addressed by looking at the changes that have taken place over time in the family structure of the population and the effects that those changes have had on overall poverty rates. It is indeed true, consistent with popular perceptions, that family structure has changed dramatically over the past few decades, away from traditional married-couple families: in 1959, 85.8 percent of the population lived in male-headed families; in 1983, 74.4 percent did. Figure 9.1 graphs these changes separately for blacks and whites. Household composition has changed much

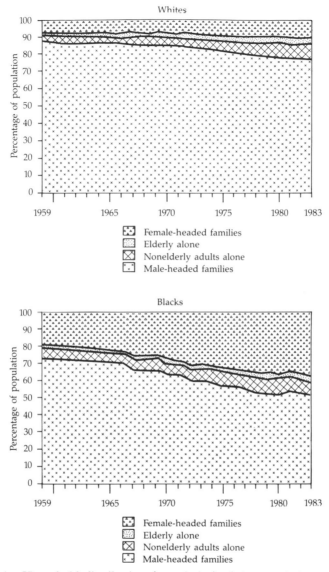

Figure 9.1. Household distribution (cumulative) of the population, whites and blacks, 1959–1983. Sources: U.S. Bureau of the Census, Current Population Reports, ser. P–20, *Household and Family Characteristics,* various years.

more dramatically among blacks over the two decades, with the percentage living in female-headed families rising from 19.0 percent in 1959 to 36.7 percent in 1983.

Since 1959 the composition of the population, especially among blacks, has shifted toward household types that are most likely to be poor. Female-headed families and individuals living alone have both grown as a proportion of all households. The major decline is seen in husband-wife families, the group that is by far the least likely to be poor.

But how much effect have these changes in family structure had on the overall poverty rate? One way to answer that question is to calculate the extent to which total poverty in the United States would have been different in 1979 and 1983 if the poverty rates within household composition categories had changed as they did since 1959, but if age and household composition had remained at 1959 levels. The results are consistent with other work but nonetheless somewhat surprising:

> The poverty rate in 1979 would have been about 16 percent lower than it was had family composition remained as it was in 1959. Family composition changes contributed almost nothing to the increase in poverty between 1979 and 1983.
>
> Family composition effects are more dramatic for blacks than for whites. Nonetheless, most of the difference between blacks and whites comes from higher poverty rates for blacks within household composition types. And the accounting framework may well overestimate the effects of family structure on black poverty.

Table 9.2 shows the effects on overall poverty rates of various family composition adjustments. The first row of each panel shows actual poverty rates, the second row, the effects in 1969, 1979, and 1983 of holding household composition constant at the 1959 level. Consider 1979, when the actual poverty rate was 11.6 percent. If household composition had remained as it was in 1959 but poverty rates were at their 1979 levels, the poverty rate would have been 9.7 percent, or 16 percent lower. If we hold family structure at the 1979 level, we find that family changes between 1979 and 1983 account for only 0.2 percentage points of the actual 3.4-percentage-point increase for all races.

These calculations hold both age structure and household composition constant at earlier levels. It is possible, however, to remove the age structure effect and look only at the changes in household composition within broad age categories. The age-adjusted figures in Table 9.2 indicate that

Table 9.2. Effects of household composition changes on overall poverty rate, by race, 1959–1983

	1959	1969	1979	1983
All races				
Actual poverty rate	22.4	12.1	11.6	15.0
If 1959 composition	—	11.4	9.7	13.0
With age adjustment		11.4	9.5	12.4
If 1979 composition	—	—	—	14.8
Whites				
Actual poverty rate	18.1	9.5	9.1	12.0
If 1959 composition	—	9.0	7.8	10.8
If 1979 composition	—	—	—	11.9
Blacks				
Actual poverty rate	55.1	32.2	30.9	35.5
If 1959 composition	—	29.7	24.2	28.5
If 1979 composition	—	—	—	35.3
If white composition	51.8	25.2	20.6	25.1

Sources: Calculated from data from U.S. Bureau of the Census (1981c, 1984c, 1984d).

the differences are not very great, but household composition effects are larger when age structure is adjusted to its current levels. The age structure shift has been toward a larger representation of nonelderly adults in the population, with the decrease in children more than balancing the increase in the elderly. Nonelderly adults are less likely to be poor than either children or the elderly, so, other things equal, an increase in the proportion of nonelderly adults would be expected to decrease poverty.

A comparison for blacks and whites shows that the effects of household composition changes have been more dramatic among blacks. In 1979 the actual poverty rate for blacks was 30.9 percent. If household composition among blacks had not changed since 1959, the poverty rate would have been 24.2 percent, or 22 percent below its actual level. For whites the 1959 household composition yields a 1979 poverty rate 14 percent below its actual level.

Estimates of what black poverty rates would have been if their household composition had been the same as whites show that in 1983 differences in household composition account for 44 percent of the differences in overall poverty rates between blacks and whites. Thus 55 percent of the difference between blacks and whites comes from higher poverty rates for blacks *within* household composition types.

Given the dramatic changes in family composition that have taken place and the popular perception of the importance of these changes, these family composition effects are surprisingly small. But small as they are, they are almost certainly overstated since the accounting framework holds family composition constant at earlier levels while assuming that poverty rates changed over time as they did. The calculations assume that poverty rates are associated with household composition types, and that the people who moved, for example, from male-headed families to female-headed families between 1959 and 1979 were essentially the same, on average, as people who remained in husband-wife families.

This assumption is not necessarily correct. It could be that the increased numbers in female-headed families in 1979 were people who were more likely to be poor, whatever type of family they lived in. Had they remained in husband-wife families, the poverty rate among that group would have been higher and the overall poverty rate perhaps not much different from what it turned out to be. This scenario represents a reshuffling of poor people into different household types rather than a change in poverty caused by household changes.

Some light can be shed on the differences between popular perceptions of the importance of family structure changes for poverty and the data on estimated effects by a more explicit look at the feminization of poverty and the factors contributing to it. This analysis can also help our understanding of the extent to which the estimated effects may be overstated.

THE FEMINIZATION OF POVERTY

With a rather broad definition of the feminization of poverty—including everyone not living in husband-wife or other male-headed families—it is clear that poverty has become more and more feminized.

Members of female-headed and single-person households made up 60 percent of the poor in 1979, up from 30 percent in 1959. Both the level of feminization and the amount of change were much greater among blacks.

Figure 9.2 shows these changes separately for blacks and whites. The data for all races combined show that members of female-headed families and men and women living alone made up 30.3 percent of the poor in 1959, rose to 58.9 percent of the poor in 1979, and decreased slightly to 53.7 percent of the poor in 1983. By far the greatest increase between 1959 and 1979 occurred among members of female-headed families. During recessions it appears that members of female-headed families and men and women living alone decline as a proportion of the poor, presumably because

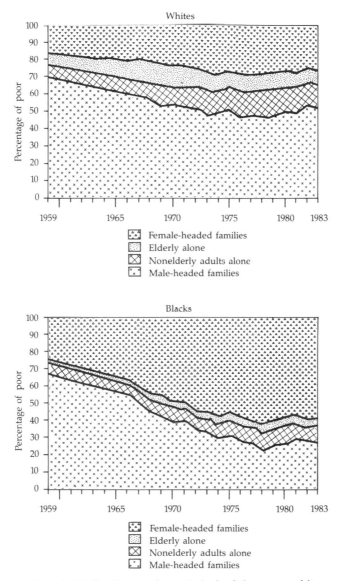

Figure 9.2.   Household distribution (cumulative) of the poor, whites and blacks, 1959–1983. Source: U.S. Bureau of the Census, Current Population Reports, ser. P–60, *Characteristics of the Population below the Poverty Level,* various years.

economic hard times push a disproportionate number of male-headed families into poverty.

Looking separately by race, we see that among whites the proportion of the poor living in female-headed and single-person families increased from 29.0 percent in 1959 to 52.1 percent in 1979. Among blacks the proportion in female-headed and single-person households more than doubled from 32.5 percent in 1959 to 75.2 percent in 1979.

These increases in the proportion of the poor living in female-headed and single-person households result from the combined effects of changes in the family composition of the population as a whole and changes in the relative poverty rates of various household groups. Figure 9.3 shows poverty rate changes. Poverty rates in general were falling over the period 1959 to 1979 and rising from 1979 to 1983. The most dramatic declines in rates appear to be among elderly whites living alone and among black male-headed families.

We can combine the data on household composition changes (Figure 9.1) and poverty rate changes (Figure 9.3) to estimate the importance of each of these changes in explaining the increased feminization of poverty. This is done by calculating what percentage of the poor would have been members of female-headed families and men and women living alone if the composition of the population had remained what it was in 1959 while poverty rates changed the way they did. The findings emphasize the importance of changes in relative poverty rates.

About 40 percent of the increase in the feminization of poverty overall is accounted for by changes in relative poverty rates. Changes in relative poverty rates were considerably more important for blacks than whites.

With 1959 composition and 1979 poverty rates, 42.3 percent of the poor would have fallen into the female-household-head and living-alone groups, compared to the actual percentages of 30.3 percent in 1959 and 58.9 in 1979. If poverty rates had stayed the same between 1959 and 1979 or had fallen in the same proportions for all groups, the calculated "feminization" rate for 1979 would be the same as the actual rate in 1959. If the poverty rates for different groups had become more alike over the time period, the calculated rate would be *lower* than the actual 1959 rate. Instead, the calculated rate is *higher* than the actual 1959 rate, implying that the gap between group poverty rates actually increased over the period. One finds that 42 percent of the increased feminization between 1959 and 1979 was due to differential changes in poverty rates, while 58 percent was due to changes in the household composition of the population.

Doing the calculation separately by race, we find that 32 percent of the

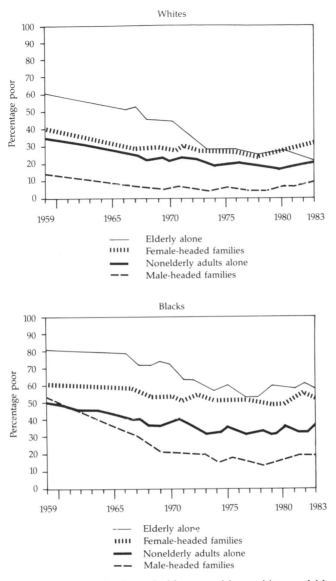

Figure 9.3. Poverty rates by household composition, whites and blacks, 1959–1983. Source: See Figure 9.2.

increase in feminization among whites can be accounted for by changes in poverty rates compared to 51 percent for blacks. Put more simply, for both races, as more people moved into female-headed families, the poverty rate gap between male- and female-headed families increased. The gap increased more for blacks than for whites.

Especially among blacks, as more female-headed families were formed, the male-headed families left intact were far less likely to be poor than they had been in earlier times. This important finding suggests that a good deal of black poverty might simply have reflected being reshuffled, with poor two-parent families breaking apart into poor female-headed and single-person households, while better-off families remained together. Among whites, the data are more suggestive of a scenario under which families that were well off before a split became poor after it (event-driven poverty).

Cross-sectional data cannot substantiate these hypotheses, however. For that we turn to longitudinal data.

Transitions into Poverty

It is clear that certain household types are much more likely to be poor than others and that aggregate changes in household composition may have slowed the declines in poverty over the 1959–1979 period. The next question, hinted at by the feminization analysis, is the extent to which the poverty of female-headed and single-person households is actually associated with the transition from a nonpoor into a poor household.

Consider the different ways in which a female household head and her children might have become poor. She might have been poor *before* she became a household head, living with her own poor parents or with a husband who was also poor, and in a sense carried that poverty over into her new situation. She might have become poor *after* she became a household head, either by losing earnings, child support, or another source of income or by adding a member to the family whose increased needs put sufficient pressure on family income to drive them into poverty.

Alternatively, she might have become poor *at the same time* she became a household head; that is, moving from the nonpoor household of her parents or a marriage into a poor household headed by herself. In these cases there could have been a simultaneous change in needs; for example, the birth of a child to a woman who moved away from home at the time of the birth. There could have been a change in resources; for example, the woman also stopped working. Or her poverty could have come about even though the total resources available to household members remained approximately the same: Household resources could have been divided up in such a way that one of the households after the split became poor; or the loss of economies of scale could have made both households poor after the split.

The distinction among these three routes into poverty is important, I believe, because of the way we think about individual and family responsibility, a set of issues that are discussed in the last section of this chapter. The extent to which poverty in the late 1970s appears to have come about from the various routes is derived from two analyses: one of transitions into poverty and one of transitions into female-headed or single-person households. The first analysis looks at people in the first year of a spell of poverty and asks whether the beginning of the poverty spell occurred at the same time as a change in household structure. This analysis yields estimates of the relative importance, for members of poor female-headed and single-person households, of poverty spells that began *simultaneously with* household changes versus poverty spells that began *after* household changes.

The analysis of transitions does not allow examination of the extent to which the poverty spells of female-headed and single-person households begin *before* household changes. This information, however, can be inferred from an analysis of transitions into female-headed and single-person households. This analysis, like that of poverty spell beginnings, identifies simultaneous household and poverty transitions. In addition, it identifies households that are poor both before and after the household transitions.

Ideally, one would want a large sample of years of poverty, covering a long period after the beginning of poverty spells, to estimate a distribution of beginning types for the poor at a point in time. A very rough approximation of this can be obtained by combining the two analyses described above.

These analyses use longitudinal data from the first fifteen years of the Panel Study of Income Dynamics (PSID), a longitudinal study that began with a sample of about 5,000 households in 1968 and included more than 20,000 individuals in 1982. The study oversampled low-income areas and thus generates relatively large unweighted samples of blacks. The sample, the data, and the weighting procedures are described extensively in the *User Guide* (Survey Research Center, 1984) and in other work from Michigan. The representativeness of the sample is examined in Becketti et al. (1983).

POVERTY SPELL BEGINNINGS

The first PSID analysis identifies spells of poverty, defined as periods of one or more years when an individual's household income falls below the poverty line, and examines the events associated with the move into poverty. The rationale for looking at poverty spells, the methods for identifying spells, and the procedures for identifying beginning types are the same as those used by Bane and Ellwood (1983b).[3] This analysis uses a somewhat different set of beginning types and includes elderly men and women.[4] In all, 6,794 poverty spell beginnings were observed during the fifteen years, 2,613 for whites and 4,181 for blacks.

Tables 9.3 and 9.4 show the distribution of beginning types, for whites and blacks, by household relationship in the first year of the poverty spell. They distinguish poverty spells that began at birth, both those in which the household was poor before the birth and those in which the birth was simultaneous with the movement into poverty. They show three types of movement into female-headed families, that of children from male-headed into female-headed families, that of women in male-headed families (mostly wives but also female children in male-headed families) into female headship, and that of women from other types of families into female headship. This last category includes girls who move from their mothers' households into their own female-headed families and women living alone who have children and thus become female household heads. It shows movements from various types of families into single-person households for both elderly and nonelderly adults. The final set of categories shows needs and earnings changes. If a household's needs increased proportionately more than its income, either because income did not keep up with inflation or because the household increased in size, the poverty spell beginning was attributed to a needs change. Otherwise, income was defined as the precipitating event, either the earnings of the head, the earnings of others, or unearned, mostly transfer, income.[5]

The tables show a number of interesting facts, most of them similar to those reported and discussed in Bane and Ellwood (1983b). For the purposes of this chapter, though, the most interesting concern the proportion of spells of poverty that begin with a movement into a female-headed or single-person household.

Among whites about a quarter of all poverty spell beginnings were associated with the move into a female-headed or single-person household.

For members of female-headed families in the first year of their poverty spells, the table shows that about 50 percent of their spells began with the

Table 9.3. Distribution of types of poverty spell beginnings among whites, by household structure in first year of poverty spell

Primary reason for beginning of individual's poverty spell	Individual's household structure in first year of spell				
	Male-headed family	Female-headed family	Single nonelderly adult	Single elderly person	All
Birth					
Born into poor household	3.4%	5.3%	—	—	3.1%
Born when household became poor	2.6	4.4	—	—	2.4
Transition to female-headed family	—	50.5	—	—	11.3
By child from male-headed family	—	(25.6)	—	—	(5.8)
By wife or adult daughter from male-headed family	—	(20.7)	—	—	(4.7)
By woman from female-headed or single household	—	(3.7)	—	—	(0.8)
Transition to single living	—	—	66.5	30.9	13.3
Income or needs changed					
Household needs increased	9.8	5.1	1.1	8.0	7.3
Head's earnings dropped	51.3	10.8	21.1	23.7	36.5
Earnings of other household members dropped	10.5	12.0	—	—	8.7
Nonearned income dropped	20.7	12.5	6.6	37.5	17.4
Percentage of beginnings	58.0	21.6	16.2	4.3	100.0
Number of observed beginnings	1,579	560	378	96	2,613

Source: Tabulations from the Panel Study of Income Dynamics.

household change. Some proportion of the birth beginnings may also have occurred simultaneously with a household change if the birth itself was the precipitating event for the formation of a female-headed household. About 40 percent of the poverty spells of white members of female-headed families

Table 9.4. Distribution of types of poverty spell beginnings among blacks, by household structure in first year of poverty spell

Primary reason for beginning of individual's poverty spell	Individual's household structure in first year of spell				
	Male-headed family	Female-headed family	Single nonelderly adult	Single elderly person	All
Birth					
Born into poor household	8.1%	17.5%	—	—	11.6%
Born when household became poor	1.8	4.0	—	—	2.6
Transition to female-headed family	—	23.2	—	—	10.9
By child from male-headed family	—	(12.1)	—	—	(5.7)
By wife or adult daughter from male-headed family	—	(7.9)	—	—	(3.7)
By woman from female-headed or single household	—	(3.2)	—	—	(1.5)
Transition to single living	—	—	50.3	32.8	5.9
Income or needs changed					
Household needs increased	14.2	10.4	0.4	0.0	11.3
Head's earnings dropped	40.3	14.0	31.3	23.3	27.1
Earnings of other household members dropped	19.4	15.5	—	—	15.5
Nonearned income dropped	15.7	15.3	10.6	44.0	15.5
Percentage of beginnings	43.1	46.3	9.1	1.5	100.0
Number of observed beginnings	1,859	1,963	338	21	4,181

Source: Tabulations from the Panel Study of Income Dynamics.

began with an earnings or needs change. Changes in the earnings of others—mostly adult children, one suspects, but perhaps also roommates or partners—are surprisingly important. These could have come about when the adults left the household, and some of them might have thus been more accurately classified as a different type of household change. Changes in transfer ("other") income are also important, with both of these categories somewhat more important than changes in the earnings of the female household head.

Among adults living alone, the table shows that an even larger proportion of poverty spell beginnings were associated with movements into single-person households. These adults are largely, one assumes, young men and women who are moving out of their parents' households to live independently. Among the elderly living alone, in contrast, less than a third of poverty spell beginnings were associated with the movement into a single-person household—which among the elderly mostly means widowhood. The major source of poverty spell beginnings for the elderly living alone was changes in "other income," primarily, one assumes, Social Security.

Among blacks, even though a much larger proportion of the poor are members of female-headed households, only about 17 percent of poverty spell beginnings are associated with movement into a female-headed or single-person household. Among those blacks in female-headed or single-person households in the first year of the poverty spell, about 23 percent of all poverty spell beginnings were associated with the household change.

There are many indications in the data on blacks of the lesser importance of event-caused poverty.[6] Birth into poverty is the source of 12 percent of poverty spell beginnings among blacks and 17.5 percent of the beginnings of those in female-headed families. The movement into female-headed families accounts for less than a quarter of the poverty spell beginnings of those in female-headed families. More than half of the poverty spells of these families begin with an income or needs change that occurs after the formation of a female-headed household, although only 14 percent began with a change in the earnings of the head. Changes in needs, in the earnings of others, and in transfer income are all surprisingly important in generating poverty among families headed by women. Adults living alone account for a smaller proportion of poverty spell beginnings among blacks than whites, and the movement into those households is a somewhat less important beginning type.

When interpreting these data, one should be aware that beginning types were tabulated for all spells of poverty. An individual could have more than one spell; Duncan (1984), also using PSID data, reported a substantial amount of what he called intermittent poverty. We could be seeing, therefore, indications of chronic low income, which manifests itself in many poverty spells brought about by rather small income or needs changes.

TRANSITIONS INTO FEMALE-HEADED AND SINGLE-PERSON HOUSEHOLDS

A different, and perhaps better, indication of the importance of event-driven poverty can be derived from looking at transitions into female-headed and single-person households. The PSID can be used to look for such transitions, since over the period of the panel study a great many transitions took place. The analysis reported here found 5,867 transitions into female-headed or single-person households, 3,010 among whites and 2,857 among blacks. It is thus possible to ascertain the poverty status of the individual making the transition both before and after the transition took place.

Table 9.5 shows the results of such an analysis, using data from years two to fourteen of the PSID. Income in three years was observed to determine poverty status: the year of the transition and the years before and after. (This analysis does not include births.)

The table shows that the majority of the whites and about half of the blacks who moved into female-headed and single-person households were

Table 9.5. Changes in poverty status before and after household transition, by race[a]

	% not poor after transition	Poor after transition		Unweighted number
		% not poor before	% poor before	
Transition by whites				
Into female-headed family				
From male-headed household	75.8	76.5	23.5	1,308
From other household	80.3	63.7	36.3	163
Into nonelderly adult single household	77.4	81.0	19.0	1,374
Into elderly single household	78.1	71.8	28.2	165
Transition by blacks				
Into female-headed family				
From male-headed household	43.5	38.2	61.8	1,515
From other household	48.4	23.5	76.5	384
Into nonelderly adult single household	62.3	48.7	51.3	906
Into elderly single household	20.5	25.5	74.5	52

Source: Tabulations from the Panel Study of Income Dynamics.
a. Income observed in year before transition, year of transition, and year following transition.

not poor after their household transitions. Most of these were not poor before the transition either. A small proportion (not shown in the table but less than 10 percent in most categories) were poor before the transition and not poor after.

Among those who were poor in the first year after the transition into female-headed or single-person households, the table shows very different patterns for blacks and whites: three-quarters of whites who were poor in the first year after moving into a female-headed or single-person household became poor simultaneously with the transition; in contrast, of the blacks who were poor after the transition, about two-thirds had also been poor before.

These data suggest very clearly the importance of poverty associated with split-ups of male-headed families among whites but the much lesser importance of event-caused poverty among blacks. This is especially true for movements into female-headed families, but even for movements into single-person adult households, the difference between blacks and whites is clear: for whites more than 80 percent of poverty after a split is associated with the event, while among blacks less than half appears to be event-caused.

RELATIVE IMPORTANCE OF HOUSEHOLD TRANSITION IN INITIATING POVERTY

The PSID does not, unfortunately, provide an ideal sample for looking comprehensively at event-caused versus reshuffled poverty. Ideally one would have a large sample of years of poverty observed over a long enough time that the beginning types of all current years of poverty could be observed. Even better, one would observe the beginning of the *first* spell of poverty for each individual, so as to better characterize intermittent poverty of chronic low income. But because many spells of poverty, especially among blacks, last a very long time (Bane and Ellwood, 1983b) and because much poverty is intermittent, even with fifteen years of data many beginnings are simply not observed.

What is reported here is only a rough approximation of the ideal analysis. It combines the two analyses described above by using the first years of poverty spells of single-person and female-headed households and the first years of poverty after transitions, eliminating the double counting of years when a transition and a poverty spell beginning occurred simultaneously. It thus approximates a sample of years of poverty occurring to female-headed or single-person households. The sample, however, almost certainly underrepresents the later years of long-term poverty spells and more generally persistent poverty. It is likely to overrepresent intermittent poverty, since the first year of each spell is included.

With those caveats, Table 9.6 indicates the relative importance of poverty that begins simultaneously with, before, and after a household transition to a female-headed or single-person household. It basically corroborates the patterns observed earlier.

About 49 percent of poor white members of female-headed families began their spell simultaneously with a household transition, 37 percent began after the transition, and 14 percent began before the transition.[7] Event-caused poverty is clearly important among whites. Falling into poverty because of an earnings or needs change after becoming a female household head is also important, however.

About 22 percent of the poverty of poor blacks in single-parent families began simultaneously with a household transition, 45 percent began after the transition, and 33 percent began before. Falling into or back into poverty while a female household head is surprisingly common. Poverty that carries over from male- to female-headed households appears to be more than twice as common among blacks as whites.

Among nonelderly adults in single-person households, about 65 percent of the poverty of whites and 56 percent of the poverty of blacks began

Table 9.6. Beginning of poverty spells in relation to household transition, by race (percentages)

Onset of spell	Female-headed household	Adult alone	Elderly adult alone
Whites			
Simultaneous with household transition	49	65	30
After transition	37	24	59
Before transition	14	11	11
Blacks			
Simultaneous with household transition	22	56	17
After transition	45	8	34
Before transition	33	36	49

Source: Estimated from data reported in Tables 9.3, 9.4, and 9.5.

simultaneously with beginning to live alone. Among the elderly living alone, only about 30 percent of the poverty of whites and 17 percent of that of blacks began with the transitions into a single-person household.

It is hard to know how much the underrepresenation of long-term poverty distorts this analysis. We know from both Bane and Ellwood (1983b) and Duncan (1984) that blacks have much longer poverty spells than whites. Bane and Ellwood also reported that poverty spells that began with birth are much longer than those that began in other ways. Their analyses did not, however, find much difference in duration between poverty spells that began with family changes and those that began with earnings or needs changes. It is quite possible that poverty carried over into female-headed or single-person households generates longer spells of poverty for those households than poverty that began with or after the transition. That issue, however, must wait for later research.

THE IMPORTANCE OF ECONOMIES OF SCALE

When poverty does occur simultaneously with a household transition, it can come about either because of the way household resources are divided after the split or because of the loss of economies of scale. The latter can lead to the onset of poverty because economies of scale are taken into account in establishing the poverty level.[8]

Poverty can conceivably be created, therefore, simply by the loss of the economies of scale that are assumed in defining poverty. For example, imagine a family of four with 1983 income of $11,500, which was about 113 percent of the poverty line for a family of that size ($10,178). Suppose the family splits up while the total resources available to the family remain the same. The mother and two children take $7,500 and the husband $4,000. Both families now fall below the poverty line, since the poverty line was $7,938 for a family of three and $5,061 for a single-person household.

If income is split according to a ratio reflecting the poverty line, as in the example above, the creation of poverty because of a family split-up can occur only in a relatively narrow band of family incomes. The income level below which poverty occurs for at least one of the split-off households because of the loss of economies of scale (the break-even point) depends on household sizes before and after the split. It ranges from about 116 percent of the poverty line for a household of six that breaks into two households of three each, to about 156 percent of the poverty line for a household of two that breaks into two single-person households.

The importance of the loss of economies of scale can thus be roughly estimated by looking at households for which a poverty spell occurred simultaneously with the transition and seeing whether household income fell between the poverty line and the break-even point before the split.[9] That analysis suggests that only a small proportion of the poverty that is generated by household splits occurs because of the loss of economies of scale. Of those who became poor when they moved into female-headed households, about 16 percent of whites and 28 percent of blacks became poor because of the loss of economies of scale.

This analysis, although rough, suggests that enough resources were available to many split-up households to avoid poverty for both households if total resources were divided up after the break proportionately to total need.[10] This is especially true among whites: although about half of all poverty among white female-headed households begins simultaneously with a household split, it appears that less than 10 percent (16 percent of that half) follows inexorably from the break. Among blacks, consistent with other findings in this chapter, we find the loss of economies of scale to be more important. Just as there are more poor black combined households that split into two poor independent households, so are there more black households just above the poverty level who are pushed into poverty by a split.

Individual and Family Responsibility

These findings are important because most family structure changes are to some extent voluntary, for at least one of the parties involved. (The obvious exception is widowhood, but the transition to poor widowhood accounts for only a small proportion of poverty.) Couples decide whether or not to break up; children (or their parents) whether to leave home, adults whether to live with others. To the extent that poverty is "chosen," to the extent that people make the decision to accept poverty to achieve privacy by moving from a nonpoor joint household to a poor independent household, society in the aggregate is less willing to assume the responsibility for supporting the person who has made or suffered from the decision.

Thus it is important to recognize that less than half of the poverty of female-headed and single-person households and therefore only about a quarter to a fifth of all poverty appears to have come about *simultaneously with* changes in household composition. Family composition changes in the early 1980s made only a trivial contribution to the increase in poverty.

Most poverty, even that of female-headed families, occurs because of income or job changes.

It is also important that only about a fifth of the poverty among black female-headed and single-person households appears to be driven by the events of household composition changes. Among blacks poor female-headed and single-person households are much more likely to be formed from households that were already poor. They are also much more likely to fall into or back into poverty after the break-up, perhaps testifying to the chronic economic problems of black families and resultant intermittent poverty. Although there has indeed been a dramatic and shocking increase in female-headed households among blacks and an equally dramatic feminization of black poverty, one cannot conclude that much of the poverty could have been avoided had families stayed together. The serious problems in the black community appear to be intertwined, as Wilson and Neckerman, in this volume, point out, rather then stemming primarily from family break-ups.

This analysis indicates that the problem of poverty should be addressed by devoting attention to employment, wages, and the development of skills necessary for productive participation in the labor force rather than hand-wringing about the decline of the family. Nonetheless, it is still true that perhaps a fifth of all poverty occurs simultaneously with family break-up, and only a small proportion of that is attributable to the loss of economies of scale. Thus, perhaps about 15 percent of all poverty could be alleviated by more attention to the allocation of resources after household splits.

The problem of enforcing legal support responsibilities for children and spouses has rightfully received a good deal of recent attention—and deserves a good deal more. We may also want to move to the next steps: expanding notions of legal responsibility and providing more incentives for generosity.

It is extremely important to note, however, that if the argument of this chapter is correct, child and spousal support may help alleviate the poverty of many white households, but it can make only the smallest dent in the problem of black poverty. The poverty of blacks is indeed concentrated among women, children, and split-up households, but its roots cannot be found in decisions about family structure. That problem is a much larger one, which we can no longer afford to misunderstand or to ignore.

10 Poverty and Family Structure: The Widening Gap between Evidence and Public Policy Issues

William Julius Wilson
Kathryn M. Neckerman

IN THE EARLY AND MID-1960s social scientists such as Kenneth B. Clark (1965), Lee Rainwater (1966), and Daniel Patrick Moynihan (1965) discussed in clear and forceful terms the relationship between black poverty and family structure and sounded the alarm even then that the problems of family dissolution among poor blacks were approaching catastrophic proportions. These writers emphasized that the rising rates of broken marriage, out-of-wedlock births, female-headed families, and welfare dependency among poor urban blacks were the products not only of race-specific experiences but also of structural conditions in the larger society, including economic relations. And they underlined the need to address these problems with programs that would attack structural inequality in American society and thereby, in the words of Moynihan, "bring the Negro American to full and equal sharing in the responsibilities and rewards of citizenship" (1965, p. 48).

The virulent attacks on the Moynihan report on the Negro family in the latter half of the 1960s created a lull in serious research on the subject. Recently, however, increases in teenage pregnancies and the sharp rise in female-headed families, especially in the inner city, have generated a good deal of public interest, leading to a revival of scholarly research on the relationship between poverty and family structure.

There is a distinct difference in the way the problems of poverty and family structure were viewed in the major studies of the 1960s and the way they are viewed today, however. Unlike the earlier studies, discussions of the relationship between black family instability and male joblessness in the current research have been overshadowed by analyses that link family instability with the growth of income transfers and in-kind benefits. Because, as we demonstrate in this chapter, the factors associated with the rise of single-parent families—not only among blacks, but among whites as well—are sufficiently complex to preclude overemphasis on any single variable, the recent trend among scholars and policymakers to neglect the role of male joblessness while emphasizing the role of welfare is especially questionable. But first let us examine the problem of poverty and family structure in its historical context.

Historical Perspective

In the early twentieth century the vast majority of both black and white low-income families were intact. Although national information on family structure was not available before the publication of the 1940 census, studies of early manuscript census forms of individual cities and counties make it clear that even among the very poor a substantial majority of both black and white families were two-parent families (Furstenberg, Hershberg, and Modell, 1975). Moreover, most of the women heading families in the late nineteenth and early twentieth centuries were widows (Pleck, 1972; Furstenberg, Hershberg, and Modell, 1975). Evidence from the census indicates that divorce and separation were relatively uncommon (Farley, 1970; Farley and Hermalin, 1971).

It is particularly useful to consider black families in historical perspective because social scientists have commonly assumed that the recent trends in black family structure that will be of concern in this chapter could be traced to the lingering effects of slavery. E. Franklin Frazier's classic statement of this view in *The Negro Family in the United States* (1939) informed all subsequent studies of the black family, including the Moynihan report (see Walker, 1985). But recent research has challenged assumptions about the influence of slavery on the character of the black family. Reconstruction of black family patterns from manuscript census forms has shown that the two-parent nuclear family was the predominant family form in the late nineteenth and early twentieth centuries. Historian Herbert Gutman (1976) examined data on black family structure during this period in northern urban areas (Buffalo and Brooklyn, New York), southern cities (Mobile, Alabama, Richmond, Virginia, and Charleston, South Carolina), and several counties and small towns and found that between 70 and 90 percent of black households were "male-present" and that a majority were nuclear families. Similar findings have been reported for Philadelphia (Furstenberg, Hershberg, and Modell, 1975), rural Virginia (Shifflett, 1975), Boston (Pleck, 1972), and cities of the Ohio Valley (Lammermeier, 1973). This research demonstrates that neither slavery, nor economic deprivation, nor the migration to urban areas had seriously affected black family structure by the first quarter of the twentieth century.

The poverty and degraded conditions in which most blacks lived were not, however, without their consequences for the family. For the most part, the positive association between intact family structure and measures of class such as property ownership, occupation, and literacy generally reflected the higher rate of mortality among poor men (Pleck, 1972; Furstenberg, Hershberg, and Modell, 1975). Widowhood accounted for about three-quarters of female-headed families among blacks, Germans, Irish, and native white Americans in Philadelphia in 1880 (Furstenberg, Hershberg, and Modell, 1975). In addition, men sometimes had to live apart from their families as they moved from one place to another in search of work (Pleck, 1972). Given their disproportionate concentration among the poor in America, black families were more strongly affected by these conditions and therefore were more likely than white families to be female-headed. For example, in Philadelphia in 1880 25.3 percent of all black families were female-headed, compared to only 13.6 percent of all native white families.

The earliest detailed national census information on family structure is available from the 1940 census. In 1940 female-headed families were more prevalent among blacks than among whites and among urbanites than among rural residents for both groups. Yet, even in urban areas 72 percent of black families with children under eighteen were male-headed. Moreover, irrespective of race and residence, most women heading families were widows.

The two-parent nuclear family remained the predominant type for both blacks and whites up to World War II. As shown in Table 10.1, 10 percent of white families and 18 percent of black families were female-headed in 1940. The relative stability in gross census figures on female-headed families between 1940 and 1960 obscures the beginnings of current trends in family break-up. More specifically, widowhood fell significantly during those two decades, and marital dissolution was rising.[1] Furthermore, the proportion of out-of-wedlock births was growing. By the 1960s the proportion of female-headed families had begun to increase significantly among blacks, rising from 22 percent in 1960 to 28 percent in 1970 and then to 42 percent by 1983. This proportion also rose among white families, from 8 percent in 1960 to 12 percent in 1983. The increase in female-headed families with children under eighteen is even more dramatic. By 1983 almost one out of five families with children under eighteen were headed by women, in-

Table 10.1. Percentage of female-headed families, no husband present, by race and Spanish origin, 1940–1983

Year	White	Black	Spanish origin	Total families
1940	10.1	17.9	—	—
1950	8.5	17.6[a]	—	9.4
1960	8.1	21.7	—	10.0
1965	9.0	24.9	—	10.5
1970	9.1	28.3	—	10.8
1971	9.4	30.6	—	11.5
1972	9.4	31.8	—	11.6
1973	9.6	34.6	16.7	12.2
1974	9.9	34.0	17.4	12.4
1975	10.5	35.3	18.8	13.0
1976	10.8	35.9	20.9	13.3
1977	10.9	37.1	20.0	13.6
1978	11.5	39.2	20.3	14.4
1979	11.6	40.5	19.8	14.6
1980	11.6	40.2	19.2	14.6
1981	11.9	41.7	21.8	15.1
1982	12.4	40.6	22.7	15.4
1983	12.2	41.9	22.8	15.4

Sources: U.S. Bureau of the Census (1965b, 1971b, 1972, 1973a, 1973b, 1974, 1975a, 1975b, 1976a, 1976b, 1977b, 1978a, 1979a, 1979b, 1980, 1981b, 1982b, 1983b, and 1984b).
a. Black and other.

cluding 14 percent of white families, 24 percent of Spanish origin families, and 48 percent of black families (U.S. Bureau of the Census, 1984b). To understand the nature of these shifts, it is necessary to disaggregate these statistics and consider factors such as changes in fertility rates, marital status, age structure, and living arrangements.

Changing Family Structure and Demographic Correlates

The unprecedented increases in the proportion of births out-of-wedlock are a major contributor to the rise of female-headed families in the black community. In 1980 68 percent of births to black women aged fifteen to twenty-four were outside of marriage, compared to 41 percent in 1955 (National Office of Vital Statistics, 1957; National Center for Health Statistics, 1982a). According to 1981 figures, almost 30 percent of all young single black women had borne a child before the age of twenty (U.S.

Bureau of the Census, 1983a). The incidence of out-of-wedlock births has risen to unprecedented levels for young white women as well, although both rates and ratios remain far below those for black women (see Table 10.2).

These increases in births outside of marriage reflect trends in fertility and marital status as well as changes in population composition. Age-specific fertility rates for both white and black women have fallen since the peak of the baby boom in the late 1950s. Even fertility rates for teen-agers (aged fifteen to nineteen) have fallen overall. What these figures obscure, however, is that the fertility rates of young unmarried women have risen or declined only moderately, while those of married women of these ages have fallen more substantially (see Table 10.2). In addition, growing proportions of young women are single. Recent data show not

Table 10.2. Fertility rates and ratios by race and age, 1960–1980

Age group and year	Fertility rate		Marital fertility rate[a]		Nonmarital fertility rate		Illegitimacy ratio	
	Black	White	Black	White	Black	White	Black	White
15–19								
1960	158.2	79.4	659.3	513.0	76.5	6.6	421.5	71.6
1965	136.1	60.7	602.4	443.2	75.8	7.9	492.0	114.3
1970	133.4	57.4	522.4	431.8	90.8	10.9	613.5	171.0
1975	106.4	46.4	348.0	311.8	86.3	12.0	747.2	229.0
1980	94.6	44.7	344.0	337.6	83.0	16.0	851.5	329.8
20–24								
1960	294.2	194.9	361.8	352.5	166.5	18.2	199.6	21.9
1965	247.3	138.8	293.3	270.9	152.6	22.1	229.9	38.4
1970	196.8	145.9	267.6	244.0	120.9	22.5	295.0	51.8
1975	141.0	108.1	192.4	179.6	102.1	15.5	399.5	60.9
1980	145.0	112.4	232.8	198.2	108.2	22.6	560.2	114.9
25–29								
1960	214.6	252.8	225.0	220.5	171.8	18.2	141.3	11.4
1965	188.1	189.8	188.6	177.3	164.7	24.3	162.8	18.8
1970	140.1	163.4	159.3	164.9	93.7	21.1	180.6	20.7
1975	108.7	108.2	130.8	132.4	73.2	14.8	226.8	26.2
1980	115.5	109.5	149.7	148.4	79.1	17.3	361.7	50.2

Sources: National Center for Health Statistics, *Vital Statistics of the United States,* annual volumes 1960–1975 and 1984.

a. Marital fertility rates for 1980 are unavailable; 1979 figures are substituted.

only that the incidence of premarital conception has increased but also that the proportion of those premarital pregnancies that are legitimated by marriage has decreased (O'Connell and Moore, 1980; Cherlin, 1981). Thus, out-of-wedlock births now comprise a far greater proportion of total births than they did in the past, particularly for black women. The black illegitimacy ratio (see Table 10.2) has increased as precipitously as it has in recent years not because of substantial increases in the rate of extramarital births but because the percentage of women married and the rate of marital fertility have both declined significantly.

The decline in the proportion of women who are married and living with their husbands is a function of both a sharp rise in separation and divorce rates and the substantial increase in the percentage of never-married women. The combined impact of these trends has been particularly drastic for black women as the proportion married and living with their husbands fell from 52 percent in 1947 to 34 percent in 1980 (U.S. Bureau of the Census, 1948, 1981a). Black women have much higher separation and divorce rates than white women, although the differences are exaggerated because of a higher rate of remarriage among white women.[2] Whereas white women are far more likely to be divorced than separated, black women are more likely to be separated than divorced. Indeed, a startling 22 percent of all married black women are separated from their husbands (U.S. Bureau of the Census, 1981a).

Just as important a factor in the declining proportion of black women who are married and living with their husbands is the increase in the percentage of never-married women. Indeed, as shown in Table 10.3, the proportion of never-married black women increased from 65 percent in 1960 to 82 percent in 1980 for those aged fourteen to twenty-four and from 8 to 21 percent for those aged twenty-five to forty-four. On the other hand, while the proportion of black women who are separated or divorced increased from 22 percent in 1960 to 31 percent in 1980 for those aged twenty-five to forty-four and from 17 percent to 25 percent for those aged forty-five to sixty-four, the fraction divorced or separated actually fell for younger women.

For young women, both black and white, the increase in the percentage of never-married women largely accounts for the decline in the proportion married with husband present (see Table 10.3). For black women aged twenty-five to forty-four increases in both the percentage of never-married women and in marital dissolution were important; for white women of the same age group marital dissolution is the more important factor. Marriage has not declined among white women aged forty-five to sixty-four; how-

Table 10.3. Marital status of women by race and age, 1947–1980

Age group and marital status	1947		1960		1970		1980	
	White	Black	White	Black	White	Black	White	Black
14–24								
Married[a]	33.5	30.9	33.6	25.7	29.6	21.3	26.8[b]	13.1[a]
Never married	62.9	59.5	63.3	65.0	66.4	72.3	68.6	82.4
Separated/divorced/husband absent	3.3	8.4	3.0	9.0	3.8	6.2	4.5	4.3
Widowed	0.4	1.3	0.1	0.3	0.1	0.1	0.1	0.2
25–44								
Married	80.3	67.2	85.1	64.9	85.0	62.0	75.5	44.7
Never married	11.5	10.5	6.8	8.2	6.3	12.2	9.8	21.3
Separated/divorced/husband absent	5.8	14.4	6.3	22.4	7.6	22.2	13.6	30.8
Widowed	2.4	8.0	1.8	4.5	1.2	3.6	1.1	3.2
45–64								
Married	70.2	57.6	74.1	52.8	73.5	54.1	74.0	46.0
Never married	8.0	5.3	6.4	5.3	5.9	4.7	4.4	6.8
Separated/divorced/husband absent	5.0	8.3	5.7	16.6	7.3	20.4	9.8	25.4
Widowed	16.8	28.7	13.7	25.3	13.3	20.4	11.8	21.8

Sources: U.S. Bureau of the Census (1948, 1960, 1971a, 1981a).
a. Married, husband present.
b. Includes only ages 15–24.

ever, among black women in the same age group the proportion married with husband present has fallen, mainly owing to increases in marital dissolution.

Although trends in fertility and marital status are the most important contributors to the rise of female-headed families, the situation has been exacerbated by recent changes in the age structure, which have temporarily increased the proportion of young women in the population, particularly in the black population. Whereas in 1960 only 36 percent of black women aged fifteeen to forty-four were between fifteen and twenty-four years of age, by 1975 that proportion had increased to 46 percent; the comparable increase for white women was from 34 percent in 1960 to 42 percent in 1975 (U.S. Bureau of the Census, 1965c, 1982e). These changes in the age structure increase the proportion of births occurring to young women and, given the higher out-of-wedlock birth ratios among young women, inflate the proportion of all births that occur outside of marriage as well.

Finally, the rise in proportions of female-headed families reflects an increasing tendency for women to form independent households rather than to live in subfamilies. Until recently, Census Bureau coding procedures caused the number of subfamilies to be significantly underestimated (Bane and Ellwood, 1984a); therefore, an accurate time series is impossible. However, other research suggests that women are becoming more likely to form their own households. For example, Cutright's analysis of components of growth in female-headed families between 1940 and 1970 indicates that 36 percent of the increase in numbers of female family heads between the ages of fifteen and forty-four can be attributed to the higher propensity of such women to form their own households (Cutright, 1974). Bane and Ellwood (1984a) show that these trends continued during the 1970s. In the period 1969–1973 56 percent of white children and 60 percent of black children born into single-parent families lived in households headed by neither mother nor father (most lived with grandparents). During the years 1974–1979 those proportions declined to 24 percent for white children and 37 percent for black children.

Thus, young women compose a greater proportion of single mothers than ever before. For example, while in 1950 only 26 percent of black female family heads and 12 percent of white female family heads were under the age of thirty-five, in 1983 those proportions had risen to 43 percent for blacks and 29 percent for whites (U.S. Bureau of the Census, 1979b, 1984b). The number of black children growing up in fatherless families increased by 41 percent between 1970 and 1980, and most of this growth occurred in families in which the *mother had never been married* (U.S. Bureau of the Census, 1971a, 1981a). This is not surprising, according to Bane and Ellwood's research: whereas the growth of single white mothers over the past decade is mainly due to the increase in separation and divorce, the growth of single black mothers is "driven by a dramatic decrease in marriage and increased fertility among never-married women" (Bane and Ellwood, 1984a, p. 3). In 1982 the percentage of black children living with both parents had dipped to 43 percent, only roughly half the proportion of white children in two-parent homes.

As Bane and Ellwood point out, "Never married mothers are more likely than divorced, separated or widowed mothers to be younger and to be living at home when they have their children" (1984a, p. 23). Younger mothers tend to have less education, less work experience, and thus fewer financial resources. Therefore they are more likely initially to form subfamilies, drawing support from parents and relatives. However, it appears that most children of single mothers in subfamilies spend only a small part of their life in such families. Bane and Ellwood (1984b) suggest that by the time children born into subfamilies reach age six, two-thirds will have moved into different living arrangements. Among blacks two-thirds of the moves are into independent female-headed families, whereas among whites two-thirds are into two-parent families. However, whether the focus is on subfamilies or on independent female headed families, less that 10 percent of white children and almost half of the black children born into non-two-parent families remain in such families "for their entire childhood" (Bane and Ellwood, 1984b, p. 27). And, as we shall see in the next section, these families are increasingly plagued by poverty.

The Poverty Status of Female-Headed Families

The rise of female-headed families has had dire social and economic consequences because these families are far more vulnerable to poverty than are other types of families. Indeed, sex and marital status of the head are the most important determinants of poverty status for families, especially in urban areas. The poverty rate of female-headed families was 36.3 percent in 1982, while the rate for married-couple families was only 7.6 percent. For black and Spanish-origin female-headed families in 1982, poverty rates were 56.2 percent and 55.4 percent respectively (U.S. Bureau of the Census, 1983d).

Individuals in female-headed families constitute a growing proportion of the poverty population—fully one-third of the poor in 1982. Forty-six percent of all poor families and 71 percent of all poor black families were female-headed in 1982. These proportions were higher for metropolitan areas, particularly for central cities, where 60 percent of all poor families and 78 percent of all poor black families were headed by women (U.S. Bureau of the Census, 1983d). The proportion of poor black families headed by women increased steadily from 1959 to 1977, from less than 30 percent to 72 percent, and has remained slightly above 70 percent since then. The total number of poor black female-headed families continued to grow between 1977 and 1982, increasing by 373,000; their proportion of the total number of poor black families did not continue to increase only because of the simultaneous sharp rise in male-headed families in poverty (from 475,000 to 622,000 in 1982). The proportion of poor white families headed by women also increased from less than 20 percent in 1959 to a high of almost 40 percent in 1977 and then dropped to 35 percent in 1983.

Female-headed families are not only likely to be in poverty; they are also more likely than male-headed families to be persistently poor.[3] For example, Duncan (1984) reports that 61 percent of those who were persistently poor over a ten-year period in the Michigan Panel Study of Income Dynamics were in female-headed families, a proportion far exceeding the prevalence of female-headed families in the general population. Hill (1981) found that almost half of the persistently poor were in female-headed families with children.

Bane and Ellwood (1983a, 1983b) report that most people who become poor during some period of their lives endure poverty for only one or two years. However, the long-term poor, about 60 percent of those in poverty at any given point in time, are in the midst of a poverty spell that will last eight or more years. Female-headed families are likely to have longer than average spells of poverty: at a given point in time, the average child who became poor when the family changed from male-headed to female-headed is in the middle of a poverty spell lasting almost twelve years. Bane and Ellwood report, "Some 20 percent of poverty spells of children begin with birth. When they do, they tend to last ten years. The average poor black child today appears to be in the midst of a poverty spell which will last for almost two decades" (1983a, p. 36). Their findings on spells of welfare receipt are similar. The groups indentified as being at high risk of long-term spells of welfare receipt include unwed mothers, nonwhites, and high school dropouts.

Causes of the Rise in Female-Headed Families

As the foregoing discussion suggests, to speak of female-headed families and out-of-wedlock births is to emphasize that they have become inextricably tied up with poverty and dependency, often long-term. The sharp rise in these two forms of social dislocation is related to the demographic changes in the population that we discussed in the previous section. For example, the drop in the median age of women heading families would lead one to predict a higher rate of poverty among these families, all other things being equal. We only need to consider that young women who have a child out-of-wedlock, the major contributor to the drop in the median age of single mothers, are further disadvantaged by the disruption of their schooling and employment.

Although consideration of demographic changes may be important to understand the complex nature and basis of changes in family structure, it is hardly sufficient. Indeed, changes in demographic factors are generally a function of broader economic, political, and social trends. For example, as we noted, the proportion of out-of-wedlock births has risen among young black women as a result of a decline in both marriage and marital fertility coupled with relative stability in out-of-wedlock birth rates (the number of births per 1,000 unmarried women). This increase in the proportion of extramarital births could be mainly a function of the increasing difficulty of finding a marriage partner with stable employment, of changes in social values regarding out-of-wedlock births, or of increased economic independence afforded women by the availability of income transfer payments. Broader social and economic forces may also be influencing married women to have fewer children. By examining the role of these broader social and economic trends in family formation and family structure, we hope to establish the argument that, despite the complex nature of the problem, the weight of existing evidence suggests that male joblessness could be the single most important factor underlying the rise in unwed motherhood among poor black women. Yet it has received scant attention in recent discussions of the decline of intact families among the poor. Let us first examine the contribution of other factors, including social and cultural trends and the growth of income transfers—which in recent years has become perhaps the single most popular explanation of changes in family formation and family structure.

THE ROLE OF CHANGING SOCIAL AND CULTURAL TRENDS

As indicated previously, extramarital fertility among teenagers is of particular significance to the rise of female-headed families. Out-of-wedlock birth rates for teens are generally not falling as they are for older women. Almost 40 percent of all illegitimate births are to women under age twenty (National Center for Health Statistics, 1982a). Moreover, adolescent mothers are the most disadvantaged of all female family heads because they are likely to have their schooling interrupted, experience difficulty finding employment, and very rarely receive child support. They are also the most likely to experience future marital instability and disadvantages in the labor market.

Any attempt to explain the social and cultural factors underlying the rise of teenage fertility must begin with the fact that most teenage pregnancies are reportedly unwanted. Surveys by Zelnik and Kantner have consistently shown that the majority of premarital pregnancies are neither planned nor wanted. In 1979, for instance, 82 percent of premarital pregnancies to fifteen- to nineteen-year-olds (unmarried at the time the pregnancy was resolved) were unwanted (Zelnik and Kantner, 1980).

However, unpublished tabulations from a recent Chicago study of teen-age pregnancy indicate that adolescent black mothers reported far fewer pregnancies to be unwanted than did their white counterparts (Hogan, personal communication, 1984). Moreover, as Dennis Hogan has stated, the Chicago data suggest that "it is not so much that single motherhood is wanted as it is that it is not sufficiently 'unwanted.' Women of all ages without a strong desire to prevent a birth tend to have limited contraceptive success" (Hogan, personal communication, 1984). This argument would seem especially appropriate to poor inner-city black neighborhoods. In this connection, Kenneth Clark (1965, p. 72) has argued:

> In the ghetto, the meaning of the illegitimate child is not ultimate disgrace. There is not the demand for abortion or for surrender of the child that one finds in more privileged communities. In the middle class, the disgrace of illegitimacy is tied to personal and family aspirations. In lower-class families, on the other hand, the girl loses only some of her already limited options by having an illegitimate child; she is not going to make a "better marriage" or improve her economic and social status either way. On the contrary, a child is a symbol of the fact that she is a woman, and she may gain from having something of her own. Nor is the boy who fathers an illegitimate child going to lose, for where is he going? The path to any higher status seems closed to him in any case.

Systematic evidence on expected parenthood prior to first marriage is provided in two studies by Hogan (1983, 1984). Drawing upon data collected in a national longitudinal survey of high school students conducted for a National Center for Educational Statistics study, Hogan (1983) found that whereas only 1 percent of the white females and 1.4 percent of the white males who were single and childless in 1980 expected to become a parent prior to first marriage, 16.5 percent of black females and 21 percent of black males expected parenthood before first marriage. In a follow-up study that focused exclusively on black female adolescents and excluded respondents "who were pregnant or near marriage at the time of the initial interview [1980]," Hogan (1984) found that only 8.7 percent expected to become single mothers in 1980, and of these, 19.5 percent actually became unmarried mothers by 1982. On the other hand, of the 91 percent who reported that they *did not* expect to become unmarried mothers, only 7.4

percent gave birth to a child by 1982. Unpublished data from this same study reveal that 20.1 percent of the black girls becoming single mothers by 1982 *expected* to do so in 1980 (Hogan, personal communication, 1984). Thus, although only a small percentage of these adolescent girls expected to become single mothers, those who expressed that view were almost three times as likely to become single mothers as the overwhelming majority who did not.

A number of social structural factors, which may influence the development of certain behavior norms, may also be directly related to single parenthood. Hogan's (1983, 1984) research shows that girls from married-couple families and those who live in households with both mother and grandparent are much less likely to become unwed mothers than those from independent mother-headed households or nonparental homes. The fact that the rate of premarital parenthood of teens who live with both their single mothers and one (usually the grandmother) or more grandparents is as low as that of teens who live in husband-wife families would "suggest that the critical effects of one-parent families are not so much attributable to the mother's example of single parenthood as an acceptable status as to the poverty and greater difficulty of parental supervision in one-adult families" (Hogan, 1984, p. 21). Furthermore, Hogan and Kitagawa's (1985) analysis of the influences of family background, personal characteristics, and social milieu on the probability of premarital pregnancy among black teenagers in Chicago indicates that those from nonintact families, lower social class, and poor and highly segregated neighborhoods have significantly higher fertility rates. Hogan and Kitagawa estimated that 57 percent of the teenage girls from high-risk social environments (lower class, poor inner-city neighborhood residence, female-headed family, five or more siblings, a sister who is a teenage mother, and loose parental supervision of dating) will become pregnant by age eighteen compared to only 9 percent of the girls from low-risk social backgrounds.

Social structural factors also appear to affect the timing of marriage. Hogan reports that although black teenagers expect to become parents at roughly the same ages as whites, they expect to become married at later ages (Hogan, 1983). Analysis of the High School and Beyond data reveals that when social class is controlled, black adolescents have expected age-specific rates of parenthood that are only 2 percent lower than those of whites but expected age-specific rates of marriage that are 36 percent lower (Hogan, 1983). While Hogan notes that many whites are delaying marriage and parenthood because of educational or career aspirations, he attributes blacks' expectations of late marriage to the poor marriage market black women face. Indeed, available research (Easterlin, 1980; Hogan, 1981; Evans, 1983) has demonstrated a direct connection between the early marriage of young people and an encouraging economic situation, advantageous government transfer programs, and a balanced sex ratio (Hogan, 1983). These conditions are not only more likely to obtain for young whites than for young blacks, but as we shall try to show, they have become increasingly problematic for blacks.

This evidence suggests therefore that attitudes and expectations concerning marriage and parenthood are inextricably linked with social structural factors. Since we do not have systematic longitudinal data on the extent to which such attitudes and aspirations have changed in recent years, we can only assume that some changes have indeed occurred and that they are likely to be responses to broader changes in the society. This is not to ignore the import of normative or cultural explanations; rather it is to underline the well-founded sociological generalization that group variations in behavior, norms, and values often reflect variations in group access to channels of privilege and influence. When this connection is overlooked, explanations of problems such as premarital parenthood or female-headed families may focus on the norms and aspirations of individuals and thereby fail to address the ultimate sources of the problem, such as changes in the structure of opportunities for the disadvantaged.

But it is also important to remember that broader social and cultural trends in society affect in varying degrees the behavior of all racial and class groups. For instance, sexual activity is increasingly prevalent among all teenagers. Growing proportions of adolescents have had sexual experience: according to one survey, the proportion of metropolitan teenage women who reported having premarital intercourse increased from 30 percent in 1971 to 50 percent in 1979 (Zelnik and Kantner, 1980). These proportions have risen particularly for white adolescents, thereby narrowing the differentials in the incidence of sexual activity. And they have more than offset the increase in contraceptive use over the past decade, resulting in a net increase in premarital pregnancy (Zelnik and Kantner, 1980). Rising rates of sexual activity among middle-class teens may be associated with various social and cultural trends such as the sexual revolution, the increased availability of birth control and abortion, and perhaps the growing sophistication of American adolescents or their adoption of adult social behaviors at an increasingly early age. These trends may also have influenced the sexual behavior of teens from disadvantaged backgrounds, but it is difficult to assess their effects independent of the complex array of other factors. Our meager state of knowledge permits us to say only that they probably have some effect, but we do not even have a rough idea as to the degree.

Although our knowledge of the effect of social and cultural trends on the rise of extramarital fertility is scant, we know a little more about the effect of some of these trends on marital dissolution. Multivariate analyses of marital splits suggest that the women's labor force participation (Hoffman and Holmes, 1976; Danziger et al., 1982) and income (Ross and Sawhill, 1975) significantly increase marital dissolution among white women. Labor force participation rates of white women have nearly doubled in the past forty years (see Table 10.4), owing in part to a decline in marriage and in part to an increase in labor force participation among married women, particuarly those with children present. The labor force partici-

Table 10.4. Labor force participation rates by age, race, and sex, 1940–1980[a]

Age group and race	Male					Female				
	1940	1950	1960	1970	1980	1940	1950	1960	1970	1980
16–19										
White	46.4	51.5	51.1	48.9	55.5	26.7	32.1	33.8	36.4	49.0
Black	59.5	55.8	42.4	35.8	36.5	28.6	24.0	23.9	25.4	30.3
20–24										
White	88.0	82.1	86.8	81.6	84.3	45.7	43.4	44.7	56.1	69.5
Black	88.5	80.4	82.0	76.4	73.5	44.9	39.5	45.5	56.3	61.4
25–34										
White	95.4	92.8	95.7	94.7	94.3	31.7	30.3	33.5	42.9	64.2
Black	92.4	86.2	88.5	87.6	83.5	46.1	44.3	48.6	58.9	71.6
35–44										
White	94.9	95.0	96.3	95.6	95.2	25.1	33.4	41.1	46.0	64.0
Black	92.4	90.6	89.8	88.1	86.3	45.1	48.5	55.8	60.4	71.0
45–54										
White	92.9	92.8	94.0	93.3	91.3	20.9	31.8	45.8	51.9	58.5
Black	89.9	88.4	87.6	85.0	81.0	40.0	43.5	54.7	58.0	61.7
55–64										
White	83.9	83.7	83.9	81.3	72.2	15.8	22.9	34.5	41.8	41.4
Black	84.6	80.2	75.9	72.4	62.3	31.1	31.4	40.3	44.9	44.1

Source: U.S. Bureau of the Census (1984a).

a. Figures for 1940, 1950, and 1960 refer to nonwhite; figures for 1970 and 1980 refer to black.

pation of black women has also increased, but not as dramatically; black women have always worked in greater proportions than white women, a pattern that still holds today for all age groups except women aged sixteen to twenty-four, an age category with high fertility rates.

Accompanying the increasing labor force participation of women has been the feminist movement, which validates work as a source of independence from men and of personal fulfillment, and which has provided practical support not only through legal and political action but also by promoting organizational resources for women in the labor market. Feminism as a social and cultural movement may have had direct influence on the marriage decisions of women; it may also have had an indirect effect through its role in women's more active labor force participation. In the absence of systematic empirical data, the effect of the activities of the feminist movement on the marital dissolution of women, particularly white women, can only be assumed.

It can be confidently asserted, however, that women's increasing employment makes marital break-up financially more viable than in the past. Although marital dissolution means a substantial loss of income and sometimes severe economic hardship—median income of white female-headed families in 1979 was $11,452, compared to $21,824 for white married-couple families (U.S. Bureau of the Census, 1984a)—most white women can maintain their families above poverty with a combination of earnings and income from other sources such as alimony, child support, public income transfers, personal wealth, and assistance from families. In 1982 70 percent of white female-headed families were living above the poverty line (U.S. Bureau of the Census, 1983d). In addition, many white single mothers remarry. For most black women facing marital dissolution, the situation is entirely different, not only because they tend to have fewer resources and are far less likely to remarry but also because the major reasons for their increasing rates of marital disintegration have little to do with changing social and cultural trends.

THE ROLE OF WELFARE

A popular explanation for the rise of female-headed families and out-of-wedlock births has been the growth of liberal welfare policies, in particular broadened eligibility for income transfer programs, increases in benefit levels, and the creation of new programs such as Medicaid and food stamps. Charles Murray (1984), for example, argues that relaxed restriction and increasing benefits of AFDC enticed lower-class women to forego marriage or prolonged childlessness in order to qualify for increasingly lucrative benefits. Likewise, Robert Gordon (in Feldstein, 1980, p. 341) depicts "welfare provisions as a major influence in the decline in two-adult households in American cities."

The effect of welfare on out-of-wedlock births and marital instability became even more of an issue after the costs and caseloads of public assistance programs dramatically increased during the late 1960s and early 1970s. Since that time a good deal of research has addressed this issue. Because all states have AFDC and food stamps programs, there can be no true test of the effects of welfare on family structure: there is no control population that has not been exposed to these welfare programs. However, substantial interstate variations in levels of AFDC benefits and in eligibility rules have provided opportunities for researchers to test the effects of program characteristics. Most studies have examined the level of welfare benefits as one of the determinants of a woman's choice between marriage and single parenthood. Some use aggregate data; others use individual-level data; still others examine the effect of providing cash transfers to intact families under special conditions, such as the income maintenance experiments. But whether the focus is on the relationship between welfare and out-of-wedlock births or that between welfare and marital dissolution, the results have been inconclusive.

Many of the studies concerning welfare and out-of-wedlock births have compared illegitimacy rates or ratios across states with varying AFDC benefit levels. Cutright (1973) found no association between out-of-wedlock birth rates and benefit levels in 1960 or 1970. Using aggregate data, Winegarden's (1974) state-level analysis showed no association between measures of fertility and benefit levels, although he did report a small positive association with benefit availability. Fechter and Greenfield (1973) and Moore and Caldwell (1977) both used state-level cross-sectional data in a multivariate analysis and found no effects of welfare benefit levels on out-of-wedlock births. Finally, Vining (1983) showed that for blacks the illegitimacy ratio in the south was only slightly lower than that in nonsouthern states, despite levels of AFDC payments that were less than half those of the rest of the country; for whites the difference was somewhat larger.

This type of research is vulnerable to the criticism that, in Vining's words, "the overall incidence of illegitimacy could have been rising over time in concert with an overall rise in welfare payments, despite the lack of correlation between cross-state variation in illegitimacy and cross-state variation in welfare levels at any point in time" (1983, p. 108). However, despite frequent references in the literature to rising welfare expenditures, benefit levels have fallen in real terms over the past ten years, while illegitimacy ratios have continued to rise. Both Cutright (1973) and Ellwood and Bane (1984) examined changes over time in state benefit levels and in illegitimate birth rates and found no association.

Other studies using different approaches and data sets have also yielded inconclusive, largely negative results. Placek and Hendershot (1974) analyzed retrospective interviews of three hundred welfare mothers and found that when the women were on welfare, they were significantly *less* likely to refrain from using contraceptives, *less* likely to desire an additional pregnancy, and *less* likely to become pregnant. Similarly, Presser and Salsberg (1975), using a random sample of New York women who had recently had their first child, reported that women on public assistance desired fewer children than women not on assistance and were less likely to have planned their first birth. Based on a longitudinal study of low-income New York City women, Polgar and Hiday (1974) reported that women having an additional birth over a two-year period were no more likely to be receiving welfare at the start of the period than women who did not get pregnant. Moore and Caldwell (1976) reported no relationship between characteristics of AFDC programs and out-of-wedlock pregnancy and childbearing from a microlevel analysis of survey data. Ellwood and Bane (1984) examined out-of-wedlock birth rates among women likely and unlikely to qualify for AFDC if they became single mothers and found no significant effect of welfare benefit levels; a comparison of married and unmarried birth rates in low and high benefit states also yielded no effects.

Finally, results from the income maintenance experiments have been inconclusive. Reports from the New Jersey experiments indicate no effect (Cain, 1974). In the Seattle and Denver experiments, effects of income maintenance payments on fertility varied by race/ethnicity: white recipients had significantly lower fertility, Mexican-Americans had higher fertility, and blacks showed no effect (Keeley, 1980); because of the relatively short duration of the study, it is not clear if maintenance payments affected completed fertility or simply the timing of births.

The results of studies focusing on the relationship between welfare and family stability have also been inconclusive. Researchers using aggregate data ordinarily look for correlations between rates of female family headship and size of AFDC payments, while controlling for other variables. In some cases the unit of analysis is the state (Cutright and Madras, 1974; Minarik and Goldfarb, 1976); in others, most notably Honig (1974) and Ross and Sawhill (1975), various metropolitan areas were examined. Analytic models used in most of these studies are similar, but disagreement over specification of the variables and other aspects of the analysis has produced mixed results. Honig (1974) found positive effects for AFDC payments on female family headship, although by 1970 the effects had diminished; Minarik and Goldfarb (1976) reported insignificant negative effects; Ross and Sawhill (1975) found significant positive effects for nonwhites but not for whites; and Cutright and Madras (1974) found that AFDC benefits did not affect marital disruption but did increase the likelihood that separated or divorced mothers would head their own households.

As Ellwood and Bane observe, despite the sophistication of some of these multivariate analyses of aggregate data, they have "largely ignored the problems introduced by largely unmeasurable differences between states" (1984, p. 2). Introducing a unique and resourceful solution to these problems, they present estimates of welfare effects based on comparisons of marital dissolution and living arrangements among mothers likely and unlikely to be AFDC recipients and among women who are or are not mothers (and thus eligible for AFDC) in high- and low-benefit states. They also examine changes over time in benefit levels and family structure. The findings based on these three different comparisons were remarkably similar. Ellwood and Bane estimate that in 1975 a $100 increase in monthly AFDC benefits would have resulted in a 10-percent increase in the number of divorced or separated mothers, with a more substantial effect for young women; the same increase in AFDC benefits would have contributed to an estimated 25- to 30-percent increase in the formation of independent households, again with much more substantial effects for young mothers.[4]

Studies using individual-level data have yielded mixed results, with some finding modest effects and some reporting no effect at all of welfare on marital dissolution or family headship. Hoffman and Holmes (1976) analyzed Michigan PSID data and reported that low-income families living in states with high AFDC benefits were 6 percent more likely than the average to dissolve their marriages, whereas similar families in states with low benefit levels were 6 percent less likely to do so; Ross and Sawhill (1975), in a similar analysis of the same data, found no significant welfare effects, even in a regression performed separately for low-income families. In a recent study Danziger et al. (1982) modeled headship choices using data from 1968 and 1975 Current Population Surveys and concluded that a reduction in welfare benefits would result in only a slight decrease in the number of female household heads; the authors also reported that the increase in female-headed families between 1968 and 1975 was greater than the model would have predicted, given the changes in the relative economic circumstances of female heads and married women occurring during that period. It seems likely that the decreasing supply of marriageable men (to be examined below) is a constraint on women's marriage decisions not accounted for in the model.

Studies of intact families receiving income transfers under the income maintenance experiments show that providing benefits to two-parent families did not tend to reduce marital instability: the split rates for these families were higher, not lower, than those of comparable low-income families (Bishop, 1980), although the results were not consistent across maintenance levels. The income maintenance experiments "increased the proportion of families headed by single females. For blacks and whites, the increase was due to the increase in dissolution; for Chicanos, the increase was due to the decrease in the marital formation rates" (Groeneveld, Hannan, and Tuma, 1983, p. 344). Groeneveld, Tuma, and Hannan (1980) speculate that nonpecuniary factors such as the stigma, transaction costs, and lack of information associated with the welfare system caused the income maintenance program to have a greater effect on women's sense of economic independence.

To sum up, this research indicates that welfare receipt or benefit levels have no effect on the incidence of out-of-wedlock births. AFDC payments seem to have a substantial effect on living arrangements of single mothers, but only a modest impact on separation and divorce. The extent to which welfare deters marrriage or remarriage among single mothers is addressed only indirectly, in studies of the incidence of female-headed households, and here the evidence is inconclusive.

However, if the major impact of AFDC is on the living arrangements of single mothers, it could ultimately have a greater influence on family structure. As we emphasized in our discussion of Hogan's (1983, 1984) research on the premarital parenthood of adolescents, young women from independent mother-headed households are more likely to become unwed mothers than those from married-couple families and those from female-headed subfamilies in the home of their grandparents.

Nonetheless, the findings from Ellwood and Bane's (1984) impressive research and the inconsistent results of other studies on the relationship between welfare and family structure and welfare and out-of-wedlock births raise serious questions about the current tendency to blame changes in welfare policies for the decline in the proportion of intact families and legitimate births among the poor. As Ellwood and Bane emphatically proclaim, "Welfare simply does not appear to be the underlying cause of the dramatic changes in family structure of the past few decades" (1984, p. 8).

THE ROLE OF JOBLESSNESS

Although the structure of the economy and the composition of the labor force have undergone significant change over the past forty years, the labor force participation patterns of white men have changed little. As shown in Table 10.4, the labor force participation rate of white men declined from 82 percent in 1940 to 76 percent in 1980, in part because of a drop in the labor force activity of men over the age of fifty-five. Labor force participation of white men twenty-four and under actually increased over the past decade.

For blacks the patterns are different. The labor force participation of black men declined substantially, from 84 percent in 1940 to 67 percent in 1980. Labor force trends for older black men parallel those of white men of the same ages. But the decline in labor force participation of young black men and, to a lesser extent, prime-age men has occurred while the participation of comparable white men has either increased or remained stable.

Economic trends for black men, expecially young black men, have been unfavorable since the end of World War II. Whereas the status of young blacks who are employed has improved (Duncan, 1984), with the percentage of white collar workers among all black male workers rising from 5 percent in 1940 to 27 percent in 1983, the proportion of black men who are employed has dropped from 80 percent in 1930 to 56 percent in 1983 (U.S. Bureau of the Census, 1979b; U.S. Bureau of Labor Statistics, 1984a). Unemployment rose sharply for black male teenagers during the 1950s and remained high during the prosperous 1960s; similarly, unemployment rates for black men twenty to twenty-four years of age rose sharply during the mid-1970s and have remained high. In 1979, when the overall unemployment rate had declined to 5.8 percent, the rate of black male teenagers was 34.1 percent (U.S. Bureau of Labor Statistics, 1984a). In addition, although blacks have historically had higher labor force participation levels, by the 1970s the labor force participation of black men had fallen below that of white men for all age groups, with particularly steep declines for those aged twenty-four and younger and those aged fifty-five and older.

The adverse effects of unemployment and other economic problems on family stability are well established. Studies of family life during the

Depression document the deterioration of marriage and family life following unemployment (Bakke, 1940; Komarovsky, 1940; and Elder, 1974). More recent research, based on longitudinal data sets or on aggregate data, shows consistently that unemployment is related to marital instability and the incidence of female-headed families (Honig, 1974; Ross and Sawhill, 1975; Sawhill et al., 1975; Hoffman and Holmes, 1976). Indicators of economic status such as wage rates, income, and occupational status may also be related to marital stability or female-headedness, although the evidence is not as consistent (Bishop, 1980). For instance, Cutright's (1971) analysis of 1960 census data indicates that divorce and separation rates are higher among lower-income families. Sawhill et al. (1975) find that unemployment, fluctuations in income, and lack of assets are associated with higher separation rates but that the level of husband's earnings has an effect only among low-income black families. However, Cohen (1979) reports that when husband's age is controlled, the higher the husband's earnings, the less likely both black and white couples are to divorce.

Nonetheless, the weight of the evidence on the relationship between the employment status of men and family life and marriage life suggests that the increasing rate of joblessness among black men merits serious consideration as a major underlying factor in the rise of black single mothers and female-headed households. Moreover, when the factor of joblessness is combined with high black male mortality (Farley, 1980) and incarceration rates (Blumstein, 1982), the proportion of black men in stable economic situations is even lower than that conveyed in the current unemployment and labor force figures.

The full dimensions of this problem are revealed in Figures 10.1 and 10.2, which show the effect of male joblessness trends, in combination with the effects of male mortality and incarceration rates, by presenting the ratio of employed civilian men to women of the same race and age groups.[5] This ratio may be described as a male marriageable pool index. The number of women is used as the denominator in order to convey the situation of young women in the marriage market. Figure 10.1, for men eighteen to twenty-four years of age, shows similar patterns: a sharp decline in the nonwhite ratios beginning in the 1960s, which is even more startling when compared with the rising ratios for white men. Figure 10.2, for men twenty-five to forty-four years of age, shows a more gradual decline for black men relative to white men. Clearly, this male marriageable pool index reveals a long-term decline in the proportion of black men, and particularly young black men, who are in a position to support a family.

A detailed explanation of the deteriorating employment status of black

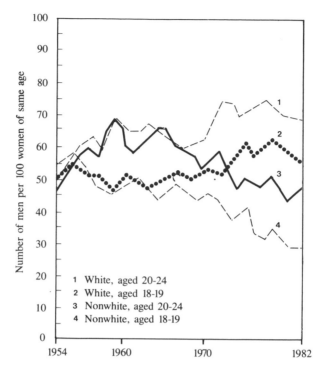

Figure 10.1. Employed civilian men per 100 women of same age and race, aged 18–24, 1954–1982. Source: Numbers of employed men by age and race, U.S. Bureau of Labor Statistics (1980, 1984a); numbers of women by age and race, U.S. Bureau of the Census (1965c, 1978b, 1983c).

men, particularly young black men, is beyond the scope of this paper. But we would like to note that a number of studies have attempted to account for the changing employment experiences of young blacks. In a recent review of some of these studies, Mare and Winship (1980) conclude that increasing school enrollment, military service, and the displacement of blacks from southern agriculture are well-documented factors in trends in the labor force status of young blacks. They found mixed evidence for the effects of structural changes in the economy, changes in the patterns of industrial and residential location, cohort size, labor market crowding, and the minimum wage.

Two more recent studies on youth employment (Cogan, 1982; Ellwood and Wise, 1983) deserve special attention. Cogan (1982) argues that the reduction in the aggregate black teenage employment ratio from 1950 to 1970 was not due to such commonly cited factors as the growth in welfare programs, the sudden increase in number of black teenagers, and the

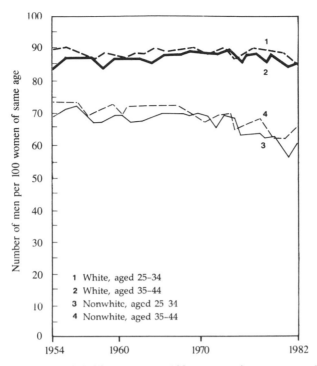

Figure 10.2.   Employed civilian men per 100 women of same age and race, aged 25–44, 1954–1982. Source: See Figure 10.1.

relocation of firms from the central city but to "the decline in the demand for low-skilled agricultural labor" (1982, p. 635). And, he suggests, the reason these displaced teenagers were not absorbed into the nonagricultural sector of the South was the barriers imposed by the minimun wage law. Nonetheless, Cogan emphasizes that the decline in agriculture cannot be used to explain the sharp drop in black teenage employment ratios through the 1970s because agriculture had ceased to be important as a source of employment for black teenagers after the 1960s. Also, since the employ-ment ratios of black teenagers in the North in 1950 were substantially lower than those of white teenagers, they cannot be attributed to the federal minimum wage law because it did not apply to low-skilled service industry and retail trade industry workers in 1950.

Ellwood and Wise (1983) found that although school enrollment, military service, demographic factors, household formation, family background, and public policy concerning youth employment in the 1970s accounted for white employment trends, they had only limited explanatory value for blacks. Military service, school enrollment, family background, and macroeconomic conditions "all contributed to the decline in civilian employment of blacks relative to whites" (1983, p. 68), but a large part of the gap between white and black employment rates remained unexplained even after these factors had been taken into account.

Although the state of our knowledge about the factors contributing to the joblessness problem among young black males is rudimentary, the relationship between joblessness and marital instability is well established, as we noted above, in the literature. Moreover, available evidence supports the argument that among blacks increasing male joblessness is related to the rising proportions of families headed by women.[6] By contrast, for whites trends in male employment and earnings appear to have little to do with the increase in female-headed families. Although lower-income families have higher rates of marital dissolution, trends in the employment status of white men since 1960 cannot explain the overall rise in white separation and divorce rates.

It seems likely that the chief cause of the rise of separation and divorce rates among whites is the increased economic independence of white women as indicated by their increasing employment and improving occupational status. It is not that this growing independence gives white women a financial incentive to separate from or to divorce their husbands; rather, it makes dissolution of a bad marriage a more viable alternative than in the past. That the employment status of white males is not a major factor in white single motherhood or female-headed families can perhaps also be seen in the higher rate of remarriage among white women and the significantly earlier age of first marriage. By contrast, the increasing delay of first marriage and the low rate of remarriage among black women seem to be directly tied to the increasing labor force problems of men.

IN THE 1960s scholars readily attributed black family deterioration to the problems of male joblessness. However, in the past ten to fifteen years, in the face of the overwhelming focus on welfare as the major source of black family break-up, concerns about the importance of male joblessness have receded into the background. We argue in this paper that the available evidence justifies renewed scholarly and public policy attention to the connection between the disintegration of poor families and black male prospects for stable employment.

We find that when statistics on black family structure are disaggregated to reveal changes in fertility rates, martital status, age structure, and residence patterns, it becomes clear, first of all, that the black illegitimacy ratio has increased rapidly not so much because of an increase in the incidence of out-of-wedlock births but mainly because the rate of marital fertility and the percentage of women married and living with their husbands both declined significantly. And the sharp reduction of the latter is due both to the rise in black divorce and separation and to the increase in the percentage of never-married women. Inextricably connected with these trends are changes in the age structure that have increased the fraction of births to young women and thereby inflated the proportion of all births occurring outside of marriage. The net result has been a 41-percent increase in the number of black children growing up in fatherless families during the 1970s, with most of this increase occurring in families in which the mother has never been married. Furthermore, the substantial racial differences in the timing of first marriage and the rate of remarriage underscore the persistence of black female-headedness. And what makes all of these trends especially disturbing is that female-headed families are far more likely than married-couple families to be not only poor but mired in poverty for long periods of time as well.

Although changing social and cultural trends have often been invoked to explain some of the dynamic changes in the structure of the family, they appear to have more relevance for shifts in family structure among whites. And contrary to popular opinion, there is little evidence to provide a strong case for welfare as the primary cause of family break-ups, female-headed households, and out-of-wedlock births. Welfare does seem to have a modest effect on separation and divorce, especially for white women, but recent evidence suggests that its total effect on the size of the population of female householders is small. As shown in Ellwood and Bane's (1984) impressive study, if welfare does have a major influence on female-headed families, it is in the living arrangements of single mothers. And we explained why this could ultimately and indirectly lead to an increase in female family headship.

By contrast, the evidence for the influence of male joblessness is much more persuasive. Research has demonstrated, for example, a connection between the early marriage of young people and an encouraging economic situation. In this connection, we have tried to show that black women are more likely to delay marriage and less likely to remarry. We further noted that although black teenagers expect to become parents at about the same ages as whites, they expect to marry at later ages. And we argue that both the black delay in marriage and the lower rate of remarriage, each of which is associated with high percentages of out-of-wedlock births and female-headed households, can be directly tied to the labor market status of black males. As we have documented, black women, especially young black women, are facing a shrinking pool of marriageable (that is, economically stable) men.

White women are not faced with this problem. Indeed, our male marriageable pool index indicates that the number of employed white men per 100 white women in different age categories has either remained roughly the same or has increased since 1954. We found little reason, therefore, to assume a connection between the rise in female-headed white families and changes in white male employment. That the pool of marriageable white men has not shrunk over the years is reflected, we believe, in the earlier age of first marriage and higher rate of remarriage among white women. For all these reasons, we hypothesize that increases in separation and divorce among whites are due chiefly to the increased economic independence of white women and related social and cultural factors.

Despite the existence of evidence suggesting that the increasing inability of many black men to support a family is the driving force behind the rise of female-headed families, in the past ten to fifteen years welfare has dominated explanations of the increase in female headship. Low unemployment rates in the late 1960s seemed to invalidate economic explanations. For example, from the Great Depression to 1960 unemployment accounted in large measure for dependency: the correlation between the nonwhite male unemployment rate and the number of new AFDC cases opened was nearly perfect during this period. Considering this relationship, Moynihan observed: "It could not be established that the men who lost their jobs were the ones who left their families, but the mathematical relationship of the two statistical series—unemployment rates and new AFDC cases— was astonishingly close" (1973, p. 93). Suddenly, however, the relationship began to weaken at the beginning of the 1960s, evaporated by 1963, and completely reversed itself during the rest of that decade with a steady decrease in the nonwhite male unemployment rate and a steady increase in the number of new AFDC cases.

Some observers quickly seized upon these figures to argue that welfare dependency was rising as a result of increases in the level of public assistance benefits because, they argued, even during periods of an economic upswing the welfare rolls were expanding. However, even though the rate of nonwhite male unemployment did drop during the 1960s, the percentage of the nonwhite civilian population out of the labor force (the labor force nonparticipation rate) rose steadily, thereby maintaining a positive relationship between joblessness and the number of new AFDC cases.

The common-sense assumption that welfare regulations break up families, affirmed by liberals and conservatives alike, buttressed the welfare explanations of trends in family structure. The Subcommittee on Fiscal Policy of the Joint Economic Committee initiated a program of research on the topic in 1971; according to Cutright and Madras (1974), recognition of the increasing monetary value of noncash benefits, in the context of economic theories of marriage (see Becker, Landes, and Michael, 1977), persuaded the Subcommittee that welfare was related to the rise of female-headed families despite inconclusive evidence. And despite frequent references to rising social welfare expenditures, the real value of welfare benefits has declined over the past ten years while the number and proportion of female-headed families continues to climb.

Only recently has it been proposed that the rise in female-headed families among blacks is related to declining employment rates among black men (Center for the Study of Social Policy, 1984; Wilson, 1984a, 1984b; Walker, 1985). Evidence such as that displayed in Figures 10.1 and 10.2 and in other studies discussed in this chapter makes a compelling case for once again placing the problem of black joblessness as a top priority item in public policy agendas designed to enhance the status of families. Perhaps the Center for the Study of Social Policy comes closest to capturing the seriousness of the problem: "The persistent alienation and attrition of black men constitutes a formidable challenge to both researchers and policymakers, a challenge that is only now beginning to be recognized. How to study, understand, and eventually respond to this phenomenon are fresh and troubling issues. But they are, as well, critical issues; if we do nothing, the turn of the century will see 70 percent of all black families headed by single women and fewer than 30 percent of all black men employed. The human costs of such continued erosion of the black family are socially, politically, and morally unacceptable" (1984, pp. 13, 14).

11 Legal Rights and Welfare Change, 1960–1980

Michael R. Sosin

THE MOST WIDELY DISCUSSED trends in the administration of social services during the 1960–1980 period are increasing regulation from above, progressive standardization, specification of appeals procedures, and growing bureaucratization of the local offices (Handler and Sosin, 1983; Simon, 1983). These trends occurred in institutions as diverse as juvenile courts and mental health facilities, but nowhere have they been as profound as in the administration of the AFDC program, in which the entire character of the system seemed to be transformed.

Many believe that the transformations in AFDC occurred as a result of the growth of the legal rights perspective. But commentators vary in their evaluation of the changes. Some argue that legal rights reforms allowed the development of legal and political challenges that turned the system into one in which public control became impossible (Friendly, 1975). Others argue that the legal rights movement produced moderate reforms—guaranteeing due process and reducing arbitrary behavior—which merely protected the social services client from the most severe abuses (Handler, 1979). Still others now insist that the high degree of legal regulation backfired, producing a system so concerned with rules that it has established new barriers to client access and to satisfying the needs of enrolled clients (Brodkin and Lipsky, 1983; Simon, 1983).

Yet a careful examination of actual changes in administrative practices demonstrates a more complicated pattern than that envisioned by any of the three groups of commentators. Although the early legal rights advocates believed that legal rights reforms would greatly alter the system, only moderate changes actually developed from this advocacy. After the reform movement lost its zeal, there was a second movement, toward bureaucratization and restrictiveness, that I argue was only loosely tied to legal rights reforms and instead reflected other social goals. Further, the present system is best characterized as a mixed one in which the client's right to welfare is established more fully than it was before the 1960s as a result of the legal rights revolution, even though recently established rigid rules restrict access and significantly alienate clients.

The Elements of Change

This modern history of welfare in the United States is partly an unfolding of traditional ideas about the poor. These include but are not limited to concerns about the moral integrity and honesty of recipients, desires to reform as well as to aid clients, discussions about how adequate aid should be, and a belief that work is superior to welfare and should be encouraged (Handler and Hollingsworth, 1971; Steiner, 1971; Handler, 1972).

During the 1960–1980 period, however, these traditional concerns were augmented by some additional factors. One was the new political philosophy mentioned above, the legal rights perspective. A second factor, not as often considered, was the growth of a movement of social activists, perhaps spurred to action by other social changes. The way their activity was structured helped to define the nature of the reforms (Turner, 1981). Yet another factor was the growth of bureaucracies that could fashion or refashion policies in reaction to the activists' and the legal rights approach.

I believe that the limits and nature of change in welfare practice partly reflected the essential nature of all of these new elements as they interacted with the more traditional constraints, not just the legal rights ideology. Accordingly, a first task of this chapter must be to examine the three elements; we will then demonstrate their contribution to change in the 1960–1980 period.

LEGAL RIGHTS

The legal rights position was partly a reaction to the traditional rehabilitative ideal (Allen, 1982) that professionals, dealing on a one-on-one basis with those in need, can utilize their skills to treat pathology (Leiby, 1978). Those espousing the traditional perspective, which dominated AFDC before the 1960s, insist that the structure of social services should maximize the autonomy of the expert, freeing professionals to make decisions on the basis of client needs rather than rigid bureaucratic procedures. According to the legal rights view, however, the discretion made available under the professional model might be abused. While in theory a professional worker acts in a disinterested manner, the pressures brought to bear on actual social service delivery systems by bureaucracies, rules and regulations, and community norms tend to overwhelm professional standards (Allen, 1964). This results in decisions being made, on too many occasions, on the basis of personal preferences or irrelevant criteria (Davis, 1971; Jowell, 1975).

The legal rights perspective proposed a new view of the relationship between government—the main provider of financing for services since the New Deal—and clients. As Reich (1964) argued, governmental benefits have traditionally been considered a privilege, dispensed at the will of the state. However, the government has become a "major source of wealth" in the society as a whole. The relation to government is now as important to economic survival as private property had been in the past, so that it stands to reason that the benefits government provides should be treated as a right, comparable to property rights.

In the central case of social welfare, Reich was concerned that the resources available to workers could enable them to "buy up" constitutional rights if benefits were not protected as a right. Not only might benefits be denied to those whose lifestyles or behaviors are considered unattractive (notably, women living with men to whom they were not married), but once benefits are granted, the worker might demand changes in behavior that are irrelevant to the program. Reich thus argued that in economic benefit systems privacy should be respected, lifestyles should not be a bar to eligibility, and individuals should be able to obtain a fair hearing if they disagree with decisions about their receipt of benefits.

This position, in some form or another, was adopted by many reformers. To some it seemed to argue for a tremendously reformed system: new appeal procedures, standardized rules concerning program eligibility, and a much more trusting, positive view of recipients by the welfare bureaucracy. This is why some feared that the rights revolution might create a system that would be out of control, one in which "equity claims" (Janowitz, 1976) would be so strong that nearly anyone could make a case for receiving economic support.

On closer examination, however, it is apparent that the legal rights approach will not cause control to be lost. As Mashaw (1983) notes, if used to obtain guarantees of fair treatment, the perspective merely encourages procedural changes that enable individuals to have their say but do not change the outcomes that result. The benefit programs still might condition benefits upon particular behavior, such as cooperating with a work program, even if they adopt appeal procedures, standard rules, and so forth.

Nevertheless, it can be argued that, at least if one judges by the Supreme Court decisions, the norms of fundamental fairness that are implicit in the legal rights perspective seem to have implications that go beyond fair procedures. For example, the legal rights revolution has successfully argued that criteria that are irrelevant to the major goals of the program, such as lifestyle criteria in AFDC, are not constitutional.

The limit is that courts, normally the prime forum for such changes, often respond most favorably to narrow requests for appeal procedures, some right to privacy, and equal application of the law; the Constitution seems unambiguous on the issues. But as Mashaw (1983) notes, when the courts begin to consider more substantive rights, they tend to balance the right to privacy and individualism against other social ends. The right to a hearing is tempered by the acknowledgment that too many hearings or too lengthy hearings will place an undue burden on the bureaucracy; procedures may be denied if the government needs to address other social goals. In striking a balance, courts then may be affected by the traditional classical themes in welfare policy, and the resulting policy changes will thus be small.

Given the limits of procedural changes in achieving welfare reform, the legal rights approach must go further to reach the ends Reich had in mind. One such argument is for economically fair treatment (compared to the more wealthy) and revised benefit levels. The broad view of rights then becomes an income redistribution philosophy. The negative income tax movement, as advocated by some, looks at shares of the income pie and views a particular share as a "right" of the lowest income group.

A somewhat more narrow approach looks at benefits across aided individuals in terms of "horizontal equity." Here the assumption is that individuals in the same situation should be treated equally. Those with the same need for resources should obtain the same amount of resources from government, regardless of the state in which they live, their ability to influence case workers, and so forth.

Legislatures, not courts, are involved in adjudicating these equity issues. And to a small degree, legislatures may accept such fairness arguments. But while the views may imply significant reform, political problems may develop for all proposals but incremental changes. One problem is that what is a right to some people might not be a right to others. For example, does horizontal equity mean that all individuals in families of the same size must receive identical benefits, regardless of locality, or does it mean that special needs or geography should be taken into account? How is it balanced with perceptions that those who might refuse work or misrepresent themselves need to be weeded out and that costs should be controlled? Differences among advocates or politicians on the issues can limit reform.

The second element in the new reform movement comprised organizations in a position to advocate for legal rights (some, though, had other philosophies), including community action agencies, legal aid offices, and welfare rights groups. Such organizations may play key roles in bringing issues to the public attention, thus activating the political process. They initiate court appeals and administrative hearings; they may publicize existing inequalities; and they advocate for specific legislative proposals. When groups are active, welfare rights may be kept on the political center-stage. Group-initiated court challenges might also help to ensure that reforms that are obtained continue to be implemented. The demise of the groups may thus limit or end reform.

These groups are often called "social movement organizations." A recent literature suggests conditions that might lead to or detract from their success, and some are particularly important for understanding the extent of change during the 1960–1980 period (Oberschall, 1973; Wilson, 1973; Gamson, 1975; McCarthy and Zaid, 1977; Fireman and Gamson, 1978; Handler, 1978). The literature stresses that change brought about by a social movement organization depends on the ability of the organization to sustain itself. But theory and research suggest that the existence of an interest in bringing about change may not be enough to attain this goal. Olson (1965) thus claims that, even with a common interest, there is a disincentive to organize. Whereas the success of an organization may depend on the activity of a number of activists, each specific individual might realize that he or she makes very little difference. Given the cost of participation, it is thus in the interest of each individual to allow others to do the work while he or she reaps the benefits; and if all think that way, the organization will not form.

The disincentives might be overcome in many ways. One important element is the *perception* that one really can make a difference (Moe,

1980). In other words, at times individuals may feel that they can obtain alterations in policy that exceed their contribution—whether this is the case or not. Another way of maintaining an organization is to provide incentives to individuals. For example, some may simply find organizing pleasurable; others may gain status or financial rewards by joining the organization. And there is the possibility that, if the cost of participation is low, the popularity of the issue and a feeling of social solidarity might be enough to attract adherents.

Some of the reasons for partial successes of legal rights reforms are evident from this brief overview of incentives. One reason for success is that certain ideas about fairness can mobilize support. The great inequities between local areas, and especially between clients within one area, seem unjust to many. Activism was particularly likely when the civil rights movement was strong; welfare rights activists could be encouraged by the successes, others might be sympathetic to claimed inequities, and the public might view problems in welfare as linked to legitimate civil rights demands. The poor can be organized if they perceive a high probability of obtaining improved benefits, and, given a general perception of the inequities, financial support can be gained from outsiders.

However, judged from this perspective, advocacy in social welfare also appears to be very fragile. Since the problems of poverty do not normally attract substantial political attention, the chances for success are usually limited to brief periods. In fact, owing to the lack of a strongly held direct commitment to social welfare, it is likely that the mobilization of individuals and the perception of success by members and leaders must depend upon external events. Thus, although the civil rights movement may provide a sense of common meanings, a source of funds, and an ideology for a welfare rights organization, the demise of the movement can reduce funding, legitimacy, and donations for welfare reform advocacy.

In addition, perceptions of success depend on the access of movement leaders to those who make political decisions. Not only does this encourage leaders to adopt a level of cooperation that might inevitably result in reducing the scope of the issues, but it is also unstable. When public sentiments change so that the issue is no longer popular, external leaders may prefer to reduce their contacts, and the social movement organization may no longer be able to attain enough success to maintain the needed loyalty (Moe, 1980). Because welfare reform costs money and may cause a severe backlash, public leaders may take this path after a very short period of time; reforms can then be limited.

BUREAUCRATIC RESPONSES

Bureaucracies and the governments they represent were the third element shaping reforms. Because bureaucracies are under political pressures from many sources in addition to those of advocates, their response to activists depends on many factors. It may be to their advantage to acquiesce in advocates' demands when protests disrupt the staff, reduce efficiency, and have public support. But repression may also be in their interest: When the basic nature of the system is threatened or when the public is not sympathetic to change, the bureaucracy can arrest those whose protest involves disobedience to the law; they can coopt the leadership; or they can respond more narrowly to a specific appeal or protest and not change the system more generally (Gamson, 1975). Their responses determine the direction and success of reform.

When do bureaucracies strongly favor, oppose, or reconstruct demands for reform? One possibility is that they choose policies that protect themselves. When not under much pressure, they prefer discretion. When under pressure, they prefer standard, clear rules, so that they can claim that by following the rules they are carrying out agreed-upon policy and should not be blamed for problems. But the rules may differ slightly from what many who fought for change demand, making them less objectionable to opponents and easier to administer—as long as the differences do not cause new controversy. And when an issue is even more controversial but some rules must be developed, they attempt to delegate implementation decisions to lower levels, which can be blamed when objections arise (Handler and Sosin, 1983).

When the legal rights groups place much pressure on the system, one would thus expect challenges to be met with the formation of apparently satisfactory rules. But such rules might be adjusted to serve the ends of the bureaucracy. They can also be redirected toward meeting objections from opponents of change, particularly once legal rights groups are no longer active. The bureaucracy can even use an equity argument to develop rules that turn substantive criticism into an apparent disagreement over form. It can promote and argue for any standardized system as a way of reducing substantive unfairness. Although such a system would not mute criticisms from active legal rights groups, it may, by appearing equitable, forestall new mobilizations of a legal rights movement that has calmed. Bureaucracies at the federal level can also develop broad guidelines that force local authorities to implement and take the blame for restrictive policies.

Indeed, bureaucracies can use standardizing reforms to reduce the extent of advocacy and pave the way for more rigid rules—rules that protect the bureaucracy from advocates while satisfying those who desire to reduce the scope of welfare. For example, Piven and Cloward (1977) imply that the trend toward legalism and bargaining with bureaucracies about new rules deflected the National Welfare Rights Organization from disrupting the system and thereby perhaps obtaining substantive benefits. All such behaviors thus limit reform in the long run; it is readily apparent that it is difficult for legal rights activists to sustain significant reforms.

Welfare "Reform," 1960–1980

Welfare change between 1960 and 1980 covers three eras: (1) an early reform period in which concerns with rehabilitation and political power were played out, (2) the legal rights "revolution," itself; and (3) a period of increasing bureaucratization and restrictiveness. As we describe these periods, we identify the forces that led to change, the nature of reforms, the ways in which reforms might have affected clients, and the way in which the interaction of legal rights, advocates, and the bureaucracy helps explicate the changes.

CHANGE FROM THE INSIDE AND OUTSIDE, 1962–1967

AFDC before the mid-1960s was characterized by a large amount of discretion. States, as well as establishing benefit levels, varied widely in their procedures. Social workers were given substantial discretion in dispensing benefits within a structure of complex rules and regulations.

The combination of discretion and rules was often used to limit eligibility and grant amounts. Many states and counties adopted residence requirements, requirements to prove destitution, and other criteria so difficult to meet that they discouraged many from applying. Some AFDC offices closed down during the summer, claiming that there was sufficient cotton-picking to substitute for AFDC (Piven and Cloward, 1971). Workers could also restrict eligibility if the home was not deemed suitable, if a man lived in the house some of the time, or if the applicant did not cooperate with work requirement or another regulation. And when benefits were obtained, they could be easily reduced or withdrawn.

Looking at the 1960 system in terms of the theory presented in the first portion of this chapter, there were few incentives for change. The ideology

of legal rights was not well developed, whereas the rhetoric of professionalization suggested that any change should come from technical advances
among social workers, not from large-scale system reforms. In addition,
local and state bureaucracies viewed discretion as functional (Handler and
Hollingsworth, 1971), since the bureaucracy could ward off criticism of too
much leniency or restrictiveness by claiming that professional judgments
were being made. This was an era in which Edelman's (1977) notion of
symbolic language was important, as virtually any worker decision should
be legitimated on "therapeutic grounds."

Activism from those directly served—potential and actual AFDC recipients—seemed unlikely. The poor were aware that they had a low probability of success in changing the system, given their lack of political power,
their apparent small numbers, their lack of organizing skills, and their
limited monetary sources. Allies were few; state and local differences created barriers across localities; stigma could result from joining a coalition
and thus admitting welfare dependency; and few external funds were available to organize the poor.

Clearly, however, there was substantial ferment and reform during the
1960s, owing to many destabilizing influences. The Kennedy administration
determined that poverty was a political issue worth pursuing. Johnson's
War on Poverty received impetus from those views. The civil rights movement publicized racial disparities in earnings and in income and highlighted
the problems of inner city ghetto life. The civil rights leaders were themselves surprisingly ill-informed about AFDC (West, 1981), but at least in
the public mind poverty and race became linked, particularly after urban
riots began. Legislative progress in the area of race led to further concerns
about welfare.

Nevertheless, the earliest changes in welfare during the 1960s stemmed
from traditional professional service ideologies. Most notable were the
1962 Social Security amendments which, among other things, provided 75-
percent reimbursement to states for social services and also allowed states
to contract social services (Steiner, 1971). It was held that an upgrading
of social services would result in a higher quality of counseling and therefore
a reduction in poverty, as those in need learned how to adjust to job roles
and to the society as a whole.

This goal of reducing the welfare rolls by providing services has never
been reached—although service provision has become a major task of local
welfare offices. Yet when Johnson became president he took the service
ideology even further. The Office of Economic Opportunity (OEO) in

general, and most local community action agencies and community action programs (CAPs), were designed to reduce poverty through services.

As a result of the changes brought about by the civil rights movement, by urban riots, and by a general liberalization of government, the OEO programs as later implemented demonstrated more ambiguity than they had originally. With the provision for maximum feasible participation added to the charter of the OEO, local agencies were expected to gain the political participation of the poor.[1] One-third of each board of directors was to be composed of local, elected community representatives. Although most agencies remained service providers rather than advocates, advocacy grew in some CAPs. The legal arm of OEO also took on cases that led to reforms of welfare (Friedman, 1977; Peterson and Greenstone, 1977).

OEO and related movements were precursors of the legal rights movement. Concern for the poor was also growing, to be reflected in policy. As the theory section predicts, the perception of a potential for reform, along with the availability of resources through OEO, enabled organizations for welfare clients to come into being. These became important in the next period. In the short run, welfare workers and urban systems became less restrictive. Participation in AFDC grew to somewhere between 45 and 55 percent of those eligible in 1967, far above the 1960 level of about 33 percent (Bendick, 1980; Michel and Willis, 1980).

THE INFLUENCE OF LEGAL RIGHTS, 1967–1972

Proponents of social services had always claimed that professional services would reduce welfare dependency through counseling the poor. When the number receiving benefits increased instead, providing services was gradually discredited as a way of reducing poverty. The attempt of community action agencies to gain political power also failed. Urban governments readily altered federal regulations in order to maintain political control of welfare when confronted by community action groups. The groups had some success as advocates but never gained political power.

The political advantage of the fairness doctrine, particularly as practiced by legal rights advocates, was that it did not make promises to reduce welfare rolls, nor did it claim to alter the power structure. Its claim was that changes in procedure were needed to guarantee constitutional rights and basic fairness. As a result, given a general environment favoring change, this movement gained ground during the mid- and late-1960s. Legal services workers, in particular, changed their emphasis from an OEO-related power strategy to a narrow legal rights approach in which court challenges of procedures as well as administration appeals played major roles (Johnson, 1974).

The National Welfare Rights Organization (NWRO), active from about 1967 until 1973, was involved in legal and administrative challenges. Early in its history, NWRO adopted the fairness doctrine. George Wiley, the group's leader, realized that welfare laws and policies were not being carried out. Many believe that his long-range goal was to disrupt the welfare system to the point at which a negative income tax would be adopted (Kotz and Kotz, 1977; Moynihan, 1973). Whether one accepts this or not, it is clear that his focus was on a legal rights approach in the short run. He was thus quoted:

> We very consciously chose welfare rights as the battleground for our struggle. First, it was a very repressive nationwide system geared to disseminate economic benefits to large numbers of people, but it operated totally out of conformity with the Constitution, with the Social Security act under which it was supposed to operate, and most strongly, with its own rules and regulations. Second, if the system were found to deliver anything like the amounts of cash benefits to which poor people were legally entitled, that system would collapse of its own weight.   (Kotz and Kotz, 1977, p. 198)

The most important organizing tool for NWRO, as well as its most important success, was the application of a legal rights viewpoint to the "special needs" provisions of AFDC benefit programs. Although allowances for many special needs (ranging from refrigeration to cod-liver oil) were on the books, workers often used their discretion and refused to dispense them. Legal aid attorneys successfully fought for many of them as legal entitlements. NWRO offered to help individuals gain these special benefits, through appeals or case advocacy, in exchange for membership. As a result, the organization grew and exercised more power. In both Massachusetts and New York, for example, NWRO-sponsored demonstrations and extended campaigns to increase demands for benefits under the special needs programs overwhelmed the bureaucracy. It became simpler to give in to demands and avoid the appearance of illegally restricting access than to continue to deny benefits to individuals or to demand discretion (Bailis, 1974; Gelb, 1975).

Not only were local offices affected, but the new legal rights view was accepted in part by the Supreme Court, so that some restrictive procedures were overturned when challenged by NWRO and other reformers. Shapiro

v. Thompson (1969) held that residency requirements, which prevented those who had recently moved into the jurisdiction from receiving benefits, were unconstitutional. Reversing the typical one-year residency requirements increased potential eligibility in an era in which migration from the South to the North was high.

The Supreme Court also voided man-in-the-house rules, noting in King v. Smith (1968) and Lewis v. Martin (1970) that an AFDC recipient could receive benefits even if cohabiting with another adult. (Benefits could only be reduced if a financial contribution of the party could be proved.) The right of clients to appeal decisions to alter individual benefits was guaranteed in Goldberg v. Kelly (1970).

At the same time, federal and state policies helped simplify the application process. One federal suggestion was that states adopt eligibility by declaration, relieving workers of the need to verify all statements of clients on a simplified application form. Roughly twenty states responded in the short run and had simplified their process by 1970 (Steiner, 1971). As Grønbjerg (1977) notes, the average "total eligibility score," that is, a summing of the types of state requirements needed for clients to prove eligibility, decreased from 22 to 14 between 1960 and 1970.

Caseworkers also became more sensitive to need and less likely to use their discretion to withhold benefits. Social services workers with some professional training had been hired. Given the tenor of the time (including the Supreme Court and lower court decisions, in addition to more case advocacy), most social workers apparently believed that higher benefits and eased eligibility were justified. A 1968 administrative order separated services workers from those who determined eligibility, but few states complied for two or three years. This meant that professional workers with a new view of clients were determining eligibility. Perhaps as a result, applicant acceptance rates increased slightly (Michel and Willis, 1980), and many local areas improved outreach (Gelb, 1975). Grants also increased during the period, from an average of $6,946 in 1968 to $8,649 in 1972, and the new benefit programs such as food stamps and Medicaid grew.

At least in some jurisdictions, appeals were used with increasing frequency. With the aid of OEO projects in New York, for example, roughly 8 percent of recipients filed appeals in one year; this was perhaps double early figures. The appeals were often successful because rules had been simplified to the point that clear legal challenges were possible, and hearing examiners seemed receptive to challenges (Baum, 1974).

Nevertheless, it does not appear that the number of appeals represented anything like a crisis in the vast majority of jurisdictions; those who believe that the welfare system was unmanageable, administered more by appeals decisions than by workers and supervisors, take an exaggerated view (Friendly, 1975). The 8-percent figure for New York was probably the extreme, and it was only temporary. More typical was Milwaukee, in which less than 2 percent of all terminations were appealed during the 1969–1976 period, and only about 4 percent of all denials. Only in the transition year, 1974, when new procedures encouraged a large but temporary upsurge in appeals, did they climb to twice the normal rate (Hammer and Hartley, 1978). The greatest impact of appeals was that they led to the perception by the general public and the local officials that welfare was a right.

It is thus no surprise that caseloads expanded fairly dramatically during this period. The number of AFDC recipients rose from 5 million in 1967 to 10.9 million in 1972. The increase was partly attributable to increases in the rate at which those who were theoretically eligible were able to obtain benefits. The participation rate rose to 90 percent (Michel and Willis, 1980).

The elements of change, discussed earlier, all contributed to this reform of the welfare system. Widespread belief that the AFDC system was inequitable, no doubt bolstered by concerns about racial discrimination, helped convince the Supreme Court, local courts, welfare offices, and the federal government that rights-related changes were needed to ensure basic fairness. The War on Poverty and civil rights movements provided skilled advocates, and the growing liberalism of the system made the chances for success appear high and mobilization more possible. The stigma associated with welfare also diminished, allowing recipients to mobilize without experiencing repercussions. Funding could also be garnered. Legal aid groups were often supported by the government (OEO). The NWRO was able to amass a budget from liberal church groups and even from the government (Kotz and Kotz, 1977; West, 1981).

Because more benefits became available as rules were changed, some might argue that the reformers went further than an attempt at increasing fairness and access and helped to institutionalize new programs such as Medicaid and food stamps and raise welfare budgets. On the face of it, this does not seem to be the case. Many of the new programs were implemented earlier, a result of the War on Poverty and not the legal rights revolution. Further, average AFDC grants, plus food stamps, decreased in value after 1971, in the middle of the period of activism (Cole, forthcoming). In general, legal rights in the broad sense of giving the poor a greater share in the nation's wealth were not implemented.[2] As other data imply, the increases in grant size until 1971 probably reflected the availability of state and federal government budget surpluses as the GNP grew (Swank, 1983).

BUREAUCRATIZATION, 1972–1980

Between 1972 and 1980 advocates came to realize the limitations of the narrow legal rights approach they had been using. Although they had changed procedures, they were unsuccessful in their attempts to raise benefit levels. Benefits were determined by the states, and the Supreme Court in decisions such as Rosado v. Wyman (1970) rejected demands that states adopt adequate standards of need on which to base AFDC benefits or calculate grants so as to meet all discovered needs.

Many even believed that the balance of the court had changed and that little could be accomplished at lower court levels. The fight thus turned toward challenges of the bureaucracy and attempts to alter legislation. But activists began to have a decreasing impact. The NWRO, which outlasted activism in civil rights, fell apart by 1973. Internal conflicts forced out Wiley, and the funding sources he cultivated began to turn elsewhere— especially after the counter-movement within the bureaucracies, which we will describe below. Federal policies also limited the role of CAP agencies and legal aid offices. In the political arena concern about equity lost ground to concern about loss of financial control and fear of fraud and abuse. The movement for a negative income tax did not succeed as advocates lost membership and as it became apparent that there was an insufficient political constituency for even moderate reform. Over time, changes slowly evolved away from legal rights proposals.

One change involved in the reaction but still tied to legal rights was an alteration in the division of labor in public welfare. During the last few days of the Johnson administration, in 1967, Wilbur Cohen, outgoing Secretary of the Department of Health, Education, and Welfare, issued regulations calling for a separation of social services from income maintenance. At all levels, from the state bureaucracy to the local office, it became necessary to separate those activities that involve individual counseling, family planning, mental health referrals, and so forth from the distribution of income maintenance benefits.

Cohen is fond of claiming that separation was the first step in creating a negative income tax system, in which the provision of fair, equitable, simplified benefits would be expanded across states and in which social services would not be viewed as a requirement for obtaining benefits. Many legal rights scholars applauded the move, believing that it reduced the extent to which workers could condition the receipt of financial benefits on recipient cooperation with service activities. However, further development of a negative income tax did not occur. Instead, shortly after separation actually took place in most areas—in about 1971—services began to lose visibility. The trend was toward provision of "hard" services such as day care, rather than counseling. The budget for services ceased to be open-ended, and the dollars soon began to shrink. Because social workers were no longer involved in income maintenance, they no longer had a strong interest or ability to lobby for further changes. This situation may have reduced the interest in legal rights in government agencies at all levels.

Even more ambiguously tied to the rights movement was the alteration in the character of the AFDC basic income maintenance grant. When NWRO demands for those special needs provisions attached to the discretionary AFDC program began to increase, a few states—notably California, New York, and Massachusetts—replaced their programs, which required provisions for specified special needs, with a flat or consolidated grant. A flat grant is one in which workers no longer cost out specific items. Instead, the grant is calculated from a standard that takes into account only a few variables, such as family size and structure, work expenses, income, and perhaps region of the state.

The first flat grants, established in 1969 and 1970, were relatively liberal. Average grants were calculated by combining the cost of basic needs and some special needs. Generally some sort of large increase above the average needs was allocated in the first year. But after 1971 the flat grants continually lost their value relative to inflation in all but a small handful of states (Handler and Sosin, 1983).

However, the flat grant, adopted in nearly all states by 1975 (Sosin, 1982), was as much a bureaucratic reaction to the rights movement as a part of the movement. Although it was partly adopted because it made it more difficult for advocates to use fairness issues to mobilize support, it was also adopted in states without special needs provisions or NWRO lobbying, because it was useful to some administrators. It promised to bring local programs under state control; this was particularly important as costs rose in response to the legal rights revolution. To be sure, others believed that such control would increase horizontal equity, but administrators linked equity to efficiency, not rights (Handler and Sosin, 1983).

In fact, flat grants were largely a response by state bureaucracies to the institutionalization of "error rate" controls by the federal government. An error was defined as an instance in which the grant was incorrect according to state or federal rules, and these rules appeared to be remarkably high in the early 1970s. To cut errors but also to control expanding costs, a regulation mandated that sanctions be applied to states that continued to have high error rates. Although this regulation was not enforced, legislative action of 1978 reinstituted the penalty. As research on the subject indicates, errors are more common when calculations are more complex (Piliavin, Masters, and Corbett, 1979); administrative simplification was virtually required to bring error rates under control (Touche, Ross & Co., 1977).

It is true that some states developed separate emergency assistance or special needs programs to compensate for the flatness of the grants, but the existence of specialized programs should not be taken to imply that no substantial change had occurred. Only about half the states adopted an AFDC Special Needs or Emergency Assistance program. And the programs made individualized benefits available only under very specific circumstances, ensuring low demand. The programs also tended to be funded in sum-certain fashion by states or by counties, limiting both benefits and the legal entitlement (Handler and Sosin, 1983).

Further reforms sprang almost completely from the bureaucracy and not the rights movement. Owing perhaps to increasing costs, the focus from about 1975 to 1980 was clearly on increasing administrative efficiency, even if this meant reducing access to the system. (Advocates, even when they rejected the changes, no longer had public support.) Many states began using computers, adopted fraud controls, and developed more complicated application forms. It is no exaggeration to state that the AFDC workers, in theory professionals in 1970, had become more like clerks ten years later. Their primary interests were in meeting rules, filling out forms, and taking deadlines into account, not in dispensing social services or referring clients to service workers.

Toward the end of the decade, experiments on monthly reporting threatened to increase the level of standardization even further. This reform was a product of the income maintenance experiments of the late 1960s. While conducting the experiments, a consulting firm discovered that financial savings might result from the experiment's reporting requirements, under which experimental families reported income every month rather than every six months. According to the experiment, grants were more accurate. And since recipients were more likely to underreport changes in status that increased income than those that decreased income, accuracy would save money (Williams et al., 1979; Crespi, Kaluzny, and Tidwell, 1980). By 1981 monthly reporting was mandated by law.

Although there is no particular reason why the flat grant or the separation of services from eligibility should have altered participation rates in AFDC, it is relatively clear that, when combined with the types of error rate control and monthly reporting that were implemented, these reforms tended to reduce the proportion of eligible individuals who participated in the program. Rules resulting from the reforms began to weed out otherwise eligible recipients, and complicated procedures and insensitive workers discouraged individuals from applying. In short, those who claim that the reforms reduced access are more accurate when considering the post-1976 period than when considering the earlier period.

Error rate control thus tends to create administrative structures that reduce participation rates—at least as the controls were implemented by federal regulations. While the federal government gathers figures on both the extent to which individuals are overpaid and the extent to which they are underpaid, it imposes economic sanctions only in cases of overpayment. (A small reward was offered, but only briefly.) As Brodkin and Lipsky argue (1983), there is thus a clear incentive for state bureaucracies to establish rules that control overpayments—even if this is at the expense of allowing many people to be underpaid or declared ineligible. One study demonstrates that, within the existing bureaucratic procedures, concentration on the control of overpayments means underpayments are more likely to go undetected (Mills, 1981).

Administrative control of overpayments tends to reduce access to the system in many ways. For example, federal reviewers often check on actual earnings to a far greater degree than do individual workers, and they call any discrepancy an error. Accordingly, 93 percent of the states increased verification requirements to meet error rate control standards, bringing them in line with reviewers' standards. At the same time, if an individual is not registered for the work incentive program or has not cooperated with attempts to find an absent parent, payments are considered errors; consequently, one-third of the states increased verification of participation in the work incentive program in order to reduce errors (Bendick, Lavine, and Campbell, 1978).

It seems likely that increases in verification in the grant program and in the work incentive program decrease participation. The verification requirements may demand an unusual amount of proof from clients about income, rent payments, and so forth; those who cannot provide it may become discouraged from applying or may be denied. And since the burden is on recipients to prove registration in the work incentive program, clients can be discontinued, at least temporarily, when administrative errors occur. Indeed, Grønbjerg (1977) demonstrated that strict eligibility requirements correlate with reduced caseloads, and Cunningham (1977) noted an increase of denials for procedural nonconformity. And, as Brodkin and Lipsky (1983) indicate, Massachusetts reported a very large decrease in the acceptance rate when reducing the error rate. There was also an increase in the rate at which appeals were successful, apparently indicating that workers were no longer necessarily following all the rules. They focused instead on avoiding the overpayments, because they might be sanctioned for them.

Data also support the idea that monthly reporting, as adopted in some states before 1980, was implemented in a manner that tended to reduce participation of those who are eligible (Price, 1981; Crespi, Kaluzny, and Tidwell, 1980; Williams et al., 1979). The data from the original Colorado experiment indicate that, although monthly reporting saves money, the savings do not come from accuracy, as was originally believed. While the system decreases underreporting of income, it also decreases overreporting. And although the former is more common, the latter involves larger amounts per case. They roughly balance out. The savings actually occur because a small percentage of individuals do not return the form each month. The percentage is low, perhaps 5 percent, but the data indicate that many among these 5 percent are eligible for very substantial benefits. Some of them reapply, but about 1 to 2 percent do not. Although the system has procedures for handling late forms, apparently discouragement follows from lost forms, the inability to read forms, and repeated client or worker errors that result in letters of terminations. This small drop in participation, cumulating each month, can add up to large decreases in AFDC caseloads, because the average length of stay in AFDC is about two years. (There is, it should be noted, other evidence questioning any effect of monthly reporting in payments, caseloads, or error rates.)

In any system some discretion continues to exist. Another reason for the decrease in participation is that the administrative changes over the course of the 1970s, by changing the focus of workers, may have changed the way they used discretion. Because the service workers were separated from income maintenance technicians, those who were involved in eligibility decisions no longer had a professional orientation. During the late 1960s it is likely that the former desired to keep benefits as high as possible, but the latter had little incentive to do so. Indeed, when faced with a choice, requirements to handle cases quickly (if they take too much time, an error is declared) and to avoid overpayments were likely to result in uses of discretion that discouraged applicants.

Simon (1983), reflecting on his years as a legal aid attorney, provides many examples of the ways in which discretion is misused. Clients who report to the wrong worker to apply for aid are not referred to another worker; those who fail to report a Social Security number are denied aid; levels of proof concerning the availability of various sources of income are occasionally unmanageable. In addition, appeals are less successful because decisions came to be made with efficiency and cost-cutting in mind (Baum, 1974; Hagan, 1983; Hammer and Hartley, 1978).

In an admittedly exploratory article, McDonald and Piliavin (1984) present information about another source of discretion that might affect program participation. They note that 30 percent of individuals in Wisconsin who originally received an application did not complete it. In many cases failure to complete the application occurred either because a conversation with the worker convinced the applicant that he or she was not eligible or because the procedures were such that the applicant felt that he or she would be treated unfairly (combined, these account for half to two-thirds of reasons given by those who did not follow through). The authors note that, from the income data they could gather, two-thirds of those who did not complete the process appeared to be eligible. Although this lack of follow-through might always be a problem, it appears that workers currently have special reasons to discourage potentially eligible applicants.

The data comparing potentially eligible individuals to those actually receiving aid, although limited, show that program participation rates decreased. In 1975, when flat grants had been adopted and assistance was separated from services, participation apparently remained relatively high, at 90 percent. However, with the institution of quality control procedures and related state reforms, the estimated rate decreased to 87 percent in 1976 and to 74 percent in 1977, the last year for which rates have been calculated (Bendick, 1980).[3] Also, it appears that clients found workers less sympathetic (Piliavin and Gross, 1977).

These restrictive reforms could occur because conditions that might lead to support of the legal rights revolution no longer existed. As costs rose and the economy cooled off, there was more concern for controlling the system than for guaranteeing rights. And because reformers found that narrow legal rights approaches were nearly exhausted, they turned to broader approaches that simply never received sufficient support; a negative income tax was not achieved. As a result of this reduction in support, new limits of public sympathy for rights in all forms, and fewer successes to point to, the legal rights movement lost adherents and financial backing.

At the same time, the bureaucracy helped bring about change. After the rights movement lost influence, bureaucracies were faced with a dilemma. They could not completely abandon the rules implementing legal rights without encouraging new mobilizations or unfavorable court deci sions, but they had to balance rights with such newly popular concerns as cost contol. Error rate control and other types of standardization seemed to do just that. They created rules that seemed equitable, but they also increased control and reduced access. If individuals who appeared to deserve aid did not receive it, other levels of government could be blamed. Federal officials could blame state implementation of the controls; states could blame federal rules or county implementation. All levels could blame clients for not participating in what could be legitimated as a fair system.

Role of the Legal Rights Revolution

Clearly the legal rights movement and the reformers' efforts have not come to dominate the system as some feared earlier. It is true that standardization reduced the amount of discretion permitted to states and localities. Further, there was an increase in centralization, so that some efforts to alter caseloads could be launched from Washington—by error rate control, for example (Derthick, 1970). But the states continue to set grant levels, and the post-1972 adjustments in these levels have been so limited as to raise doubts about the belief that the system could not be controlled (although, for reasons beyond the scope of this chapter, the number of eligible individuals continued to rise). Further, federal changes in the post-1972 period indicate an ability to control the system from another level.

These changes also argue against Simon's (1983) idea that the legal rights philosophy, the first of the three new elements in our theory, is largely responsible for the decreases in grant amounts, the bureaucratization of the system, and the reduction in participation rates (Handler, 1983). Simon may claim that post-1972 limits in grant increases are a result of the new philosophy, based on legal rights, which favors a flat grant that is not sensitive to increasing needs because workers do not gather information on needs. But because the literature suggests a strong relation between economic growth and welfare expenditures (Wilensky, 1975; Swank, 1983), it may very well be that the failure of grants to keep up with inflation is due not to introduction of the flat grant but to changing economic conditions, increases in welfare costs during the 1970s, and resulting taxpayer backlash. Indeed, even much of the growth, while perhaps preconditioned by increases in the participation rate up to 1972, occurred after this point as need increased dramatically. From this perspective, one can at best argue that the rights revolution helped establish rules that allowed caseloads to rise to the point at which costs would skyrocket and some level of decreases would be demanded by others (Bernstein, 1982). And not only is the reaction tied to the return of traditional themes rather than legal rights, but it is limited: the decreases did not reduce grant levels to below prereform levels.

Simon also argues that the reforms of the early rights movement helped encourage bureaucratization and later restrictiveness. Actually the relation is indirect and depends more on the bureaucratic reaction (the third element of the theory) than on the movement for reform. It was perhaps inevitable that, given the types of arguments that might be politically acceptable, the successful challenges to the existing order used an equity argument. Courts were used in order to assure equity within the system, and complaints about unequal application of the rules were used to obtain special needs grants. Very little else would have succeeded at all. The problem is that the bureaucracy often reacted by increasing equity in a way that was not to the liking of the reformers: less for everyone is as equitable as more. For example, when the NWRO fought to increase coverage of special needs, New York and Massachusetts responded by eliminating special needs provisions. This reduced the influence of the NWRO and even eliminated its major tool of organization, interest in special needs. Whereas the effort increased grants in the short run, once flat grants were instituted they could remain unchanged as inflation increased; changes in real income did not mobilize supporters. Similarly, as long as some basic due process elements are included, it is possible to have very stringent rules about work or child support that cannot easily be challenged within the legal rights framework. Such changes reveal how fragile welfare rights were; the coalition could quickly be torn apart, even by success. But it is clear that the restrictiveness was not directly encouraged by the basic goals of legal rights.

The characterization of calls for reform in equity terms indeed successfully coopted the reformers and allowed for further restrictive changes. One of the early developments of the period was the Nixon administration proposal for a family assistance plan (FAP). This plan, which unsuccessfully wound its way through both houses of Congress from 1970 to 1972, called for centralization of the income maintenance system. It combined a basic federal income maintenance guarantee with stronger work programs; it also reduced worker discretion by promoting standardized rules (Burke and Burke, 1974).

From the point of view of NWRO (basically an urban and northern-oriented organization), the proposal was a step back because it strengthened work requirements and did little for benefits in the North. However, this reform directed attention away from NWRO because it made the role of advocates moot. It was difficult to continue to mobilize states for change when FAP seemed just around the corner, and NWRO could actually do little to affect the plan directly.

The bureaucratic order, with its assumed rationality and equity, could itself act as a cover for other types of reforms. Error control appears reasonable, and all agree that individuals should work and parents should support their children. It appears to make sense to demand verification of income and of past work experience and to expect recipients to fill out one form a month in order to obtain benefits. Yet such changes at the federal level induced states to become more restrictive and may actually have reduced the participation of the eligible. The attitude of workers toward clients shifted from one of trust to one of skepticism, as was often seen in the 1950s. Because the claims of promoting equity and of setting reasonable standards are so powerful, these restrictive measures are difficult to challenge. In other words, it appears that the bureaucracy itself reacted to the earlier reforms, restricted access, and avoided complaints as it changed from justifying itself by the political language of professionalization to justification on the basis of the myth and ceremony of bureaucracy (Meyer and Rowen, 1977). The myths in question clearly have substantive anticipated impacts. This crucial change in the post-1972 period was caused more by attempts to limit the system than by a rights ideology.

Despite all of this, one cannot say that advocacy did not succeed. The legal rights movement gained some lasting changes, institutionalizing new pressures on the bureaucracies. The Supreme Court decisions remain in effect, appeals are possible, fewer individuals are arbitrarily denied benefits, and a basic statewide grant standard remains. Error rate controls restrict access only indirectly; they are a far cry from dismantling the system, and they (and other changes) do not seem to threaten to reduce participation rates to the levels of the 1950s. It is even possible that a new, somewhat more advanced definition of fairness has been adopted by the political process, one that makes it politically difficult to directly remove the legal entitlement. Because a program is in place, any alterations must be justified in terms of their fairness compared to present policies; there thus must always be a "safety net" to avoid complaints.

Judging from their responses to the new federalism, state bureaucracies have come to rely on the somewhat enlarged federal system. Decentralization would cost the states money; it would decrease the flow of income into the states; it would put the blame on state officials if individuals went hungry; and it would force states to make politically painful decisions about who deserves aid and under what type of system. Congress thus seems under pressure to resist dismantling the program. The transformations in the welfare system brought about by size and by the legal rights revolution helped alter the form and length of the swing of the policy pendulum, even though they did not prevent the swing.[4]

The Future of Reform

What changes might one expect in the future? The new standardized system offers few opportunities for mobilizing opposition and thus for further change from the outside. Previously the facts that procedures were not followed and that individuals were treated inequitably were important in forging reform coalitions and in obtaining political support. But the new system does not have as many such inequities. In addition, special needs provisions, which formerly helped mobilize clients, are now controlled. Also, an increased percentage of influential administrative policies stem from Washington, where advocates may have many problems in putting their issues on the crowded national agenda (Sosin, 1979b).

From the point of view of administrators, flat grants, administrative control, and the use of the computers have many advantages. They can protect the system from claims of conservatives that the programs are wasteful; the reforms make welfare appear to be efficient and businesslike. They also help protect executives from claims from the left, since the rules appear to be equitable. Administrators have now come to view standard-ization as a sought-after goal (Handler and Sosin, 1983). One can argue that predictability is so important and standard rules so entrenched that further lessening of bureaucratization is nearly impossible without the growth of a new ideology. To the extent to which welfare benefit levels and access are the ways of reducing poverty, the legal rights revolution appears impotent to do any more about the issue.

What might be successful in changing the welfare system? One possibility might be to increase state discretion and decentralization, but the current administration's attempt to use this as a rationale has not profoundly reformed administrative policies. States depend too much on the present system. Another possibility would be to link welfare reform to the women's movement, but so far that movement has paid scant attention to nonmarket problems and may not be able to do so without losing adherents.

A return to professionalism, suggested by Simon (1983), also appears unlikely. For all of the reasons mentioned above, the standardized system appears to be too firmly entrenched. The attempts to use a services (professional) strategy in the early 1960s demonstrate additional problems with this approach. A professional model can only be instituted if it can claim to reduce the level of poverty; it is unlikely that such an argument can be made. The techniques of the part of social work that deals with individual change are not sufficiently advanced (if poverty can ever be dealt with by individual counseling—many social workers now doubt this), and the public has lost its faith in the rehabilitative ideal (Allen, 1982).

It should be noted that some modifications of the present system are being considered. For example, it is possible that a new definition of equity, one that includes elements of discretion, could be adopted (Handler, forthcoming). Such a definition might encourage cooperation between citizens and the bureaucracy, mobilize interest groups, and, ideally, convince bureaucracies that they need cooperation and not restrictiveness to succeed.

Another possibility would be to transfer services away from the large bureaucracies to smaller units with different approaches. I have suggested, for example, that emergency assistance programs might be more efficiently delivered and more appropriately individualized if dispensed by publicly supported private agencies rather than by the public sector (Sosin, forthcoming). There appears to be citizen support for private sector involvement, and it is possible that the bureaucracy may allow flexibility in contracted programs as long as public programs dispense basic benefits and remain standardized. While dispensing services, these agencies may even be able to perform some of the useful advocacy activities that disappeared with the demise of the NWRO in the mid-1970s.

In other words, I believe that it would not be productive to talk about turning back the clock and attempt to reintroduce discretion into the public system. Rather, it may be more useful to look for alternative methods of dealing with situations and events that cannot be appropriately handled within the current public system's conceptualization of equity and rights.

Comment by Lawrence M. Mead

This chapter is an able review of policy and administrative developments in welfare since 1960. I would differ mainly with some of the author's interpretations of events. His main theme is the inherent limits of legal rights as an approach to expanding welfare. Many of the mechanisms that restricted benefits before the 1960s, such as man-in-the-house rules and special grants controlled by social workers, were highly discretionary. In attacking them as invidious, the rights movement stood on strong legal and political ground. Its victories, in court and in federal and state policymaking, sharply reduced discretion, forcing agencies to grant benefits to most applicants on the basis of need alone. Easier access, in turn, helped double the AFDC rolls in the years around 1970.

But, as Sosin emphasizes, these legal claims did not directly address the fairness or adequacy of welfare in more substantive senses. The rule of law might justify a niggardly welfare system as well as a generous one. Conservatives saw that they could reimpose limits on welfare provided they did so using impersonal statutory rules. During the 1970s state legislatures restricted special needs grants, on which the rights movement had concentrated its pressure, and allowed real benefits to decline with inflation. The federal government added new regulations to reduce fraud and abuse and enforce child support and work obligations. Rights advocates could not call these steps unjust unless they shifted from a procedural to a social or economic definition of equity, something much tougher to sell politically.

While this analysis helps to explain the frustrations of the welfare movement, it implies that the movement's strengths were legal, its weaknesses political. Actually, the claims rights advocates could make in court were quite limited. The Supreme Court did overturn residency and man-in-the-house rules and grant recipients due process in disputes over benefits, but it did not accept that welfare or any other social benefit was a constitutional right. The Charles Reich "new property" argument for welfare entitlement was decisively rejected, a critical defeat that Sosin barely mentions. The verdict left legislatures free to set the parameters of welfare largely as they wished; conservatives could therefore limit benefits or attach conditions to them.

Conversely, Sosin underestimates the political resources of the rights movement. He discusses its political problems as if it faced a completely hostile environment. In reality, the poor have always depended on support from the larger society, and during the 1960s that support was generous. In those years liberal currents among public and politicians alike led virtually all of social policy in an expansive direction. Perhaps "poverty [did] not normally attract political attention" before 1960, but it has since, as recent outcries over increased poverty, hunger, and homelessness attest. Political rhetoric may currently be conservative, but polls show no diminution of public commitment to the welfare state or to helping the poor. Even the Reagan cuts have only slightly trimmed the benefits available to the needy.

My interpretation is that the rights movement had considerable political assets but squandered them through one-sided claims. Advocates asserted new rights for the poor but rejected reciprocity. They demanded that a minimum income be assured to everyone without any serious requirements, for instance, that the employable work or pay child support in return. The damage this did can be seen from the struggle prompted by welfare reform, the proposals from the late 1960s to the late 1970s to liberalize welfare benefits and extend coverage beyond the female-headed families eligible for AFDC. The defeat of reform is usually blamed on standard left-right disagreement over the scale of support. My own reading is that work was much more contentious than welfare. Few Congressmen opposed expanded welfare as such, even for the "working poor," but the majority did oppose welfare without conditions. They wanted the employable to earn their benefits by working or at least looking seriously for work, much as the middle class earns social insurance benefits by first working and paying employment taxes. Had liberals accepted this condition, guaranteed income would probably have passed. But they refused.

I think Sosin misinterprets the bureaucratization of welfare since 1970. It is true that work, child support, and fraud and abuse programs have attached more conditions to benefits and made eligibility determination more exacting. But the motivation was not basically antiwelfare as Sosin suggests. If politicians had wanted simply to cut the AFDC rolls, they could have excluded families with employable members or tried to reinstitute by statute the restrictive rules struck down by the courts, steps Congress has never seriously considered. The chief aim of work and child support requirements is not to restrict eligibility but to make welfare more respectable. If employable welfare mothers work and their spouses pay child support, they are functioning in ways society reasonably expects, and their dependency generates less negative response.

Such stipulations often were invidious when imposed locally, in the decades before welfare rights. They are much less so now that they are levied by federal statute. In essence, Congress has accepted the concept of welfare rights but also has affirmed that obligations must accompany such rights. In this, it merely reflects public opinion, which does not oppose assistance as such but is very much against perceived abuses by welfare recipients, particularly nonwork. Such legislation actually elevates the status of welfare: benefits are no longer an act of charity but are given according to a legal definition of claims and duties that amounts to an operational definition of citizenship for the dependent.

Sosin's contention that the new requirements have restricted welfare seems to me weakly supported. It is true that since the early 1970s welfare mothers have been made to establish need regularly, referred to work programs if employable, and required to help the authorities locate absent fathers. It is also true that the proportion of potential AFDC eligibles actually on the rolls has declined in the same period. The author says the two trends are connected, but none of the sources he cites strictly proves it. How do we know that applicants deterred from applying were really eligible? They may have been in income terms, but the whole point of the new requirements is that need alone is not enough to justify support. Recipients must also meet reasonable social expectations about behavior, just like the nondependent. Short of disability, if they decline to assume these obligations and are denied aid, there is no injustice.

The new bureaucratization exposes the ambivalence of the welfare movement about legal rights. Was the rule of law in welfare an end to be sought in itself, or was it only a means to maximize assistance for the poor? If the former, then rights advocates ought to applaud the new rule-based administration, even if it means some restrictions on aid. If the latter, the rule of law must after all be questioned. Sosin's recommendations indicate his own disillusionment with law. He suggests that the restrictive mold of the new bureaucracy might be broken by such steps as greater delegation to the states, a return to a "professional" administrative style, and expanded emergency assistance programs. It sounds like a return to the discretionary regime of the past.

The poor would be better served if the legal revolution in welfare were completed, not disowned. The real weakness of welfare recipients today is that they have run out of the obligations that they, like other people, need in order to justify claims. Exactly by reducing welfare discretion, the rights movement took away from them many of the burdens they could claim to bear. While that step was necessary, it left them in the position of petitioners, dependent on society's goodwill, as anyone is who possesses *only* rights.

To establish further claims, the poor and their advocates must assert new obligations. They should accept, rather then resist, the new bureaucratic requirements, especially work tests. If more welfare mothers worked, their claim to support would be fundamentally stronger. There is, of course, room for argument about what the requirements for recipients should be. But a focus on obligations is much more likely than continued one-sided claims to rights to justify further benefits for the poor. Exactly because welfare rights in a narrow sense have been achieved, serious discussions of obligations must begin.

12 Social Policies, Civil Rights, and Poverty

Charles V. Hamilton
Dona C. Hamilton

DISCUSSIONS OF SOCIAL POLICIES and civil rights in the United States traditionally focus primarily on racial discrimination. A prolific literature has been generated on the efforts of civil rights organizations to overcome *de jure* segregation and discrimination, concentrating largely on the courts and the achievement of goals normally perceived to be within the purview of constitutional rights (Franklin, 1947; Vose, 1959; Bennett, 1962; Lewis, 1964; Miller, 1966; Kellogg, 1967; Bell, 1973; Kluger, 1976). Less attention has been paid to the efforts of such organizations in the social policy arena (referring mainly to social insurance and public assistance), dating back to the New Deal. Such efforts have been made, although they have not achieved the prominence or results of more traditionally understood civil rights efforts and goals.

This chapter will chart the course of social policy strategies of some national civil rights and welfare rights groups from the New Deal to the present. The fifty-year historical context is important for understanding current and evolving agendas. Groups concerned with alleviating the economic plight of their constituents were constantly mindful of those constituents as members of an exploited racial group and what that likely meant in terms of the lack of political influence as well as the kinds of benefits they would receive. Race, in other words, has always been fused with class in the political struggle to obtain equitable policies to alleviate poverty.

We will include in our study certain New Deal programs and legislation, the Fair Employment Practices Committee, the Full Employment Act of 1946, antipoverty programs of the Great Society, the Family Assistance Plan (FAP), and the Humphrey-Hawkins Act of 1978, and discuss their implications for prospective policy emphasis. In addition, we will focus on such matters as the nature of benefits provided (for example, welfare versus employment) and decisions relating to implementation. The latter is especially relevant in reviewing the federal versus state/local approach.

We will also be concerned with the extent of the involvement of advocacy groups. Some of them (for example, the National Association for the Advancement of Colored People and the National Urban League) did not take a leading role in generating support for certain programs (for example, the FAP). In some cases a lack of adequate resources to broaden the programmatic agenda limited the group's involvement. In others there was a strong organizational policy view that the constitutional civil rights agenda was paramount and should not be diluted by devoting attention to other, albeit important, matters. Still another reason for noninvolvement was a tacit division of labor between the groups; certainly the last rationale prevailed in the FAP struggle, with several groups following the lead of the National Welfare Rights Organization in 1969–70.

Recent organizational efforts, what we will refer to as the economically oriented civil rights movement (as distinguished from the constitutionally oriented movement), are seen by some observers as a new emphasis for the groups. We will document that this is only partially correct. At the same time, some maintain that this economic orientation is not properly civil rights at all and therefore should not be accorded the same moral or political support as the other orientation (Abram, 1984). This is not an inconsequential debate, and in many ways it reflects basic policy concerns that must be addressed. Indeed, a contrary view is that the economic agenda is a logical and necessary consequence of a substantially successful constitutional agenda; the latter laid the foundation for engaging the former. In fact, it can be argued that the socioeconomic issues could not be dealt with until certain basic conditions of constitutional status and citizenship rights, such as the right to vote and to participate politically, were established.

Assuming, as we do, that there is more than a modicum of truth to this premise, it is important to make some observations about the political policy orientations of the organizations we will be examining. That is, since our terrain will be mainly the legislative and executive (as opposed to the judicial) arenas, it is useful to identify what we perceive to be certain consistent policy preferences and organizational strategies. These substantive and procedural characteristics, we suggest, constitute persistent attributes, and they offer useful guides to examining our subject throughout the period and programs under study. We note the following characteristics:

Civil rights organizations have been traditionally associated with social policies favoring a pro-active government, one willing to intervene in the economy for purposes of helping those unable to benefit from the more laissez-faire market economy. They have been "liberal-progressive" but not readily available to appeals from groups and ideologies commonly associated with socialist platforms. And the organizations have been wary of private voluntarism as viable means for alleviating poverty.

Civil rights organizations have traditionally sought to form alliances with other liberal groups. They are usually willing to adopt pragmatic political bargains, but they always focus on non-discrimination and antisegregation. This has led to a running battle with organized labor, because of the latter's history of discriminatory practices while at the same time being in the forefront of much liberal-progressive legislation.

Civil rights organizations have traditionally preferred national government action to that of state and local governments.

A preference for jobs over welfare characterized the social policy orientation of the groups, especially during the New Deal. This preference was not particularly pronounced, however, during the initiation and development of the antipoverty programs of the 1960s, and this difference has important implications for civil rights groups increasingly turning their attention to an economically oriented policy agenda.

These policy orientations will serve as guides as we discuss the history of social policies, civil rights/welfare rights groups, and poverty, and as we comment on the implications for future organizational agendas and strategies.

Historical Context

The Great Depression was an era of great political and economic turmoil that resulted in a significant change in social welfare policy. During this decade two national black organizations, the National Urban League (NUL) and the National Association for the Advancement of Colored People (NAACP), advocated for New Deal policies that would be advantageous to black Americans. They believed, even before the onset of the Depression, that unemployment and lack of employment opportunities were at the heart of the problems confronting black Americans and welcomed government intervention in the resolution of these problems. Their evaluations of New Deal programs and legislation were very much related to how these provided jobs and income security to black workers. They paid minimal attention to relief (welfare) policies. As the Depression waned in 1940, both organizations advocated for some kind of permanent public works program (NAACP, 1939; Hamilton, 1984). Black workers were not being absorbed into the private sector labor force as rapidly as white workers were. It was feared that blacks were becoming permanently dependent on relief, which was viewed as having negative consequences on the status of blacks in a society with a strong work ethic. Dependence on relief would stigmatize and deter the advancement of the race.

New Deal programs and legislation that were of special interest to the NUL and the NAACP were work and work-relief programs; the National Recovery Administration (NRA); the Agricultural Adjustment Administration (AAA); the Social Security Act; the National Labor Relations Act; and the Fair Labor Standards Act. In all of these programs and legislation each of the organizations developed certain policy preferences related to eligibility, administration, and the form of benefits. Each attempted to influence the shaping of policy in these areas.

NATIONAL RECOVERY ADMINISTRATION

The NRA was an early and short-lived program established in 1933 whose purpose was to stimulate private industry to produce more and thus enable it to hire more workers. It set out to establish fair practice codes in all industries that would regulate hours and wages in the private sector (Leuchtenburg, 1963). When President Roosevelt issued a blanket code to promote compliance with the regulations (the "blue eagle agreement"), it caused widespread displacement of black workers, especially in the South where employers refused to pay the minimum wage to blacks. Furthermore, two-thirds of black workers, those in domestic and agriculture work, were excluded from coverage (Reed, 1934; National Urban League [henceforth NUL] Papers, 1933a).

To counteract this displacement and exclusion, the Joint Committee on National Recovery was founded, composed of twenty-two national fraternal, civic, and church groups (Cayton and Mitchell, 1939). Evidence of discrimination in applying the codes was collected, and code hearings affecting large numbers of black workers were attended. The NRA was accused of legislating black workers into a new industrial slavery (Davis, 1934; NAACP Annual Report, 1933; NUL Papers, 1933b). But the combined efforts of the organization did not accomplish much. Part of the problem was that organized labor did not involve black workers in its movement to organize workers in large-scale industries (NUL Papers, 1933c).

NATIONAL LABOR RELATIONS ACT (WAGNER ACT)

The National Labor Relations Act, passed in 1935, gave considerable power to organized labor. Two main features of the act were the right of labor to bargain collectively and the prohibition of employers from interfering in the establishment of unions in their plants (Leuchtenburg, 1963).

Neither the NUL nor the NAACP was enthusiastic about the bill because it legalized closed shops. Since many black workers were excluded from unions, they feared that thousands would be shut out of employment (NAACP Annual Report, 1934). The NUL testified against adoption of the bill. Although it approved any measure that would equalize the bargaining powers of employers and employees and encourage amicable settlement of labor disputes, it was not in favor of the bill for several reasons. The bill permitted labor organizations to exclude blacks from membership; it denied the status of "employees" to black workers engaged in "strike-breaking" in occupations that excluded black workers and did not allow them to join unions; it failed to protect black workers from discriminatory practices by labor unions, both as union and non-union members; and it permitted the establishment of competitive unions based on race, thereby weakening the bargaining power of all workers. The NUL supported its testimony with evidence of trade union exclusion and depicted strike-breaking as the only means for the black workers to "break the stranglehold that certain organized labor groups have utilized in preventing his complete absorption in the American labor market" (NUL, 1934, p. 2).

NEW DEAL WORK AND WORK-RELIEF PROGRAMS

The NUL was initially enthusiastic about New Deal work and work-relief programs and was at the forefront of the struggle to help black workers obtain benefits from these programs. But as New Deal programs were implemented, the NUL realized that the programs were not the panacea it had anticipated. It became clear that certain program policies were impediments to black workers becoming gainfully employed. As a result the

League developed certain policy preferences that it believed would be helpful to the black unemployed. Major policy preferences were benefits in the form of work rather than relief; federal administration of programs with limited state and local autonomy; prevention of discrimination in programs; and the inclusion of blacks in the administration of programs. In addition, the NUL was in favor of policies that specified a set wage rate and regulated hours of work, preferably without geographic differentials. They also urged inclusion of an antidiscriminatory clause in all government contracts (Hamilton, 1984).

Although many of the New Deal programs did have an antidiscriminatory clause, there was no enforcement mechanism. The involvement of black administrators in New Deal programs proved to be a deciding factor in preventing discrimination. Robert Weaver, a young black economist, served as Advisor for Negro Affairs under Harold Ickes, secretary of the Department of the Interior, the department responsible for the administration of the Public Works Administration (PWA). Weaver, very much aware of the discriminatory policies of local contractors and organized labor, developed a plan to prohibit discrimination on government construction projects. To test the plan, he used a special PWA administrative unit responsible for slum clearance and the construction of low-cost housing. All PWA projects in this unit were required to hire a certain percentage of skilled black craftsmen based on the total number of skilled black craftsmen in specific cities throughout the country. If this percentage was not met, it was prima facie evidence of discrimination. A year and a half after his plan was implemented, Weaver thought it was "a workable solution to a difficult problem" (Weaver, 1936), but it was never extended to other programs (Hamilton, 1984).

Mary McLeod Bethune, a member of the NUL board, served as Advisor for Negro Affairs in the National Youth Administration (NYA). In spite of the fact that NYA was a program in which a great deal of local autonomy was allowed, there appears to have been less discrimination in this program than in other programs with similar policies. This implies that Bethune had a great deal of influence; she was able to funnel thousands of dollars to black youth (Hamilton, 1984; Kirby, 1980).

AGRICULTURAL ADJUSTMENT ADMINISTRATION

The AAA was established in 1933 to deal with the problems of depressed prices for farm products and mounting crop surpluses. Perhaps to speed passage of the farm bill, Roosevelt wanted a decentralized administration that allowed for participation at the local level (Leuchtenburg, 1963). Thus the AAA vested its authority in local committees, and as a result great variations were seen in the treatment of black sharecroppers under this administration (Wolters, 1970). The autonomy of local committees in the South meant, too frequently, that large landowners controlled government benefits, benefits that were incentives for a reduction of cotton acreage. Although the program set forth clear guidelines as to how benefits were to be allocated between owner and tenant, many sharecroppers and tenants were not given their fair share.

The NAACP presented evidence of widespread discrimination of share-croppers and tenant farmers along with a proposal regarding acreage re-duction contracts and the administration of the program. It supported the Southern Tenant Farmers' Union and conducted a letter-writing campaign demanding fairer treatment of blacks in New Deal agriculture programs (NAACP Annual Reports, 1935–1937). But it was difficult for a black organization to compete with the southern bloc of the Democratic Party and little was accomplished. Nonetheless, the NAACP was one of the groups that helped to focus national attention on the AAA cotton reduction program and its negative effect on poor blacks in the South.

SOCIAL SECURITY ACT

The Social Security Act of 1935 was a giant step in the federal government's participation in and responsibility for a broad range of social welfare pro-grams to help individuals meet the loss of earnings or absence of income caused by unemployment, old age, death, and other hazards of life. The NUL's analysis of the bill focused on unemployment compensation and old age security and ignored other aspects of the bill, including aid to dependent children. It testified in favor of the coverage of all workers, total federal administration, and allocation of benefits based on economic need (Hill, 1935; NUL, 1935). The NAACP also testified in favor of the bill, with many of the same concerns as the NUL, particularly coverage of all workers (NAACP Annual Report, 1935). The NAACP was not in favor of "lily-white social security" (Haynes, 1935).

The two organizations were most disappointed when the bill was passed without providing coverage for domestic and agriculture workers. This meant that more than two million workers (two-thirds of the black labor force) would not receive benefits from the act and would have to rely on welfare when they were unable to work. Both organizations continued to advocate coverage for these workers (Wood, 1939; Wright, 1936).

FAIR LABOR STANDARDS ACT

The Fair Labor Standards Act was passed in 1938 to establish maximum hours of work and a minimum wage (Leuchtenburg, 1963). It was a highly controversial act, and even the NUL and the NAACP were not in full agreement about it. The NUL was in favor of the bill, believing that it would improve working conditions, but the NAACP opposed it in the belief that it would pass only if the South were granted concessions allowing for a special wage level for blacks that would be fixed for years (NAACP Annual Report, 1937; NUL Papers, 1938).

Although the act was very weak when it was finally passed (too many concessions were made to various industries), it caused some layoffs of black workers, especially in the South. The NUL saw this as a temporary problem that would pass with time, but the NAACP believed that its reservations about the act had been well substantiated (NAACP Annual Report, 1938; NUL, 1938).

FAIR EMPLOYMENT PRACTICES COMMITTEE

The growth of the defense industry in the early 1940s rapidly expanded the private sector labor market. The NAACP and the NUL viewed this expansion as an opportunity for black workers to gain regular employment and urged them to apply for jobs at all defense plants. Although working independently, the NUL and the NAACP conducted a nationwide campaign for jobs.

It was not uncommon for employers at defense plants to regard black workers as lacking the skills necessary to qualify for jobs. To counteract this attitude, the campaign for jobs was coordinated with an effort to help black workers receive a fair share of vocational training in programs that were being offered throughout the country. In addition, the organizations documented incidents of discrimination and sent this information to federal officials. Although discrimination was prohibited in vocational training programs supported by federal funds, black workers experienced much difficulty both in becoming enrolled in these programs and in securing employment at defense plants (Carter, 1941; NAACP Annual Report, 1940).

Part of the problem was the failure of unions to take any action against discriminatory employment policies. The NAACP, the NUL, and the Brotherhood of Sleeping Car Porters (BSCP) met with the President, other federal officials, and American Federation of Labor (AFL) officials to discuss discrimination in hiring (Garfinkel, 1959). A. Philip Randolph, president of BSCP, came to the conclusion that meetings with the President and officials in Washington were not productive. He believed that some kind of mass action by blacks was needed to call attention to the problem. He solicited and received the support of the NUL, the NAACP, and prominent black ministers and educators. A March on Washington Committee was formed as well as a Sponsoring Committee to help publicize the march and to contribute funding (Carter, 1941; Granger, 1941).

The march never occurred, but the threat of the march succeeded in convincing Roosevelt to issue Executive Order 8802, which stated: "There shall be no discrimination in the employment of workers in defense industries because of race, creed, color, or national origin . . ." The order was to be enforced by a temporary Fair Employment Practices Committee (FEPC), which would investigate complaints of discrimination and "take appropriate steps to redress grievances" (Anderson, 1972; Carter, 1941).

Executive Order 8802 did not result in the immediate hiring of large numbers of blacks at defense plants. In spite of the crucial need for workers, employers continued to be reluctant to hire blacks. The critical demand for labor during World War II was the significant factor in expanding employment opportunities for black workers. Even union membership among blacks increased substantially, especially in the Congress of Industrial Organizations (CIO), which made more of an effort to recruit black members. The tendency to place blacks in lower-paying, unskilled jobs continued, but there was a notable improvement in the number of black workers employed (Foner, 1974).

The NAACP and the NUL worried about what would happen when the war ended. Black workers were the last hired, and it seemed likely that they would be the first fired. It was very possible that industry would revert to its former discriminatory hiring practices without some enforcement against discrimination. They advocated for a permanent FEPC that would take strong action against discrimination in employment (NAACP Board of Directors Meeting, 1945; Garfinkel, 1959). Government action to prohibit discriminatory employment practices continued to be a focal point for the organizations. Their efforts culminated many years later in the establishment of the Equal Employment Opportunity Commission under Title VII of the Civil Rights Act of 1964.

THE FULL EMPLOYMENT ACT OF 1946

As World War II ended, the upheaval related to the change from a wartime economy to one of peace was a major concern of the NUL and the NAACP.

They feared high unemployment among black workers and also worried about how returning black servicemen would react if they were not given equal consideration for jobs after risking their lives defending their country. Neither organization was satisfied with the plans outlined by the Department of Labor to help key areas adjust to a peacetime economy. The plans were based on 1940 data and did not take into consideration the population changes that had occurred since then. During the war thousands of blacks had migrated to areas where jobs were available, and a significant amount of reverse migration seemed unlikely, particularly when there did not appear to be jobs at the other end. This black population would probably remain in the areas where it had settled during the war. Since these individuals would need employment, a difficult situation could ensue: competition for jobs in these areas might result in racial conflict (Johnson, 1945; NAACP Board of Directors' Meeting, 1945).

Consequently, it is not surprising that the NUL and the NAACP were in favor of H.R. 2202, "a bill to establish a national policy and program for assuring continuing full employment in a free competitive economy, through the concerted efforts of industry, agriculture, labor, state and local governments, and the federal government." They perceived it to be a very strong and important piece of legislation that would give citizens a "right" to a job; they testified in favor of it (Congressional Testimony, 1945; Bailey, 1964). If it passed, it would mean that black workers would be gainfully employed and not dependent on welfare during times of recession. However, the compromise that finally assured the passage of the bill resulted in a very diluted version of its original intent: The act did not give workers the right to a job; it merely promoted "maximum employment, production, and purchasing power" and required the President to give an annual Economic Report to Congress that would be referred to a Joint Committee. The lobbying efforts of organizations representing private industry, which hoped to defeat the bill, were too strong for the passage of a bill with "teeth" in it (Bailey, 1964). One can only speculate about the effect the act might have had if it had given citizens the "right" to a job. It would seem that it would have made a significant difference to black workers who have experienced higher rates of unemployment and who are more vulnerable to economic recessions than other groups in the country.

Recent Social Policy Initiatives

We began this chapter with a discussion of the New Deal and subsequent experiences prior to the 1960s because we believe that that historical context is essential to an understanding of civil rights and welfare rights groups from the mid-1960s on. Too frequently, assessment of policy matters is undertaken within a too-narrow framework. This is especially the case with this subject, where social activism and policy responses are frequently perceived as starting almost *de novo* after a period of relative quiescence in the 1950s.

As we have seen, black organizations in the 1930s and 1940s were keenly concerned with the economic plight of their black constituents. They believed that racial barriers—in many instances, sanctioned by law—had to be overturned before the benefits of social policies could be realized by black Americans. At the same time, they constantly emphasized measures that would provide incomes as opposed to charity or relief. "Jobs not alms" was more than an idle slogan for those groups. But always they had to contend with the fact that many of the policies begun in the New Deal would likely have minimal, if not negative, consequences for blacks unless specific steps were taken to avoid such results—thus the concentration on eliminating racial segregation and discrimination. This meant consciously calling to the forefront the overriding issue of racial subordination. In addition, it is difficult to miss the underlying orientation of an ultimate desire to be treated "just like everybody else" and to join with other progressive forces in the society to obtain social policies that would benefit all.

These advocacy efforts, for various and obvious reasons, tend to be obscured when we turn our attention to the 1960s and 1970s, the years of mounting civil rights activity—in the streets, the courts, Congress, and the Executive branch. Masses marched in Washington, in Birmingham, at local construction sites in the North, against city halls. Rioting began a string of "long hot summers" from 1964 to 1969. Nationalist cries of "black power" were heard, bringing different messages and demanding seemingly different goals. Local community groups began to insist on community control, while at the same time calling on the national government to appropriate more resources for the alleviation of what had come to be a new term on the American social policy agenda—poverty.

At first glance, all of this seems like a sharp departure from the relatively mild pleadings and proddings chronicled in the first part of this chapter. Quiet, sober letters and meetings asking for equitable treatment gave way to loud, defiant demands (with raised clenched fists) for "power to the people." Protracted debates were held extolling the virtues of coalition politics or condemning the vices of "separatism." Many of these discussions, it is sad but accurate to say, were held almost in a historical vacuum. Few knew, or at least alluded to, the previous history of polite struggle discussed in the first part of this chapter. We should not repeat those errors in understanding. Social struggle is continuous, seldom *in vacuo*.

THE GREAT SOCIETY PROGRAMS

We preface this section by noting the lack of historical perspective because one of the debates concerning the origins of Great Society programs centers on the issue of initiation. More than a few accounts tell us that the myriad of programs that were put forward during the Kennedy and Johnson administrations were initiated by a few scholar-policymakers who conceived what should be done based on their theories and experiences with youth gangs (Sundquist, 1968). Some point to the traumatic impact of West Virginia poverty conditions on candidate Kennedy in the spring of 1960, and his reading of Michael Harrington's influential *The Other America* (1962). Still others point to the mounting unrest in urban black communities and to the desire of the national Democrats to forge a new viable political force for their party among potential black voters (Piven and Cloward, 1971).

In any case, the country witnessed a burst of new social policy initiatives in the 1960s. A substantial literature describes the differing motives and goals of the policymakers, the varying views of the Shriver people, the Bureau of the Budget people, the Mobilization for Youth people, and others (Moynihan, 1969). Our interest here is not to recount those often-told tales. We propose to maintain our focus on the positions taken by the traditional and new civil rights and welfare rights organizations in the face of this emerging agenda.

As the story is told, policymakers began to think consciously about poverty when President Kennedy reportedly said to Walter Heller, his chairman of the Council of Economic Advisers in December 1962: "Now look! I want to go beyond the things that have already been accomplished. Give me facts and figures on the things we still have to do. For example, what about the poverty problem in the United States?" (Sundquist, 1968, p. 112) There was a sense that the several existing programs were not addressing the core problems of the poor. Urban renewal was, in the assessment of Morris and Rein, flawed: "Where were the slum dwellers to be relocated? . . . Urban renewal became, for the city's poor, a cynical expropriation in the interests of business, real estate, and the tax base" (Morris and Rein, 1973, p. 14). The 1962 Manpower Development and Training Act was aimed at retraining displaced workers. It was not, however, reaching the chronic unemployed. Many of the latter were not educationally equipped to benefit from available jobs; they were functionally illiterate. Thus, MDTA was expanded in 1963 "to permit training in literacy and basic work skills in addition to the regular occupational training" (Sundquist, 1968, p. 131).

Throughout 1963 the Kennedy advisers worked on a set of proposals that subsequently constituted the legislative package attacking poverty introduced by President Lyndon Johnson early in 1964. Community action programs were endorsed, with the urging of the Ford Foundation which had had experience with its "grey areas" program. The Office of Economic Opportunity (OEO) was created to administer all poverty programs. Essentially, the "war" consisted of a set of strategies designed to deliver services to poor people to enable them to improve their skills, their health, and their basically inadequate educational backgrounds in order to be better equipped to function in the market economy.

But there was one major dissenter—Willard Wirtz, secretary of labor. He emphasized the need for jobs and even favored a "proposed 5-cent tax on cigarettes expected to yield $1.25 billion per year to be earmarked for employment programs for the adult poor" (Moynihan, 1969, p. 99). This idea was not implemented; employment strategy was not the centerpiece of the War on Poverty. What emerged was a service strategy with emphasis on community action programs.

Moynihan observed that although urban black communities were to be the most affected, the various CAP planning groups consisted exclusively of middle-class whites. One major statement and suggested proposal on the economic condition, a "Freedom Budget for All Americans" announced in 1966 by the A. Philip Randolph Institute, was developed by several black and white economists and policy analysts (including Leon Keyserling, Vivian Henderson, Tom Kahn, and Bayard Rustin). It called for a ten-year allocation of $180 billion; full employment was at the top of the list, along with an adequate minimum wage, a guaranteed income to all those unable to work, and other programs aimed at eradicating slums and improving housing.

This proposal was apparently not taken seriously in Washington policy councils, which were then heavily involved in implementing and amending the service-oriented War on Poverty. Indeed, not only is the Freedom Budget not discussed in the classic literature chronicling that period, but there is virtually no evidence that the civil rights and welfare rights groups that testified before congressional committees from 1966 through 1970 felt compelled to advocate forcefully in its behalf. Instead, the many organizations, national and local, that went to Washington in the late 1960s to testify before Congress concentrated their efforts on seeking more funds for the poverty programs, supporting the "maximum feasible participation" features of Title II of the Economic Opportunity Act (maximum feasible participation implied that the poor should be involved in planning and implementation of Title II programs), and generally calling for increased support for the service-oriented strategy of the various programs. Scant attention was paid directly to job-creating measures for the unemployed.

For example, on May 8, 1967, Arthur C. Logan, chairman of the Anti-Poverty Committee of United Neighborhood Houses in New York City, testified before the Senate subcommittee on Employment, Manpower, and Poverty of the Committee on Labor and Public Welfare, which was holding hearings to examine the then three-year-old antipoverty program. Senator Clark (Pa.) was chairman and Senator Javits (N.Y.) was present. Logan suggested that the subcommittee carefully consider the Freedom Budget because this "would be of very great value" in directing legislators' thinking toward the eradication of poverty rather than "remediation of the effects of poverty." Logan's suggestion was rebuffed by Senator Clark, who flatly stated, "I don't think our constituents are anywhere near ready for that budget" (Congressional Testimony, 1967a). This states the issue quite clearly: Whatever the substantive merits of the Freedom Budget, the politics of the time dictated other emphases—emphases that even then were recognized by many to be less than sufficient to come to grips with the basic poverty problems in the society.

Therefore, the social policy situation throughout the latter years of the 1960s was one in which antipoverty supporters were attempting to adjust to a program stressing services and the allocation of relatively minimal resources to those services. To be sure, proponents constantly paraded before congressional committees pleading for more money for Head Start, day-care, job counseling, health services, community action agencies. Whitney M. Young, Jr., executive director of the National Urban League, told a U.S. Senate subcommittee: "my criticism is directed not to the structure of the Office of Economic Opportunity, but to the scale on which the war on poverty is being conducted, a scale still far too limited to do much more than act as a palliative. . . . The OEO has launched important programs with a need unmatched by any Federal agency since the New Deal. What is needed is more, not less." Young, when asked, recommended at least $10 billion for fiscal 1968, adding "I would probably have to go up after that. We need at least that" (Congressional Testimony, 1967b).

Young also complained that not enough antipoverty funds were allocated to established civil rights organizations. He pointed out that these organizations have had a "half-century or more of experience, . . . thoroughly representative boards, and the established confidence of the community." If poverty funds had been given to them, they would have been "able to implement some of the tangible programs sought within the ghettos" (Congressional Testimony, 1967b).

Another theme that constantly occupied the attention of the civil rights and welfare rights groups during the late 1960s was related to the maintenance of the Office of Economic Opportunity (OEO) as a distinct viable agency. This concern increased after Nixon's election, when proposals were made to transfer some functions of OEO to established cabinet departments. Generally, this plan was not well received by the groups. In June 1969 the NUL urged a House of Representatives Committee not to transfer OEO functions and to maintain it as an independent agency reporting directly to the President: "Its only constituency must be the poor . . . Successfully developed programs should be transferred from OEO to other Federal agencies only after a careful determination that the receiving agency can effectively carry on the unique features of the program, such as involvement of the target population and utilization of the private sector" (Congressional Testimony, 1969a).

As early as 1967 the National Sharecroppers Fund (NSF) voiced its strong disagreement with any attempt to dismantle OEO: "We need the Office of Economic Opportunity as the nerve center and general staff of the war on poverty." Eliminating OEO "would end the most important accomplishment of the antipoverty campaign: a beginning voice for the poor in the highest council of governments and the establishment and celebration of an end to poverty as a national goal." Transferring antipoverty programs to other departments would mean that "they would lose their driving force" (Congressional Testimony, 1967a). It was felt that antipoverty programs would get lost in intrabureaucratic struggles over funds and turf, and therefore the programs would be likely to be "more conservative and less adventurous, less willing to take a chance" (Congressional Testimony, 1967b).

Clearly, the civil rights and welfare rights groups saw the OEO as *their* special agency in the higher councils of government. If other interest groups— big business, organized labor, farmers—had particular departments to which they could turn, then this new OEO structure represented the focus for the representatives of the poor. This view made the advocacy of community control on the one hand consistent with the recognition of the growing centralization of power on the other. What the newly politicized antipoverty groups were pushing for was a direct linkage between funds-dispensing authority in Washington and themselves in the local communities. This meant, to the extent possible, circumventing state and local official structures. For the most part, old structures and relationships of the federalist system were dysfunctional to the best interests of the community-based groups.

Thus, the following observation of the National Sharecroppers Fund was reasonably illustrative:

> The move towards state-operated community action programs serving rural and smaller communities is bad and should be reconsidered. The southern states where NSF works have already shown a most unwise tendency to use what veto power they have to stop programs needed by the poor particularly in the rural communities. (NSF itself has just had one important program for training local leadership approved for funding by OEO and then vetoed by the State of Alabama.) The participation of the poor in planning and directing a program in such a top-down arrangement would be at maximum a token gesture. The reason poverty, illiteracy, and migration are so prevalent in wide areas of the rural south is in large part due to calculated neglect of these areas by state and local agencies. To turn over vital parts of the poverty program to the whim of state agencies would be to abandon the poor. (Congressional Testimony, 1967c)

The NAACP, represented by Clarence Mitchell, was also convinced that a nationally based OEO with power to curtail obstructionist state and local politicians was essential (Congressional Testimony, 1969b). Mitchell was likewise convinced that a separate OEO was needed, and that its responsibilities should not be given to established departments. He used the New Deal as his reference, arguing that New Deal agencies were set up because existing agencies were not flexible enough "to do the job that they had to do." OEO programs were established for the same reason and should not be turned over to other federal administrations. For example, Head Start should not be placed under the Office of Education, "a conduit of Government interests and funds to local communities and schools," and some of the functions of the Job Corps and Labor should not be given to the Employment Service, "one of the worst discriminators in this country" (Congressional Testimony, 1969b).

As could be expected, the role of the private sector in business as well as in the social service delivery system was of major concern to policymakers and social activists. Invariably, antipoverty activists conceded the need to involve the business community in various ways: as partners with local groups (such as Opportunities Industrialization Centers); in offering job-training and apprenticeship programs; in providing summer jobs for youth; and in working with local organizations (such as the Bedford-Stuyvesant Restoration Corporation) in multiple community economic development ventures. Essentially, this limited partnership role was about as far as most thinking and expectations went. The emphasis on a service strategy basically assumed that if people were educationally equipped and sufficiently trained, jobs would be available in the private sector for those willing to work.

This was not the exclusive view, however. As one might expect, organized labor, especially the AFL-CIO, focused its efforts on the need to create jobs. Following Willard Wirtz's preference for an income emphasis to poverty, an early and frequent position of labor could be summed up in a 1966 statement to Congress, which asserted that "half of America's poverty problem is directly related to the lack of enough jobs at decent pay." Poverty could not be "reduced quickly and permanently" unless OEO projects were meshed with programs that provided jobs at a decent wage for the "millions of working poor" and with programs that provided adequate income-maintenance payments for "impoverished families without a member in the labor force." Labor advocated a continuing effort to ensure full employment, believing that "the resources we are allocating toward this purpose are altogether insufficient in terms of both the need and of our abilities" (Congressional Testimony, 1966).

But in the middle of the riotous summer of 1967, Parren Mitchell (Democratic Congressman from Baltimore, then executive director of Baltimore's Community Action Agency) told a House committee that jobs were not enough. Although he was totally in favor of manpower training and job development, he felt that the situation required "simultaneous action in the area of civil rights that erased the last vestiges of discrimination" (Congressional Testimony, 1967d).

For the most part, however, at that time social policies dealing with poverty focused mainly on providing a range of services to poor people, services aimed at preparing them to take advantage of employment opportunities that many policymakers thought were (or would be) available in the market economy.

THE FAMILY ASSISTANCE PLAN

When the Nixon administration introduced a guaranteed annual income proposal (disguised for political reasons as welfare reform) in 1969, liberals, and especially several black organizations, were surprised and suspicious. The plan was not approved by Congress, and Daniel P. Moynihan, its architect, ultimately blamed those liberals and especially George Wiley and the National Welfare Rights Organization (NWRO).

The Family Assistance Plan (FAP) included two principles that most agreed with: a minimum income for everyone and help for "working poor" families (Kotz and Kotz, 1977). It also provided for "workfare." Initially, the National Urban League and the National Council of Negro Women were inclined to support the proposal, but they and others ultimately took their lead from the NWRO. Basically, NWRO felt that the floor was too low ($1,600, instead of a preferred $5,500), and some welfare rights benefits would be lost.

In addition, George Wiley of NWRO accused Moynihan of the same fault voiced earlier by Moynihan regarding formulation of the War on Poverty; namely, excluding the poor in drafting the proposal (Kotz and Kotz, 1977). Essentially, the debate revolved around whether the plan should be accepted at least as a start, a "foot in the door," that would establish for the first time the concept of a guaranteed annual income. If so, the argument went, greater benefits could be added later. The NWRO was not convinced or not optimistic that this strategy would work. Some people later suggested that this was a strategic error on the part of the liberals.

Even the sixteen members of the Congressional Black Caucus initially endorsed the plan, but the NWRO kept up the pressure for liberalization. It was not opposed to the workfare provision (its own version allowed for that) but fundamentally objected to the low benefit level. And this objection prevailed among liberals, notwithstanding that many southern poor blacks would likely immediately benefit from the plan.

The established civil rights groups apparently decided to follow the lead of Wiley and the NWRO because they were impressed with Wiley's command of the subject. Vernon Jordan of the National Urban League stated: "George did the best organizing job of anybody after the sixties had their peak. When it came to welfare legislation, I was very impressed with his detailed knowledge. He wasn't just a podium type who could raise the rights of people and exhort. He would quote from page four of the bill and he knew what section A meant, and that was important. He commanded support" (Kotz and Kotz, 1977, p. 276).

It can be argued (as we do) that failure to support this concept of an income floor (in spite of its low level) was a missed opportunity for those ultimately concerned about jobs/income versus welfare/charity. An important feature of FAP was its inclusion of the working poor, which is politically necessary, one would suspect, in any effort to undertake major social policy reform in the United States.

To be sure, FAP was not a jobs bill or even a minimum step toward full employment. It was, however, a significant conceptual leap toward understanding and treating poverty as a permanent basic social policy responsibility of the national government. Its specific provisions were flawed; its social policy purposes were, in balance, positive.

FULL EMPLOYMENT AND BALANCED GROWTH ACT OF 1978

The problem of unemployment has been a longstanding concern of black organizations. Congressman Augustus Hawkins (D-Calif.) called attention to the problem again when he introduced the Equal Opportunity and Full Employment bill in the House in 1975. The title of the bill caused some to regard it as an antidiscriminatory measure. Hawkins was quick to point out that this was not the bill's primary goal, stating, "Equal employment opportunity and genuine full employment are interwoven. When there are in fact 'useful and rewarding opportunities for adult Americans, willing and able to work,' employment discrimination . . . is necessarily largely minimized" (Hawkins, 1975).

Long-term structural unemployment prompted Hawkins to introduce his bill, but it was criticized because it seemed to lack comprehensive economic and job-creating policies. It was eventually linked to the Balanced Growth and Economic Planning bill introduced by Senator Hubert Humphrey (D-Minn.), a bill that was criticized because it had no discernible goals. The combined bills became the Full Employment and Balanced Growth bill in March 1976. It was an expansion of the Full Employment Act of 1946, but its goals went far beyond the 1946 act. It called for the development of a long-range plan to provide for economy in government, to ensure that monetary and fiscal policies were used to achieve annual economic goals, and to develop and support long-range goals and priorities. It was a strong bill that would give all adult Americans able, willing, and seeking work the *right* to useful paid employment at a decent wage. The responsibility for promoting full employment was given to the federal government. The bill required the President and Congress to set specific employment goals annually along with a plan to meet those goals. Public service employment, public works, antirecession grants to states and local governments, and skill training in the public and private sectors were to be used to reach full employment. Programs would be implemented when national unemployment exceeded 3 percent and discontinued when they were no longer needed.

A full employment policy was very appealing to the black community. The Full Employment Action Council was formed and consisted of labor, business, church, and civil rights groups, including the NUL and the NAACP. Coretta Scott King, president of the Martin Luther King Center for Social Change, was a co-chair along with Murray H. Finley, president of the Amalgamated Clothing Workers of America. The Council coordinated lobbying efforts, encouraged the formation of local councils thoughout the country, testified in favor of the bill, and attempted to educate the general public about the need for the bill (Full Employment Action Council Newsletters, 1976). The Congressional Black Caucus (CBC) was solidly behind the bill, and it too worked to get the bill through Congress.

Black leaders focused on the potential of the bill to resolve social problems—crime, discrimination, and the waste of human resources. Attempts were made to counteract the criticism that the bill was too costly by pointing out the high cost of unemployment—the payment of unemployment compensation, welfare benefits, and efforts to counteract high crime. It was argued that it was unfair to attempt to control inflation by maintaining high unemployment. In addition, it was pointed out that the Phillips curve was not valid; there appeared to be no relationship between the proportion of unemployed workers and the rate of inflation. Both were going up (National Committee for Full Employment, 1976; Lekachman, 1976).

The fate of the bill was similar to the fate of the 1946 bill. The 1978 Act was a watered-down version of the 1976 Full Employment and Balanced Growth bill. It did not give Americans a constitutional right to a job, nor were the job programs outlined in the original bill developed (see text of the Full Employment and Balanced Growth Act of 1978). The Act was a disappointment to the black community. Reducing inflation was given higher priority than full employment, and efforts to reduce inflation included maintaining a certain percentage of unemployment. The Act would not reduce unemployment in the immediate future nor did it appear that it would resolve the problem of unemployment among black workers in the years ahead. The strong support the bill received from organizations with black constituents illustrates again their preference for work rather than relief, for government intervention to provide jobs, and for federal administration of employment programs.

ALTHOUGH THE major thrust of this chapter has been employment opportunities for black Americans, it is certainly not our intent to imply that the civil rights movement was not important to this goal. It is clear that civil rights policies and the expansion of employment opportunities for black workers are not separate policy issues. Blacks certainly benefited from the civil rights policies formed during the 1960s. But at the present time, despite a popular civil rights movement and an antipoverty program, unemployment remains a crucial problem among blacks, particularly among black youth. The civil rights struggle to obtain and protect economic equality should continue to be a critical concern. Job discrimination is still a major impediment to the economic advancement of blacks. Blacks, once hired, continue to be slower to advance and more vulnerable to periods of economic retrenchment. The "new" service economy places blacks in their usual position—the lowest-paying occupations without fringe benefits, without job security through union affiliation, and frequently without full-time employment. Therefore, it is important for civil rights organizations to continue to press for more employment opportunities for blacks, to monitor career advancement patterns and litigate cases where there is suspicion of discrimination, and to seek ways to limit the impact of cutbacks on those blacks who have the least amount of seniority in the labor market, public and private.

We conclude this chapter by examining Moynihan's interesting, but obviously unanswerable, speculation on whether black involvement in the planning process of Great Society programs would have led to the same emphasis of those programs on a service strategy rather than on jobs and incomes. Clearly, the weight of the evidence from the New Deal tells us that black civil rights groups definitely favored socioeconomic programs aimed at work, not relief. This preference persisted throughout the 1940s into the early 1960s. It is equally clear, however, that one cannot overlook the political environment in which social policies are hatched and implemented. We would suggest that organizations such as the National Urban League and the NAACP were able to make the case—if, indeed, not entirely to prevail—for an employment emphasis during the New Deal because unemployment *for whites* likewise was of primary national concern. Such groups keenly understood the value of work over relief in a society predicated on the work ethic. In fact, as we have discussed, black organizations fifty years ago were more than wary about policies that could conceivably leave too many black Americans reliant on public assistance. This would make them vulnerable to stigmatization and to the vagaries of a charity system that would, at best, only reluctantly provide a minimum of security to recipients. During the New Deal black organizations were decidedly unsupportive of policies that for reasons of inadequate coverage and discriminatory implementation would likely mandate a dependent status for black Americans.

Would the Great Society thrust have taken a different turn in the mid-1960s if blacks had persisted manifestly in this New Deal general policy orientation? It is difficult to be optimistic that things would have come out differently—which, we hasten to add, is probably not sufficient justification for virtually abandoning the attempt.

As we have seen, on the few occasions when jobs were high on the black social policy agenda after the New Deal—FEPC, the Employment Act of 1946, the 1963 March on Washington, the Freedom Budget, the Humphrey-Hawkins bill in the late 1970s—there was not much political support from the larger society. Again, when the market economy is performing reasonably well for the majority of Americans, it is very difficult to generate the support required for concerted government intervention to create and maintain jobs for those not benefiting from economic prosperity. This political reality severely constrains the influence of economically vulnerable racial minorities. We must not forget Senator Clark's blunt but honest admonition to Arthur Logan that the Freedom Budget was politically "utterly unrealistic" and that his and Senator Javits' constituents (Pennsylvania and New York, not Alabama and Mississippi) were not "ready for that budget" (Congressional Testimony, 1967a).

To be sure, organized labor was seemingly "ready" in the 1960s, but if they were willing then to be part of the solution, they (certainly, AFL) were also part of the problem in the 1930s and 1940s. Why this shift on its part? The answer very likely lies in the proposition stated earlier: blacks can get others focused on jobs when those others are concerned about their own jobs or the lack of employment. Thus, in the late 1960s organized labor recognized the threat to their ranks of developing economic conditions. They could see—even if many of their employed members could not—the uncertain employment outlook, as described in two news items published in later years. In 1972 a front-page *Wall Street Journal* story stated: "The realization that companies can operate effectively with far fewer employees than they dreamed possible back in 1969 may be comforting to top corporate brass and shareholders. But it's not particularly good news for job-hunting graduates, former middle-management executives, technicians and other salaried employees. Nor is it very happy news for factory hands. . . . Many companies can increase output substantially without adding to the work force" (March 8, 1972).

Eleven years later (May 1983) in the *New York Times* there was an account of a three-day meeting of the Business Council in Hot Springs,

Virginia. The corporate leaders assembled there clearly stated what they perceived to be the employment situation from their vantage point. James H. Evans, chairman of the Union Pacific Corporation, said that 6,000 of his company's 44,000 employees were on layoff. "Will they come back?" he asked rhetorically. "The answer is probably not. We're running 40 percent more freight tonnage than we did 20 years ago—with half as many employees. If we had the same number of employees we had then, we would have priced ourselves out of the market. How have we done it? Automation" (*New York Times,* May 16, 1983).

Our point is that the political process is embedded in these economic realities. If and when jobs and job security—which have always been the social policy concerns of blacks—become important to many others, then, and probably only then, will the wider community become politically active in job creation efforts.

That community was distinctively inattentive to the long-term job-creating needs of blacks in the 1960s and 1970s. The presumption was that if jobs were available for most, then those who were left out very likely needed special training and/or other services before they could be employed. This was sufficient and reasonable justification for the creation of an elaborate set of service-oriented programs, Willard Wirtz and others notwithstanding. For whatever political and organizational reasons (and they were probably many and varied), most black organizations subscribed to this approach. In the process the country embarked on an experiment probably more laden with policy risk than at any other time in its history.

And a curious phenomenon ensued. Proponents of the programs complained from the outset that the experiment was bound to fail unless more resources were committed. Some more funds were allocated, but according to the supporters, never really enough. Subsequently, when critics accused the programs of failure, the proponents were forced to defend what modicum of achievements they identified. Throughout—and now—the criteria for measurement were confused and complicated. Supporters talked in broad terms of eliminating poverty. Poverty increased. Programs were implemented that were aimed at addressing various pieces of the problem, but all too frequently assessments were made on the whole.

It is important to note some consistent themes extending from the New Deal through to the present. Civil rights and welfare rights groups have consistently preferred national government responsibility to that of state and local governments, and a distinct, independent national agency to assigning functions to various established bureaucratic departments. Keen to the machinations of the politics of federalism and interagency struggle, black groups sought to locate authority and responsibility in a particular entity that could be held administratively and politically accountable to their needs. Competing for congressional authorization and funds was difficult enough without having to engage in an additional struggle over inept enforcement and implementation of already minimal programs.

Likewise, we see consistency, not too frequently noted in discussions of these issues, in the emphasis on the need for special treatment, or quotas. Many students of modern social policy date the attention to affirmative action from President Lyndon B. Johnson's 1965 speech at Howard University, where he called for "equality of results," not just for "equality of opportunity." Overlooked is the Weaver plan for PWA to require a certain percentage of blacks to be hired on work programs. Then, as now, the primary motivation was to guard against racially discriminatory hiring practices and to provide a reasonably firm criterion for monitoring compliance.

One is moved to compare the contexts of the two periods and to ask why the furor associated with present-day plans was apparently not generated during the Depression. What comes to mind immediately is the fact that during the Depression the federal government clearly assumed responsibility for providing jobs for those out of work, and therefore, although there was a hiring plan with quotas, there was no sense, in all probability, of zero-sum. If a certain percentage of skilled craftsmen on a PWA job had to be black, this would not necessarily prevent other workers from getting jobs. The quota could realistically be seen as a "floor" below which blacks should not fall, and whites did not have to fear that they would be left out altogether, inasmuch as the federal commitment to employment was more direct and active. This is clearly not the case today: now, whether in the public or private sector, when the federal government (or any other public authority) imposes antidiscrimination hiring percentages, the government is not at the same time assuming the responsibility to "hold harmless" those whites not covered. They might well be harmed—by not getting a job—and it is understandable that such circumstances would create a political backlash. In this sense the New Deal lesson and experience should not be lost on those advocating *and* opposing affirmative action plans in the 1980s. Our analysis is not intended necessarily to denigrate the opposition today based on principle, but it is relevant to note that there was no such discernible opposition during the Depression.

We also believe that civil rights and welfare rights organizations missed a major opportunity when they failed to support the Family Assistance Plan. This was a strategic policy error on their part. To be sure, the annual income figure was abysmally low. But the price at the time was probably worth it in order to establish the principle. The federal government was moving toward assuming responsibility for income maintenance. One is reminded of the political debate around the Fair Labor Standards Act forty-seven years earlier. It was worth supporting, if only to establish the principle. Therefore, when the next round of political struggle ensued, it could concentrate on raising the floor, not on establishing the policy. To fail to support FAP in 1969–70 meant that the political struggle in the 1970s and 1980s would be very different and, we would argue, much more difficult. In addition, FAP would have broadened the base of political alliance to include the working poor.

Finally, we are of the opinion that the heightened focus on welfare rights that emerged in the late 1960s and early 1970s drastically changed the tone of the social policy–civil rights struggle. Unlike the New Deal, when the organizations virtually eschewed emphasis on welfare/relief, the thrust in the 1970s was in that direction. This policy focus on services and welfare was, in our judgment, unfortunate. The earlier concern was primarily on getting blacks into the labor market, not on the welfare rolls. This does not imply that we disagree with the need for civil rights organizations to give attention to welfare policies. There is a need for this, especially since the black population continues to be overrepresented on the welfare rolls. Yet the extent to which the central concern about jobs waned—or at least became less prominent—has been detrimental. It has shifted attention away from examining the implications of major structural changes in the economy. Those people who continue to insist on the necessity for devoting attention to such issues are faced with a much more difficult and resistant audience. It has neglected to address the stigma issue in a society still imbued with the work ethic. If the political environment in the late 1960s was not "ready" for a discussion of the Freedom Budget, it is hardly now amenable to a serious consideration of welfare as a right. One would suspect, however, the concept of a right to a job would be more politically palatable. That emphasis, stressed in the New Deal, should be the emphasis as we move further into the 1980s. It was sound then; it is no less relevant today.

13　The Political Foundations of Antipoverty Policy

Hugh Heclo

THIS CHAPTER FOCUSES on the political past and future of antipoverty policy of the United States. How much and what kinds of federal antipoverty effort will U.S. political society tolerate? Without some rough understanding of political constraints and opportunities, statistical studies are likely to remain academic exercises and policy prescriptions untempered by political prudence.

Unfortunately, the short, scientific, and unhelpful answer to the political question is that we know very little for sure. Most data are anecdotal. The few relevant quantitative studies that exist are often not comparable and are subject to a variety of interpretations. So far as I know, no nationally representative study has explored American elite or mass attitudes regarding social welfare in any great depth.[1] Compared with what we know regarding the relation between poverty and income transfers, family structure, labor markets, and other subjects dealt with in this volume, any information on political feasibilities is—to put it as politely as possible—the softest of the soft variety.

Nor is the problem simply one of information gaps that can be filled by supplying missing data. Political leadership and other such infrequent occurrences can perform a reconstitutive teaching function that may greatly alter the scope of what is feasible politically. Calculations of political benefits and costs are shaped at least as much by changeable perceptions and interpretations as by "real" facts regarding who gains and loses from public programs.

Yet the lack of hard data does not, I think, mean that interpretations must be arbitrary. The history of antipoverty policy provides rough guidelines for assessing political factors. So too does the sparse information available regarding public attitudes. It is also possible to draw inferences relevant to antipoverty policy from what we know more generally about the way our various political institutions work. Putting all this together yields a sketch, not a political blueprint, for thinking about the prospects of federal commitments to the poor.

In the following pages I examine the problem of political feasibility by presenting evidence that is relevant to two contrasting interpretations. In one view the main constraint is public opinion—what the American public will and will not accept with regard to policies affecting poor people. According to another line of thought, the chief impediments to effective antipoverty policies derive from the way our political institutions work— the kinds of policies that can and cannot be produced under existing political structures and procedures. Of course these two views are not mutually exclusive; the real problem is to try to disentangle the patterns of interrelationship.

Antipoverty Policy in Two Historical Moments

In retrospect it is always easier to divide political life into neat historical stages than it is to appreciate the complexities that prevail at given moments of time. This is certainly true of antipoverty policy. Looking back to the New Deal of the 1930s, liberal antipoverty warriors in the 1960s tended to see a promising first stage of development in social welfare policy that they would try to complete under the rubric of a War on Poverty. Looking back to the 1960s, conservative policymakers in the 1980s have typically seen a period of reckless commitment to social redistribution and big government in Washington; in their view a new stage of restraint and selectivity is called for.

These caricatures pay little attention to the crosscurrents, confusion, and gropings for meaning that typically have preoccupied those living amidst what will be history to other people. The following review of political forces at work during two particularly important moments in our history suggests that there never has been a clear, unambiguous political commitment to antipoverty policy in the United States. To understand the enduring sources of that ambivalence is one way of gaining perspective on what the future might portend.

THE NEW DEAL

Poverty as a lasting social problem was rarely a dominant issue on the domestic agenda during the New Deal period. To the extent that it did command attention, political factors severely constrained anything attempted through national programs. Many of those who sought in the 1960s to reinvigorate the Roosevelt coalition for social reform ignored the equivocal political history on which they were building. Here there is space to review only the most prominent developments that touched on questions of poverty policy during the 1930s and early 1940s.

It is worthwhile disentangling three strands of New Deal programming as these affected poor people. Probably the greatest amount of attention and effort was spent on the emergency relief of immediate distress. With masses of formerly employed Americans and their families facing destitution, federal resources were mobilized on an unprecedented scale to help tide people over. In the depths of the winter of 1933–34, more than one-fifth of the American population was receiving help from federal relief programs that had not existed a year before. This felt political need to engage in relief spending continued throughout the 1930s, but as economic hard times lingered the Roosevelt administration shifted its emphasis from emergency cash support to more publicly acceptable forms of work relief.

Several aspects of this relief spending have important implications for antipoverty policy. First, federal relief efforts were conceived, implemented, and politically sold as strictly temporary measures. In accord with mainstream progressive thinking of the time, Roosevelt himself rejected the notion of any continuing federal responsibility for cash relief ("a subtle destroyer of the human spirit," Rosenman, 1938, pp. 19–21; see also Romasco, 1983) and never sought to extend work relief into any long-term program of public employment (Bremer, 1984; Bremner, 1985). Second, relief programs claimed only to be helping tide people over; producing educational or other measures to qualitatively change the life prospects of recipients was not part of this effort. Finally, while relief programs may have created new expectations about the social role of government, the actual operation of these programs also appears to have reinforced many Americans' doubts about the efficacy of government action. Often the program's failings had less to do with the federal bureaucracy than with political requirements imposed on relief programs by Congress, local political machines, and administrative breakdowns at grassroots level. But the highly visible examples of abuse were the topics of discussion on Main Street and tarnished the image of New Deal accomplishment.[2]

A second strand of public programming related more directly to the older, less unemployment-related forms of poverty: the chronically ill, homeless, abandoned, and otherwise misfortunate persons who lived on or were constantly struggling to stay off public assistance even before the 1930s. Their ranks were, of course, greatly swollen by unemployable or scarcely employable persons in the Depression. By and large the New

Deal's political exertions were not focused on poverty in this sense of the term. The government activities with by far the largest direct effect were public assistance programs (which were only gradually emerging from the traditional poor law approaches of earlier centuries). On this front the New Deal introduced only very modest changes. The essence of Roosevelt's strategy was to place all responsibility for general cash assistance on state and local governments. Supporting more than four million families annually between 1936 and 1940, general assistance aided more Americans than any other social program, and it was the one antipoverty measure to which New Deal reform and the national government made almost no contribution (Patterson, 1981, p. 63).

For certain other categories of very needy and presumably more deserving persons, the New Deal created a new financial mechanism by which the federal government matched state public assistance spending for needy aged and blind persons and dependent children (mainly of widows). The key political actors interested in such reforms were a few liberals and a small circle of professional social workers. Countering their efforts to impose more equitable and professional standards nationwide, conservative and southern Democratic segregationist forces in Congress were generally able to ensure that local political preferences in administration would prevail. Frequently this meant a punitive poor law approach and blatant racial discrimination.

In the long term a very important policy change had occurred: federal matching grants to certain categories of the poor were assured without the vagaries of the annual congressional appropriation process. But politically this change and everything else relating to the public assistance system was little noticed and easily forgotten. No one ever said so, but what might be called the New Deal's revealed preference regarding the unemployable and chronically poor was simply that they should go away—either into the labyrinth of state and local general assistance or into a new and better future when social insurance would prevent all but the most extraordinary occurrences of destitution.

The third strand of New Deal programming sought to transcend an agenda of relief and recovery by instituting permanent structural changes in economic and social affairs. Insofar as these efforts concentrated on those at the bottom of American society, their thrust was usually frustrated by a variety of political forces. Insofar as structurally oriented programs did produce more enduring changes, they did so by incorporating the poor through the political back door. Structural change *and* visible concentration on the poor were politically incompatible.

Social insurance was the greatest social policy change with long-term implications for reducing poverty. But in its original New Deal conception social insurance was of no benefit to those who were too poor to help provide for their own security. Under the 1935 law Social Security offered an insurance-based annuity for those who enjoyed a stable attachment to the work force and who were well enough off to achieve security by combining a modest government pension or unemployment check with personal savings and private insurance. Roughly 90 percent of the black work force were thereby excluded from Social Security coverage. Those blacks who were included could anticipate an old-age pension amounting to between $4.50 and $54 per *year* (Wolters, 1975, p. 194). When social insurance rules began to be liberalized in 1939, the somewhat better deal being given lower-income persons was (more or less) hushed up politically by program executives. Rather than trying to make the political case and garner support for a more equalizing system of income redistribution, proponents effected the changes by elaborating and expanding the concept of contributory insurance to new levels of mythology regarding individual accounts and earned benefits. Over time a significant antipoverty dimension developed in the Social Security program, but it did so by trading public understanding of the social welfare commitments being created for ease of passage (Derthick, 1979; Cates, 1983).

By contrast, programs aimed at structural changes in American life bearing directly on poor people encountered considerable political trouble and usually could not be sustained. For example, public housing legislation was mainly of interest to political constituencies in large northern cities, and southern Democrats in Congress easily succeeded in limiting the degree to which funds could be targeted on such major urban areas.

Rural poverty accounted for the major proportion of permanently destitute families, and nowhere were the political limitations of antipoverty policy more transparently exposed. When government lawyers sought to protect farm tenants' right to organize, they were unceremoniously squashed by New Deal political leaders of the Department of Agriculture who were worried about congressional reaction to such "radicalism." Efforts to improve the lot of landless tenants and the poorest farmers were subject to constant attack and underfunding by congressmen of both parties unwilling to disturb local power structures. For example, to more than one million black tenants, the Farm Security Administration (FSA) made a total of less than 2,000 tenant purchase loans. To win congressional approval, the FSA concentrated loans on those with the best chances for repaying rather than those in greatest needs. When Washington officials in the Agricultural Adjustment Administration sought to increase the participation of the rural poor in the local system of agricultural planning committees, the Farm Bureau and conservative coalition in Congress had little difficulty in thwarting the effort and maintaining agricultural policies that were in the interests of larger commercial farmers (Campbell, 1962; Baldwin, 1968). Again it was the more indirect methods of tackling longer-range problems of rural poverty, such as Rural Electrification and the Tennessee Valley Authority, that were more successful. Here too, however, it was the more liberal, social-engineering aspects of the TVA that were the first to be eliminated as the experiment proceeded, and plans for a series of TVA projects around the nation were stillborn.

What then can be said about the politics of antipoverty policy in the New Deal era? For America's poor, the New Deal domestic agenda was an exercise in social stabilization and not social engineering. This was a source of great political strength in the near term but of considerable political weakness in the longer term. On the positive political side, FDR's social programs never strayed very far or for very long from the main lines of contemporary political acceptability. New Deal relief programs were responsive to a widely felt need for action at the national level, and the emphasis on work in return for income support for the employable was fully in tune with public desires. Social programs that went beyond stabilization to produce structural changes either succeeded by tucking the poor away from view (as in the Social Security program) or else failed (as in most rural antipoverty efforts) when forced to confront the realities of local and commercial power expressed in Congress.

Another advantage of the New Deal's approach was that government administrators by and large knew how to do what they were being asked to do. Veteran practitioners from the state level (especially Wisconsin and New York) were brought to Washington to carry out reforms in social insurance and public relief spending that built on a base of practical knowledge. Often these experienced, nonradical reformers stayed on in Washington to develop their programs and cement enduring collaborative arrangements with selected congressional committees (Altmeyer and Witte at the Social Security Administration; Jane Hoey at the Bureau of Public Assistance).

In the long run, however, the New Deal experience produced major problems for any subsequent attention to antipoverty policy. Few political resources were expended in trying to legitimize any larger norms of redistribution. As time passed, the Roosevelt administration's political survival and success became divorced from any domestic policy agenda capable of mobilizing and educating a mass political base. To have developed this capacity would have required time-consuming efforts to build a much more extensive organizational machinery linking the Democratic Party, trade unions and a grassroots membership, usually in the face of hostile local Democratic power structures.[3]

At the same time, the President's and the nation's attention was increasingly concentrated on foreign rather than domestic affairs. There seems little chance that either Roosevelt or the liberal New Dealer faction of the Democratic Party interested in long-term social policy reforms could have prevailed after 1937 unless a conscious effort had been made to promote further social reform in such a way as to take advantage of the powerful nationalistic sentiments of the war effort.

To be sure, during World War II there appears to have developed at least a potentially favorable public sentiment that might have been tapped for further social policy reforms. But Roosevelt was disinclined to launch controversial ideas about domestic reconstruction, and for good political reasons. Such initiatives could be expected to distract attention from the war effort; they could threaten congressional support for FDR's international diplomacy; and a new social agenda could be counted on to alienate businessmen whom the President needed to participate in the war mobilization effort. Moreover, war brought prosperity to Americans rather than the physical destruction that European social reformers could use to emphasize norms of social solidarity (Brody, 1975).

Thus, the New Deal demonstrated the vulnerability of antipoverty policy to localism and congressional power structures, to political expediency and ambiguities of public opinion, to the need for presidential commitments and to the uncertainty of such commitments, especially as the foreign affairs concerns of a world power might intervene. In 1937 FDR spoke eloquently about one-third of the nation living in material want, but this statement coincided with the sunset of New Deal domestic victories in Congress. When the President in 1944 declaimed an economic bill of rights for all Americans, it was only an intimation of something that he would never live to talk about again. These speeches were announcements of something that never happened in any real political or policy terms. Rather than being the first act for the Great Society of the 1960s, the New Deal was more a dress rehearsal for frustration (Patterson, 1967; Polenberg, 1975).

THE GREAT SOCIETY

As Congress was passing the 1964 War on Poverty program, President Lyndon Johnson stood on the courthouse steps in Gainesville, Georgia (where Franklin Roosevelt had once braced himself), and pledged to carry on the war against want that Franklin Roosevelt had started. As we have seen, however, it is pure romance to think that an unambiguous or popular New Deal agenda for combating poverty ever existed. In fact in 1935 a twenty-six-year-old political entrepreneur named Lyndon Johnson used his position in Texas as the New Deal's youngest state National Youth Administration (NYA) director to build a local political base that promoted his own rather than the Roosevelt administration's ambitions. Had the Johnson of the Great Society reflected on the Johnson of the NYA he might have proceeded more cautiously (Caro, 1983, pp. 341–368, 397–398). In any event, the types of political factors that stalemated the New Deal were often the same ones that sapped the strength of antipoverty warriors in the Great Society.

If the historiography of the 1960s suggests anything, it is the extremely fragile political bases on which new antipoverty policy commitments were built. Public opinion polls from the period 1960 to 1965 indicate that Americans were fairly evenly divided as to whether welfare spending should be increased or reduced, rather more inclined to attribute poverty to lack of effort than to circumstances beyond a person's control, and clearly reluctant to see more spent on the needy if it meant raising taxes (Schiltz, 1970, pp. 153, 158–160; Lander, 1971). In general there appears to have been little public demand for launching a major attack on poverty and a great deal of skepticism about eliminating poverty in the United States. Likewise, histories of the period show that the political parties did little to prepare the intellectual or political groundwork for putting poverty on the national agenda; in a sense antipoverty policy adopted the Democratic Party rather than the other way around. Interest groups do not appear to have been clamoring for a war on poverty, although as always many groups were zealous in protecting and advancing their piece of the action once President Johnson declared such a war (Matusow, 1984).

There seems to be one major exception to these generalizations—the civil rights movement. A form of political mobilization embracing blacks and whites was clearly under way before and during the national government's commitment to an explicit antipoverty policy. Unfortunately a rather unproductive argument has developed among scholars as to which factor was the most important in generating the War on Poverty—the civil rights movement, social science theories, elite strategies for social control, or something else.[4]

Identifying the interconnections among these and other factors is probably more worthwhile than trying to weigh which single factor was dominant over the others. Without doing too much violence to the historical record, it can be said that the War on Poverty, like other policy initiatives, grew out of the brief convergence of three largely separate streams of development (Kingdon, 1984).

From the so-called problem stream came a series of focusing events that caught many people's attention in such a way that previously accepted conditions came to be defined as a "problem" and eventually acquired a collective name of their own: poverty. A representative sample would include events such as the increased attention to indicators of juvenile delinquency and popular dramatizations of community breakdown such as *Blackboard Jungle* and *West Side Story;* feedback from past policies regarding, for example, the social displacements resulting from urban renewal programs; dramatic revelations in the print and rapidly growing TV media of human distress, such as Harrington's *Other America* or Homer Bigart's study of eastern Kentucky in the *New York Times;* and the Birmingham demonstrations and stirrings of violence from the civil rights movement in 1963.

The second stream, which can be labeled "political" in the partisan sense of that term, also had many currents. One was the presence of a young and activist president, eager to use the presidency for setting the nation's agenda as an instrument of national purpose and to push beyond the party appeals of an older generation. Another factor was a growing level of prosperity that made poverty seem anomalous and combating it easily affordable. Another set of political opportunities came from liberals' willingness to embrace a Cold War stance and use it to justify domestic initiatives; America could not set an anti-Communist standard for the world if it countenanced poverty and injustice at home. The good Cold Warrior was a good Poverty Warrior. Kennedy's assassination and Johnson's desire for bold domestic legislation with the Johnson stamp on it provided an even greater political opportunity for antipoverty policy, a theme that could be seen as both helping to unify a traumatized nation and offering partisan advantages in the election year of 1964. At the same time, congressional politicians of both parties had strong incentives to take bold actions that would seem to be in keeping with the postassassination theme of moving forward and being responsive to the increasingly vocal complaints of blacks. On the face of it, combating poverty seemed a highly attractive political issue.

The third stream—policy proposals—flowed from networks of policy experts who basically had to wait for attention to problems and political openings to develop but who then had substantial scope for injecting their own preferred approaches into the opportunities of the moment. As the War on Poverty got underway, proposals were forthcoming from several such expert sources. Those put forward through standard bureaucratic channels often simply extended existing policy approaches relating, for example, to job training programs for adults and young adults (Jobs Corps, Neighborhood Youth Corps, extended Manpower Development Training Act activities) and to special education for the children of the poor (Head Start, Upward Bound, Teacher Corps, and Title I of the Elementary and Secondary Education Act). Another and more novel source for antipoverty proposals was sociologists and others enjoying special executive access through the Kennedys' interest in government programs to combat delinquency. From this source came support for community action and efforts to increase participation by the poor in making local services more responsive to their needs. Throughout the life of the Johnson administration these bureaucratic and antibureaucratic strands of programming operated virtually independent of each other and at times in open conflict.

The three streams of problems, politics, and proposals converged in the mid-1960s with what seemed a winning combination of presidential leadership, social science expertise, congressional and bureaucratic logrolling— all wrapped in a concept of *opportunity* for the disadvantaged that seemed fully in tune with the American public philosophy. By way of contrast, there was little inclination at that time on anyone's part to take on the much more politically difficult task of selling the American people on a major program of social reconstruction and income redistribution.

In retrospect, it now seems clear that the nature of the connections between the poverty problem, its political backing, and policy choices contained severe shortcomings. Let me briefly indicate four political weaknesses that seem to have been most damaging for the overt antipoverty policy commitment that had been undertaken. The effect of all four together was devastating. It meant that when economic growth slowed and Vietnam destroyed any consensual linkage between anti-Communism and domestic reform, antipoverty efforts were left high and dry with no base of independent political support.

Weak linkages between the policy community and political backers. The most enduring policy reforms of the New Deal era grew out of a shared background of progressive politics that linked policy people active in developing working reform programs (such as state social insurance laws) with people active in day-to-day partisan political work. By contrast, the antipoverty policies of the Great Society did not develop from an organic political-intellectual linkage of this nature. The corps of poverty policy professionals inside government or shuttling between government and the academy were largely detached from important centers of party and local political power. Likewise, virtually none of the key political figures endorsing the antipoverty effort (Johnson, Shriver, the Kennedys) had any experience or operational knowledge of the field (unlike Roosevelt, Hopkins, Perkins, and Robert Wagner). And unlike New Dealers who were dealing with the relatively familiar tasks of creating relief and social insurance programs, the Kennedy/Johnson people aspired to the much more difficult tasks of social engineering (through education and community action) that no one was sure how to carry out. Missing links between policy commitments and political backing were nowhere clearer than in the community action component of the Great Society. On the one hand, community action programs sought to mobilize and empower the poor as a new political force challenging local power centers. On the other hand, community action sought to elicit a coordinated response from local social agencies that were heavily dependent on established political structures. The result was an even more rapid erosion of political support than had greeted similar New Deal aspirations for the rural poor.

The weaknesses of president-centered reform. It seems a truism that any major policy realignment in the American political system requires strong backing at the presidential level. Antipoverty policy in the 1960s, however, went beyond that requirement to become almost *wholly* identified with the initiative of a particular president and his advisors. This fact left antipoverty policy highly vulnerable on a number of counts. It meant that in an area of great complexity and uncertain solutions, there were immense pressures to come up with dramatic proposals and quick results that would satisfy political needs in the Oval Office. Thus, scarcely tested social theories of opportunity became received doctrine in a small circle of Kennedy people committed to "action." And so too under Lyndon Johnson even larger presidential ambitions transformed what were cautious plans for a handful of demonstration projects into an expansive proposal for eradicating poverty on a national basis. In fact no one seriously informed on the subject claimed to know how to accomplish that presidential objective (Matusow, 1984, pp. 109–123).

President-centered antipoverty policy became highly personalized, and when the President's popularity declined, it became much easier politically to attack antipoverty commitments—an erstwhile "motherhood" issue— as another case of Johnson's failures. The ultimate problem, however, was that the presidency, for all its public appearance of power, was simply too small a piece of the political system to sustain anything as broad as a national antipoverty effort. The presidential office could not itself take the place of an enduring political coalition of congressmen, state officials, mayors, and interest groups. The confusion and contention associated with the staffing of the new poverty agency (the Office of Economic Opportunity) simply reflected this deeper reality (Schott and Hamilton, 1983, chapter 6).

The vulnerability of a black-dominated coalition. Clearly the one point at which the Great Society antipoverty program did tap into a larger political coalition was in the civil rights movement, a movement that by the early 1960s was taking on mass dimensions. To be sure, the intellectual rationale for the antipoverty program was delineated by white liberals concerned about juvenile delinquency and white economists interested in an income "poverty gap," but it was into black hands that fell most of the day-to-day grassroots political work of campaigning on behalf of the poor. The federally sponsored community action programs, once envisioned as a traditional good government device for coordinating bureaucratic efforts, were soon transformed into a means of attacking the local political exclusion of blacks. The creation of separate, largely black urban bureaucracies to administer antipoverty programs, the welfare rights initiatives advanced through the court system, and the drama of black urban riots in Watts and the North all helped to publicly identify antipoverty policy with minority claims on a dominant white majority.

In the long run, the disadvantages of this identification probably outweighed any short-term operational advantages. Blacks themselves were a divided constituency, with a majority supporting strategies of compromise and nonviolence, a much more clamorous minority advocating militant resistance to white liberal policies, and an even more visible subset of troublemakers gaining access to the evening news by ripping off anybody in sight. But divisions within the black community were not the main problem. The minority status of all blacks left antipoverty policy highly vulnerable to white liberal doubts and antiblack racist sentiment. The civil rights movement generated powerful white support so long as it concentrated on issues perceived as moral questions (such as segregation, voting rights, antiblack violence); it lost that capability when the movement's focus shifted to the economic aspects of racial inequality. As the civil rights movement moved north after 1964 and pressed demands for open housing, busing, and affirmative action, the northern white civil rights constituency began melting away and undermining the political foundations of antipoverty policy. By the spring of 1968 the Poor People's campaign and Resurrection City in Washington aroused scarcely any response from the Johnson administration and the shattered antipoverty constituency of white liberals, independents, and unionists.

Program effectiveness as the price of passage. The antipoverty efforts of the Johnson administration played out a familiar story in American public policy. To put the point bluntly, the necessary conditions for legislative success were usually sufficient conditions for operational failure. This general tendency reappeared in any number of guises. For example, OEO struggled through its first year without a deputy director because the most appropriate candidate for the job, Adam Yarmolinsky, had antagonized several southern senators by launching Defense Department initiatives to counter racial discrimination near military bases. The price for passage of the Economic Opportunity Act creating OEO in 1964 was a White House pledge to keep Yarmolinsky out of the deputy's job. No one will ever know how much of the early mismanagement that undermined the poverty program's standing might have been avoided had this price not been exacted (Schott and Hamilton, 1983, pp. 117–118).

Usually the policy costs paid for political support were much less blatant and personalized. To soothe bureaucratic jealousies within the executive branch, antipoverty functions were divided up among a number of federal agencies, thereby ensuring continued fragmentation of effort. In education, housing, and health programs, attempts to target resources on the most disadvantaged ran afoul of congressional desires to distribute benefits to broader constituencies; perfunctory targeting was usually the price paid for congressional support. Likewise, powerful local political forces—local school districts, state social bureaucracies, and private providers—could be counted on to resist any program designs for strong central administration from Washington. As a result, most antipoverty programs operated through financial inducements, third parties, and loose forms of national, subnational, and private sector interaction rather than through central bureaucratic direction. Later commentators would look back to the 1960s as a time when "big government" in Washington took excessive powers unto itself and carried through its own high-handed redistributive agenda. Actually, nothing could be further from the truth. Antipoverty officials might have aspired to be more directive in favoring the poor than was customary in Washington, but these aspirations were typically stalemated in practice.

The four sets of political problems we have mentioned related most directly to the explicit antipoverty policy of the Great Society. Meanwhile, there was underway what might be called the covert antipoverty programs of this period, namely those policies affecting the poor that were not a formal part of President Johnson's War on Poverty. Included in this category would be the rapid growth of food stamp and child nutrition programs after the mid-1960s, Medicare and Medicaid, and the largest antipoverty measure of all in terms of persons lifted above the poverty line—the liberalization of Social Security benefits.

Each of these programs had its own complex patterns of politics, with Congress rather than the President in the lead during the Nixon/Ford years. The important point for present purposes is that covert antipoverty policies had in common the fact that they reduced the visibility of the poor within some larger more encompassing set of program commitments. The problem of hunger and maladies caused by inadequate child nutrition served this function. So too did the obvious burden of paying health care costs. But by far the most politically successful program for helping the poor by not talking about them was Social Security. The huge number of beneficiaries and the doctrine of entitlements earned via contributory insurance produced a political safehouse for some categories of poor persons. It seems fair to say that few Americans understand the complex rules by which otherwise poor persons are advantaged far beyond their contributory entitlements. Neither during nor after the Great Society was there a serious public debate regarding the massive income redistribution that lies buried in the Social Security program's benefit and taxation formulas and that has done so much to reduce income poverty for some.

This history indicates that the New Deal and the Great Society encountered similar problems with regard to the political barriers facing major federal efforts to directly affect the conditions of the poor. If anything, Great Society programming had an even shallower reservoir of public demand for government action and a more ambitious agenda for change than anything attempted in the New Deal under the imprimatur of the President. Whereas Roosevelt (to the frustration of his wife and liberal New Dealers) was cautious in pushing any domestic reform beyond the bounds of immediate political acceptability and carefully avoided jeopardizing support for his foreign policy priorities, Lyndon Johnson became personally identified with the reverse situation—a politically reckless domestic agenda combined with a crumbling foreign policy consensus. Curiously enough (given all the rhetoric in 1964 about enhancing opportunity not handouts), any enduring concern for poverty after the mid-1960s came to be associated with economists' analytic preference for income and poverty-line conceptions of need. For many antipoverty warriors seeking to reform the welfare system, economic status itself—that is, low income—created a presumptive right to assistance; this thinking fit in well with a liberal view that poverty was not the fault of the poor. The problem with this attention to poverty income lines and rates was that not many Americans outside the antipoverty community seemed to accept the concept of a right to income as such but only to the necessities income might buy. Caught between the politically unpopular idea of treating poverty by guaranteeing income, on the one hand, and, on the other, congressional unwillingness to accept the administrative and financial costs of effective work requirements for employable poor persons, welfare reform died a lingering, painful death during the Nixon, Ford, and Carter administrations (Mead, 1985).

However, if one steps back from all the details, it can be argued that the political results in the New Deal and Great Society eras were much the same for antipoverty policy. Structural reforms focused solely on the disadvantaged were thwarted. Policies with a covert antipoverty component were carried forward in the late 1960s and early 1970s, but these changes occurred largely as special interest pleading in Congress and not by mobilizing any broad-based political commitment to the redistribution that was under way. There was no political construction put on policy developments that could promote a mature public understanding of the country's immense social policy apparatus. And so Americans were left to nurture their own particular brand of love-hate relationship with the welfare state.

Public Attitudes and Institutional Constraints

What are the public's preferences regarding antipoverty policy? How well or poorly does what our political institutions can produce fit these preferences? Answers to these questions may go a long way in defining the political prospects for future antipoverty policy in the United States. Put crudely, it often seems that when it comes to antipoverty policy, what Americans want from their policymaking system they cannot have, and what they can have they do not want.

PUBLIC ATTITUDES

There is no such thing as unitary public opinion that produces a logically consistent set of propositions regarding government programs affecting the poor. In probing the so-called public mind (and indeed our own individual minds for that matter) one is trying to characterize a range of sentiments that can serve as political constraints and opportunities for policymaking.

Academics have a vested interest in complicating such matters, and politicians and the media are inclined to oversimplify attitudes into convenient shibboleths.

A great deal more analysis of public images and attitudes toward poverty and government programs needs to be done. My operating premise in what follows is that relatively straightforward opinion survey questions can tap at least some politically relevant dimensions of most people's thinking. The danger with more sophisticated analysis is that asking people more and more about what they "really" think may create responses that are simply an artifact of continual questioning. Tortured long enough, almost anyone or any body of data will eventually yield the desired results.

The main features of public attitudes toward poverty policy can be grouped into five broad characterizations.

Americans have no principled objection to national government actions on behalf of the poor. At much earlier times in our history the question of whether helping the poor is an appropriate role for the federal government was a major political issue. That these kinds of boundary arguments seem passé today is probably part of the legacy of the New Deal and Great Society debates and not least of all the devaluation of states' rights appeals achieved by the civil rights movement. Attempts early in the Reagan administration to revive the theory of federalism by proposing to sort out functions between national and subnational levels raised not a whiff of interest in the general public. Surveys show that Americans consider the national government to be less responsive and efficient than other levels, but these appear to be technical, not principled, objections to federal activity (Keene, 1984; Goodman, 1984; see Table 13.1). If anything, the past five years may have helped to entrench further the public legitimacy of national action; having rhetorically endorsed the concept of a social "safety net," the Reagan administration has made it much more difficult for any subsequent conservative government to contend that there is no national responsibility pertaining to social policies for the poor.

At the same time, *Americans are typically ill at ease with comprehensive ideological justifications for national action in social policy.* This phenomenon seems to go deeper than noting that Americans criticize general taxing and spending levels but support specific programs. Recent studies have suggested rather deep splits in our thinking. Norms of democratic equality and solidarity are accepted in the realm of political affairs, while norms of inequality, individual competition, and the like are applied to what are regarded as economic matters. Questions of social relations are the terrain on which these diverging views are puzzled over and never resolved. Social

Table 13.1. Public attitudes toward the poor, 1948–1984 (percentages)

Allocations of government resources for the poor

	Should be increased	Should be kept the same	Should be reduced
1948: "Over the course of the years a number of measures have been taken by the government to improve the conditions of the poor people. Generally speaking do you think the government should do more to improve the conditions of the poor people, or that the government is doing just about the right amount of things now, or that the government has already done more for the poor people than is good for them?"	45	34	13
1961: "How about help for needy people? Do you think the government should be spending more money, less money, or about the same amount?"	60	28	7
1984: "Do you think federal spending on programs for the poor should be increased, decreased, or kept about the same?"	51	41	8

Need for government to work to decrease the income gap between rich and poor

	Agree	Disagree
1981: "I'm going to read a few statements . . . Can you please tell me if you tend to agree or disagree . . . ? The government should work to substantially reduce the income gap between rich and poor."	67	33

Sources: For 1948, Roper, quoted from Schiltz (1970), p. 196; for 1961, Mueller (1963), p. 214; for 1984, survey by CBS/*New York Times,* Jan. 14–21, 1984; for 1981, survey by ABC/*Washington Post,* Feb. 19–20, 1981.

policy inevitably requires choices among applications of social values that are criss-crossed by considerations of political realities, economic incentives, and personal caring about one's own versus the claims of unknown untrusted strangers. Comprehensive theories of social policy, whether of the rightist libertarian or the leftist social solidarity variety, seem to resolve too many things that Americans do not *want* to be clear about in their own minds (Free and Cantril, 1968; Hochschild, 1981; McClosky and Zaller, 1984).

In supporting the concept of government activity Americans apply a very strong needs-based orientation. Although it is not a simple or unconditional commitment, substantial public support exists for the general idea of committing government resources to help the poor. Nor does this view appear to have changed significantly in the past thirty-five years.[5] For example, in 1948, 1961, and 1984 the overwhelming majority of Americans favored maintaining or increasing government resources devoted to the poor (see Table 13.1). Even when the issue was put in the much stronger terms of government action to substantially reduce income gaps between rich and poor, a majority of Americans has seemed willing to endorse government activity.

Potentially then, antipoverty programs tap an important set of preferences, the main concern of which is to deal with presumed need. But all needs, it turns out, are not created equal.

Americans distinguish among kinds of needs and seem to invoke fairly well-structured sets of ideas regarding deserts. Social welfare policies tend to be assessed and supported in terms of their ability to enhance personal independence. Thus, there is a very strong emphasis on good faith efforts of people to help themselves, especially through work. There is little generalized willingness to provide cash assistance to poor persons capable of work but widespread public support for educational and other services that might give such people a second chance. Where disability, injury, or other special circumstances intervene, attitudes again become tailored to circumstances.

Consider several examples of such tailoring of preferences. Public funding for child care is seen to be appropriate for a widow trying conscientiously to support three children (81 percent view this as a good use of public funds); this approval diminishes somewhat when the father is merely absent and mother not working (to 52 percent) and virtually disappears when the mother has never married and is not interested in working (to 15 percent). This seems to indicate less a sense of sexual moralism and more a matter of expecting adults, mothers and absent fathers, to take responsibility for themselves and their own. Publicly funded services for medical care, foster homes, child protection, and the like rank very high with the public as a good use of funds, but counseling on unwanted pregenancy is regarded as a waste of funds. But again there are distinctions drawn by the public, with almost two-thirds supporting public funds to counsel teenage mothers but only one-third thinking such counsel is a good use of public funds if applied to women in their thirties with an unwanted pregnancy. The view seems to be that the teenager needs support and deserves a second chance but that a woman in her thirties, while possibly needing such a chance, should be expected to take responsibility for herself (Carter, Fifield, and Shields, 1973; Cook, 1979).

Asked to consider more than slogans regarding welfare spending, the public seems to prefer drawing distinctions and calibrating various forms of desert and responses to them. The overwhelming preference is for neither indiscriminate help nor laissez faire approaches that abandon people to their fate but rather an emphasis on policies to *support*—and not re-place—people's taking responsibility for themselves and for those dependent upon them. Although life may be seen as a race based on individual effort, there is a desire for policies that help to provide a fair start, that offer support over the rough spots and give people a second chance. Policies that seem to provide a free ride or guaranteed outcomes can be expected to incur widespread disfavor. So too can approaches that espouse a devil-take-the-hindmost philosophy.

A paradoxical finding is that *Americans favor government action to help the poor, but they generally dislike the subset of government programs that are intended to be targeted on the poor.* There appears to be little variation in this finding over time, or indeed among the developed nations. The truly popular programs are the huge, mass-based social programs at the core of the welfare state—pensions, health care, education, and (to cast the net more broadly) environmental protection. By contrast, considerable unpopularity is attached to programs that are most directly relevant to the poor: public assistance, food stamps, social services, and the like (Coughlin, 1980; Lipset and Schneider, 1981; Sears and Citrin, 1982). The general pattern has varied little since the New Deal: since 1935 a majority of Americans have *never* wanted to spend more on welfare (or for "relief and recovery" as the survey question was phrased in the 1930s). However, appearances can be deceiving. In an experimental design in 1984 the Roper organization varied the phrasing of questions and produced the interesting results shown in Figure 13.1: the public was much more supportive of "caring for the poor" or "assistance for the poor" than for "welfare."

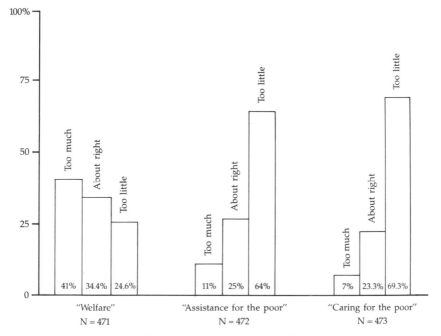

Figure 13.1.   Percentage of respondents supporting different levels of spending for "welfare," "assistance for the poor," and "caring for the poor," 1984. Source: National Opinion Research Center (1984).

The difference in response between a compassionate public when asked about the poor versus a more hard-hearted public when asked about welfare relief seems to derive from the public's understanding of these terms. "Welfare" (or in the earlier period "relief") probably suggests to Americans income transfers going mainly to the working age population. A strongly embedded work ethic from the economic sphere casts a long shadow of doubt over any presumptions of need in this group. The notion of work, not government intervention per se, appears to be the key. Despite Americans' endorsement of free enterprise and many antigovernment attitudes with respect to the economy, one of the most enduring findings is the continual public support for government guarantees of a job for all those who want to work. This strong support for work, including government support for the labor market if necessary, places in special jeopardy any programs offering non-work-related benefits to persons of employable age.

Adding to the problems for means-tested cash assistance programs is a widespread perception (across all income groups and races, including those on assistance) that significant cheating and maladministration occur in delivering these benefits. Much of the support and nonsupport for welfare probably reflects conclusions about the efficiency of the programs rather than judgments about the desirability of government activity itself. In effect, most Americans do not seem to object to targeting resources on the poor; they simply do not believe it happens very often. Thus, doubts about unearned income grants for working-age people and about any real targeting of such support combine to undermine public support for "welfare."

INSTITUTIONAL CONSTRAINTS

An antipoverty policy designed along the lines of general public preferences would have some identifiable if not always well-defined characteristics. The nation's antipoverty policy would be presented as part of the normal course of events, so to speak, and not as part of any larger philosophical or political project to redefine the role of government or meaning of social obligations. Such policy would place heavy emphasis on the idea of tailoring programs to meet readily identifiable needs and personal circumstances. The implication is a desire for coherent and highly sensitive administration. Work would have a central place in antipoverty policy for those able to work; so would educational and other assistance to give people a second chance. Along with the receipt of public support would go the obligation to behave in personally responsible ways (Mead, 1985). Whether on issues of work, family relations, or long-term dependencies, policy would support personal efforts and not be seen as taking over individual responsibilities or guaranteeing outcomes.

These general ideas are, of course, bound to become more complicated when translated into the details of program design and administration. And yet the complexity inherent in any antipoverty program should not necessarily be seen as a barrier to public acceptability. Political factors are important to consider precisely because they are devices for simplifying the presentation of complex choices and transforming contradictions into acceptable public understandings.

Views will differ on an issue as controversial as this, but my reading of the evidence suggests that the American public seems quite tolerant of major federal efforts to deal with poverty. The key political problem is not public hostility to the poor or to social benefits. The problem is that our political institutions do not seem to have the capacity to produce the kinds of antipoverty policy that would be likely to command public support. If I overstate the case in this way, it is because so much attention in popular accounts has been given to what an American political culture of individualism and antistatism will not allow; little attention has been devoted to analyzing what people might want but our political institutions cannot produce. For a people reputed not to believe in government and economic redistribution, we have certainly managed to create an immense federal role in the distribution of income and services and to do so for many more than those who are poor (Lampman, 1984). More than two-fifths of Americans receive income transfers, and immense sums are being publicly spent to assure personal health care, education, affordable housing, and individual retirement accounts—these are not the signs of a people seized by rugged individualism. There must be more to the story than the intellectual hammerhold of John Locke.

At least four characteristic features of our political institutions deserve attention. All are contained within the record of past antipoverty "moments" and can be expected to continue their influence in the future.

First, a strong need for overselling whatever is to be done seems to be built into the structure of our politics. Effective power is widely distributed not only between Congress and the executive but also among the different parts of Congress, different parts of the executive, different levels of national and local government, and different kinds of public and private organizations. To capture attention in this situation and galvanize the many different power centers into action, policy advocates have a strong incentive to overdramatize problems and oversell solutions (Light, 1982). In few cases is this more clearly demonstrated than with regard to the presidency. Presidents as different as Johnson, Nixon, Ford, and Carter have concerned themselves with welfare reform, promising a sweeping attack on a problem declared to be reaching crisis proportions. In all cases, to the surprise of White House advisers hyping the subject, little broad-based public interest in the issue could be generated. Overselling has simply devalued the coin of antipoverty policy.

Second, a number of interacting features in our national political institutions reduce the odds of effectively targeting resources on the poor. One such feature is the tendency of our political processes to accord special treatment only to groups that are well organized, politically active, and sophisticated in pursuing a uniform set of interests. The poor—who vote rarely, who represent a varied set of problems and interests, and whom daily life tutors into passivity—are hardly such a group.[6] Larger surrogate organizations that in other countries sometimes take up the cause of the poor—for example, strong labor union movements and/or Social Democratic and Catholic parties—are weak or absent in the United States.

Another feature important in inhibiting any concentration of resources on the poor is the weakness of priority-setting mechanisms within government. The diminished power of congressional and party leadership has created strong incentives for legislative coalitions to be formed by spreading program benefits across many congressional districts rather than by concentrating resources on greatest needs. The dilution of effort and resources for the poor is a natural result. As Senator Paul Douglas once summarized the distributive tendency, in order to provide crumbs for the poor it is necessary to set a banquet for the rich. Moreover, as government domestic programs have become a more prominent part of legislative business since the late 1950s, congressmen have become increasingly self-conscious and adept at calculating the benefits and costs of any proposal to their individual constituencies, particularly those parts of the constituency that can affect reelection prospects. These are not the poor. Driving results in the same direction is the fact that legislative and bureaucratic powers are fragmented into a number of powerful veto points capable of blocking actions that adversely affect their interests. Each of these veto points enforces what Charles Schultze has called the Hippocratic oath of our political system: "never be seen to do direct harm" (Mills and Palmer, 1984, p. 383). Harm is typically defined as not only the loss of existing benefits and privileges but also the failure to obtain a piece of whatever is being passed around. The design becomes self-replicating. Each committee, subcommittee, and government bureau nourishes its own veto power and distributive preferences by means of an implicit agreement not to attack the comparable power of other units to do the same.

Hence the distributive tendency and antiredistributive veto centers inside government, combined with the weak electoral connection externally to the poor as a constituency, converge to bias results against needs-based targeting. If a person tried to design a system with the goal of reliably preventing redistribution from the privileged to the most disadvantaged members of society, he would find it difficult to improve on what exists.

A third and related general feature is the institutional difficulty of dealing with any policy having a large number of separate components. An anti-poverty policy that calibrated support across a range of differentiated needs, as the public seems to prefer, would require close coordination of income transfers, employment programs, social services, health care, and probably more. But in fact jurisdictional divisions and jealousies within the national bureaucracy reflect and reinforce comparable divisions within Congress, and these divisions are often linked in turn to local government divisions of power of a geographic and professional nature (Leman, 1985). Rather than combining government assistance in ways appropriate to complex human needs, the tendency is to simplify human beings into categories to accommodate complex government programs. The resulting administrative confusion of responsibilities for meeting the needs of the poor has plagued operation of antipoverty programs in the past, and if anything, the difficulty has become more acute in recent years.

Finally, although public preferences place heavy emphasis on the employment aspects of antipoverty policy, labor market policy constitutes an area of the federal government where administrative capacities are at their weakest. The history of employment and training programs—from trade adjustment assistance, to public service jobs, to work programs for welfare recipients—presents a sorry chronicle of vacillating objectives, bungled relations with the private sector, and sheer administrative incompetence in what has typically been a backwater of national policymaking. If this judgment seems harsh, it nevertheless represents the fairest summary of a lengthy record of overpromising and underperforming. From the work of the Manpower Demonstration Research Corporation we know how financially and administratively demanding it is to enhance the employment prospects of the very poor, although with a concerted effort the results are not discouraging. From public opinion surveys we know how important such activities are in eliciting support for antipoverty policy. But the existing capacities of government institutions to actually repond to this challenge are extremely limited and constitute an immense barrier to any serious progress (Robertson, 1984; Van Horn and Baumer, 1984).

It is possible to argue that all these political barriers are simply another reflection of public preferences for limited and fragmented government power and a refusal to tolerate the kind of dangerous authority that could produce concerted action and coherent administration. Americans would rather have markets than governments distribute their incomes. But this view is much too simple. Immense government redistribution is already in place and accepted. Moreover, it is difficult to believe that Americans would consider their individual liberties to be threatened somehow by coherent labor market policies or careful coordination of income and social service support but not by the relatively coherent operations of the Federal Reserve Board, NASA, or the Social Security Administration. The theory of revealed preferences that says antipoverty policies are what they are because that is what people want misses too much of the real world. One must also take into account what people are taught to think and what they can get from established political processes and prevailing structures of power.

Political Prospects

The implementation of effective antipoverty policy is a matter of considerable concern to many of us, and some of the conclusions regarding
political feasibility may not be those we would prefer to draw. However,
in looking at the record of the past twenty years as realistically as possible,
one has to acknowledge that antipoverty programs have had no worse
enemy than their uncritical and permissive friends.

As we look forward, it would be wise to recall that the wide swings
between liberal and conservative epochs that historians sometimes identify
in domestic policy more generally are largely absent in this area. One of
the most striking aspects of public attitudes with regard to the poor and
government programs is their immense stability. Delete the dates from
relevant opinion survey questions and it is often difficult to determine
whether one is reading results from the present time or from the last half
of the 1930s. If there are moments of collectivist altruism affecting poverty
policy, they appear as passing eddies in an immense seascape of traditionally individualistic and work-oriented "conservative" sentiments. Those
instants, as in 1964–65, are the oddities requiring special explanation.
Having said this, we need to recognize that public preferences regarding
antipoverty policy are not monolithic but textured and complex. Often this
fact does not become clear unless Americans are asked to think beyond
the stereotypical questions of being for or against more welfare spending
(Bishop, Oldendick, and Tuchfarber, 1978).

One route to the future, hoped for by some, is probably closed: any
attempt to ground American antipoverty policy in a highly egalitarian,
social democratic vision of society is trying to recreate a possibility that
has passed, if such a chance ever existed at all. It is at least conceivable
that in the 1930s and 1940s a proegalitarian movement might have succeeded by harnessing widely acknowledged domestic needs with the nationalistic fervor of the last "good war" and by linking the local community,
political party, and workplace dimensions of ordinary people's lives. Today,
with political parties finding it increasingly difficult to play a role even as
nominating and electoral devices, that social democratic moment has surely
passed. By the same token, then, we should disenthrall ourselves from the
idea that there is some advanced, more "complete" version of the welfare
state in the world that America as a laggard in social policy should try to
emulate. If the predictions of the predecessor volume to this one ten years
ago had been correct, we should now be engaged in a great national debate

for increasing economic equality. The failure of that prediction should tell us something (Haveman, 1977, pp. 18, 278).

Broad economic conditions can be expected to play an important although not necessarily simple role in shaping the political conditions for antipoverty policy. The most obvious generalization is that there is more tolerance for poor people's programs in periods of rising real incomes, as in the 1960s, and greater insistence on retrenchment when the average American is experiencing stagnant or declining real income, as in the 1970s and early 1980s. The relationships are more complex than that, however. The boom years of the 1920s were hardly a period of social policy expansion compared to the economically hard-pressed 1930s; likewise today, those states with the strongest economic performance (Sunbelt areas such as Texas, Arizona, and Oklahoma) are often the least generous in support for the poor (as indicated, for example, through AFDC benefit levels). The most reasonable position is to recognize a large degree of indeterminism surrounding economic conditions and political responses. Prosperity can throw the anomalous conditions of the poor into sharper relief and release spare resources to finance more generous programs for the poor, but it can also make it easier to be very judgmental and ignore the poor (by generating a feeling that "I'm making it, why can't they"). By the same token, hard economic times can intensify conflict over scarcer financial resources and desensitize the nonpoor struggling to make ends meet; but economic adversity can also expand the constituency needing assistance and create a sense of shared vulnerability. Which of these forces holds sway probably depends heavily on political leadership and on the kind of antipoverty effort that has been undertaken. It seems quite likely that a poverty policy grounded in the politics of mere generosity (what "we" are going to do for "them") will be most prone to ebb and flow with the state of the economy. A policy grounded in mutual self-interest extending across social groups will have greater staying power.

In substantive terms the main political problem with antipoverty policy is that it is antipoverty policy. The concept of income poverty is a statistical construction capable of interesting and animating economists and policy analysts but lacking a political reality capable of animating social action. Orienting the policy debate around the simple economic conception of poverty makes it plausible to argue (as the Reagan administration has) that funds spent on those above the poverty line are wasted, a notion that a socially relevant and politically usable conception of need would never countenance. If the poor are a weak constituency, the poverty-line poor are a nonexistent political constituency in an institutional system designed to reflect constituency pressures outside and organizational champions within the federal government. Without the protective coloration of a larger program agenda that—as with Social Security—embraces the felt needs of many Americans, antipoverty efforts are likely to remain a political afterthought.

If a program's defining category of need is low income, the poor can expect to lose almost every time politically, because Americans do not endorse a publicly guaranteed right to income as such. Politically viable forms of categorization must be based on more or less widely shared needs, although for budgetary and other reasons these socially inclusive categories will often have to be applied in a selective (i.e., income-based) way.[7] Children's need for support from their parents is one such category. Helping any child obtain support from an absent parent could be one part of the picture; so too could public supplementation when the personal circumstances of that absent parent do not permit adequate child support to be paid. A politically feasible family policy would be one that supports people's right to make choices without abdicating responsibilities; it would not be one that tries to prescribe living arrangements (should today's single parent with custody of a child be asked by government to think of itself as a defective or "spoiled" social unit?). The need for work is another such socially inclusive category. Potentially it is capable of linking policies dealing with dislocated workers, new entrants to the labor force, and welfare families with employable persons.[8] In these and other cases the general political lesson remains the same: when developing programs designed to serve the best interests of the poor, we should not think only of the poor.

By and large the Reagan administration has been effective in tapping not only the resentments accumulated during the past twenty years of antipoverty programs but also some parts of the deeper structure of public preferences. In the realm of resentments, there was much raw material with which to work. The social programs cut deepest in the first half of the 1980s (education, employment and training, social services, and health) would seem in theory to be programs favored by the public, inasmuch as they were usually targeted broadly and were intended to enhance chances for becoming self-supporting. But these programs also had the most unfortunate reputations for ineffectiveness, bloated professional bureaucracies, and the like (Wholey, 1984). Compared with the much larger social entitlements, means-tested programs also took their lumps (see Figure 13.2). This retrenchment typically took the form of tightening eligibility requirements in the name of concentrating resources on the neediest. Of

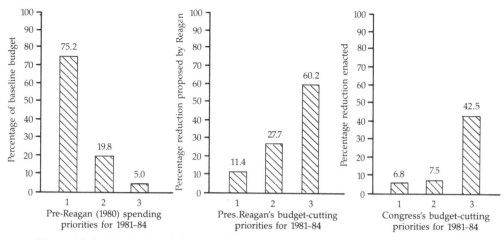

Figure 13.2. Federal social expenditures before the Reagan administration, re-ductions proposed by Reagan, and reductions enacted by Congress. Source: Data from Palmer and Sawhill (1984, pp. 185–186). *Key: 1 = Social insurance entitle-ments:* Social Security (retirement and disability), veterans' compensation, un-employment insurance, Medicare, other health services, guaranteed student loans, veterans' readjustment benefits. *2 = Means-tested income assistance:* veterans' pensions; Supplemental Security Income; Aid to Families with Dependent Chil-dren; food stamps; child nutrition programs; Food Program for Women, Infants, and Children; housing assistance; low-income energy assistance; Medicaid; other student financial assistance. *3 = Other programs for those of low income:* com-pensatory education, Head Start, vocational education, Social Services Block Grant, Community Services Block Grant, general employment and training, Public Service Employment, Job Corps, work incentive program.

course, some highly targeted programs have enjoyed substantial political support and have been protected in Congress, but this is largely because of special connections to notions of needs and deserts (Supplemental Se-curity Income where the rights of the aged are often assumed, Medicaid with its tie to health needs, and the Earned Income Tax Credit with its link to work; insofar as the food stamp program has gradually been per-ceived as income support rather than a food program, it has become po-litically suspect).

In effect, the Reagan administration preempted the touchstone question posed by antipoverty warriors of the 1960s: What does it do for the poor? If income poverty lines are to be the criterion for action, poverty spending for those above that line would represent an inefficient use of resources. And the cash value of noncash benefits (medical insurance, housing sub-sidies) should be added to the incomes of the poor to determine how many persons are or are not living in need. Poverty experts objected to these assertions, but not many American voters or congressmen were really listening.

They were not listening because the Reagan administration—quite apart from economic circumstances of the time—went beyond exploiting resentments and touched a chord within the deeper structure of public preferences. Attacking the administrative slackness of welfare, demanding work from able-bodied persons claiming income support, targeting the poor's share of resources on those presumably most in need—these were positions in tune with mainstream American attitudes regarding antipoverty policy. In contrast to the preceding well-intentioned but somewhat tepid and permissive standards (economic incentives to "encourage" parental responsibility, work effort, and so on), the Reagan administration's proposals simply assumed those traditional norms and unhesitatingly sought to enforce them. The results as enacted by Congress and implemented by the states were not everything Reagan's supporters might have wanted, but compared to the previous generation of efforts at welfare reform in the permissive liberal mode, the Reagan administration's policy victories were impressive.

The story will not end, however, with Reaganism. Across the spectrum of political opinion there is a strong residual concern that as we grow economically we should not shrivel socially. Few Americans wish to live amid two nations of children, or two nations of the elderly, or in a society that is willing to ignore some fraction of its inhabitants because they can be regarded as economically superfluous. The Reagan administration has also sought to tap this caring side of the American social philosophy (Berger, 1984; Bendick and Levinson, 1984), but its message is ultimately self-defeating. It is unlikely that Americans can be taught to think of themselves as caring individuals at the level of the family, the local community, volunteer groups, and the business sector—but not when it comes to the national government.

The economy may or may not need the poor. The poor themselves may or may not need to have their self-esteem enhanced by hearing that they are part of a deliberately inclusive society. Rather, the message of social inclusiveness is one that we all need to hear, for our own welfare, as part of a self-conscious national community. Acting on this vision demands that rarest combination of scarce resources—political leadership and social statesmanship.

14   The Main Themes

Edward M. Gramlich

I WOULD LIKE TO HIGHLIGHT three important and related themes that come up repeatedly in this book, and then discuss a fourth theme that I think deserves more attention than it received. This analysis tends to confirm the standard pessimism about the likelihood that events of policy will cause important changes in the nature of the poverty problem, but there are at least some signs that the clouds will break.

The Family Structure Problem

One important phenomenon, dealt with at length by Wilson and Neckerman, Ellwood and Summers, and Bane, is the family structure problem. The incidence of single-parent families has been rising for all racial groups, dramatically for blacks, and we do not know why. In combination with other trends (improvement in transfers for the elderly and, in some years, economic expansion for two-parent families) this has led to a phenomenon sometimes referred to as the feminization of poverty.

Four major research questions have been raised by the complex of issues surrounding the family structure problem.

1. What does family splitting mean in terms of the ultimate welfare of individuals? A puzzling result from the income maintenance experiment in Seattle and Denver illustrates the question. Most people assumed that the existing AFDC program (of which the control subjects were part) subsidized family splitting by making it difficult for two-parent families to qualify for support. The income maintenance treatments, intended to be neutral with respect to living arrangements, seemed to increase splits. On inspection, it turned out that this increase was prominent both for families

without children and for families in certain counseling programs. That raises the question: what does a split mean? If two people living at the margin of subsistence are given more money and split, perhaps the union was not a very happy one in the first place. Perhaps it was occasioned by economic hardship and nothing more. Perhaps the female was even being physically harmed. These are all questions and not answers, but they should caution against oversimplified interpretations of the nature of this problem. A better understanding is required of what is meant by family break-ups and whether and in what circumstances they are desirable or undesirable.

2. Do splits or separate living arrangements increase poverty? Bane analyzes this issue in terms of changes in family income and needs in response to splits. Slight increases in poverty as officially measured occur when splits rise, but these increases are not very meaningful given the well-known arbitrariness of poverty-line calculations when applied to microdata. But there is a related long-run question: if splits increase, are the separate individuals and their children more or less likely to climb out of low-income status in the long run? Analyses of the Panel Study of Income Dynamics lead to the rather surprising conclusion that AFDC itself does not lead to higher welfare incidence in the next generation. There are many difficulties with such analyses and the results need further scrutinization, but similar calculations should be done with income status and living arrangements.

3. What causes splits or arrangements where individuals are never married? The Ellwood and Summers chapter is convincing in arguing that whatever caused the high and rising incidence of poor single-headed families, it was not the AFDC system. On a time-series basis, much of this rise occurred while real AFDC benefit levels were falling; on a cross-section basis, the family structure statistics look much the same in high and low AFDC benefit states. The Wilson and Neckerman chapter provides suggestive evidence that, at least for blacks, the rise in numbers of single-parent families was related to the decline in employment of black young males. Their notion of a marriageable pool seems a useful concept.

That still leaves two problems. First, the relationship with black young adult employment is based on a simple eyeball comparison of two time series. One would think that much more could be done in the way of controlling for outside influences, using cross-sectional data, and so forth. In particular, it is possible that explained or unexplained increases in the prevalence of the underground economy explain both movements. Second, even if the statistical puzzles are resolved and black employment does turn out to be the main causal variable (a cost of recessions not tallied up by

Blank and Blinder), the nation still has a major policy puzzle because, as explained below, it has proven so difficult to raise black employment.

4. What evidence is admissible? As is so often the case in the social sciences, convincing evidence is hard to come by. Time-series evidence is useful, but it is not incontrovertible. If time series are too long, the structure may have changed; if too short, there may not be enough turning points in the data. Cross-section evidence might be better, but there may be time effects, and conditions in some states may influence behavior in others. Pooled cross-sections, as used by Ellwood and Bane (the careful work underlying the gross results reported by Ellwood and Summers), seem to be the best answer, but even these data have various mixtures of the problems mentioned above. Given the weak evidence for testing hypotheses, they must be tested and retested on quite different bodies of data before firm notions of what the data imply can be developed.

The Jobs Problem

The most promising explanation for the high and rising incidence of single-parent households seems to be the low and falling level of employment opportunities. The second popular theme of this book, arising particularly in the chapters by Ellwood and Summers and by Blank and Blinder, is how employment opportunities for low-income groups can be expanded.

Unlike the family structure issue with its not very solid research results, more substantial conclusions can be affirmed regarding employment increases. The problem in this case is not that research has not answered the questions but that the answer is always no.

The frustrations involved in economists' search to find ways of stimulating employment are immense and long-standing. Formerly there was hope in simple macroeconomic stimulation of the economy, but for fifteen years almost all economists have believed that such sustained overstimulation would simply generate accelerating inflation. To the extent that there is policy content in Blank and Blinder's finding of strong cyclical influences on poverty, it is only that severe recessions must be avoided; vigorous booms cannot be created.

Some observers hold out hope for large-scale public jobs programs, but there are at least two serious empirical objections. One is that public employee unions strongly resist creating low-wage jobs. It sounds preferable to create high-wage jobs, but in fact it would not be good for the poor. High-wage jobs would be attractive to and taken by middle-class workers; in addition, they would make the programs expensive and difficult to run on a large scale. The second objection involves "displacement"— when a jobs program is created, ultimately it may be impossible to prevent state and local governments from using the new workers to displace others they would otherwise have hired. The consequence is that public employment programs have not seemed to stimulate very much employment, certainly of disadvantaged workers, at the state and local level.

Conservatives argue that reductions in the minimum wage will stimulate increased youth employment. While most existing empirical studies of this oft-studied problem do find significant minimum wage effects, the effects are rather small. As if to illustrate these small effects, we should note that the real minimum wage has declined sharply in the past five years as the government has followed the simple expedient of not raising the level in nominal terms; but, as Wilson and Neckerman show, the employed marriageable pool for black males has not only not expanded but has plummeted in this time of falling real minimum wages. Further evidence that what economists call substitution effects for low-wage workers are not very powerful comes from the disappointing results of various wage subsidies and employment tax credits.

Perhaps the best hope for expanding opportunities for low-wage workers lies in training programs, the subject discussed at length by Bassi and Ashenfelter. Here the story is much like that for family structure. Certain kinds of training programs might be worthwhile, but so few studies have been done with good control groups that evaluation is very difficult. There is also a further imponderable that is likely to make it very difficult to stimulate aggregate employment through training: if employment opportunities for low-income and/or young workers are constrained by inadequate demand, a proposition for which there is a great deal of evidence, additions to the supply of competent workers by added training will accomplish very little. The newly trained and credentialed workers will get jobs but others will lose them (and then need training). Training will not improve the employment situation until there are plentiful job opportunities.

Categorization

In contrast to the pessimism about creating jobs, by now quite standard, some new and hopeful thoughts were expressed regarding the categorization of support.

Fifteen years ago most economists were in favor of a general negative income tax that would apply to all of the poor and possibly even the rich as well (that is, a continuous schedule could translate pretax into posttax income for the entire population, implying positive or negative taxes as the case may be). This volume enumerates a number of reasons why that policy strategy is unwise and why a categorical strategy is much more likely to be successful.

1. Categorization by recipients is economically efficient. This point, made by Ellwood and Summers, refers to the fact that some poor people, such as the disabled, have quite inelastic labor supplies, whereas others, such as youths, have quite elastic supplies. Since the cost of the distortions attributable to the transfer system depends on supply elasticities, it makes sense to treat different groups differently. Both support levels and implicit tax rates should be high for the disabled, low for youths.

2. Categorization by goods and services actually consumed by the poor is economically efficient as well. Starr defends Medicaid on the ground that it is helping to improve the health of low-income individuals. Even if it were hard to establish that, it would seem to make eminent sense to subsidize or provide health care for the poor if one of the reasons society aids the poor in the first place is that it is bothered by inadequate health care among low-income individuals. Categorization by consumption goods makes sense in view of what seem to be the likely motives for income support programs.

3. Categorization on the taxpayer side can improve both efficiency and equity. This calls forth Garfinkel's much-discussed plan for increasing the level of support required of absent fathers, hence bringing the income support system more into line with popular notions of appropriate responsibility.

4. Categorization by recipients and certain consumption goods is politically acceptable, or at least more acceptable than general support. Heclo cites evidence from polls that suggests that the public approves of helping certain types of individuals and of supporting certain of their consumption activities, often while condemning AFDC itself.

Despite all these points in favor of categorizing assistance both by recipients and certain consumption types, there remains a significant question: do taxpayers favor categorized income support programs so much that they will pay the cost? Mead, in his discussion of Sosin's chapter, asserts that the nation should expect that transfer recipients have a "normal obligation" to work, as a condition of receiving income support. Presently both the food stamp program and AFDC contain clauses to that effect, although the clauses are rendered irrelevant by the paucity of steady jobs for low-income workers. To make these nominal obligations real obligations, the government would have to create both more low-income jobs (through public service employment if need be) and more day care centers. Possibly the two programs could be combined to save on costs, but a crude estimate of the cost of government provision of both the necessary public jobs and day care is on the order of $15 billion, about $7 billion more than the federal government now pays for AFDC. The question is whether the government should enforce the "normal obligation" clause even if it costs taxpayers more than the present unenforced normal obligation system. My own answer is no, and I would discount any polling evidence indicating the contrary on the grounds that respondents are simply unaware of how little waste, fraud, and abuse there is in the public welfare system. Mead argues strenuously that public opinion would opt for a "yes" answer. Whatever the case, responses to questions such as this could provide guidance on how serious American public opinion is about enforcing work obligations.

Regionalism

To this point I have tried to weave together some recurrent themes of this volume. I close by mentioning one that is surely very important but rarely emerged.

When discussing programs, populations, or whatever, most of the authors have written about the United States as if it were one country. In many ways it is more like two. One region, call it the Rust Belt, has per capita GNP levels perhaps slightly above the national average but has seen little growth in these GNP levels for the past decade, has above-average unemployment (excepting a few states in the far Northeast), and has AFDC guarantee levels that amount to about $7,000 per year for a family of four. These guarantee levels rose rapidly from the mid-1960s to the early 1970s, but since then they have been declining in real terms.

The other region, call it the Sun Belt, has per capita GNP levels slightly below those in the Rust Belt but rising rapidly. AFDC guarantee levels are much lower, now about $3,500 per year per family of four (excepting a few states in the Far West); they too have been dropping in real terms for a decade, from a much lower base amount.

The fact that this country contains regions with such diverse experience should facilitate analytic studies. In efforts to assess the impact of AFDC and economic growth on unemployment, labor supply, family structure, or whatever, regional data can be used to give more independent variation. That was profitably done by Ellwood and Summers in explaining the impact of AFDC levels on family structure, but in no other chapter. As one example, regional data could also have been used to test the marriageable pool–family split connection alluded to by Wilson and Neckerman.

As policy recommenders, on the other hand, regional variations complicate the situation. While the "taste" for paying income support in the form of AFDC benefits is modest enough in the Rust Belt—even here AFDC is no longer enough to keep families without other resources out of poverty—it is much more modest in most Sun Belt states. Benefits are very low, even though with federal matching most states are paying only about one-fourth of their AFDC cost. Without federal matching and using reasonable elasticity estimates, benefits would drop to almost nothing.

The favorite policy recommendation from the Institute for Research on Poverty these days, made especially in the chapter by Danziger, Haveman, and Plotnick, is to nationalize AFDC. What this means is that the national government would establish a national minimum benefit level, assumed to be well above that now obtaining in the Sun Belt. States could then supplement this level as they wish. I favor such a measure too, but I think we should understand that the economic rationale for such a proposal is rather tenuous. The story gets very complicated when there is migration of beneficiaries from one region to another, along with federal matching. Elsewhere (Gramlich and Laren, 1984) I have tried to work out these complications, and the bottom line is that they are all dwarfed by massive differences in taste for redistribution from region to region. This means first that if a standard national benefit level is established, median voter principles might put it much closer to the low Sun Belt level than the higher Rust Belt level. And second, one can wonder why a national benefit level should be established, in view of the fact that taste differences are so large compared with migration inefficiencies. Such regional issues constitute an important area for future research.

15 A Poverty Research Agenda for the Next Decade

Daniel H. Weinberg

PRIMARY RESPONSIBILITY for supervising the federal government's involvement in research on poverty was given to the Office of Economic Opportunity in 1964. When that office was disbanded in the early 1970s, most of its research functions were transferred to the U.S. Department of Health, Education, and Welfare, now Health and Human Services (HHS). To my five-year involvement in poverty research at HHS, I add a modicum of introspection, a dose of perspective, a number of conversations with colleagues, and the chapters included in this volume. The resulting mixture provides the basis for my personal speculations on issues regarding poverty that need additional research. In the spirit of full disclosure, however, I freely admit that I look on these issues with an economist's bias.[1]

My choice of topics is motivated mainly by my perception of their potential policy relevance. The economic and social situation affecting the poor is not static. Even the basic issue of how we count the number and types of people in poverty is currently controversial. The topics below cover a broad range of issues—from the macroeconomic environment and how it is affected by both the private sector and government actions to the effects of incentives on individual behavior. The research topics are organized into seven broad areas: (1) family and household structure, (2) work and welfare, (3) in-kind transfer programs, (4) labor market studies, (5) the relationship of poverty to the broader society, (6) fiscal federalism, and (7) methodological issues. These topic areas are not mutually exclusive; questions often cut across the categories.

Family and Household Structure

Changes in the structure of the typical American household or family affect and are affected by government programs; moreover, they affect the concepts and the definitions of income support and poverty that guide these programs. The complex interaction between the determinants of family structure (marriage, divorce, and childbearing), living arrangements (for example, subfamilies), and economic circumstances (employment and earnings, education, and welfare recipiency) should be investigated in depth. The analytic effort should include not only traditional economic-type approaches focusing on response to incentives created by the government but also ethnographic studies involving cultural and attitudinal considerations and demographic studies of trends in and determinants of marriage, divorce, fertility, and migration (see Ellwood and Bane, 1984).

More than two-fifths of the nonelderly poor are children; many live in female-headed families (see Chapter 9). How has the phenomenal growth of female-headed families and the concurrent growth in female labor force participation affected the well-being of children? Of both single-parent and two-parent families? Are there viable government interventions that will reduce the number of out-of-wedlock births and increase the number of fathers taking financial (and moral) responsibility for their children? Questions that could be addressed include how changes in community attitudes have affected teenage pregnancy and how the availability and generosity of welfare benefits have affected the probabilities of marriage and divorce, of living in a subfamily, and of having a baby while unmarried.

Demographic studies of poverty should also examine welfare recipiency, program participation, and income sources of particular minority groups such as native Americans, recent immigrants, and refugees. The extent of immigration (both legal and illegal) will continue to be a major determinant of the well-being of the low-income population as a whole. Research questions include the following: How has immigration affected the low-wage labor market in the United States? How has it affected the poverty population? Do recent immigrants differ from past cohorts in their use of public support programs? Can we predict future trends in refugee flows and immigration and how these trends will affect income support programs?

The homeless are yet another group in need of analysis; their poverty is obvious, yet it is unmeasured by any national statistics. Can a scientific study of this population be undertaken that characterizes their situation, evaluates causes, and suggests solutions? In particular, what is the effectiveness of the provision of social services, housing, or income transfers in alleviating the poverty of the homeless? What proportion of the homeless are deinstitutionalized mental patients; what proportion of those are or are not being helped by community-based mental health resources, and why?

Another set of issues concerning the family involve financial responsibility. For example, research is needed on the determinants of the payment and nonpayment of child support by absent parents, since the nonpayment of child support contributes to the poverty of custodial parents (typically female). We need a reliable description or profile of the absent-parent population. Are they supporting other families? Do they live geographically close to their children? What are their economic circumstances? Why do only a minority pay full child support? What factors (such as enforcement action, proximity, exercise of visitation rights, presence of new family members) appear to affect payment of child support?

Intergenerational financial responsibility between adults and their parents is another emerging issue. The improvement in longevity has increased and will further increase the number of elderly persons, especially those over eighty years of age (the "old old"). What has been the typical role of younger generations in supporting poor parents and how has this changed in the past several decades? Has the tax system discouraged families from taking financial responsibility for their older members? How has the growth in both benefits from and availability of Social Security, Supplemental Security Income, Medicare, Medicaid, and other programs affected intergenerational relationships and encouraged the provision of long-term care in institutional rather than family settings? Analysts should consider the legal issues (impact, implications, equity, and enforceability), historical trends, and the underlying social philosophy associated with a legal requirement that children support their parents.

Work and Welfare

What are the appropriate roles and effectiveness of work incentives and jobs programs as part of welfare programs? How do individuals perceive the trade-off between a job on the one hand and public income transfers on the other? How has this changed over time? How does the presence of public support programs (welfare, unemployment insurance, workers' compensation) affect the compensation (wages plus fringe benefits) offered for jobs with different risk of unemployment or injury? The desire of individuals to seek employment? How does the different risk aversion of different individuals affect their choice of occupation, job, or career? Their decision to apply for welfare?

The role of work experience within a welfare program should be studied. Can the concept of reciprocity (establishment of a quid pro quo in exchange for welfare benefits) lead to increased exit from welfare by promoting the self-sufficiency of recipients or would it merely reduce the welfare rolls by denying benefits? Given limited resources, which welfare recipients should be selected for employment, education, and training programs? Specifically, should mothers with pre-school-age children or infants be expected to work in exchange for welfare benefits? What happens to the children in families where the mother decides not to work and is thereby denied benefits? What are the different effects of voluntary versus mandatory work programs for welfare recipients?

Aaron (1984) posed what he termed "six questions that go to the heart of the ongoing debate about welfare policy": (1) who should be eligible for aid? (should this be determined solely by income or should demographic categories also play a role?) (2) what is the effect of welfare on pretransfer income (in other words, on earnings)? (3) what obligations do the recipients of assistance owe to society? (4) can large-scale work requirements be made to operate? (in other words, can they be made to do more than harass?) (5) to what extent is the rising incidence of single-parent families traceable to increased assistance? and (6) what reliance should be placed on in-kind assistance?

The development of improved econometric techniques and the availability of longitudinal data provide an important opportunity for better understanding the dynamics of poverty and welfare recipiency. These analyses should attempt to distinguish among the causes and correlates of poverty and welfare participation—general labor market conditions, changes in government programs, changes in family structure, and changes in health status.

Another broad question is whether there is any content to the concepts of a "culture of poverty," a "welfare class," or an "underclass." These designations are typically tied closely to characterizing the effect on children and youth of living in poor female-headed families that rely on income transfers for a substantial part of their income and living in concentrations of such people. One possible approach might be through a thorough, ethnographic-oriented study of urban neighborhoods—perhaps by contrasting poor neighborhoods with and without large concentrations of welfare recipients.

Social services (such as day care) have been an important part of the support system for low-income families for many years, yet we know little about the way they affect work and welfare, or for that matter, poverty. To what extent do particular social services enhance the success of work programs, reduce poverty and welfare dependency, or overcome the obstacles to employment that some welfare recipients confront (health, language, transportation, child care problems)? How is success affected by program design and sponsorship (private vs. public)? Does the provision of day care by welfare recipients for the children of other welfare recipients enable both groups to gain valuable labor market experience and thereby improve their chances of escaping poverty?

In-Kind Transfer Programs

The War on Poverty and subsequent related developments transformed the federal government's approach to the provision of in-kind benefits. Medicare and Medicaid made health care services available to many of the poor; the food stamp, child nutrition, and Women, Infants, and Children (WIC) programs improved the general nutrition of the poor. At the same time, housing assistance was expanded (see Chapter 2 for further background). We need a better understanding of why the Congress finds it so much easier to provide in-kind benefits to all poor Americans (the food stamp program has been called a straightforward negative income tax) whereas cash assistance is available only to some (single parents, the aged, the blind, and the disabled). We also need a comprehensive examination of the role public preferences play in determining public policy toward poverty (see Chapter 13). Does the perception of poverty change in response to changes in real income? Are there cycles in public opinion opening "windows of political opportunity" for increasing or reducing benefits for the poor?

Medicaid is now the largest welfare program. How does it affect the well-being of the poor? How has the availability of health benefits to the poor (in particular the elimination of all benefits when eligibility is lost) changed their work behavior? Does "free" medical care (national health insurance) in other countries lead to different behavior by their low-income populations?

The most equitable and efficient way of providing housing assistance remains open to debate. Since providing adequate shelter for all poor (particularly the homeless) is apparently beyond the capability of local governments, should federal aid focus on the supply side (expensive construction programs) or the demand side (less expensive but still costly housing vouchers)? (Of course, providing vouchers raises other concerns. See, for example, Friedman and Weinberg, 1982.) How can one reconcile providing housing assistance to one family but denying it to an otherwise identical family simply because funds are limited? In administering a housing program, how does one trade off between physical adequacy of existing housing and its affordability?

Education is another major in-kind benefit provided by government, although not the federal government. The methods educators can use to improve the ability and achievement of children from low-income environments have been the focus of policy since the War on Poverty began. What approaches show the most promise? Is there any further role for educational experimentation or should the move "back to basics" be endorsed?

Labor Market Studies

Understanding the structure and operation of both demand and supply in low-wage labor markets is critical for evaluating the role they can be expected or encouraged to play in alleviating pretransfer poverty. What kinds of jobs offer stable employment and/or on-the-job training and/or good fringe benefits (for example, health insurance) to low-wage workers, and what kinds of employers offer these jobs? What other characteristics are associated with these jobs? What selection criteria do employers use to hire and retain employees for these jobs? How do employers respond to changes in the availability of different kinds of workers; in other words, how are jobs created? Are there structural and discrimination barriers to upward mobility ("dual" labor markets)? What is the role of part-time work and has it been changing over time? Under what circumstances do current or former welfare recipients find jobs that offer stable employment or on-the-job training and in what fields? Can any guidance be obtained to help improve the work programs provided to welfare recipients?

The U.S. experience in creating jobs in response to baby boom pressures has been quite different from and apparently much more successful than the West European experience. Is it also different in the role that the private sector plays in alleviating poverty by providing employment? Can lessons from this comparison be applied effectively in alleviating U.S. (or European) poverty? How has the continuing transformation of the U.S.

economy toward a service-oriented one and away from a manufacturing-oriented one affected poverty? What are the long-range implications for the labor market of the changing age structure of the population?

The problem of youth unemployment is so serious and the solution so elusive that it deserves special attention. Further analysis of job programs for youth and dissemination of knowledge about what works is required. Apparently, Job Corps, the Youth Incentive Entitlement Pilot Project, and the Summer Youth Program (public service employment on a temporary basis) all work to some extent (see Chapter 6, and Crane and Ellwood, 1984). On the other hand, the minimum wage seems to reduce their employment (see Wise, 1984b). How can we translate some of the lessons learned from those programs to a broader national context?

What are the long-run consequences of youth unemployment for those individuals' later poverty and marriage (see Chapter 10)? Does welfare discourage educational attainment and the employment prospects of youth? To what extent does success for individuals in training programs occur at the expense of nonparticipants as opposed to benefiting society as a whole?

The income maintenance experiments answered many questions about the effects of transfer programs on labor supply (U.S. Department of Health and Human Services, 1983). There are a number of unanswered questions about other effects of a negative income tax. For example, there is still some controversy about the impact of a negative income tax on marital stability (see Aaron, 1984, p. 8). What explains the rise and fall of the negative income tax as a policy approach to helping the poor (see, for example, the conclusion of Ellwood and Summers in Chapter 4 that categorical programs are preferable to universal ones)?

While it has been argued that social insurance programs (Social Security, disability insurance, and unemployment insurance, in particular) reduce the labor supply of recipients (see Danziger, Haveman, and Plotnick, 1981, for a summary of the literature), there is little consensus on the magnitudes of these effects. For example, a number of investigators (Leonard, 1979; Parsons, 1980; Halpern and Hausman, 1984; Haveman, Wolfe, and Warlick, 1984) have estimated behavioral models of the "decision to become disabled," but there is still controversy about the results. In addition, these studies have not addressed health issues. The prevalence of impairment and pathology and thus the extent of disability in the future will be influenced by a number of factors, including changes in the age distribution of the population, trends in the incidence and duration of various medical conditions, and improvements in medical technology.

The Relation of Poverty to the Broader Society

Secular economic growth is clearly important in reducing poverty (see Chapter 4), but the effects of business cycles are not borne evenly across demographic groups (see Chapter 8). Nonetheless, further attention should be given to the links between macroeconomic theory and microeconomic evidence on behavior. For example, what are the theoretical and practical links between labor market processes (for example, job search) and macroeconomic outcomes (the unemployment rate)?

Research addressing the determinants of the overall distribution of income is important as well. The distribution of earnings has become more unequal and pretransfer poverty has increased (see Chapter 3). To what extent is this situation the result of the growth of transfer programs and changes in the tax system and to what extent is it the result of increases in the participation of the poor in the "underground" economy or the result of other factors? Low-income families are affected by the tax system as well as the welfare system. What aspects of the tax system have particularly pernicious or particularly salutary effects? How does the taxation of the working poor (including payroll taxes, tax credits such as the Earned Income Tax Credit, state and local income taxes, property taxes, sales taxes) affect poverty? The need for income transfer programs?

Another issue involves the treatment of particular disadvantaged groups. To what extent does discrimination—as compared to cultural and market factors and private choices—contribute to the lower economic well-being of various minority groups and women? Has this effect moderated in the period of civil rights, equal opportunity, and affirmative action legislation? How does discrimination affect the process of social mobility and social and economic integration? That is, what are the relative roles of discrimination, social networks (personal contacts and relatives), cultural conditioning, education, and experience in facilitating or hindering economic mobility? How much does discrimination as compared to private choice affect occupational choice, job search methods, or career strategies?

Fiscal Federalism

Meeting the needs of the poor has been the joint responsibility of all levels of government. How does the division of responsibility for the poor among federal, state, and local governments determine the options available for restructuring that division and how has the division shifted over time? How does it affect the mix and delivery of services and the differential growth of programs? What have been the effects of recent changes in the fiscal environment (such as the federal fiscal crisis, state surpluses and deficits, and block grants) on benefits? On the trade-off between taxes and spending at the local level? To what extent has policy been affected by the willingness of the private sector to provide support for the poor through philanthropy and charity?

Since most welfare programs are administered by state and local governments, we need further research on how improved administrative practices, such as monthly reporting of income, can make programs more effective and reduce fraud, waste, error, and abuse. What role can local initiatives play in demonstrating new technologies (such as computers) to improve administration of welfare? Can welfare bureaucracies be made more responsive to individual needs without sacrificing equitable treatment (see Chapter 11)?

Methodological Issues

Research into the definition of poverty should build on the current debate about methods of valuing noncash benefits, and it should also include studies on the purpose of a poverty measure and its policy uses. What is the appropriate treatment and valuation of such noncash transfers as fringe benefits? Should poverty be measured in relative or absolute terms? What is the validity of the current implicit equivalence scale as opposed to a subjective equivalence scale, or one that adjusts for regional and state differences in the cost of living? What would be the effect of changing the time period to a subannual accounting period for the magnitude and coverage of income support programs, and so forth? Other questions involve how we should treat "unrelated individuals," the institutionalized population, and the homeless. (Note that the latter two groups are not included in any official measure of poverty.)

Political debate about improving the welfare system often rests on unproven assertions about the unmeasured costs and benefits of the proposed changes. Can we improve the technology, methodology, and rhetoric of cost-benefit and regulatory analysis as well as program evaluation by quantifying more accurately the social benefits (income security, health coverage, reduction of income poverty) and the social costs (reduction in labor supply, saving, and capital formation; incentives for family break-up; loss of productivity) of welfare programs? Even though not all benefits and costs can be measured, can this new methodology be applied to look at proposed or actual changes in welfare programs, such as evaluating the extent of displacement that occurs when public service employment or other work programs for welfare recipients are implemented?

IN AN ERA of limited resources for both programs and research, this represents an enormous research agenda. From a policy analyst's perspective, the questions that should be given priority are those most likely to affect policy decisions, particularly in the areas of family and household structure and work and welfare. Despite what we have learned over the past twenty years, considerably more study is required if efforts to improve the welfare system are to be successful.

References

Aaron, Henry J. 1978. *Politics and the professors: The Great Society in perspective.* Washington, D.C.: Brookings Institution.

―――― 1982. *Economic effects of social security.* Washington, D.C.: Brookings Institution.

―――― 1984. Six welfare questions still searching for answers. *Brookings Review* 3:12–17.

Abram, Morris B. 1984. What constitutes a civil right? *New York Times Magazine,* June 10, pp. 52–54, 58–64.

Abt Associates. 1984. State medical inpatient hospital reimbursement: Summary of state programs. Cambridge, Mass. Photocopy.

Adams, C. F., Jr. 1981. A summary of statistically derived estimates of the job creation impact of public service employment grants to large cities, 1977–79. School of Public Administration, Ohio State University. Mimeo.

Adams, C. F., Jr., R. Cook, and A. Maurice. 1983. A pooled time-series analysis of the job-creation impact of public service employment grants to large cities. *Journal of Human Resources* 18:283–294.

Aday, L., R. Andersen, and G. Fleming. 1980. *Health care in the U.S.: Equitable for whom?* Beverly Hills, Calif.: Sage Publications.

Albritton, Robert. 1979. Social amelioration through mass insurgency? A reexamination of the Piven-Cloward thesis. *American Political Science Journal* 73:1003–1012.

Allen, Francis. 1964. *The borderland of criminal justice: Essays in law and criminology.* Chicago: University of Chicago Press.

―――― 1982. *The decline of the rehabilitative ideal: Penal policy and social purpose.* New Haven: Yale University Press.

Anderson, Jervis. 1972. *A. Philip Randolph: A biographical portrait.* New York: Harcourt Brace Jovanovich.

Anderson, Martin. 1978. *Welfare: The political economy of welfare reform in the United States.* Stanford, Calif.: Hoover Institution.

―――― 1984. The objectives of the Reagan administration's social welfare policy.

In *The social contract revisited,* ed. D. Lee Bawden. Washington, D.C.: Urban Institute Press.

Anderson, W. H. Locke. 1964. Trickling down: The relationship between economic growth and the extent of poverty among American families. *Quarterly Journal of Economics* 78:511–524.

Ashenfelter, Orley. 1978. Estimating the effect of training programs on earnings. *Review of Economics and Statistics* 60:47–57.

Asher, Martin A. 1983. Macroeconomic activity and income distribution in the postwar United States: Comment. Brookings Institution, Washington, D.C. Mimeo.

Bailey, Stephen Kemp. 1964. *Congress makes a law.* New York: Vintage Books.

Bailis, Lawrence N. 1974. *Bread or justice: Grassroots organizing in the welfare rights movement.* Lexington, Mass.: Lexington Books.

Bakke, W. E. 1940. *Citizens without work.* New Haven: Yale University Press.

Baldwin, Sidney. 1968. *Poverty and politics: The rise and decline of the Farm Security Administration.* Chapel Hill: University of North Carolina Press.

Bane, M. J., and D. T. Ellwood. 1983a. The dynamics of dependence: The routes to self-sufficiency. Report supported by U.S. Department of Health and Human Services grant, Contract no. HHS-100–82–0038. John F. Kennedy School of Government, Harvard University. Mimeo.

—— 1983b. Slipping into and out of poverty: The dynamics of spells. Working Paper 1199. National Bureau of Economic Research, Cambridge, Mass.

—— 1984a. The dynamics of children's living arrangements. Working paper, supported by U.S. Department of Health and Human Services grant, Contract no. HHS-100–82–0038. John F. Kennedy School of Government, Harvard University. Mimeo.

—— 1984b. Single mothers and their living arrangements. Working paper, supported by U.S. Department of Health and Human Services grant, Contract no. HHS-100–82–0038. John F. Kennedy School of Government, Harvard University. Mimeo.

Bassi, Laurie. 1981. Evaluating alternative job creation programs. A report to the National Commission for Employment Policy. Washington, D.C.

—— 1983. The effect of CETA on the postprogram earnings of participants. *Journal of Human Resources* 18:539–556.

—— 1984. Estimating the effect of training programs with nonrandom selection. *Review of Economics and Statistics* 56:36–43.

Bassi, L., L. Burbridge, M. Simms, and C. Betsey. 1984. Measuring the effect of CETA on youth and the disadvantaged. Final report, Urban Institute, Washington, D.C.

Bassi, L., and A. Fechter. 1979. *The implications for fiscal substitution and occupational displacement under an expanded CETA Title VI.* Washington, D.C.: GPO.

Baum, Daniel J. 1974. *The welfare family and mass administrative justice.* New York: Praeger.

Beach, Charles M. 1977. Cyclical sensitivity of aggregate income inequality. *Review of Economics and Statistics* 59:56–66.

Becker, G. S., E. M. Landes, and R. T. Michael. 1977. An economic analysis of marital instability. *Journal of Political Economy* 85:1141–1187.

Becketti, Sean, William Gould, Lee Lillard, and Finis Welch. 1983. *Attrition from the PSID*. Santa Monica, Calif.: Unicon Research Corporation.

Bell, Derrick A., Jr. 1973. *Race, racism, and American law*. Boston: Little, Brown.

Bendick, Marc, Jr. 1980. Failure to enroll in public assistance programs. *Social Work* 25:268–274.

Bendick, Marc, Jr., Abe Lavine, and Toby H. Campbell. 1978. *The anatomy of AFDC errors*. Washington, D.C.: Urban Institute Press.

Bendick, Marc, Jr., and Phyllis M. Levinson. 1984. Private sector initiatives or public-private partnerships? In *The Reagan presidency and the governing of America,* ed. Lester M. Salamon and Michael S. Lund. Washington, D.C.: Urban Institute Press.

Benham, L., and A. Benham. 1975. The impact of incremental medical services on health status, 1963–1970. In *Equity in health services,* ed. R. Andersen, J. Kravits, and O. W. Andersen. Cambridge, Mass.: Ballinger.

Bennett, Lerone, Jr. 1962. *Before the Mayflower: A history of the Negro in the United States*. Chicago: Johnson Publishing.

Berger, Renee A. 1984. Private-sector initiatives in the Reagan era. In *The Reagan presidency and the governing of America,* ed. Lester M. Salamon and Michael S. Lund. Washington, D.C.: Urban Institute Press.

Bergthold, L. 1984. Crabs in a bucket: The politics of health care reform in California. *Journal of Health Politics, Policy and Law* 9:203–222.

Bernstein, Blanche. 1982. *The politics of welfare*. Cambridge, Mass.: ABT Books.

Birdsall, William. 1984. The value of the official poverty statistics. Paper presented at the annual conference of the Association of Public Policy Analysis and Management, New Orleans.

Bishop, George F., Robert W. Oldendick, and Alfred J. Tuchfarber. 1978. Effects of question wording and format on political attitude consistency. *Public Opinion Quarterly* 42:81–92.

Bishop, J. H. 1980. Jobs, cash transfers, and marital instability: A review and synthesis of the evidence. *Journal of Human Resources* 15:301–334.

Bishop, John, and Robert Haveman. 1979. Selective employment subsidies: Can Okun's Law be repealed? *American Economic Review* 69:124–130.

Blank, Rebecca M. 1985. Disaggregating the effects of economic growth on the distribution of income. Discussion paper 780–85, Institute for Research on Poverty, University of Wisconsin–Madison.

Blank, Rebecca M., and Alan S. Blinder. 1985. Macroeconomics, income distribution, and poverty. Paper presented at a conference of the Institute for Research on Poverty, University of Wisconsin–Madison (a more detailed version of the chapter in this volume).

Blinder, Alan S. 1980. The level and distribution of economic well-being. In *The American economy in transition,* ed. M. S. Feldstein. Chicago: University of Chicago Press.

Blinder, Alan S., and Howard Y. Esaki. 1978. Macroeconomic activity and income distribution in the postwar United States. *Review of Economics and Statistics* 60:604–609.

Blinder, Alan S., and William Newton. 1981. The 1971–1974 controls program and the price level. *Journal of Monetary Economics* 8:1–23.

Bloom, H., and M. McLaughlin. 1982. CETA training programs: Do they work for adults? Joint report of the Congressional Budget Office and the National Commission for Employment Policy, Washington, D.C.

Blumstein, A. 1982. On the racial disproportionality of United States prison populations. *Journal of Criminal Law and Criminology* 73:1259–1281.

Bodie, Zvi. 1976. Common stocks as a hedge against inflation. *Journal of Finance* 31:459–470.

Bonanno, J., and T. Wetle. 1984. HMO enrollment of Medicare recipients: An analysis of incentives and barriers. *Journal of Health Policy, Politics and Law* 9:41–62.

Boudon, Raymond. 1974. *Education, opportunity, and social inequality.* New York: Wiley.

Bound, John. 1985. The health and earnings of rejected disability insurance applicants. Department of Economics, Harvard University.

Bovbjerg, R. R., and J. F. Holahan. 1982. *Medicaid in the Reagan era: Federal policy and state choices.* Washington, D.C.: Urban Institute Press.

Brauer, Carl. 1982. Kennedy, Johnson, and the War on Poverty. *Journal of American History* 69:98–119.

Bremer, William W. 1984. *Depression winters: New York social workers and the New Deal.* Philadelphia: Temple University Press.

Bremner, Robert H. 1985. The New Deal and social welfare. In *Fifty years later: The New Deal evaluated,* ed. Harvard Sitkoff. Philadelphia: Temple University Press.

Brodkin, Evelyn, and Michael Lipsky. 1983. Quality control in AFDC as an administrative strategy. *Social Service Review* 57:1–34.

Brody, David. 1975. The New Deal and World War II. In *The New Deal: The national level,* ed. John Braeman, Robert Bremner, and David Brody. Columbus: Ohio State University Press.

Bronfenbrenner, Urie. 1974. Is early intervention effective? U.S. Office of Child Development, Washington, D.C. Mimeo.

Brown, Rexford. 1983. Public policy and pupil achievement. *State Legislatures* (October): 39–41.

Burke, Vincent J., and Lee Burke. 1974. *Nixon's good deed: Welfare reform.* New York: Columbia University Press.

Burkhauser, Richard, and Robert Haveman. 1982. *Disability and work: The economics of American policy.* Baltimore: Johns Hopkins University Press.

Burtless, Gary. 1983. Why is insured unemployment so low? *Brookings Papers on Economic Activity* 1:225–253.

—— 1984. Unemployment insurance and poverty. In Committee on Ways and Means, U.S. House of Representatives, *Poverty rate increase hearings.* Serial 98–55. Washington, D.C.: GPO.

—— 1985. Are targeted wage subsidies harmful? Evidence from a wage voucher experiment. *Industrial and Labor Relations Review* 39 (in press).

Burtless, Gary, and Haveman, Robert. 1984. Policy lessons from three labor market experiments. In *Employment and training R&D: Lessons learned and future directions,* ed. Thayne Robson. Kalamazoo, Mich.: Upjohn Institute for Employment Research.

Burton, Nancy W., and Lyle V. Jones. 1982. Recent trends in achievement levels of black and white youth. *Educational Researcher* 11(4):10–17.

Cain, G. 1968. Benefit-cost estimates for Job Corps. Discussion paper 9–68, Institute for Research on Poverty, University of Wisconsin–Madison.

———— 1974. The effect of income maintenance laws on fertility in results from the New Jersey–Pennsylvania Experiment. In *Final report of the Graduated Work Incentive Experiment in New Jersey and Pennsylvania*. Madison and Princeton: Institute for Research on Poverty, University of Wisconsin, and Mathematica Policy Research.

Campbell, Christiana. 1962. *The Farm Bureau and the New Deal*. Urbana: University of Illinois Press.

Cantril, Hadley. 1951. *Public opinion, 1935–1946*. Princeton: Princeton University Press.

Card, David E. 1983. Cost-of-living escalators in major union contracts. *Industrial and Labor Relations Review* 37:34–38.

Caro, Robert. 1983. *The years of Lyndon Johnson: The path to power*. New York: Random House.

Carter, Elmer. 1941. The editor says. *Opportunity* 19 (January): 2–3, (May) 130–131, (July) 194–195.

Carter, Genevieve, Lillene H. Fifield, and Hannah Shields. 1973. *Public attitudes toward welfare: An opinion poll*. Los Angeles: Regional Research Institute in Social Welfare, University of Southern California School of Social Work.

Carter, Launor F. 1984. The sustaining effects study of compensatory and elementary education. *Educational Researcher* 13(7):4–13.

Cates, Jerry. 1983. *Insuring inequality: Administrative leadership in Social Security, 1935–54*. Ann Arbor: University of Michigan Press.

Cayton, Horace, and George Mitchell. 1939. *Black workers and the new unions*. Chapel Hill: University of North Carolina Press.

Center for the Study of Social Policy. 1984. The "flip-side" of black families headed by women: The economic status of black men. Working paper. Washington, D.C.

Chall, Jeanne S. 1983. Literacy: Trends and explanations. *Educational Researcher* 12(10):3–8.

Cherlin, A. 1981. *Marriage, divorce, remarriage*. Cambridge, Mass.: Harvard University Press.

Clark, K. B. 1965. *Dark ghetto*. New York: Harper and Row.

Clark, Kim, and Lawrence Summers. 1981. The demographic composition of cyclical variations in employment. *Journal of Human Resources* 16:61–79.

Coe, R. D. 1978. Dependency and poverty in the short run and long run. In *Five thousand American families: Patterns of economic progress*, vol. 6, ed. G. J. Duncan and J. N. Morgan. Ann Arbor: Institute for Social Research, University of Michigan.

Cogan, J. 1982. The decline in black teenage employment: 1950–70. *American Economic Review* 72:621–638.

Cohen, A. 1979. Economics, marital instability and race. Ph.D. diss., University of Wisconsin–Madison.

Cohen, J. 1984. Success and failure in containing Medicaid costs: Twelve states' experience between 1981 and 1982. Working paper, Urban Institute, Washington, D.C.

Cohen, J., and J. Holahan. 1984. Medicaid eligibility after the Omnibus Budget Reconciliation Act of 1981. Working paper, Urban Institute, Washington, D.C.

Cohen, W. J. 1977. Discussion. In *A decade of federal antipoverty programs: Achievements, failures, lessons,* ed. Robert H. Haveman. New York: Academic Press.

—— 1984. Medicare: 1965–1985–2000. Speech at conference on Medicare: Reaffirming the Vision, Retooling the Instrument, Woodrow Wilson School of Public and International Affairs, Princeton University, November.

Cole, Steven. Forthcoming. The trend in AFDC benefit levels, 1970–1983: A comparison of Wisconsin and the United States. Institute for Research on Poverty, University of Wisconsin–Madison.

Congressional Testimony. 1945. Hearings before the Committee on Expenditures in the Executive Departments, House of Representatives (September, October, November).

—— 1966. Hearings before the Subcommittee on the War on Poverty Program of the Committee on Education and Labor, House of Representatives (July 20).

—— 1967a. Hearings before the Subcommittee on Employment, Manpower, and Poverty of the Labor and Public Welfare Committee, Senate (May 8).

—— 1967b. Hearings before the Subcommittee on Employment, Manpower, and Poverty of the Labor and Public Welfare Committee, Senate (June 8).

—— 1967c. Hearings before the Subcommittee on Employment, Manpower, and Poverty of the Labor and Public Welfare Committee, Senate (June 9).

—— 1967d. Hearings before the Committee on Education and Labor, House of Representatives (July 12–19).

—— 1969a. Hearings before the Ad Hoc Task Force on Poverty of the Education and Labor Committee, House of Representatives (May 8).

—— 1969b. Hearings before the Subcommittee on Employment, Manpower, and Poverty of the Labor and Public Welfare Committee, Senate (June 4).

Cook, Fay Lomax. 1979. *Who should be helped?* New York: Sage Publications.

Cook, R. 1980. Public service employment in 1980. Woodrow Wilson School of Public and International Affairs, Princeton University. Mimeo.

Cook, Thomas, et al. 1984. *Black achievement and school desegregation.* Washington, D.C.: National Institute of Education.

Cooley, T., T. McGuire, and E. Prescott. 1979. Earnings and employment dynamics of manpower trainees: An exploratory econometric analysis. In *Research in labor economics,* ed. F. Bloch. Greenwich, Conn.: JAI Press.

Corcoran, Mary, G. J. Duncan, and Patricia Gurin. 1983. Psychological and demographic aspects of the underclass. Paper presented at the annual meetings of the Population Association of America, Pittsburgh.

Corcoran, Mary, and Christopher Jencks. 1979. The effects of family background. In Christopher Jencks et al., *Who gets ahead? The determinants of economic success in America.* New York: Basic Books

Coughlin, Richard. 1980. *Ideology, public opinion, and welfare policy*. Berkeley: Institute for International Studies, University of California, Berkeley.

Covello, Vincent T., ed. 1980. *Poverty and public policy*. Boston and Cambridge, Mass.: G. K. Hall, Schenkman Publishing.

Crane, Jon, and David T. Ellwood. 1984. Summer youth employment programs: Private job supplement or substitute? Report prepared for the Department of Health and Human Services under ASPE grant no. 92A–82. John F. Kennedy School of Government, Harvard University. Mimeo.

Crespi, Irving, Richard L. Kaluzny, and Billy Tidwell. 1980. *Final report: A survey of participants in the Denver Monthly Reporting Experiment*. Princeton: Mathematica Policy Research.

Cunningham, M. 1977. Eligibility procedures for AFDC. *Social Work* 22:21–26.

Curtin, Richard T., and Charles D. Cowan. 1975. Public attitudes toward fiscal programs. In *Surveys of Consumers 1972–73*, ed. Burkhard Strumpel et al. Ann Arbor: Institute for Social Research, University of Michigan.

Cutright, P. 1971. Income and family events: Marital instability. *Journal of Marriage and the Family* 33:291–306.

——— 1973. Illegitimacy and income supplements. *Studies in public welfare*. Paper no. 12. Prepared for the use of the Subcommittee on Fiscal Policy of the Joint Economic Committee, Congress of the United States. Washington, D.C.: GPO.

——— 1974. Components of change in the number of female family heads aged 15–44: United States, 1940–1970. *Journal of Marriage and the Family* 36:714–721.

Cutright, P., and P. Madras. 1974. AFDC and the marital and family status of ever married women aged 15–44: United States, 1950–1970. *Sociology and Social Research* 60:314–327.

Danziger, Sheldon, and Peter Gottschalk. 1985. The impact of budget cuts and economic conditions on poverty. *Journal of Policy Analysis and Management* 5:587–593.

Danziger, Sheldon, Robert Haveman, and Robert Plotnick. 1980. Retrenchment or reorientation: Options for income support policy. *Public Policy* 28:473–490.

——— 1981. How income transfer programs affect work, savings, and the income distribution: A critical review. *Journal of Economic Literature* 19:975–1028.

Danziger, Sheldon, and George Jakubson. 1982. The distributional impact of targeted public employment programs. In *Public finance and public employment*, ed. Robert H. Haveman. Detroit: Wayne State University Press.

Danziger, Sheldon, George Jakubson, Saul Schwartz, and Eugene Smolensky. 1982. Work and welfare as determinants of female poverty and household headship. *Quarterly Journal of Economics* 97:519–534.

Danziger, Sheldon, and Robert Plotnick. 1982. The war on income poverty: Achievements and failures. In *Welfare reform in America*, ed. Paul Sommers. Boston: Kluwer Nijhoff.

Darlington, Richard B., and Irving Lazar. 1984. Letter. *Phi Delta Kappan* 66:231–232.

Darlington, Richard B., et al. 1980. Preschool programs and later school competence of children of low income families. *Science* 208 (April 11): 202–204.

Davis, James A. 1980. Conservative weather in a liberalizing climate. *Social Forces* 58:1129–1156.

Davis, John P. 1934. NRA codifies slavery. *Crisis* (October): 298–299, 304.

Davis, Karen. 1977. A decade of policy developments in providing health care for low-income families. In *A decade of federal antipoverty programs: Achievements, failures, and lessons,* ed. Robert H. Haveman. New York: Academic Press.

Davis, K., M. Gold, and D. Makuc. 1981. Access to health care for the poor: Does the gap remain? *Annual review of public health,* vol. 2. Palo Alto, Calif.: Annual Reviews.

Davis, K., and R. Reynolds. 1976. The impact of Medicare and Medicaid on access to medical care. In *The role of health insurance in the health services sector,* ed. R. N. Rosett. New York: Neale Watson Academic Publications for the National Bureau of Economic Research.

Davis, K., and D. Rowland. 1983. Uninsured and underserved: Inequities in health care in the United States. *Milbank Memorial Fund Quarterly/Health and Society* 61:149–176.

Davis, K., and C. Schoen. 1978. *Health and the War on Poverty: A ten-year appraisal.* Washington, D.C.: Brookings Institution.

Davis, Kenneth C. 1971. *Discretionary justice: Preliminary inquiry.* Urbana: University of Illinois Press.

Derthick, Martha. 1970. *The influence of federal grants: Public assistance in Massachusetts.* Cambridge, Mass.: Harvard University Press.

——— 1979. *Policymaking for social security.* Washington, D.C.: Brookings Institution.

Dickinson, K., T. Johnson, and R. West. 1984. An analysis of CETA programs on components of earnings and other outcomes. Final report, SRI International, Menlo Park, Calif.

Digest of Education Statistics. 1984. Washington, D.C.: National Center for Education Statistics, U.S. Department of Education.

Duncan, G. J. 1984. *Years of poverty, years of plenty.* Ann Arbor: Institute for Social Research, University of Michigan.

Easterlin, Richard. 1980. *Birth and fortune: The impact of numbers on personal welfare.* New York: Basic Books.

Economic report of the President. 1984. Washington, D.C.: GPO.

Edelman, Murray. 1977. *Political language: Words that succeed and policies that fail.* New York: Academic Press.

Education Week. 1984a. Increase found in handicapped pupils enrolled in special-education classes. February 22.

Education Week. 1984b. State education statistics. January 18.

Elder, G. H., Jr. 1974. *Children of the Great Depression.* Chicago: University of Chicago Press.

Ellwood, D. T. Forthcoming. The mismatch hypothesis: Are there teenage jobs missing in the ghetto? In *The black youth employment crisis,* ed. Richard B. Freeman and Casey Echniowski. Chicago: University of Chicago Press.

Ellwood, D. T., and M. J. Bane. 1984. The impact of AFDC on family structure and living arrangements. Report prepared for the U.S. Department of Health and Human Services under grant no. 92A–82. John F. Kennedy School of Government, Harvard University. Mimeo. (Forthcoming in *Research in Labor Economics* [Greenwich, Conn.: JAI Press].)

Ellwood, D. T., and D. A. Wise. 1983. Youth employment in the seventies: The changing circumstances of young adults. In *American families and the economy: The high costs of living,* ed. Richard Nelson and Felicity Skidmore. Washington, D.C.: National Academy Press.

Erskine, Hazel. 1975. The polls: Government's role in welfare. *Public Opinion Quarterly* 39:257–274.

Evans, M. D. 1983. Modernization, economic conditions, and family formation: Evidence from recent white and nonwhite cohorts. Ph.D. diss., University of Chicago.

Farley, Reynolds. 1970. *Growth of the black population.* Chicago: Markham.

———— 1980. Homicide trends in the United States. *Demography 17:*177–188.

Farley, R., and A. I. Hermalin. 1971. Family stability: A comparison of trends between blacks and whites. *American Sociological Review* 36:1–18.

Fechter, A., and S. Greenfield. 1973. Welfare and illegitimacy: An economic model and some preliminary results. Working paper, Urban Institute, Washington, D.C.

Feder, J., J. Hadley, and R. Mullner. 1984a. Poor people and poor hospitals: Implications for public policy. *Journal of Health Politics, Policy and Law* 9:237–250.

———— 1984b. Falling through the cracks: Poverty, insurance coverage, and hospitals' care to the poor, 1980 and 1982. Working paper, Urban Institute, Washington, D.C.

Feldstein, M. S. 1974. Social security, induced retirement, and aggregate capital accumulation. *Journal of Political Economy* 82:905–926.

———— 1982. Inflation, capital taxation, and monetary policy. In *Inflation,* ed. R. E. Hall. Chicago: University of Chicago Press.

Feldstein, M. S., ed. 1980. *The American economy in transition.* Chicago: University of Chicago Press.

Fireman, Bruce, and William A. Gamson. 1978. Utilitarian logic in the resource mobilization perspective. In *The dynamics of social movements: Resource mobilization, tactics, and control,* ed. M. N. Zald and J. D. McCarthy. New York: Sage Publications.

Florida Task Force on Competition and Consumer Choices in Health Care. 1984. *Florida health issues: "An opportunity for leadership."* Tallahassee: Office of the Governor.

Foner, Philip S. 1974. *Organized labor and the black worker, 1619–1973.* New York: Praeger.

Fraker, T., R. Maynard, and L. Nelson. 1984. An assessment of alternative comparison group methodologies for evaluating employment and training programs. Final report, Mathematica Policy Research, Princeton.

Franklin, John Hope. 1947. *From slavery to freedom: A history of Negro Americans.* New York: Knopf.

Frazier, E. F. 1939. *The Negro family in the United States.* Chicago: University of Chicago Press.

Free, L., and Hadley Cantril. 1968. *The political beliefs of Americans.* New York: Simon and Schuster.

Freeman, Richard B., and H. J. Holzer. 1985. Young blacks and jobs—What we now know. *Public Interest* 78 (Winter):18–31.

Friedman, Joseph, and Daniel H. Weinberg. 1982. *The economics of housing vouchers.* New York: Academic Press.

Friedman, Lawrence. 1977. The social and political context of the War on Poverty: An overview. In *A decade of federal antipoverty programs: Achievements, failures, and lessons,* ed. Robert H. Haveman. New York: Academic Press.

Friendly, Henry. 1975. Some kind of hearing. *University of Pennsylvania Law Review* 123:1267–1317.

Fuchs, Victor R. 1967. Redefining poverty and redistributing income. *Public Interest* 8 (Summer):88–95.

——— 1979. Economics, health and post-industrial society. *Milbank Memorial Fund Quarterly/Health and Society* 57:153–182.

——— 1983. *How we live: An economic perspective on Americans from birth to death.* Cambridge, Mass.: Harvard University Press.

Full Employment Action Council. 1976. Newsletters.

Furstenberg, F. F., Jr., T. Hershberg, and J. Modell. 1975. The origins of the female-headed black family: The impact of the urban experience. *Journal of Interdisciplinary History* 6:211–233.

Gamson, William. 1975. *The strategy of social protest.* Homewood, Ill.: Dorsey Press.

Garfinkel, Herbert. 1959. *When Negroes march.* Glencoe, Ill.: Free Press.

Garfinkel, Irwin, and Robert Haveman. 1983. Income transfer policy in the United States. In *Handbook of social intervention,* ed. Edward Seidman. Beverly Hills, Calif.: Sage Publications.

Gaus, C. R., B. S. Cooper, and C. G. Hirschman. 1976. Contrasts in HMO and fee-for-service performance. *Social Security Bulletin* 39 (May):3–14.

Geiger, H. J. 1984. Community health centers: Health care as an instrument of social change. In *Reforming medicine: The lessons of the last quarter century,* ed. V. W. Sidel and R. Sidel. New York: Pantheon.

Gelb, Joyce. 1975. Organizing the poor: A brief analysis of the welfare rights movement. *Policy Studies Journal* 3:346–354.

Glazer, Nathan. 1984a. The problem with competence. *American Journal of Education* 92:306–313.

——— 1984b. The social policy of the Reagan administration. In *The social contract revisited,* ed. D. Lee Bawden. Washington, D.C.: Urban Institute Press.

Goldman, F., and Grossman, M. 1982. The impacts of public health policy: The case of community health centers. Working paper 1020, National Bureau of Economic Research, Cambridge, Mass.

Goodman, John. 1984. *Public opinion during the Reagan administration.* Washington, D.C.: Urban Institute Press.

Gottschalk, Peter. 1983. U.S. labor market policies since the 1960s: A survey of programs and their effectiveness. Discussion paper 730–83, Institute for Research on Poverty, University of Wisconsin–Madison.

Gottschalk, Peter, and Sheldon Danziger. 1984. Macroeconomic conditions, income transfers and the trend in poverty. In *The social contract revisited*, ed. D. Lee Bawden. Washington, D.C.: Urban Institute Press.

———— 1985. A framework for evaluating the effects of economic growth and transfers on poverty. *American Economic Review* 75:153–161.

Graham, G. G. 1985. Searching for hunger in America. *Public Interest* 78 (Winter):3–17.

Gramlich, Edward M. 1974. The distributional effects of higher unemployment. *Brookings Papers on Economic Activity* 2:293–336.

Gramlich, Edward M., and Deborah S. Laren. 1984a. How widespread are income losses in a recession? In *The social contract revisited*, ed. D. Lee Bawden. Washington, D.C.: Urban Institute Press.

———— 1984b. Migration and income redistribution responsibilities. *Journal of Human Resources* 19:489–511.

Granger, Lester. 1941. The President, the Negro, and the defense. *Opportunity* 19 (July):204–207, 220–221.

Groeneveld, L. P., N. B. Tuma, and M. T. Hannan. 1980. The effects of negative income tax programs on marital dissolution. *Journal of Human Resources* 15:654–674.

Groeneveld, Lyle P., Michael T. Hannan, and Nancy B. Tuma. 1983. Marital stability. Sime/Dime Final Report, pt. V. In *Design and results: Final report of the Seattle-Denver income maintenance experiment*, vol. 1. Menlo Park, Calif.: SRI International.

Grønbjerg, Kirsten. 1977. *Mass society and the extension of welfare: 1960–1970*. Chicago: University of Chicago Press.

Gueron, Judith M. 1984. *Lessons from a job guarantee: The Youth Incentive Entitlement Pilot Projects*. New York: Manpower Demonstration Research Corporation.

Gutman, Herbert G. 1976. *The black family in slavery and freedom, 1750–1925*. New York: Pantheon.

Hadley, Jack. 1982. *More medical care, better health?* Washington, D.C.: Urban Institute Press.

Hagan, Jan L. 1983. Justice for the welfare recipient: Another look at welfare fair hearings. *Social Service Review* 57:177–195.

Hagemann, Robert P. 1982. The variability of inflation rates across household types. *Journal of Money, Credit and Banking* 14:494–510.

Hahn, A., and R. Lerman. 1984. What works in youth employment policy? How to help young workers from poor families. Center for Human Resources, Brandeis University. Mimeo.

Halpern, Janice, and Jerry Hausman. 1984. Choice under uncertainty: A model of applications for the social security disability insurance program. Discussion Papers in Economics, Brookings Institution, Washington, D.C.

Hamermesh, Daniel S. 1977. *Jobless pay and the economy*. Baltimore: Johns Hopkins University Press.

———— 1983. Inflation and labor-market adjustment. Working paper 1153, National Bureau of Economic Research, Cambridge, Mass.

Hamilton, Dona Cooper. 1984. The National Urban League and New Deal programs. *Social Service Review* 58:229–243.

Hammer, Ronald B., and Joseph M. Hartley. 1978. Procedural due process and the welfare recipient: A statistical study of AFDC fair hearings in Wisconsin. *Wisconsin Law Review* 1:145–251.

Handler, Joel F. 1972. *Reforming the poor: Welfare policy, federalism, and morality.* New York: Basic Books.

———— 1978. *Social movements and the legal system: A theory of law reform and legal change.* New York: Academic Press.

———— 1979. *Protecting the social service client: Legal and structural controls on official discretion.* New York: Academic Press.

———— 1983. Discretion in social welfare: The uneasy position in the rule of law. *Yale Law Journal* 92:1270–1286.

———— Forthcoming. *The conditions of discretion: Autonomy, community, bureaucracy.* New York: Russell Sage Foundation.

Handler, Joel F., and E. J. Hollingsworth. 1971. *The "deserving poor": A study of welfare administration.* Chicago: Markham.

Handler, Joel F., and Michael Sosin. 1983. *Last resorts: Emergency assistance and special needs programs in public welfare.* New York: Academic Press.

Harrington, Michael. 1962. *The other America: Poverty in the United States.* New York: Macmillan.

———— 1984. *The new American poverty.* New York: Harper and Row.

Haveman, Robert H., ed. 1977. *A decade of federal antipoverty programs: Achievements, failures, and lessons.* New York: Academic Press.

Haveman, Robert H. 1984. How much have the Reagan administration's tax and spending policies increased work effort? In *The legacy of Reaganomics,* ed. Charles R. Hulten and Isabel Sawhill. Washington, D.C.: Urban Institute Press.

———— 1985. Antipoverty policy and the nonpoor: An economic framework and some estimates. Institute for Research on Poverty, University of Wisconsin–Madison.

Haveman, Robert, and Barbara Wolfe. 1984. The decline in male labor force participation. *Journal of Political Economy* 92:532–542.

Haveman, Robert H., Barbara Wolfe, and Jennifer Warlick. 1984. Disability transfers, early retirement, and retrenchment. In *Retirement and economic behavior,* ed. H. Aaron and G. Burtless. Washington, D.C.: Brookings Institution.

Hawkins, Augustus. 1975. Letter to the editor. *New York Times,* October 10, p. 36.

Haynes, George E. 1935. Lily white social security. *Crisis* (March):85–86.

Heller, Walter. 1966. *New dimensions in political economy.* Cambridge, Mass.: Harvard University Press.

Hibbs, Douglas A. 1976. Economic interest and the politics of macroeconomic policy. Department of Economics, Massachusetts Institute of Technology.

Hill, Martha S. 1981. Some dynamic aspects of poverty. In *Five thousand American families: Patterns of economic progress,* vol. 9, ed. M. S. Hill, D. H. Hill, and

J. N. Morgan. Ann Arbor: Institute for Social Research, University of Michigan.

―――― 1984. PSID analysis of matched pairs of ex-spouses: The relation of economic resources and new family obligations to child support payments. Institute for Social Research, University of Michigan, Ann Arbor.

Hill, T. Arnold. 1935. A statement of opinion on H.R. 2828. National Urban League Library, New York. February.

Hirsch, Barry T. 1980. Poverty and economic growth: Has trickle-down petered out? *Economic Inquiry* 18:151–158.

Hochschild, Jennifer. 1981. *What's fair?* Cambridge, Mass.: Harvard University Press.

Hoepfner, Ralph, Henry Zagorski, and Jean Wellisch. 1977. *Report No. 1: The sample for the sustaining effects study and projections of its characteristics to the national population.* Santa Monica, Calif.: System Development Corporation.

Hoffman, S., and J. Holmes. 1976. Husbands, wives, and divorce. In *Five thousand American families: Patterns of economic progress,* vol. 4, ed. J. N. Morgan. Ann Arbor: Institute for Social Research, University of Michigan.

Hogan, D. P. 1981. *Transitions and social change: The early lives of American men.* New York: Academic Press.

―――― 1983. Demographic trends in human fertility and parenting across the lifespan. Paper prepared for the Social Science Research Council, conference on Bio-Social Life-Span Approaches to Parental and Offspring Development, Elkridge, Md.

―――― 1984. Structural and normative factors in single parenthood among black adolescents. Paper presented at the annual meetings of the American Sociological Association, San Antonio, Texas.

Hogan, D. P., and E. M. Kitagawa. 1985. The impact of social status, family structure, and neighborhood on the fertility of black adolescents. *American Journal of Sociology* 90:825–855.

Holahan, J. 1984. The 1981 Omnibus Budget Reconciliation Act and Medicaid spending. Working paper (revised), Urban Institute, Washington, D.C.

Hollister, Robinson, Peter Kemper, and Rebecca Maynard. 1984. *The National Supported Work Demonstration.* Madison: University of Wisconsin Press.

Hollister, Robinson G., Jr., and John L. Palmer. 1972. The impact of inflation on the poor. In *Redistribution to the rich and the poor,* ed. K. E. Boulding and M. Pfaff. Belmont, Calif.: Wadsworth.

Honig, M. 1974. AFDC income, recipient rates, and family dissolution. *Journal of Human Resources* 9:303–322.

Howard, D. 1943. *The WPA and federal relief policy.* New York: Russell Sage Foundation.

Hurd, M. D., and J. B. Shoven. 1983. The distributional effects of social security. Working paper 1115, National Bureau of Economic Research, Cambridge, Mass.

Iglehart, J. K. 1983. Medicaid in transition. *New England Journal of Medicine* 309:868–872.

———— 1984. Cutting costs of health care for the poor in California: A two-year follow-up. *New England Journal of Medicine* 311:745–748.

———— 1985. Medical care of the poor—a growing problem. *New England Journal of Medicine* 313:59–63.

Isaac, Larry, and William J. Kelly. 1981. Racial insurgency, the state, and welfare expansion: Local and national level evidence from the postwar United States. *American Journal of Sociology* 86:1348–1386.

Jaffe, Natalie. 1978. A review of public opinion surveys, 1935–1976. In *Welfare: The elusive consensus,* ed. Lester Salamon. New York: Praeger.

Janowitz, Morris. 1976. *Social control of the welfare state.* New York: Elsevier.

Jencks, Christopher. 1984. The hidden prosperity of the 1970s. *Public Interest* 77 (Fall):37–61.

Jencks, Christopher, and Marsha Brown. 1975. The effects of desegregation on student achievement: Some new evidence from the equality of educational opportunity survey. *Sociology of Education* 48:126–140.

Jencks, Christopher, et al. 1972. *Inequality: A reassessment of the effect of family and schooling in America.* New York: Basic Books.

———— 1979. *Who gets ahead? The determinants of economic success in America.* New York: Basic Books.

Jennings, Edward T. 1983. Racial insurgency, the state, and welfare expansion: A critical comment and reanalysis. *American Journal of Sociology* 88:1220–1236.

Johnson, Earl. 1974. *Justice and reform.* New York: Russell Sage Foundation.

Johnson, George E. 1983. Unionism in a macroeconomic context: An exploratory analysis. Department of Economics, University of Michigan. Mimeo.

Johnson, G., and J. Tomola. 1977. The fiscal substitution effect of alternative approaches to public service employment. *Journal of Human Resources* 12:3–26.

Johnson, Lyndon. 1964. Letter of transmittal. In *Economic report of the President, 1964.* Washington, D.C.: GPO.

Johnson, Reginald. 1945. In-migration and the Negro worker. *Opportunity* 23:102–103.

Jowell, Jeffrey L. 1975. *Law and bureaucracy: Administrative discretion and the limits of legal action.* Port Washington, N.Y.: Kennikat Press.

Keeley, M. C. 1980. The effects of negative income tax programs on fertility. *Journal of Human Resources* 9:303–322.

Keene, Karlyn. 1984. Who's the fairest of them all? *Public Opinion* 7:47–51.

Kellogg, Charles Flint. 1967. *A history of the National Association for the Advancement of Colored People.* Baltimore: Johns Hopkins University Press.

Kemper, P., D. Long, and C. Thornton. 1981. *The supported work evaluation: Final benefit-cost analysis.* Final Report, vol. 5. New York: Manpower Demonstration Research Corporation.

Kesselman, Jonathan. 1978. Work relief programs in the Great Depression. In *Creating Jobs,* ed. John Palmer. Washington, D.C.: Brookings Institution.

Kiefer, N. 1978. Federally subsidized occupation training and the employment and earnings of male trainees. *Journal of Econometrics* 8:111–125.

———— 1979. The economic benefits from four government training programs. In

Research in labor economics: Evaluating manpower training programs, ed. F. Bloch. Greenwich, Conn.: JAI Press.

Killingsworth, M. R. 1984. *Labor supply.* New York: Cambridge University Press.

Kingdon, John. 1984. *Agendas, alternatives, and public policies.* Boston: Little, Brown.

Kinzer, D. M. 1983. Massachusetts and California—two kinds of hospital cost control. *New England Journal of Medicine* 308:838–841.

Kirby, John B. 1980. *Black Americans and the Roosevelt era: Liberalism and race.* Knoxville: University of Tennessee Press.

Kirkendall, Richard. 1985. The New Deal and American politics. In *Fifty years later: The New Deal evaluated,* ed. Harvard Sitkoff. Philadelphia: Temple University Press.

Klein, M., K. Roghmann, and K. Woodward. 1973. The impact of the Rochester Neighborhood Health Center on hospitalization of children, 1968 to 1980. *Pediatrics* 51:833–839.

Kleinman, J., M. Gold, and D. Makuc. 1981. Use of ambulatory care by the poor: Another look at equity. *Medical Care* 19:1011–1029.

Kluger, Richard. 1976. *Simple justice: The history of Brown v. Board of Education and black America's struggle for equality.* New York: Knopf.

Knox, R. A. 1984. Some local hospitals "dump" the uninsured. *Boston Globe,* February 6.

Koch, Edward. 1980. The mandate millstone. *Public Interest* 61 (Fall):42–57.

Koetting, M., and L. Olinger. 1984. A national perspective on contracting in California. Paper presented at the annual meeting of the American Public Health Association.

Komarovsky, M. 1940. *The unemployed man and his family.* New York: Octagon Books.

Kotelchuck, H., J. B. Schwartz, M. K. Anderka, and K. S. Finison. 1984. WIC participation and pregnancy outcomes: Massachusetts statewide evaluation project. *American Journal of Public Health* 74:1086–1092.

Kotz, Nick, and Mary L. Kotz. 1977. *A passion for equality: George Wiley and the movement.* New York: W. W. Norton.

Ladd, Everett Carll. 1984. Public attitudes toward policy governance: Searching for the sources and meaning of the "Reagan Revolution." In *The Reagan presidency and the governing of America,* ed. Lester M. Salamon and Michael S. Lund. Washington, D.C.: Urban Institute Press.

Lalonde, R. 1984. Evaluating the econometric evaluations of training programs with experimental data. Working paper 183, Industrial Relations Section, Princeton University.

Lammermeier, P. J. 1973. The urban black family of the nineteenth century: A study of black family structure in the Ohio Valley, 1850–1880. *Journal of Marriage and the Family* 35:440–456.

Lampman, Robert J. 1974. What does it do for the poor? A new test for national policy. In *The Great Society,* ed. Eli Ginzberg and Robert S. Solow. New York: Basic Books.

———— 1984. *Social welfare spending: Accounting for changes from 1950 to 1978.* New York: Academic Press.

Lander, Byron. 1971. Group theory and individuals: The origin of poverty as a political issue in 1964. *Western Political Quarterly* 24:514–526.

Lazar, Irving. 1981. Early intervention is effective. *Educational Leadership* 38:303–305.

Lazar, Irving, and Richard Darlington. 1978. *Lasting effects after preschool: A report of the Consortium for Longitudinal Studies.* Washington, D.C.: U.S. Department of Health, Education, and Welfare, DHEW Publication (OHDS) 79–30178.

Leiby, James. 1978. *A history of social welfare and social work in the United States.* New York: Columbia University Press.

Lekachman, Robert. 1976. *Economists at bay.* New York: McGraw Hill.

Leman, Christopher K. 1985. The forgotten fundamental: Successes and excesses of direct government. In *The tools of public policy,* ed. Michael S. Lund and Lester M. Salamon. Washington, D.C.: Urban Institute Press.

Leonard, Jonathan S. 1979. The social security disability program and labor force participation. Working paper 392, National Bureau of Economic Research, Cambridge, Mass.

Lerman, Robert I. 1984. Do welfare programs affect schooling and work patterns of young black men? Department of Economics, Brandeis University.

Leuchtenburg, William E. 1963. *Franklin D. Roosevelt and the New Deal.* New York: Harper and Row, Harper Torchbooks.

Levin, H. M. 1977. A decade of developments in improving education and training for low-income populations. In *A decade of federal antipoverty programs: Achievements, failures, and lessons,* ed. Robert H. Haveman. New York: Academic Press.

Levy, F. 1982. The structure of CETA earnings gains. Research report, Urban Institute, Washington, D.C.

Lewis, Anthony, 1964. *Portrait of a decade: The second American revolution.* New York: Random House.

Light, Paul. 1982. *The president's agenda.* Baltimore: Johns Hopkins University Press.

Lipset, Seymour Martin, and William Schneider. 1981. Lower taxes and more welfare. *Journal of Contemporary Studies* 4:35–45.

Long, D., C. Mallar, and C. Thornton. 1981. Evaluating the benefits and costs of Jobs Corps. *Journal of Policy Analysis and Management* 1:55–76.

Louis Harris and Associates, Inc. 1982. Access to health care services in the United States: 1982. Survey conducted for the Robert Wood Johnson Foundation, Princeton.

Luft, H. S. 1981. *Health maintenance organizations: Dimensions of performance.* New York: John Wiley.

Lurie, N., N. B. Ward, M. F. Shapiro, and R. H. Brook. 1984. Termination from Medi-Cal—does it affect health? *New England Journal of Medicine* 311:480–484.

Lynn, Lawrence, Jr. 1977. A decade of policy developments in the income maintenance system. In *A decade of federal antipoverty programs: Achievements, failures, and lessons,* ed. Robert H. Haveman. New York: Academic Press.

Mallar, C., et al. 1980. The lasting impact of Job Corps participation. Final report, Mathematica Policy Research, Princeton.

Manning, W. G., et al. 1984. A controlled trial of the effect of a prepaid group practice on use of services. *New England Journal of Medicine* 310:1505–1510.

Manpower Demonstration Research Corporation. 1984. *Preliminary findings from the San Diego Job Search and Work Experience Demonstration.* New York.

Mare, R. D., and C. Winship. 1980. Changes in the relative labor force status of black and white youths: A review of the literature. Report prepared for the National Commission for Employment Policy. Special report 26, Institute for Research on Poverty, University of Wisconsin–Madison.

Mashaw, Jerry L. 1983. *Bureaucratic justice.* New Haven: Yale University Press.

Masters, S., and R. Maynard. 1981. *The impact of Supported Work on long-term recipients of AFDC benefits.* Final report, vol. 3. New York: Manpower Demonstration Research Corporation.

Matusow, Allen J. 1984. *The unravelling of America: A history of liberalism in the 1960s.* New York: Harper and Row.

McCarthy, James D., and Meyer N. Zald. 1977. Resources mobilization and social movements: A partial theory. *American Journal of Sociology* 82:1212–1241.

McClosky, Herbert, and John Zaller. 1984. *The American ethos.* Cambridge, Mass.: Harvard University Press.

McCormick, M. C. 1985. The contribution of low birthweight to infant mortality and childhood morbidity. *The New England Journal of Medicine* 312:82–90.

McDonald, Thomas P., and Irving Piliavin. 1984. Failure to participate in AFDC: Some correlates and possible influences. *Social Work Research Abstracts* 20:17–22.

Mead, Lawrence M. 1985. *Beyond entitlement: The social obligations of citizenship.* New York: Free Press.

Metcalf, Charles E. 1969. The size distribution of personal income during the business cycle. *American Economic Review* 59:657–668.

Meyer, J. W., and B. Rowan. 1977. Institutionalized organizations: Formal structure as myth and ceremony. *American Journal of Sociology* 13:446–463.

Michael, Robert T. 1979. Variation across households in the rate of inflation. *Journal of Money, Credit and Banking* 11:32–46.

Michel, Richard C., and Patricia Willis. 1980. Participation rates in the Aid to Families with Dependent Children program. Working paper, Urban Institute, Washington, D.C.

Miller, Loren. 1966. *The petitioners: The story of the Supreme Court of the United States and the Negro.* Cleveland: World Publishing.

Mills, George B. 1981. Quality control in welfare administration: An analysis of payment error in Aid to Families with Dependent Children. Ph.D. diss., John F. Kennedy School of Government, Harvard University.

Mills, Gregory, and John Palmer, eds. 1984. *Federal budget policy in the 1980s.* Washington, D.C.: Urban Institute Press.

Minarik, Joseph J. 1979. The size distribution of income during inflation. *Review of Income and Wealth* 25:377–392.

———— 1980. Inflation in the necessities? *Brookings Bulletin* (Spring):8–10.

Minarik, J. J., and R. S. Goldfarb. 1976. AFDC income, recipient rates, and family dissolution: A comment. *Journal of Human Resources* 11:243–250.

Mirer, Thad W. 1973a. The distributional impact of the 1970 recession. *Review of Economics and Statistics* 55:214–224.

———— 1973b. The effects of macroeconomic fluctuations on the distribution of income. *Review of Income and Wealth* 21:385–405.

———— 1975. The distributive impact on purchasing power of inflation during price controls. *Quarterly Review of Economics and Business* 15:93–96.

Moe, Perry M. 1980. *The organization of interests: Incentives and the internal dynamics of political interest groups.* Chicago: University of Chicago Press.

Moffitt, Robert. 1983. An economic model of welfare stigma. *American Economic Review* 73:1023–1035.

Moffitt, R. A., and K. C. Kehrer. 1981. The effect of tax and transfer programs on labor supply: The evidence from the income maintenance experiments. In *Research in labor economics,* vol. 4, ed. R. Ehrenberg. Greenwich, Conn.: JAI Press.

Moloney, T. W. 1982. What's being done about Medicaid? Commonwealth Fund, New York.

Moon, Marilyn, and Isabel V. Sawhill. 1984. Family incomes: Gainers and losers. In *The Reagan record,* ed. John L. Palmer and I. V. Sawhill. Cambridge, Mass.: Ballinger.

Moore, Kristin A., and S. B. Caldwell. 1976. Out-of-wedlock pregnancy and child-bearing. Working paper, Urban Institute, Washington, D.C.

———— 1977. The effect of government policies on out-of-wedlock sex and pregnancy. *Family Planning Perspectives* 9:164–169.

Morris, Peter, and Martin Rein. 1973. *Dilemmas of social reform: Poverty and community action in the United States.* 2d ed. Chicago: Aldine.

Mosteller, Frederick, and Daniel P. Moynihan. 1972. *On equality of educational opportunity.* New York: Random House.

Moynihan, Daniel P. 1965. *The Negro family: The case for national action.* Washington, D.C.: U.S. Department of Labor, Office of Family Planning and Research.

———— 1969. *Maximum feasible misunderstanding: Community action in the War on Poverty.* New York: Free Press.

———— 1973. *The politics of a guaranteed annual income: The Nixon administration and the Family Assistance Plan.* New York: Random House.

———— Forthcoming. *Family and nation.* New York: Harcourt Brace Jovanovich.

Mueller, Eva. 1963. Public attitudes toward fiscal programs. *Quarterly Journal of Economics* 77:210–235.

Mullan, F. 1984. The National Health Service Corps and health personnel innovations: Beyond poorhouse medicine. In *Reforming medicine: The lessons of the last quarter century,* ed. V. W. Sidel and R. Sidel. New York: Pantheon.

Mullin, Stephen P., and Anita A. Summers. 1983. Is more better? The effectiveness of spending on compensatory education. *Phi Delta Kappan* 64:339–347.

Mundinger, M. O. 1985. Health service funding cuts and the declining health of the poor. *New England Journal of Medicine* 313:44–47.

Murnane, Richard. 1984. An economist's look at federal and state education policies. Economics Department, Harvard University.

Murray, Charles A. 1982. The two wars against poverty: Economic growth and the Great Society. *Public Interest* 69 (Fall):3–16.

―――― 1984. *Losing ground: American social policy, 1950–1980.* New York: Basic Books.

NAACP. 1933–1940. Annual reports.

―――― 1939. Conference resolutions. *Crisis* (September):294.

―――― 1945. Minutes of the Board of Directors' Meeting, December 10. NAACP Papers, Schomburg Library, New York.

Nathan, R. 1979. Monitoring the public service employment program: The second round. Report to the National Commission for Employment Policy, Washington, D. C.

Nathan, R.; R. Cook; V. Rawlins; and associates. 1981. *Public service employment: A field evaluation.* Washington, D.C.: Brookings Institution.

National Center for Education Statistics. U.S. Department of Education, Office of Research and Improvement. 1982. *The condition of education: A statistical report.* Washington, D.C.: NCES.

―――― 1983. *The condition of education: A statistical report.* Washington, D.C.: NCES.

―――― 1984. *The condition of education: A statistical report.* Washington, D.C.: NCES.

National Center for Health Statistics. U. S. Department of Health and Human Services. 1982a. Advance report of final natality statistics, 1980. In *Monthly vital statistics report.* Washington, D.C.: GPO.

―――― 1982b. *Vital statistics of the United States, 1978.* Vol. 3: *Marriage and divorce.* Washington, D.C.: GPO.

―――― 1984. *Vital statistics of the United States, 1979.* Vol. 1: *Natality.* Washington, D.C.: GPO.

National Committee for Full Employment, Newsletter. 1976. Focus on full employment. Washington, D.C.

National Institute of Education. 1977. *Compensatory education services.* Washington, D.C.

National Office of Vital Statistics. 1957. *Vital statistics of the United States.* Vol. 1. Washington, D.C.: U.S. Department of Health, Education and Welfare.

National Opinion Research Center. 1984. General social survey, 1972–1984: Cumulative codebook. Chicago. Mimeo.

National Urban League. 1934. A statement of opinion on Senate Bill S. 2926 (April 6). National Urban League, New York.

―――― 1935. Survey of the month. *Opportunity* 13 (March):93.

―――― 1938. The editor says. *Opportunity* 16 (November):322.

―――― 1976. *The state of black America.* New York: National Urban League.

National Urban League Papers. 1933a. New York Urban League Statistical Report, ser. IV, box 32. Manuscript Division, Library of Congress, Washington, D.C.

―――― 1933b. NUL Annual Report, ser. XIII, box 1. Minutes of Eastern Regional Conference, September 23, ser. IV, box 21. Manuscript Division, Library of Congress, Washington, D.C.

———— 1933c. Letters to William Green from T. Arnold Hill, July 5 and 15, August 21 and 29; to Hill from Green, July 15 and August 25, ser. IV, box 1. Manuscript Division, Library of Congress, Washington, D.C.

———— 1938. Memo to Executive Secretaries from Eugene K. Jones, April 19, ser. XII, box 1. Manuscript Division, Library of Congress, Washington, D.C.

New York Times. 1983. Few on layoffs may be rehired; U.S. push in world market urged; Big corporations rely on automation to aid output in a recovery. May 16, p. 1.

Oberschall, Anthony. 1973. *Social conflict and social movements.* Englewood Cliffs, N.J.: Prentice-Hall.

O'Connell, M., and M. J. Moore. 1980. The legitimacy status of first births to U.S. women aged 15–24, 1939–1978. *Family Planning Perspectives* 12:16–25.

OECD (Organisation for Economic Co-operation and Development). 1983. *The growth of social expenditure: Recent trends and implications for the 1980s.* Paris: OECD, Directorate for Social Affairs, Manpower and Education.

———— 1984a. *Economic surveys, 1983–84: United States.* Paris.

———— 1984b. Social expenditure: Erosion or evolution? *OECD Observer,* 126:3–6.

Oellerich, Donald, and Irwin Garfinkel. 1983. Distributional impacts of existing and alternative child support systems. *Policy Studies Journal* 12:119–130.

Okun, A. M. 1983. Further thoughts on equality and efficiency. In *Selected essays of Arthur M. Okun,* ed. J. A. Pechman. Cambridge, Mass.: MIT Press.

Olson, Mancur. 1965. *The logic of collective action.* Cambridge, Mass.: Harvard University Press.

Omenn, G. S., and D. A. Conrad. 1984. Implications of DRGs for clinicians. *New England Journal of Medicine* 311:1314–1317.

O'Neill, June A., and Margaret C. Simms. 1982. Education. In *The Reagan experiment,* ed. John L. Palmer and Isabel V. Sawhill. Washington, D.C.: Urban Institute Press.

Paglin, Morton. 1980. *Poverty and transfers in-kind.* Stanford, Calif.: Hoover Institution.

Palmer, John L., and Isabel V. Sawhill, eds. 1984. *The Reagan record.* Cambridge, Mass.: Ballinger.

Parsons, Donald O. 1980. The decline of male labor force participation. *Journal of Political Economy* 88:117–134.

Patterson, James. 1967. *Congressional conservatism and the New Deal.* Lexington, Mass.: Lexington Books.

———— 1981. *America's struggle against poverty, 1900–1980.* Cambridge, Mass.: Harvard University Press.

Pechman, Joseph A. 1983. *Federal tax policy.* 4th ed. Washington, D.C.: Brookings Institution.

Pechman, Joseph A., ed. 1982. *Setting national priorities: the 1983 budget.* Washington, D.C.: Brookings Institution.

Pechman, Joseph A., and Mark J. Mazur. 1984. The rich, the poor, and the taxes they pay: An update. *Public Interest* 77 (Fall):28–36.

Perl, Lewis J., and Loren M. Solnick. 1971. A note on "trickling down." *Quarterly Journal of Economics* 85:171–178.

Peterson, Paul E., and J. David Greenstone. 1977. Racial change and citizen participation: The mobilization of low-income communities through community action. In *A decade of federal antipoverty programs: Achievements, failures, and lessons,* ed. Robert H. Haveman. New York: Academic Press.

Piliavin, Irving, and Alan E. Gross. 1977. The effects of separation of services and income maintenance on AFDC recipients. *Social Service Review* 51:389–406.

Piliavin, Irving, Stanley Masters, and Thomas Corbett. 1979. Administration and organizational influences on AFDC case decision errors: An empirical analysis. Discussion paper 542–79, Institute for Research on Poverty, University of Wisconsin–Madison.

Pittenger, John C., and Peter Kuriloff. 1982. Educating the handicapped: Reforming a radical law. *Public Interest* 66 (Winter):72–96.

Piven, Frances F., and Richard A. Cloward. 1971. *Regulating the poor: The functions of public welfare.* New York: Vintage.

————— 1977. *Poor people's movements: Why they succeed, how they fail.* New York: Pantheon.

————— 1982. *The new class war: Reagan's attack on the welfare state and its consequences.* New York: Pantheon.

Placek, P. J., and G. E. Hendershot. 1974. Public welfare and family planning: An empirical study of the "brood sow" myth. *Social Problems* 21:660–673.

Pleck, E. H. 1972. The two-parent household: Black family structure in late nineteenth-century Boston. *Journal of Social History* 6:3–31.

Plotnick, Robert. 1979. Social welfare expenditures: How much help for the poor? *Policy Analysis* 5:261–289.

————— 1984. The redistributive impact of cash transfers. *Public Finance Quarterly* 12:27–50.

Plotnick, Robert, and Felicity Skidmore. 1975. *Progress against poverty: A review of the 1964–1974 decade.* New York: Academic Press.

Polenberg, Richard. 1975. The decline of the New Deal, 1937–1940. In *The New Deal: The national level,* ed. John Braeman, Robert Bremner, and David Brody. Columbus: Ohio State University Press.

Polgar, S., and V. Hiday. 1974. The effect of an additional birth on low-income urban families. *Population Studies* 28:463–471.

Presser, H. B., and L. S. Salsberg. 1975. Public assistance and early family formation: Is there a pronatalist effect? *Social Problems* 23:226–241.

Price, David A. 1981. *Study of AFDC cases discontinued by the caseloads monthly reporting system.* Princeton: Mathematica Policy Research.

Rainwater, Lee. 1966. Crucible of identity: The Negro lower-class family. *Daedalus* 95:172–216.

Rauch, J. 1984. Women and children's food program is "off limits" to Reagan budget cutbacks. *National Journal* 16:2197–2199.

Reagan, Ronald. 1982. Remarks before the National Black Republican Council, September 14, 1982. *Weekly compilation of presidential documents* 18:1152–1157. Washington, D.C.: GPO.

Reed, Gustave. 1934. The Negro worker and the NRA. *Crisis* (September):262–263, 270.

Reich, Charles A. 1964. The new property. *Yale Law Journal* 73 (5):732–787.

Research Triangle Institute. 1983. Final report: Evaluation of the 1981 AFDC amendments. Report prepared for the Office of Family Assistance, Social Security Administration, U.S. Department of Health and Human Services. Research Triangle Park, N.C. Mimeo.

Rivlin, Alice. 1984. Helping the poor. In *Economic choices: 1984,* ed. Alice Rivlin. Washington, D.C.: Brookings Institution.

Robertson, David Brian. 1984. The business-centered strategy of American labor market policy. Paper presented to the annual meeting of the American Political Science Association, Washington, D.C. Mimeo.

Rogers, D. E., R. J. Blendon, and T. W. Moloney. 1982. Who needs Medicaid? *New England Journal of Medicine* 307:13–18.

Romasco, Albert. 1983. *The politics of recovery: Roosevelt's New Deal.* New York: Oxford University Press.

Rosenman, Samuel, ed. 1938. *The public papers and addresses of Franklin D. Roosevelt.* Vol. 5: *The people approve, 1936.* New York: Random House.

Ross, H. L., and I. Sawhill 1975. *Time of transition: The growth of families headed by women.* Washington, D.C.: Urban Institute Press.

Rowland, D., and C. Gaus. 1983. Medicaid eligibility and benefits: Current policies and alternatives. In *New approaches to the Medicaid crisis,* ed. R. Blendon and T. Moloney. New York: Frost and Sullivan.

Rumberger, Russell W. 1983. Dropping out of high school: The influence of race, sex, and family background. *American Educational Research Journal* 20:199–220.

Rush, D. 1984. Some comments on the Massachusetts WIC evaluation. *American Journal of Public Health* 74:1145–1146.

Russell, L. B. 1983. Medical care. In *Setting national priorities: The 1984 budget,* ed. J. A. Pechman. Washington, D.C.: Brookings Institution.

Saunders, P. 1984. Evidence on income redistribution by governments. Paper no. 11, OECD Economics and Statistics Department, Paris.

Savage, David. 1984. Scrutinize students' test scores, and they might not look so rosy. *American School Board Journal* 171:21–24.

Sawhill, I., G. E. Peabody, C. A. Jones, and S. B. Caldwell. 1975. *Income transfers and family structure.* Washington, D.C.: Urban Institute Press.

Schiltz, Michael. 1970. *Public attitudes toward social security, 1935–1965.* Washington, D.C.: GPO.

Schott, Richard, and Dagmar Hamilton. 1983. *People, positions, and power.* Chicago: University of Chicago Press.

Schram, Sanford F., and J. Patrick Turbott. 1983a. Civil disorder and the welfare explosion. *American Sociological Review* 48:408–414.

————— 1983b. The welfare explosion: Mass society versus social control. *Social Service Review* 57:615–625.

Sears, David, and Jack Citrin. 1982. *Tax revolt.* Cambridge, Mass.: Harvard University Press.

Shifflett, C. A. 1975. The household composition of rural black families: Louisa County, Virginia, 1880. *Journal of Interdisciplinary History* 6:235–260.

Simon, William H. 1983. Legality, bureaucracy, and class in the welfare system. *Yale Law Journal* 92:1198–1269.

Skerry, Peter. 1983. The charmed life of Head Start. *Public Interest* 73 (Fall):18–39.

Smeeding, Timothy. 1975. Measuring the economic welfare of low income households and the anti-poverty effectiveness of cash and non-cash transfer programs. Ph.D diss., University of Wisconsin–Madison.

———. 1982. The antipoverty effects of in-kind transfers. *Policy Studies Journal* 10:499–521.

———. 1984. Is the safety net still intact? In *The social contract revisited,* ed. D. Lee Bawden. Washington, D.C.: Urban Institute Press.

Smith, Tom. 1982. General liberalism and social change in post–World War II America. *Social Indicators Research* 10:1–28.

Sosin, Michael. 1979. Social welfare and organizational society. *Social Service Review* 55:392–405.

———. 1982. Emergency assistance and special needs programs in the AFDC system. *Social Service Review* 58:196–210.

———. 1984. Legal rights and welfare change: 1960–1980. Paper presented at a conference of the Institute for Research on Poverty, University of Wisconsin–Madison (a longer version of the chapter in this volume).

———. Forthcoming. *Private benefits: Material assistance in private agencies.* Orlando, Fla.: Academic Press.

SRI International. 1983. *Final report of the Seattle-Denver Income Maintenance Experiment.* Vol. 1. Washington, D.C.: GPO.

Starr, Paul. 1982. *The social transformation of American medicine.* New York: Basic Books.

Steiner, Gilbert. 1971. *The state of welfare.* Washington, D.C.: Brookings Institution.

Stevens, Robert, and Rosemary Stevens. 1974. *Welfare medicine in America: A case study of Medicaid.* New York: Free Press.

Stockman, David. 1983. Statement before the U.S. House of Representatives, Committee on Ways and Means, Subcommittees on Oversight, and on Public Assistance and Unemployment, November 3. Mimeo.

———. 1984. Statement. In Committee on Ways and Means, U.S. House of Representatives, *Poverty rate increase hearings.* Serial 98–55. Washington, D.C.: GPO.

Sullivan, S., and R. Gibson, eds. 1983. *Restructuring Medicaid: A survey of state and local initiatives.* Washington, D.C.: American Enterprise Institute, Center for Health Policy Research.

Sundquist, James L. 1968. *Politics and policy: The Eisenhower, Kennedy, and Johnson years.* Washington, D.C.: Brookings Institution.

Survey Research Center. 1984. *User guide to the Panel Study of Income Dynamics.* Ann Arbor: Institute for Social Research, University of Michigan.

Swank, Duane H. 1983. Between incrementalism and revolution: Group protest and the growth of the welfare state. *American Behavioral Scientist* 26:291–310.

Swartz, Katherine. 1984. The changing face of the uninsured. Paper presented at the first annual meeting of the Association for Health Services Researchers, Washington, D.C.

Taggart, R. 1981. *A fisherman's guide: An assessment of training and remediation strategies.* Kalamazoo, Mich.: W. E. Upjohn Institute for Employment Research.

Thornton, James R., Richard J. Agnello, and Charles R. Link. 1978. Poverty and economic growth: Trickle down peters out. *Economic Inquiry* 16:385–394.

———— 1980. Poverty and economic growth: Trickle down has petered out. *Economic Inquiry* 18:159–163.

Thurow, Lester C. 1970. Analyzing the American income distribution. *American Economic Review* 60:261–269.

———— 1972. Education and economic equality. *Public Interest* 28 (Summer):66–81.

Touche, Ross & Co. 1977. *Evaluation of AFDC-QC corrective action: Final report.* Washington, D.C.: U.S. Department of Health, Education and Welfare, Social Security Administration.

Trattner, Walter. 1984. *From poor law to welfare state.* 3d ed. New York: Free Press.

Tretel, Ralph. 1976. Appeal by denied disability claimants. Staff paper 23, Social Security Administration, Washington, D.C.

———— 1979. Disability claimants who contest denials and win reversals through hearings. Staff paper 34, Social Security Administration, Washington, D.C.

Turner, Ralph. 1981. Collective behavior and resource mobilization as approaches to social movements: Issues and continuities. *Research in Social Movements, Conflict and Change* 4:1–24.

U.S. Bureau of the Census. 1943. *Census of the population.* Washington, D.C.: GPO.

———— 1948. *Characteristics of single, married, widowed, and divorced persons in 1947.* Current Population Reports, ser. P-20, no. 10. Washington, D.C.: GPO.

———— 1950. *Census of the population.* Washington, D.C.: GPO.

———— 1960. *Marital status and family status: March 1960.* Current Population Reports, ser. P-20, no. 105. Washington, D.C.: GPO.

———— 1965a. *Marital status and family status: March 1965.* Current Population Reports, ser. P-20, no. 144. Washington, D.C.: GPO.

———— 1965b. *Household and family characteristics: March 1965.* Current Population Reports, ser. P-20, no. 153. Washington, D.C.: GPO.

———— 1965c. *Estimates of the population of the United States by age, color, and sex: July 1, 1960, to 1965.* Current Population Reports, ser. P-25, no. 321. Washington, D.C.: GPO.

———— 1966. *Negro population: March 1965.* Current Population Reports, ser. P-20, no. 155. Washington, D.C.: GPO.

———— 1969. *Poverty in the United States: 1959 to 1968.* Current Population Reports, ser. P-60, no. 68. Washington, D.C.: GPO.

———— 1971a. *Marital status and family status: March 1970.* Current Population Reports, ser. P-20, no. 212. Washington, D.C.: GPO.

———— 1971b. *Household and family characteristics: March 1970.* Current Population Reports, ser. P-20, no. 218. Washington, D.C.: GPO.

———— 1972. *Household and family characteristics: March 1971.* Current Population Reports, ser. P-20, no. 233. Washington, D.C.: GPO.

———— 1973a. *Household and family characteristics: March 1972.* Current Population Reports, ser. P-20, no. 246. Washington, D.C.: GPO.

———— 1973b. *Household and family characteristics: March 1973.* Current Population Reports, ser. P-20, no. 258. Washington, D.C.: GPO.

———— 1974. *Persons of Spanish origin in the United States: March 1973.* Current Population Reports, ser. P-20, no. 259. Washington, D.C.: GPO.

———— 1975a. *Household and family characteristics: March 1974.* Current Population Reports, ser. P-20, no. 276. Washington, D.C.: GPO.

———— 1975b. *Persons of Spanish origin in the United States: March 1974.* Current Population Reports, ser. P-20, no. 267. Washington, D.C.: GPO.

———— 1975c. *Marital status and living arrangements: March 1975.* Current Population Reports, ser. P-20, no. 287. Washington, D.C.: GPO.

———— 1975d. *Historical statistics of the United States.* Vol. 1. Washington, D.C.: GPO.

———— 1976a. *Persons of Spanish origin in the United States: March 1975.* Current Population Reports, ser. P-20, no. 290. Washington, D.C.: GPO.

———— 1976b. *Household and family characteristics: March 1975.* Current Population Reports, ser. P-20, no. 291. Washington, D.C.: GPO.

———— 1977a. *Marriage, divorce, widowhood, and remarriage by family characteristics: June 1975.* Current Population Reports, ser. P-20, no. 312. Washington, D.C.: GPO.

———— 1977b. *Household and family characteristics: March 1976.* Current Population Reports, ser. P-20, no. 311. Washington, D.C.: GPO.

———— 1978a. *Household and family characteristics: March 1977.* Current Population Reports, ser. P-20, no. 326. Washington, D.C.: GPO.

———— 1978b. *Estimates of the population of the United States by age, sex, and race: 1970 to 1977.* Current Population Reports, ser. P-20, no. 721. Washington, D.C.: GPO.

———— 1978c. *Statistical abstract of the United States: 1978.* 99th ed. Washington, D.C.: GPO.

———— 1979a. *Household and family characteristics: March 1978.* Current Population Reports, ser. P-20, no. 340. Washington, D.C.: GPO.

———— 1979b. *The social and economic status of the black population in the United States: An historical view, 1790–1978.* Current Population Reports, ser. P-23, no. 80. Washington, D.C.: GPO.

———— 1980. *Household and family characteristics: March 1979.* Current Population Reports, ser. P-20, no. 352. Washington, D.C.: GPO.

———— 1981a. *Marital status and living arrangements: March 1980.* Current Population Reports, ser. P-20, no. 365. Washington, D.C.: GPO.

———— 1981b. *Household and family characteristics: March 1980.* Current Population Reports, ser. P-20, no. 366. Washington, D.C.: GPO.

———— 1981c. *Characteristics of the population below the poverty level: 1979.* Current Population Reports, ser. P-60, no. 130. Washington, D.C.: GPO.

———— 1982a. *Alternative methods for valuing selected in-kind transfer benefits and measuring their effects on poverty.* Technical paper 50. Washington, D.C.: GPO.

———— 1982b. *Household and family characteristics: March 1981.* Current Population Reports, ser. P-20, no. 371. Washington, D.C.: GPO.

———— 1982c. *Trends in the child care arrangements of working mothers.* Current Population Reports, ser. P-23, no. 117. Washington, D.C.: GPO.

———— 1982d. *Characteristics of households and persons receiving selected noncash benefits: 1980 (with comparable data for 1979).* Current Population Reports, ser. P-60, no. 131. Washington, D.C.: GPO.

———— 1982e. *Preliminary estimates of the population by age, sex, and race: 1970–1981.* Current Population Reports, ser. P-25, no. 917. Washington, D.C.: GPO.

———— 1983a. *Fertility of American women: June 1981.* Current Population Reports, ser. P-20, no. 378. Washington, D.C.: GPO.

———— 1983b. *Household and family characteristics: March 1982.* Current Population Reports, ser. P-20, no. 381. Washington, D.C.: GPO.

———— 1983c. *Estimates of the population of the United States by age, sex, and race: 1980 to 1982.* Current Population Reports, ser. P-25, no. 929. Washington, D.C.: GPO.

———— 1983d. *Statistical abstract of the United States: 1984.* 104th ed. Washington, D.C.: GPO.

———— 1984a. *Census of the population, 1980.* Washington, D.C.: GPO.

———— 1984b. *Household and family characteristics: March 1983.* Current Population Reports, ser. P-20, no. 388. Washington, D.C.: GPO.

———— 1984c. *Characteristics of the population below the poverty level: 1982.* Current Population Reports, ser. P-60, no. 144. Washington, D.C.: GPO.

———— 1984d. *Money income and poverty status of families and persons in the U.S.: 1983.* Current Population Reports, ser. P-60, no. 145. Washington, D.C.: GPO.

———— 1984e. *Estimates of poverty including the value of noncash benefits: 1979 to 1982.* Technical paper 51. Washington, D.C.: GPO.

———— 1986a. *Money income and poverty status of families and persons in the U.S.: 1985.* Current Population Reports, ser. P-60, no. 154. Washington, D.C.: GPO.

———— 1986b. *Estimates of poverty including the value of noncash benefits: 1985.* Technical paper 56. Washington, D.C.: GPO.

U.S. Bureau of Labor Statistics. 1980. *Handbook of labor statistics.* Washington, D.C.: GPO.

———— 1984a. *Employment and earnings* 31, no. 1, January. Washington, D.C.: U.S. Department of Labor.

———— 1984b. *Handbook of labor statistics.* Washington, D.C.: GPO.

U.S. Congressional Budget Office. 1979. *Profile of health-care coverage: The haves and the have-nots.* Washington, D.C.: GPO.

U.S. Congressional Budget Office and National Commission for Employment Policy. 1982. *CETA training programs—do they work for adults?* Washington, D.C.: GPO.

U.S. Council of Economic Advisers. 1964. *Economic report of the President, 1964.* Washington, D.C.: GPO.

———— 1984. *Economic report of the President, 1984.* Washington, D.C.: GPO.

U.S. Department of Commerce. Bureau of Economic Analysis. 1950–1984 (annually). *Survey of current business.* Washington, D.C.: GPO.

U.S. Department of Health and Human Services. 1983. *Final report of the Seattle-Denver Income Maintenance Experiment.* Washington, D.C.: GPO.

U.S. Department of Health and Human Services. Public Health Service. 1983. *Health: United States and prevention profile, 1983.* Hyattsville, Md.: Public Health Service.

U.S. Department of Health and Human Services. Social Security Administration. 1983. *Social security bulletin, annual statistical supplement, 1982.* Washington, D.C.: Social Security Administration.

_____ 1984. *Social security bulletin, annual statistical supplement, 1983.* Washington, D.C.: Social Security Administration.

U.S. Department of Health, Education and Welfare. 1971. *Expenditures for assistance and administration costs in public assistance and Medicaid, by source of funds: Fiscal years 1936 to present.* Washington, D.C.

_____ 1976. *The measure of poverty: A report to Congress.* Washington, D.C.: GPO.

U.S. Department of Labor. 1979. *Unemployment insurance statistics.* Washington, D.C.: GPO.

_____ 1980a. *Characteristics of major collective bargaining agreements.* BLS Bulletin 2095. Washington, D.C.: GPO.

_____ 1980b. *Earnings and other characteristics of organized workers.* BLS Bulletin 2105. Washington, D.C.: GPO.

U.S. House of Representatives. Committee on Ways and Means. 1984. *Background material and data on programs within the jurisdiction of the Committee on Ways and Means.* Serial 98–22. Washington, D.C.: GPO.

_____ Subcommittee on Oversight and Subcommittee on Public Assistance and Unemployment Compensation. 1983. *Background material on poverty.* Washington, D.C.: GPO.

U.S. Office of Management and Budget. 1984. *Major themes and additional budget details, FY 1985.* Washington, D.C.: GPO.

U.S. President's Commission for the Study of Ethical Problems in Medicine and Biomedical and Behavioral Research. 1983. *Securing access to health care.* Vol. 1: *Report of the commission.* Washington, D.C.: GPO.

Van Horn, Carl, and Donald Baumer. 1984. Policy learning and reauthorization politics: A decade of employment and training programs. Paper presented to the convention of the American Political Science Association. Mimeo.

Venti, Stephen, and David Wise. 1984. The impact of welfare benefits on the employment and schooling of youth. Report prepared for the U.S. Department of Health and Human Services under grant no. 92A–82. Department of Economics, Harvard University. Mimeo.

Vining, D. R., Jr. 1983. Illegitimacy and public policy. *Population and Development Review* 9:105–110.

Vose, Clement E. 1959. *Caucasians only: The Supreme Court, the NAACP, and the restrictive covenant cases.* Berkeley: University ~f California Press.

Walker, H. A. 1985. Racial differences in patterns of marriage and family maintenance: 1890–1980. In *Feminism, children, and the new families,* ed. S. M. Dornbusch and M. H. Strober. New York: Guilford Press.

Wall Street Journal. 1972. Companies find they can operate effectively with fewer employees. March 8, p. 1.

Weaver, Robert C. 1936. An experiment in Negro labor. *Opportunity* 14:295.

Weinberg, D. H. 1985. Filling the poverty gap: Multiple transfer program participation. *Journal of Human Resources* 20:64–89.

Weisbrod, Burton. 1977. Discussion. In *A decade of federal antipoverty programs: Achievements, failures, and lessons,* ed. Robert H. Haveman. New York: Academic Press.

West, Guida. 1981. *The national welfare rights movement: The social protest of poor women.* New York: Praeger.

Westat, Inc. 1979. The net earnings impact of the public employment program (PEP). Report prepared for the Office of Program Evaluation, Rockville, Md.

———— 1981. Net impact number 1: Impact on 1977 earnings of new FY 1976 CETA enrollees in selected program activities. Report prepared for the Office of Program Evaluation, Rockville, Md.

———— 1982. Net impact report number 1 (supplement 1): The impact of CETA on 1978 earnings. Report prepared for the Office of Program Evaluation, Rockville, Md.

Wholey, Joseph S. 1984. Executive agency retrenchment. In *Federal budget policy in the 1980s,* ed. Gregory B. Mills and John L. Palmer. Washington, D.C.: Urban Institute Press.

Wildavsky, Aaron. 1977. Doing better and feeling worse: The political pathology of health policy. *Daedalus* 6:105–124.

Wilensky, Harold. 1975. *The welfare state and equality.* Berkeley: University of California Press.

Williams, Robert G., David L. Horner, Alan M. Hershoy, and Nancy L. Graham. 1979. *First year research results: Colorado monthly reporting experiment and protest.* Denver: Mathematica Policy Research.

Wilson, J. Q. 1973. *Political organizations.* New York: Basic Books.

Wilson, W. J. 1984a. The black underclass. *Wilson Quarterly* 8:88–99.

———— 1984b. The urban underclass. In *Minority report,* ed. L. W. Dunbar. New York: Pantheon.

Winegarden, C. R. 1974. The fertility of AFDC women: An econometric analysis. *Journal of Economics and Business* 26:159–166.

Wise, David A. 1984a. Disability and work, insurance and choice: Descriptive evidence. Department of Economics, Harvard University.

———— 1984b. The effects of the minimum wage on young men and women. Report prepared for the Department of Health and Human Services under ASPE grant no. 92A–82. Department of Economics, Harvard University. Mimeo.

Wolfinger, Raymond, and Steven Rosenstone. 1980. *Who votes?* New Haven: Yale University Press.

Wolters, Raymond. 1970. *Negroes and the Great Depression.* Westport, Conn.: Greenwood Press.

———— 1975. The New Deal and the Negro. In *The New Deal: The national level,* ed. John Braeman, Robert Bremner, and David Brody. Columbus: Ohio State University Press.

Wood, L. Hollingsworth. 1939. The UL plans for the future. *Opportunity* 17 (October):314.

Wright, Louis. 1936. The 26th year of the NAACP. *Crisis* (August), pp. 244–245.

Zelnik, M., and J. F. Kantner. 1980. Sexual activity, contraceptive use, and pregnancy among metropolitan-area teenagers: 1971–1979. *Family Planning Perspectives* 12:230–237.

Zwick, D. 1974. Some accomplishments and findings of neighborhood health centers. In *Neighborhood health centers,* ed. G. Hollister, B. M. Kramer, and S. S. Bellin. Lexington, Mass.: Lexington Books.

Notes

2. Public Spending for the Poor

1. For summaries of proposed and enacted cuts, see Pechman (1982, p. 108) and Palmer and Sawhill (1984, pp. 185–186).

2. Unless otherwise noted, all years mentioned refer to federal fiscal years. Spending is measured in constant 1984 dollars, with current spending levels deflated using OMB's payments to individuals deflator.

3. It should be noted that the poverty gap is computed using pretransfer income only. Social insurance payments are therefore excluded (Weinberg, 1985).

4. Medicaid, by far the most expensive means-tested program, now spends about four dollars out of every ten on nursing home care (Russell, 1983, p. 120).

5. Note, for example, the political fates of President Nixon's Family Assistance Plan in the early 1970s and President Carter's Program for Better Jobs and Income in 1977–78.

6. The poverty gap is the amount of money required to raise the incomes of all families now in poverty above the poverty level.

7. According to Plotnick (1979), 50 percent of cash social insurance transfers went to the pretransfer poor in 1974; according to Weinberg (1985), 64 percent of Social Security and Medicare payments went to the pretransfer poor in April 1979.

8. These percentages refer to fiscal years. Estimates of future spending on Social Security, Medicare, unemployment insurance, and black lung programs and of GNP are derived from the 1986 budget.

9. See *Social Security Bulletin* (September 1984), p. 28.

10. For example, between 1975 and 1981 the number of enrollees was rising by only 2.5 percent per year. See *U.S. Department of Health and Human Services, Social Security Administration* (1984, pp. 199–200).

11. Ibid. Medical inflation has exceeded general inflation by about 20 percent since 1967.

12. For a fascinating survey, see Aaron (1978, esp. pp. 65–110).

13. These programs were formerly funded under the Comprehensive Employ-

ment and Training Act and are now primarily funded under the Job Training Partnership Act.

14. All figures come from annual budget documents published by the Office of Management and Budget. Since the categories of spending are not necessarily consistent from year to year, estimates of spending should be considered approximate.

15. For a summary of earlier evaluations of education programs, see Levin (1977, pp. 150–168). See also Chapter 7.

16. Among the more important studies or surveys are those by David A. Long, Charles D. Mallar, and Craig V. D. Thornton (1981), Robert Taggart (1981), and the U.S. Congressional Budget Office and National Commission for Employment Policy (1982).

17. For program cost data, see Robert Taggart (1981, pp. 62–72).

18. Poverty statistics are reported for calendar years rather than fiscal years. The last figure reported is the rate for 1983.

19. See, for example, Danziger and Plotnick (1982) and Chapters 3 and 4. Later in the chapter I consider whether transfers have raised the number of poor families by providing disincentives to work.

20. In addition, there may be important effects on decisions involving family formation and fertility. Although of critical interest, these effects will not be discussed here.

21. Technically, benefits are paid out of a trust fund supported by employee and/or employer payroll tax contributions. However, most economists believe that the burden of these payroll taxes—including the part paid by employers—is ultimately borne by wage earners, that is, by eventual recipients.

22. This is an oversimplification. Few workers can expect to receive eventual Social Security or jobless benefits exactly equal in value to their tax contributions. Nonetheless, the rough correspondence between contributions and benefits for many workers should greatly diminish the distortionary effects of social insurance taxes on labor supply.

3. Antipoverty Policy

1. Until 1981 sex of the head and farm-nonfarm residence were other distinctions. All official poverty statistics reported here for 1980 and prior years are based on the more detailed set of thresholds.

2. In-kind benefits are valued at market cost, cash equivalent (recipient) value, and using a "poverty budget share" method. See U.S. Bureau of the Census (1984e) for details.

3. Underreporting biases up estimates of poverty; ignoring taxes biases them down. In any year underreporting is probably a more serious problem. However, in recent years the taxes paid by the poor have increased rapidly (See Chapter 8), while underreporting has been roughly constant.

4. If in-kind benefits are valued at market cost, the 1979–1983 poverty rates are 6.8, 7.9, 9.0, 10.0, and 10.2 percent. Using the budget share method gives 9.1,

10.4, 11.5, 12.5, and 12.9 percent. Both series differ from that in column 3 of Table 3.1, but their trends are similar.

5. In 1964 in-kind transfers were negligible. Hence, the 1964 official figures and the 1983 adjusted ones are readily compared. All ignore taxes and underreporting; all include the major sources of income for the relevant years.

6. If recipient values are used, the elderly rate is 9.3 percent, however. The difference between valuation methods is larger for the elderly than for other groups because they receive Medicare and much of Medicaid expenditures.

7. This estimate is based on a partition of the population into 24 mutually exclusive groups. Poverty is measured after noncash benefits valued at market cost are included.

8. A better label would be the "pregovernment transfer poor," since private gifts, private pensions, alimony, etc. are counted as pretransfer income. Due to data constraints, public employee pensions are counted as a government transfer, like Social Security retirement benefits, not as a component of pretransfer income, like private pensions.

9. Pretransfer poverty (or prewelfare poverty), as we measure it, always understates the extent to which private incomes keep people out of poverty. Because transfers induce labor supply reductions, income in the absence of transfers would exceed measured pretransfer income. Transfers may also induce changes in living arrangements that increase pretransfer poverty, but evidence on this behavioral effect is scant. Nonetheless, even though we overstate the antipoverty impacts of transfers, our series are probably valid indicators of pretransfer trends.

10. In this discussion "economic dependence" means that a family requires income-tested assistance to escape poverty, whether or not it actually receives assistance. An alternative approach that defines "dependence" as actual receipt of welfare shows less dependence—many families who are prewelfare poor do not receive welfare, while few with prewelfare income above the line receive it. For example, if income-tested benefits were eliminated, dependence measured by prewelfare poverty would not change (ignoring work effort or other responses), while measured as program participation, it would decline.

11. Pretransfer and prewelfare poverty data are not generally published by the Census Bureau and must be computed from public use microdata tapes. Unfortunately, the earliest available tape is the 1966 Survey of Economic Opportunity (SEO), which is not strictly comparable to the Current Population Surveys (CPS), which provide our data for 1967 to 1983. SEO income appears more accurately reported, since its official 1965 rate was 15.6 percent compared with 17.3 percent reported in the CPS.

12. This measure, first used in Plotnick and Skidmore (1975), defines the relative poor as families with welfare ratios (current money income divided by the poverty line) below .44 of the median ratio. This definition was chosen so that in 1965 the relative poor and the officially poor were identical.

13. Data on the effect of in-kind transfers are not available for 1978, yet the combined poverty-reduction impact of cash and in-kind transfers is probably similar to that of 1976.

14. These results are based on the cash-equivalent valuation of in-kind transfers. If market values are used, each figure in columns 4 and 5 of Table 3.6 for 1979–

1983 would be about 11 percentage points larger. Thus, while the effects of in-kind and all transfers are larger in every year, the downward trend remains.

15. Data by demographic group for cash and in-kind transfers were unavailable for all three years.

16. Weinberg's (1985) analysis of the antipoverty effects of transfers using the poverty gap instead of the poverty rate finds similar patterns by demographic groups.

17. For reasons noted earlier, SEO data for 1965 are used in these calculations.

18. There is no residual in our decomposition of the pretransfer poverty rate because only two factors were considered.

19. These results are broadly consistent with those of Gottschalk and Danziger (1984), which are derived by a very different method.

20. An obstacle to discussing the impacts of policy on the nonpoor is their identification. In any given year the data separate the population into pretransfer poor and nonpoor groups. Yet, over time, mobility into and out of poverty is substantial. Because of data constraints, we proceed as if there is a constant group of individuals who are the official pretransfer nonpoor over the 1965–1980 period.

21. This table is patterned after the analysis in Lampman (1984). Because our focus is only on the nonpoor, our items differ substantially. A rationale for each computation in the table and the details of the estimation are provided in Haveman (1985).

22. These estimates reflect the quantitative magnitude of some of the gains and losses of a broad spectrum of policy changes to the nonpoor. They in no way form a benefit-cost analysis of the policy changes undertaken. Given the magnitude of the policy shifts, a formal benefit cost analysis would require a full general equilibrium model. Moreover, the programs grouped together are too diverse and too complex to warrant a benefit-cost evaluation. Yet our catalog facilitates appraisal of the effects of antipoverty policies on the nonpoor.

23. If, however, economic growth produces greater inequality of earnings, as appears to have been the case in recent years (Gottschalk and Danziger, 1985), pretransfer poverty may not fall very much or at all. In this case, labor market interventions to counteract rising inequality must accompany growth if poverty is to be reduced.

24. Complete indexing, however, might be inappropriate when the earnings increases of most workers lag behind price increases or when price index changes do not adequately reflect changes in the prices paid by transfer recipients.

25. The Deficit Reduction Act of 1984 expanded the EITC slightly.

4. Poverty in America

1. In fact the comparison is not quite appropriate, because elderly persons are included in the median family income figures. If elderly are included in the poverty rate, the two curves on Figure 4.2 are even more closely matched. For a far more detailed discussion of the impact of growth on poverty, see Gottschalk and Danziger (1984).

2. In his comments on this paper Timothy Smeeding expresses concern about

the apparent increase in income inequality as indicated in the final few years of the figure. Danziger and Gottschalk (1985) suggest that such a divergence may be only temporary because the income distribution always widens in times of recession.

3. In some states children of poor two-parent families can be eligible for Medicaid. States with an AFDC-Unemployed Parent program can also cover families of the unemployed, but expenditures on these groups are quite small.

4. Inferred from Table 3, U.S. House of Representatives (1983, pp. 70, 71).

5. Ibid. For a detailed discussion of the effects on measured poverty of counting in-kind benefits, see U.S. Bureau of the Census (1982a).

6. Inferred from Table 3, U.S. House of Representatives (1983, pp. 70, 71).

7. For further discussion of the effects of disability insurance, see Burkhauser and Haveman (1982) and Wise (1984a).

8. We are indebted to John Bound for pointing us in this direction. His paper (Bound, 1985) examines in more detail the issues discussed here.

9. The figures are similar for those who did and did not appeal. As one would expect, those who did not appeal had slightly higher rates of employment. See Tretel (1979).

10. Actually this is only part of the story. A second reason for the increase in the fraction of births to unmarried women is the sharp decline in the marriage rate among black women. If fewer black women marry, then the number of births to unmarried women would increase even if the number of births *per* unmarried woman was constant. The origins of the decline in marriage among black women would seem better traced to the decline in the fortunes of black men than to changes in AFDC. See Chapter 10.

11. Since the baseline for the experiment was the present system, it is hard to draw many inferences about its applicability to current policy. The experiments did not show any change in fertility, marriage, or remarriage.

12. For out-of-school youth the gaps are somewhat larger: Thirty-one percent of youths in single-parent families were working; 44 percent of those in two-parent families worked. For whites the comparable figures were 61 percent and 73 percent. The source for these figures is U.S. Bureau of the Census (1983d).

13. These figures are for both sexes because sex-specific rates are not published. We suspect the differences for men alone between the central city and suburbs would be even smaller.

5. Health Care for the Poor

1. I base this very rough estimate on (1) the differentials between fee-for-service and HMO costs (see Luft, 1981; Manning et al., 1984); (2) the differentials between median health care expenditures and costs in cities such as Seattle, Washington, and Rochester, New York; and (3) the gap that has opened up between the percentage of GNP spent on health care in the United States and that spent in Canada. (In the early 1970s both countries were spending just over 7 percent on health care; now the United States spends nearly 11 percent, the Canadians 8 percent— and the Canadians have national health insurance!)

2. The failure of the Massachusetts capitation initiative illustrates the political problems of Medicaid reform. In concert with private foundations, the administration of Gov. Edward King sought to introduce capitation payment for Medicaid beneficiaries in Boston. Some 60,000 would have been required to participate—the sponsors did not believe it would work unless enrollment was substantial—but the enrollees would have had the right to choose any of fourteen hospitals and twenty-eight community health centers. Even though only about twenty-five private office-based doctors in the entire city were accepting Medicaid clients, the plan met opposition from black organizations because of the restrictions on free choice and was abandoned after the Dukakis administration took office (Iglehart, 1983).

3. Even in the face of fiscal pressures, some steps to expand medical coverage have been taken by the federal government and the states. In 1984 Congress mandated Medicaid coverage for low-income pregnant women and infants excluded under some states' narrow eligibility rules. The Congressional Budget Office estimates that in 1986 180,000 women and 95,000 infants will receive benefits under this provision (Iglehart, 1985). In July 1985, while voting drastic cutbacks in Medicare payments to for-profit hospitals, teaching hospitals, and doctors, the House of Representatives passed a measure to require employers to offer health insurance to the surviving spouse of a deceased worker. Despite severe fiscal problems, Texas enacted a major expansion of Medicaid in 1985 as well as criminal penalties for denying emergency medical care to poor patients.

6. The Effect of Direct Job Creation and Training Programs

1. A more detailed set of results is available from the authors on request.

2. Although it is impossible to correct for this problem, it is possible to estimate the magnitude of the bias that it introduces in the estimates.

3. Ashenfelter's main estimation technique was an autoregressive earnings model, where lagged earnings was used to control for differences in unobservable characteristics between participants and comparisons.

4. Sample sizes vary from year to year, with the smallest consisting of 6,700 participants during 1975. In later years the samples were in excess of 15,000.

5. This discussion is based on the work of Bassi (1983, 1984), Bassi et al. (1984), Bloom and McLaughlin (1982), Dickinson, Johnson, and West (1984), and Westat (1979).

6. It should be noted, however, that Bassi et al. (1984) found very little evidence of significant program effects for male youths aged sixteen to twenty-two.

7. The Bloom-McLaughlin (1982) evaluation was the only study not reaching this conclusion.

8. Significant program effects were not found for young women with children.

9. Lalonde (1984) generated comparison groups from both the Panel Study of Income Dynamics and CPS while Fraker, Maynard, and Nelson (1984) relied exclusively on the CPS.

10. Private sector programs that involve wage payments are less expensive than comparable public sector programs, since public sector programs use a 100-percent

wage subsidy while private sector programs use a subsidy of less than 100 percent.

11. Kemper, Long, and Thornton (1981) provide a review of the available studies.

12. This statement would not necessarily be true if income redistribution was an objective of the program.

13. We confine our attention to the employment effects of these programs and do not consider inflationary effects.

14. Note that the concept of fiscal substitution is slightly different from that of displacement. Fiscal substitution measures a substitution of money, while displacement measures substitution rates among workers. We would expect, however, that the two measures would be highly correlated.

15. These findings are based on studies by Adams (1981), Adams, Cook, and Maurice (1983), Bassi (1981), Bassi and Fechter (1979), Cook (1980), Johnson and Tomola (1977), and Nathan (1979).

7. Education and Training Programs

1. The following figures of the U.S. Department of Education differ with respect to high school completion rates among the population aged twenty-five to twenty-nine: their statistics indicate that the percentage of whites with four years of high school education or more rose from 77.8 percent in March 1970 to 86.9 percent in March 1982; among blacks and other races from 58.4 to 82.2 percent (*Digest of Education Statistics*, 1984, p. 13). I do not know how to reconcile these figures.

2. I concentrate here on programs for youth, and in particular dropouts. For a fuller analysis of the record of training programs, see Chapter 6.

8. Macroeconomics, Income Distribution, and Poverty

1. For a more detailed discussion of these issues, see Blank and Blinder (1985).

2. The U.S. poverty line is indexed each year to the Consumer Price Index and is thus an absolute poverty standard in real terms.

3. Blank finds that women's labor market income is far less procyclical than is men's. Except among poorer households, women's hours appear to change little over the cycle.

4. Asher (1983) also used this specification, finding that the effect of unemployment diminishes as unemployment rises.

5. Specifically, the annual inflation rate was explained by five lags of itself, supplemented by variables for price controls. We also used the Consumer Price Index, rather than the GNP deflator, to be consistent with some monthly regressions reported later in this chapter.

6. Dummy variables for the pre-1958 years, not shown in Table 8.1 or in equation (8.3), were also used, because there is a change in the nature of the income distribution data after 1958.

7. The Durbin h-statistics gave no indication of serial correlation.

8. Even though a large amount of government transfers do not go to the poor but to lower- or middle-income households, total government transfers divided by

GNP provides a measure of the extent to which resources are devoted to redistributive programs.

9. Of course, the rise in unemployment should not be sustained indefinitely as the economy would return to its natural unemployment rate.

10. The equation that estimates monthly anticipated inflation includes eleven monthly dummy variables, twelve lags, and a series of variables allowing for price control effects. Its general form is similar to that used in Blinder and Newton (1981).

11. Some workers leave the labor market entirely in response to higher aggregate unemployment rates, thus lowering the reported unemployment in their race/sex/age group. The change in group-specific unemployment is therefore the difference between the total employment change and this labor supply effect. The regressions we report do not distinguish between participation rate changes and employment changes.

12. This sort of regression is very similar to those run earlier by Gramlich (1974).

13. Population ratios are omitted in aggregate equations since male/female and nonwhite/white ratios have changed little during this period. However, significant changes in the age composition of the population have occurred. Population ratios are included in all age-specific regressions to control for this cohort size effect.

14. A full set of regression results is available on request from the authors, but, in order to avoid inundating the reader with regression coefficients, we report here only the unemployment and inflation effects.

15. The sensitivity effect reported here is the marginal effect of base-level U^* on U_i. This is often referred to as the steady state effect. Using the coefficients defined in equation (8.4), we calculate the reported sensitivities in Table 8.2 as $[d_1 + 2d_2 U^*(\text{mean})] / (1-g)$. There is no simple way to calculate standard errors for this sensitivity. The underlying coefficients on unemployment (d_1) are significant in all regressions, and the coefficients on U^{*2} and the lagged dependent variable $(d_2$ and $g)$ are significant in almost all the equations.

16. This is the marginal effect of anticipated inflation on U_i. Using the coefficients defined in equation (8.4), the reported sensitivities on inflation in Table 2 are $c_1 / (1-g)$. Because there is no simple way to calculate the standard error for this term, significance levels on the coefficient c_1 are indicated.

17. No clear trends in these age, race, or sex differentials between the insured and uninsured unemployed were visible in the 1970s. Unfortunately, since the Employment and Training Administration of the Bureau of Labor Statistics stopped publishing age, race, and sex breakdowns for UI recipients in 1979, more recent data are not available.

18. The slowdown in inflation, combined with a leveling off of caseload growth, seems to have led many states finally to increase benefit levels somewhat.

19. Quintile shares are essentially relative mean nominal incomes. They are also relative mean *real* incomes if the proper deflators are the same for all groups. If the true deflator for the incomes of the poor rises faster than the CPI, then the share of the poor in real income is below their share in nominal income.

20. Under conventional accounting procedures, inflation distorts the measurement of property income, which, with unindexed tax laws, leads to high effective tax rates on real property income (Feldstein, 1982). Inflation is also bad for the

stock market, whether it is anticipated or unanticipated (Bodie, 1976), and un-anticipated inflation obviously devastates the bond market. A detailed simulation study by Minarik (1979) demonstrated that inflation was a decidedly progressive tax.

21. A possible opposing view is that most of the payroll tax is used to finance retirement annuities, which are then distributed according to a progressive formula. In this case the payroll tax is not a tax.

22. Most of the information on changes in the tax code found in this subsection and the next comes from the appendices to Pechman (1983).

23. The years selected differ from those used in other tables because these years represent significant landmarks in tax history: There was a major tax overhaul of the tax code in 1954; in 1965 the full effect of the Kennedy-Johnson tax cuts occurred; the personal exemption was gradually increased in the 1970s and the earned income credit was instituted in 1975; 1980 is the last year before the Reagan tax cuts; and 1983 is the most recent available year.

24. Instead of raising the exemption, Presidents Ford and Carter used a per capita tax credit to ease the tax burden on the poor from 1975 to 1978; then Congress eliminated it.

25. As Moon and Sawhill (1984, p. 326) observe, the lowest quintile of families gained essentially nothing from the Reagan income tax cuts.

26. The progressivity or regressivity of state and local taxes depends on one's classification of the property tax. If the property tax is viewed as progressive, the overall state-local tax structure is only slightly less progressive than the federal tax structure and also displays a trend toward diminishing progressivity. If the property tax is classified as regressive, the state-local tax structure is very regressive and displays a trend toward diminishing regressivity.

27. These calculations are complicated by the presence of the lagged dependent variable. To calculate the components of the 1983 share due to unemployment or inflation, we calculated the cumulative effect of these variables from 1973 to 1983.

28. Inflation projections are adjusted to correspond to unemployment projec-tions according to a rule of thumb by which 1 percentage point of additional unemployment for a year lowers inflation by 1 point.

29. The unemployment projections are for total civilian unemployment, whereas our regressions require the unemployment rates for prime-age males and prime-age white males. To bridge the gap, we estimated annual regressions relating these specific unemployment rates to the overall civilian unemployment rate. The un-employment rate of prime-age males is projected to run about 2 percentage points below the civilian unemployment rates. The unemployment rate of prime-age white males is projected to run a few tenths of a point lower.

9. Household Composition and Poverty

1. These data are presented for 1979, since the late 1970s represent the extreme of the feminization of poverty. Overall poverty rates at that point were very low, and the proportion of the poor in female-headed and single-person households was

very high. During the early 1980s a recession drove up poverty rates, pushed a disproportionate number of two-parent families into poverty, and decreased the proportion of the poor in other types of households. As the economy improves and poverty rates go down, I would expect to see a return to the late 1970s' family structure pattern.

2. It would have been preferable to have included noncash transfers, but the published data used here precluded that choice. Noncash transfers go disproportionately to the elderly and more to female-headed than to two-parent families (U.S. Bureau of the Census, 1982a). Their inclusion in this table would have increased the proportion of the poor in two-parent families but would not change the conclusions much.

3. The definition of poverty used for these analyses is the low-income standard included on the PSID adjusted for inflation with the CPI, which is about 125 percent of the official poverty line. Because the PSID seems to identify more income than the CPS, this is a reasonable adjustment. The definition of spells includes an adjustment to eliminate very short small changes in income (Bane and Ellwood, 1983b).

4. As noted in Bane and Ellwood (1983b), for an analysis that combines data over years, as this one does, the PSID seriously underrepresents the elderly. This occurs because people who leave the sample are removed completely, with data for the years they were in the sample deleted. The elderly, who are more likely to die than others, disproportionately leave the sample. This problem will be solved, we all hope, in later versions of the PSID tapes.

5. As was also true in Bane and Ellwood (1983b), the analysis proceeded by looking first for family structure events; income or needs changes were sought only if no family structure change occurred in the year the poverty spell began or the year before. If a family structure change occurred simultaneously with an income or needs change, the family event was identified as the beginning type. Thus the analysis somewhat overstates the importance of family events as beginning types.

6. There are also indications in these data of the greater persistence of poverty among black female-headed families, although that is not the major focus here. The last row shows that about 43 percent of all poverty spell beginnings were among blacks in male-headed families, whereas only about a quarter of the black poor in 1979 were in male-headed families. This suggests that poverty spells among blacks were much longer for those in female-headed families, a finding that was also reported in Bane and Ellwood (1983b).

7. In this analysis it was not completely obvious how to treat birth beginnings. Ideally, if a child was born into poverty, one would want to look at the mother's transition into poverty and attribute that to the child. The analysis here did not permit that. Instead, if the child's birth was simultaneous with the poverty transition, I called that a transition beginning. Births into poverty were allocated among three categories in the same proportions as nonbirth beginnings. My hunch is that this procedure overemphasizes transition and post-transition beginnings, but I have no real evidence for that conclusion.

8. Poverty lines by household size in 1983 were as follows: for household size

1, $5,061; household size 2, $6,483; household size 3, $7,938; household size 4, $10,178; household size 5, $12,049; household size 6, $13,630 (U.S. Bureau of the Census, 1984d).

9. A more accurate analysis would look not only at household income before the break but also at the income of the two households after the break, since the real issue is whether the resources available to the members of the previously combined household are being divided proportionally to needs. The analysis reported here assumes that these total resources are about the same before the break as after.

10. This finding is consistent with that of Hill (1984), who also used the Panel Study of Income Dynamics but looked specifically at the issue of child support.

10. Poverty and Family Structure

1. Farley and Hermalin's (1971) age-standardized figures show that between 1940 and 1960 the proportion of widows in the population dropped from 14 to 12 percent for white women and from 24 to 17 percent for black women. During these two decades, however, the number of divorced women per 1,000 married women rose from 27.2 to 36.8 for whites and from 29.1 to 71.3 for blacks (U.S. Bureau of the Census, 1943, 1960).

2. Whites are more likely to remarry than blacks. For instance, a 1975 Current Population Survey shows that of women aged thirty-five to fifty-four who had been divorced or widowed, 53 percent of whites had remarried and were currently married and living with their husbands, as compared with only 38 percent of blacks (U.S. Bureau of the Census, 1977a). In addition, a higher proportion of white than black marriages are remarriages, despite the fact that blacks have higher rates of marital dissolution (National Center for Health Statistics, 1982a).

3. The extent of persistent poverty has been questioned by some studies of the Panel Study of Income Dynamics data which have indicated that only a small proportion of Americans in poverty are persistently poor year in and year out. For example, Coe (1978) found that only 1 percent and Hill (1981) just 3 percent of the population was poor throughout the time span (nine and ten years respectively) of their studies. Corcoran, Duncan, and Gurin (1983) indicated that only 2.2 percent of the population was poor at least eight of the ten years (1968–1978) their study covered. However, Bane and Ellwood (1983a, 1983b) point out that studies of persistent poverty based on spells of poverty observed over a fixed period of time underestimate the length of spells because some individuals who seem to have short spells of poverty are actually beginning or ending long spells.

4. However, as Ellwood and Bane (1984) point out, a large effect of welfare on separation and divorce for young mothers implies a much larger impact on the proportion of young single mothers for whites than for blacks, because separated or divorced mothers represent a larger proportion of white single mothers (nearly 60 percent) than of black single mothers (20 percent).

5. Sources for these figures are as follows. The numerators, the numbers of employed men by age and race, are taken from U.S. Bureau of Labor Statistics

(1980, 1984a) publications. The denominators, the numbers of women by age and race, are taken from the P-25 series of the Current Population Reports (U.S. Bureau of the Census, 1965c, 1978b, 1983c).

Several objections might be raised to these figures. First, it might be argued that the ratios are biased downwards because of an undercount of young black men. This may be true, but it would seem that unenumerated men are not counted precisely because they do not have a stable attachment to labor force and family and thus would be unlikely to be included in these figures even if they had been enumerated. Second, the employment figures are for the civilian labor force only and do not include men in the armed forces. Including men who are in the armed forces would smooth out the graph for men twenty to twenty-four years of age during the late 1960s and would narrow the black-white gap a little because of slightly higher enlistment levels among blacks, but it would not change the basic trends. The slight upturn in the index after 1954 is likely to represent the return of men in the armed forces to the civilian labor force following the Korean War. Finally, it might be noted that women may marry men other than employed men of their own age and race category. This is true also, but the figures are intended to convey the marriage market constraints facing most women.

6. Rising average incomes are likely to have enhanced family stability for black men who are employed, but it is argued that the more dramatic trends in unemployment and labor force participation have outweighed increases in earnings to produce a net decline in family stability among blacks.

11. Legal Rights and Welfare Change

1. See Friedman (1977) and Peterson and Greenstone (1977) for explanations of the changes in OEO and maximum feasible participation.

2. One of Piven and Cloward's (1971) claims is that riots actually forced governments to allow participation to increase. As I read the evidence on their thesis, riots did not lead workers to use their discretion to increase participation nor did they help increase grant levels. They may have played some role in state and federal decisions to adopt less restrictive rules after 1968, but this can be debated. At best, riots thus may be defined as an additional impetus for legal rights during the 1968–1982 period. See Sosin (1984) for an extended argument, and also Albritton (1979), Isaac and Kelly (1981), Jennings (1983), Schram and Turbott (1983a, 1983b). See Piven and Cloward (1977, 1982) for their more recent statements.

3. Some may claim that the decreases in benefit levels account for the decline in participation. But using Moffitt's (1983) estimate for the relation of benefit levels and participation rates and Cole's (forthcoming) data on declines in benefit levels, it is clear that this explains only 2.3 percent of the 16-percent decline in participation rates. See Sosin (1984) for details.

4. Lawrence Mead, in his comment to the original conference paper, claims that legal rights were questioned owing to the failure of the movement to embrace work programs, which might demonstrate to the public that rights are balanced by responsibilities. But I believe that work programs generally do not help to legitimate legal rights, as witnessed by the Poor Laws of 1601 and 1834, the work incentive

program as amended in 1971, and so forth (Steiner, 1971; Trattner, 1984). They generally are instituted to increase stigma or restrictiveness.

13. The Political Foundations of Antipoverty Policy

1. The most useful recent studies would seem to be Erskine (1975), Jaffe (1978), Cook (1979), Hochschild (1981), Ladd (1984), and McClosky and Zaller (1984). My discussion has drawn heavily on these works.

2. Thus, after the New Deal's first six years, 28 percent of Americans rated relief and WPA as the Roosevelt administration's greatest accomplishment; but 39 percent listed these efforts as its worst accomplishment (Cantril, 1951, pp. 979–980; Leuchtenburg, 1963, pp. 120–130). See also Howard (1943) and Kesselman (1978).

3. The difficulty of such an enterprise was made clear in the 1938 congressional election primaries when Roosevelt unsuccessfully attempted to purge a handful of conservative Democrats (Kirkendall, 1985). Only in New York City, where there was an opportunity for liberal New Dealers to mobilize alternative local political machinery, did the President succeed in ousting an anti–New Deal Democrat (the chairman of the House Ways and Means Committee). By contrast, conservative Democrats and Republicans in the 1938 elections had an easy time playing on Americans' distaste for union agitators, working class militancy, and visions of alien communistic threats.

4. For a range of these views, see papers by Friedman and Peterson and the related comments by discussants in Haveman (1977) as well as Matusow (1984, pp. 97–127, 217–271) and Chapter 12 in this volume.

5. Useful discussions of such trends are in Schiltz (1970, p. 153), Curtin and Cowan (1975), Davis (1980), and Smith (1982).

6. For example, Wolfinger and Rosenstone (1980) show that the poor were underrepresented at the polls by about 50 percent in 1972.

7. With the new taxability of benefits, Social Security seems to be taking on even more the qualities of a universal program selectively applied.

8. While it is possible to envision a broad political base of support for social policy oriented around concepts of work (training, sheltered jobs, allowances reducing the personal costs of labor market mobility), it is much more difficult to imagine a general policy of family support that tries to be directive with regard to preferred forms of family formation. For a somewhat contrary view, see Moynihan (1985).

15. A Poverty Research Agenda for the Next Decade

1. For those interested in an historical perspective, Covello (1980) provides a sampling of views on the status of research on poverty and its role in the formulation of federal policies that affect poor people.

Acknowledgments

1. Introduction

Elizabeth Evanson gave invaluable assistance in the preparation of this chapter. Peter Gottschalk, Robert Lampman, and Eugene Smolensky provided helpful comments on an earlier draft. Any views expressed are solely those of the authors.

2. Public Spending for the Poor

I gratefully acknowledge the helpful comments of Martin N. Baily, Elise Bruml, Sheldon Danziger, Peter Gottschalk, Joseph Pechman, Alice Rivlin, and Daniel Weinberg. John L. Palmer and James T. Patterson were formal discussants of the topic at the Williamsburg conference, and Cameran Lougy provided splendid research assistance.

3. Antipoverty Policy

Matthew Rabin and Christine Ross provided valuable research assistance and Nancy Rortvedt excellent clerical assistance. Elizabeth Evanson, Edward Gramlich, Robert Lampman, Morton Paglin, Timothy Smeeding, and Daniel Weinberg gave helpful comments on a previous draft.

4. Poverty in America

We have benefited from comments by Sheldon Danziger, Robert Haveman, Morton Paglin, Timothy Smeeding, Daniel Weinberg, and Barbara Wolfe.

6. The Effect of Direct Job Creation and Training Programs

Joseph Antos and Peter Gottschalk provided helpful comments on an earlier version.

8.   Macroeconomics, Income Distribution, and Poverty

Support for this research has been provided by the National Science Foundation. We thank John Londregan for research assistance, and Joseph Antos, Peter Gottschalk, Lawrence Summers, and Daniel Weinberg for useful comments.

10.   Poverty and Family Structure

We have benefited from the significant contributions of Robert Aponte to the ideas developed here. We also wish to thank June O'Neill and Lee Rainwater for their comments on an earlier version of the chapter.

11.   Legal Rights and Welfare Change

I should like to thank Joel Handler, who helped develop this topic and also commented on an earlier draft. Thanks are also due to research assistants Jeffrey Boldt and Patricia McLaughlin, and to Lawrence Mead, Charles Nagatoshi, and Irving Piliavin.

12.   Social Policies, Civil Rights, and Poverty

We wish to thank Peter Eisinger for his helpful response to our analysis at the Williamsburg conference.

13.   The Political Foundations of Antipoverty Policy

I should like to thank Alan Brinkley, Lawrence M. Mead, John L. Palmer, and James T. Patterson for the many insights that have informed this discussion.

15.   A Poverty Research Agenda for the Next Decade

I should like to thank Thomas Ault, Gordon Fisher, Walton Francis, Paul Gayer, Martin Holmer, participants at the Williamsburg conference, and, in particular, Sheldon Danziger, Thomas Gustafson, William Prosser, and Reuben Snipper for their helpful suggestions and comments, and Robert Lampman for inspiration. The views expressed in this chapter are those of the author and should not be construed as necessarily representing the official position or policy of the Department of Health and Human Services or any office therein.

Contributors

Orley Ashenfelter, Department of Economics, Princeton University, Princeton, New Jersey

Mary Jo Bane, New York State Department of Social Services, Albany, New York, and John F. Kennedy School of Government, Harvard University, Cambridge, Massachusetts

Laurie J. Bassi, Department of Economics, Georgetown University, Washington, D.C.

Rebecca M. Blank, Woodrow Wilson School of Public and International Affairs and Department of Economics, Princeton University, Princeton, New Jersey

Alan S. Blinder, Department of Economics, Princeton University, Princeton, New Jersey

Gary Burtless, The Brookings Institution, Washington, D.C.

Sheldon H. Danziger, Institute for Research on Poverty and School of Social Work, University of Wisconsin, Madison, Wisconsin

David T. Ellwood, John F. Kennedy School of Government, Harvard University, Cambridge, Massachusetts

Nathan Glazer, Graduate School of Education, Harvard University, Cambridge, Massachusetts

Edward M. Gramlich, Department of Economics, University of Michigan, Ann Arbor, Michigan

Charles V. Hamilton, Department of Political Science, Columbia University, New York, New York

Dona C. Hamilton, Department of Sociology and Social Work, Lehman College, CUNY, Bronx, New York

Robert H. Haveman, Department of Economics and Institute for Research on Poverty, University of Wisconsin, Madison, Wisconsin

Hugh Heclo, Department of Government, Harvard University, Cambridge, Massachusetts

Christopher Jencks, Center for Urban Affairs and Policy Research, Northwestern University, Evanston, Illinois

Lawrence M. Mead, Department of Politics, New York University, New York, New York

Kathryn M. Neckerman, Department of Sociology, University of Chicago, Chicago, Illinois

Robert D. Plotnick, Graduate School of Public Affairs and School of Social Work, University of Washington, Seattle, Washington

Michael R. Sosin, School of Social Work and Institute for Research on Poverty, University of Wisconsin, Madison, Wisconsin

Paul Starr, Department of Sociology, Princeton University, Princeton, New Jersey

Lawrence H. Summers, Department of Economics, Harvard University, Cambridge, Massachusetts

Daniel H. Weinberg, Office of Income Security Policy, U.S. Department of Health and Human Services, Washington, D.C.

William Julius Wilson, Department of Sociology, University of Chicago, Chicago, Illinois

Index

Aaron, Henry: cited, 2, 45, 351, 354
Abortion, 245
Abram, Morris B.: cited, 288
Abt Associates: cited, 123
Aday, L. R.: cited, 117
Adult Education Act, 152
Agnello, Richard: cited, 181
Agricultural Adjustment Administration (AAA), 290, 292–293, 316–317
Aid to Families with Dependent Children (AFDC): GNP ratio, 4; effect on family structure, 6, 79, 93–96, 97, 102, 248–249, 250, 251, 263, 341–342, 347; benefit levels, 10, 17, 21, 75–76, 79, 95, 104, 172, 174-176, 196, 208, 247–248, 267, 271, 273, 337, 342; expenditures on, 21, 43, 76, 86–87; participation in, 21, 84, 109, 269, 272, 277, 284, 285; vs. negative income tax programs, 43; work incentives in, 44; Unemployed Parent program, 84, 392; to single-parent families, 87, 97; to children, 93–94; dependency on, 96–98, 103, 143, 258; eligibility for, 112–114, 193, 248, 271, 286; and legal rights movement, 260; reform, 267–268; special needs provisions of, 270, 274; Emergency Assistance program, 275
Alabama, 302
Allen, Francis: cited, 262, 283
American Federation of Labor, 294
American Hospital Association, 110
American Medical Association (AMA), 109, 125
Anderson, Martin: cited, 2, 117, 181
Antipoverty policies and programs, 1, 2, 13–17, 52, 73–77, 287, 301, 334; role of, 2, 15, 83–89; effectiveness of, 3–9, 11, 39, 64–69, 324; expenditures on, 4, 80–89; and able-bodied poor, 5, 340; and nonpoor, 5, 25–26, 69–74; and unemployment rate, 16; and politics, 18, 312–313, 317, 321, 332, 336–340; constraints, 19, 332–335; microeconomic effect of, 19; labor supply effect of, 44; and pretransfer poverty, 71–73, 74; and prewelfare poverty, 74; discrimination in, 75; reform, 75–77, 78, 322; cutbacks in, 78; and self-sufficiency, 83–84, 98, 103, 105; government role in, 102–105, 329; and the disabled, 103; inequality in, 104; for medical care, 106; during New Deal, 313–318; matching grants for, 315, 347; weaknesses of, 321–324; president and, 322–323; and civil rights, 323–324; covert, 324–325; public attitude toward, 326–332; administration of, 335, 356; and children, 338, 349; targeting of, 338–340
A. Philip Randolph Institute, 299
Arithmetic skills, 176, 178
Arizona, 123–124, 126–127, 337
Ashenfelter, Orley, 6, 7, 15, 17, 344; cited, 140
Asher, Martin: cited, 185
Assistant Secretary for Planning and Evaluation, 2

Bailey, Stephen: cited, 296
Bailis, Lawrence: cited, 270
Bakke, W. E.: cited, 253
Balanced Growth Act, 305–306

Health care programs (*cont.*)
of, 119–120; reform of, 121–128, 132; cost shifting in, 128, 131; competition in, 128–129, 130

Health centers, neighborhood, 111–112, 120

Health insurance, 106, 115–116, 118, 121, 122, 130; national, 16, 109–111, 132, 352; cost of, 109; selective contracting in, 124, 125; third-party, 128

Health Interview Survey, 117

Health maintenance organizations (HMOs), 112, 121, 123, 124, 125, 127, 128, 132; HMO Act, 121; and Medicaid, 125–128; and hospital services, 128, 129

Health Service Corps, 110, 111, 130

Heclo, Hugh, 13, 14; cited, 345

Heller, Walter, 298; cited, 51

Hendershot, G. E.: cited, 249

Henderson, Vivian, 299

Hermalin, A. I.: cited, 233

Hershberg, T.: cited, 233, 234

Hibbs, Douglas: cited, 189

Hiday, V.: cited, 249

High School and Beyond, 244

High school dropouts, 161, 166, 167, 168 169, 172, 394

Hill, Martha: cited, 241

Hill-Burton program, 110, 111, 130, 131

Hirsch, Barry: cited, 181

Hirschman, C. G.: cited, 127

Hoepfner, Ralph: cited, 163

Hoey, Jane, 317

Hoffman, S.: cited, 246, 250, 253

Hogan, Dennis: cited, 243–244, 245, 251

Holahan, J. F.: cited, 113, 114

Hollingsworth, Ellen Jane: cited, 261, 268

Hollister, Robinson: cited, 197

Holmes, J.: cited, 246, 250, 253

Holzer, H. J.: cited, 168

Homeless population, 349–350

Honig, M.: cited, 249, 250

Hospital(s): costs, 110, 124, 125; construction, 110, 131; rate of use, 116, 122, 127; financing of, 122–123, 129; patient dumping by, 124–125, 129, 131; and uncompensated care, 128–132

Household(s): single-person, 11, 26, 221, 226–228, 342, 343; single-parent, 26, 92; composition, 60, 210–220; student heads of, 61; affected by income transfers, 67; affected by economic growth, 181; age

composition of, 214–215; distribution, demographic, 216–218; and poverty rate changes, 218–220, 226–227; and poverty, 227–229. *See also* Family structure; Female-headed households

Housing programs, 3, 4, 18, 23, 84, 324; effect on poverty, 24; access to, 26; not counted as income, 80; for nonelderly, 87; legislation, 316; expenditures on, 333; subsidies, 339

Howard, D.: cited, 134

Human capital programs, 20–21, 34–40, 70. *See also* Education and training programs; Employment and training programs

Humphrey, Hubert, 305

Humphrey-Hawkins Act, 287, 305–306, 308

Hurd, M. D.: cited 27

Ickes, Harold, 292

Iglehart, J. K.: cited, 123, 124

Illegitimacy, 237, 248, 257

Immigration, 349

Income: guaranteed, 16, 70, 326; distribution, redistribution, 19–20, 41, 46–49, 153–154, 180–183, 184, 185, 204, 207, 317, 325, 326, 333, 335, 347, 355; underreporting of, 25, 55, 61; pretransfer, 28; current money, 53; average, and poverty, 58–59, 81–83, 88; maintenance programs, 67, 170, 248, 249, 251, 273, 275, 303, 341, 354; poverty ratio, 182, 184–189, 195–197; inequality, 182; labor, vs. total, 183

Income transfers, 20, 21, 35, 51–52, 60; effect on poverty, 3, 8, 9, 16, 50, 62, 64–65, 67–69, 79, 85–86, 88, 155, 188–189, 312; means-tested, 4, 19–20, 21–26, 30, 32–36, 38–42, 83, 331; GNP ratio, 4, 79, 85, 204, 394–395; to elderly, 5, 8, 75, 84; disincentive effects of, 5, 41, 43–44, 62, 168; and unemployed black youth, 5, 88–89; and disabled, 5, 86, 88; and single women with children, 5; and able-bodied poor, 8, 16, 74; and unemployment, 9, 193–194; real value of, 9, 10, 64, 259; indexation of, 10, 208; effect on employment, 16, 61, 88, 102, 168, 331; for those not expected to work, 17; expenditures on, 22–24, 64, 65–66, 70, 79, 88; benefit levels, 33, 52, 62, 114; counted as income, 40, 80; vs. redistribution, 41; fi-